NO PEACE
NO WAR

An Anthropology of
Contemporary Armed Conflicts

NO PEACE NO WAR

An Anthropology of Contemporary Armed Conflicts

EDITED BY PAUL RICHARDS

Professor of Technology & Agrarian Development,
Wageningen University & Research Centre, The Netherlands,
& (Honorary) Professor of Anthropology, University College London

In Memoriam Bernhard Helander

Ohio University Press
ATHENS
James Currey
OXFORD

James Currey Ltd
73 Botley Road
Oxford OX2 0BS
www.jamescurrey.co.uk

Ohio University Press
Scott Quadrangle
Athens
Ohio 45701
www.ohioedu/oupress

© James Currey Ltd, 2005
First published 2005

1 2 3 4 5 09 08 07 06 05

ISBN 0-85255-936-4 (James Currey cloth)
ISBN 0-85255-935-6 (James Currey paper)
ISBN 0-8214-1575-1 (Ohio University Press cloth)
ISBN 0-8214-1576-X (Ohio University Press paper)

British Library Cataloguing in Publication Data
No peace, no war : an anthropology of contemporary armed
conflicts : in memorium Bernhard Helander
1. War and society
I. Richards, Paul   II. Helander, Bernhard
303.6'6
Library of Congress Cataloging-in-Publication Data
available on request

Typeset in 10/11 pt Photina
by Long House, Cumbria
Printed and bound in Great Britain by
Woolnough, Irthlingborough

Contents

11

Who Needs a State?
*Civilians, Security & Social Services in
North-East Somalia*

Notes on Contributors

Sverker Finnström holds a PhD in cultural anthropology from Uppsala University, Sweden, where he also teaches and coordinates the activities of the Living Beyond Conflict Seminar. His PhD thesis, *Living with Bad Surroundings: War and Existential Uncertainty in Acholiland, Northern Uganda*, was published by Uppsala University Press in 2003.

Caspar Fithen was trained in anthropology at University College London and in diamonds in Antwerp. After experience of mining in Africa he returned to UCL, to write a PhD thesis on the anthropology of diamond mining under war-time conditions in Sierra Leone as part of a joint UCL-Wageningen research group on technology and rural transformation. He currently works as a consultant to the UN on Liberia.

Sten Hagberg is Associate Professor of Cultural Anthropology, Uppsala University. Current research considers history, religion and development in Burkina Faso. Recent publications include *Between Peace and Justice: Dispute settlement between Karaboro farmers and Fulbe agro-pastoralists in Burkina Faso* (1998), *Poverty in Burkina Faso* (2001) and the co-edited *Bonds and Boundaries in Northern Ghana and Southern Burkina Faso* (2000).

Björn Lindgren is researcher at the Nordic Africa Institute, and has carried out research on politics, ethnicity, and gender in Zimbabwe since the early 1990s. He was awarded his PhD in Cultural Anthropology by Uppsala University in 2002. His publications include 'Men Rule, but Blood Speaks' in *Changing Men in Southern Africa*, 2001, R. Morrell, (ed.). University of Natal Press/Zed Books.

Staffan Löfving is Assistant Professor at the Institute of Latin American Studies, Stockholm University. He has a PhD in cultural anthropology from Uppsala University and is the author (with Charlotta Widmark) of *Banners of Belonging: The Politics of Indigenous Identity in Bolivia and Guatemala* (Uppsala 2002).

Ivana Maček received her PhD from the Department of Cultural Anthropology and Ethnology, Uppsala University, in May 2000, with a thesis titled *War Within: Everyday Life in Sarajevo under Siege*. Currently she holds a position of assistant professor in Genocide Studies at the Programme for Holocaust and Genocide Studies, Uppsala University. Her ongoing research combines anthropological and psychological perspectives and deals with research methods in war and post-war processes.

Jan Ovesen is Associate Professor of Cultural Anthropology, Uppsala University. Recent publications include 'Indigenous peoples and development in Laos' (*Moussons* 6, 2003, with Ing-Britt Trankell) and 'Foreigners and honorary Khmers: ethnic minorities in Cambodia.' (in C. Duncan, ed., *Civilizing the Margins: South-east Asian government programs for developing minority ethnic groups*. Ithaca: Cornell University Press, 2004).

Paul Richards is Professor of Technology and Agrarian Development in Wageningen University & Research Centre (The Netherlands) and (honorary) Professor of Anthropology, University College London. He is currently studying rural post-war recovery in Liberia and Sierra Leone. His long-term research focuses on globalisation and the concept of 'common humanity'.

Åsa Tiljander Dahlström wrote her PhD thesis in the Department of Cultural Anthropology, Uppsala University. It will appear as *No Peace of Mind: the Tibetan diaspora in India* (Chennai: Earthworm). She has written a number of articles on collective and individual belonging among Tibetans in India, with a focus on 'home', 'homeland' and 'diaspora'.

Mats Utas is research fellow at the Department of Cultural Anthropology and Ethnology, Uppsala University, and postdoctoral research fellow at the Department of Sociology, Fourah Bay College, Sierra Leone. He defended his PhD thesis, *Sweet Battlefields: Youth and the Liberian Civil War* in June 2003. Current research deals with marginalised youth in urban Sierra Leone.

Editor's Note & Acknowledgements

In September 1997 I spent a month in Uppsala University at the invitation of the Department of Cultural Anthropology to work with a research group that focused on the anthropology of violent conflict and 'new wars'. An outcome was the suggestion that I should help Bernhard Helander edit a collection of essays reflecting the work of this group, a task I readily embraced. He also invited me to make my own contribution, and was happy to accept that this would be a joint piece with one of my own PhD students. The shape of the book was agreed, and we had written a couple of preliminary versions of an editorial overview when Bernhard's illness intervened. As he focused his remaining energies he asked me to continue alone. This left me with a dilemma – how properly to reflect his contribution. He was never able to draft his own chapter, but it was clearly agreed that it would expand on some of the thoughts in a short essay he had published on the provision of social services in post-war Somalia. In re-editing this piece for the present volume I have made one or two attempts to indicate Bernhard's larger aim, without departing significantly from his text. In regard to the introduction to the book it was Bernhard's final request that I would remove the sections he had drafted, which he felt he could no longer develop to his full satisfaction, and continue in my own name. This I have done (though with regret, for his line was intriguing and tone trenchant). I take sole responsibility for the chapter as it now stands, though conscious that it would not have developed as it did without our editorial interactions. I am aware, also, that there are a number of distinctive turns of phrase, in Bernhard's elegant and impeccable English, which I have been happy to absorb as my own. In the African social worlds to which Bernhard and I by marriage belong this can be accounted an aspect of ancestral blessing – in life we bear the indelible traces of those who go before us. Bernhard died in December 2001. For academics there can be no better reward than recognition of the stimulus we provide for our colleagues and students. Accordingly this book is offered not only in Bernhard's memory, but also as a living tribute to his work and influence.

Special thanks are due to ir. Hilde van Dijkhorst for her cheerful efficiency in coordinating the contributors and checking many details in the final stages of preparation, without which a distracted editor (more often in war-ravaged up-country Sierra Leone than Wageningen during the period in question) would not have been able to submit the final manuscript on time.

P.R

OBITUARY OF
Bernhard Helander
IOAN LEWIS with additional material by HUGH BEACH

Just before Christmas, 2001, after a long and courageous struggle with cancer, the well-known Swedish Somali scholar Bernhard Helander died in Uppsala. Bernhard was only forty-three years of age and leaves his wife, Jenny, and two delightful teenage girls. His funeral in Uppsala, on 8 January 2002 brought together a large number of academicians and students, including several Somalis.

This was a simple and moving ceremony, marking the loss of this very distinguished young Swedish scholar who was the leading Swedish social scientist specialising on Somalia and, indeed, the most outstanding Somali specialist of his generation in Europe. Bernhard spoke fluent Af–Maymay as well as 'standard Somali', doing his PhD research amongst the Rahanweyn, and subsequently in Puntland. He had an international reputation based on his writings and his commitment to Somali issues.

At UN request, we [BH, IL] set up the UN Somalia 'reference group' with Ambassador Sahnoun, a think-tank based in Sweden at the Life and Peace Institute, which was supposed to guide UN policy in UNOSOM. After Sahnoun resigned, however, and the UN was clearly no longer interested in seriously debating its policies, our position became untenable and we became strong critics of the UN position. This was reflected in Bernhard's remarkable *Somalia News Update* which he wrote and published between 1992 and 1994. There were sometimes as many as three editions a day, and the newsletter which was widely regarded as the most authoritative source of information on events in Somalia had over 3,000 subscribers all over the world! This tremendous undertaking naturally interfered with the flow of Bernhard's scholarly publications and did not greatly advance his university career. But Bernhard was more concerned in discovering and broadcasting the true facts about what was happening in Somalia than in achieving academic success in a narrow sense. His expertise was a constant point of reference for the Swedish media and government, and his advice and support were greatly valued by hundreds of Somali asylum seekers in Sweden. Although his major Rahanweyn study remains to be published (and we hope soon will be), and despite his other commitments, Bernhard has left us an important series of monographs and specialist articles which illustrate the range of his anthropological expertise.

Bernhard was also an inspiring teacher of social anthropology at Uppsala University and in his last days he and his family were strongly supported by Somali friends and by a devoted circle of students and colleagues. His tragic death at such a young age creates a huge gap in Somali affairs in Sweden, where he will long be remembered for his scholarship and humanitarian commitment. Bernhard had a delightful, puckish sense of humour, very far removed from the stereotype of the solemn Swedish academic. Those who had the privilege of knowing him well as a friend and collaborating with him in research will not easily forget him.

For further information see *Somalia Watch*, 3 January 2002 where Dr Jan Haakonsen, a Norwegian colleague, briefly recalls his career.

1

New War
An Ethnographic Approach

PAUL RICHARDS

New War?

The ending of the Cold War closed a chapter in world history, in which the major powers monopolised war. Until the 1980s every conflict was in some way shaped by the ideological struggle between East and West. The chief protagonists – the United States and the Soviet Union – fought wars by proxy in Africa, Southeast Asia and central America. War and the threat of war between Israel and the Arab states quickly took on the aspect of American/Russian confrontation. Perhaps unsurprisingly, intellectuals were preoccupied with how to avoid nuclear annihilation. This meant less interest in war and peace as conditions. Even though the Cold War was, ironically, only intermittently an actual war, and mostly (for Europeans and North Americans) an uneasy peace, the terms 'war' and 'peace' were often taken for granted. The priority was to find out how to win (or prevent) war, and achieve lasting peace.

Philosophers or poets might meditate on deeper meanings from time to time. Strategists used mathematical game theory to model nuclear conflict scenarios. Comparative, empirical study of war, however, was left mainly to military professionals, historians, or anthropologists with antiquarian interests. Historians were read by the strategists, or those who had fought in battles. The anthropologists had a smaller audience. Even within the discipline, the comparative analysis of 'primitive' war was seen as old-fashioned, and to propose a matching comparative anthropological study of 'peace' a very odd idea indeed. Peace was taken for granted – a default condition – despite the far-sighted Max Gluckman alerting his readers that 'custom' and 'conflict' always went hand in hand (Gluckman 1956). War – we thought we knew – was Super-Power rivalry. Peace would supervene with victory of one system over the other (or ideological accommodation).

Right-wing scholars had the option to put their anthropological skills at the service of those who campaigned for a capitalist Free World. Left-wing scholars rallied to those who opposed the crushing of a communist-led peasantry in Vietnam. The idea that any of us might actually carry out field study within a Cold War zone of conflict, and write an ethnography of war and peace, was practically unthinkable. Even to get field access would imply some kind of cosy relationship with the military.[1]

The Cold War ended in 1989, and the world changed. The expected 'peace dividend' failed to materialise. On the contrary, Africa, the Balkans and other parts of the former communist world experienced a rash of small wars. If some were unextinguished bush fires from the Cold War era, and others unfinished business from the colonial (or Soviet) era, a third group seemed new kinds of conflicts, apparently provoked by poverty, population pressure or the bizarre hatreds of international terrorists. There was a realisation that these 'new wars' were no longer the monopoly of states (van Creveld 1992), but events in inter-zones – the spaces left where weak states had withdrawn or collapsed.[2]

Once such inter-zone conflict was to prove of especial significance. After Soviet withdrawal, Afghanistan was abandoned to internal factional bickering. A modicum of order was restored by the Taleban – a movement of young scholars raised in the Deoband system of Islamic schooling (Rashid 2000). Its leaders provided refuge for the al-Qaida group, a network of 'Afghan Arabs' promoting a trans-national political Islam.[3] Al-Qaida was apparently behind the surprise terrorist attack on the United States on September 11 2001. An international alliance, led by the USA, sprang into being to deal with an unprecedented threat; a 'war against terrorism' was declared (Talbott and Chanda 2001).

Where this leads, no one knows. What is clear, however, is that rich, comfortable countries cannot risk leaving 'new wars' in poor, uncomfortable regions to blaze unattended. To cite two examples: the Lord's Resistance Movement/Army (LRM/A) in northern Uganda and the Revolutionary United Front of Sierra Leone (RUF/SL) promptly appeared on the United States' list of terrorist organisations, proscribed after September 11th. In the case of the RUF an obvious reason was that the al-Qaida network was thought to have bought alluvial diamonds from the organisation immediately prior to its attacks on the United States, to protect financial reserves previously held in banks. It would be hard to imagine a group further from the well-connected, well-funded world of international 'political Islam' than the impoverished, ragged-trousered school drop-outs of the RUF (Richards 2004). The case suggests that no war in the South, however small, will now be ignored by the Northern allies.

As 'new war' has risen on the scale of political visibility, so scholars and public intellectuals have been forced to take up the challenge. Freed from strategising 'mutually assured destruction', debate has returned to basics. What is war? Some very old answers have reappeared. War is greed. War is poverty. War is organised revenge. War is wickedness. War is human nature.

Clausewitz[4] argued we should understand war as the calculated use of violence for rational political ends. But for most commentators, 'new war' is 'mindless' mass action. It has become a behavioural phenomenon. War breaks

---

[1] Anthropology was more engaged in the struggle in SE Asia than the profession cares to remember, even if little of this work is today credited with academic respectability (Salemink 2003).

[2] The anthropologists Ferguson & Whitehead (1992) had already argued that 'tribal conflict' was less 'primitive' violence than an aspect of instability on the margins of states and empires.

[3] 'Afghan Arabs' is a conventional phrase to describe recruits to the particular brand of transnational political Islam harboured by the Taleban regime in Afghanistan. Recruits belong to many different nationalities (including Britain, France and the USA), cf. Rashid (2000).

[4] Carl von Clausewitz, *Vom Kriege*, 1832 (*On War*) trs. J. J. Graham, 1908, republished in an abridged edition with introduction by A. Rapoport, Pelican Classics, Penguin Books, Harmondsworth 1968.

out from time to time, like a midsummer riot in a jail. It spreads unaccountably, like a fashion. People apparently become 'infected' with the idea of war. 'New war' is the hazard that has first to be contained before other more cultured and desirous developments can occur.

The epidemiological image appeals especially to policy makers in rich countries, reluctant to consider 'new war' a conscious adaptation in the South to global economic restructuring dominated by Northern interests (Duffield 2001). If war is a disease, then there are no sides; coordinated international action is needed to eradicate a common threat. The tools for ending war are no longer diplomacy and hard bargaining but the peace-keeping mission, 'grass-roots' conflict resolution, police work, and humanitarian aid. This is necessary immunisation without which poor countries cannot grow. The 2001 Genoa 'G8' summit (of the heads of government of the world's largest national economies), addressing the problems of Africa, the poorest and youngest continent, resolved that dealing with the scourge of war was a *pre-condition* for the continent's economic revival. Where thirty years ago Northern countries would have been quietly planning and promoting wars in Africa to protect economic interests or favoured political dogma, they now prefer to quarantine war, and strive (in the words of Duffield, 2001: 14–15) to impose a 'liberal peace'.

There are, of course, variations on the theme. Different analysts stress different aspects. War is the way nature deals with overpopulation, war is inherent in cultural or religious difference, war is unregulated economic competition. But all these arguments – in varying degrees of sophistication – serve to set up a dichotomy between war as some kind of inherent 'bad' (the world ruled by instincts and base desire), and peace as an ideal 'good' (the world ruled by principle and law). With this kind of approach war itself becomes the enemy – indeed, the common enemy of human kind. The idea finds perfect expression in the phrase 'war on terrorism', which implies that it is a methodology of war and not a well-defined human enemy that is to be attacked.

The danger of analysing war as a disorderly 'bad' is that it tends to take war out of its social context. War is foregrounded as a 'thing in itself' and not – as we shall argue it to be – one social project among many competing social projects. Foregrounding war risks disabling precisely the strategies and tools of social organisation, culture and politics through which violence can be reduced and its adverse effects mitigated.

In this book we take a different approach. We offer a set of essays by anthro-pologists who have lived with and through the wars they describe over a number of years, reflecting an assumption that may at first seem paradoxical – that to understand war we must first deny it special status. We try to avoid quarantining war as a 'disease' – a matter for security specialists – but try instead to grasp its character as but one among many different phases or aspects of social reality. War, like peace, is organised by social agents. Often the methods are the same, as business school readers of the classics of war and strategy well know. Some-times (as Banerjee 2001 shows) non-violence is a way of waging war. We intend to place war back within the range of social possibilities, as something made through social action, and something that can be moderated by social action, rather than viewing it as so exceptional as to require 'special' explanatory effort.[5]

[5] Compare Das and Kleinman (2000) whose book of essays 'questions any established distinctions between ... times of violence and times of peace'.

To us, all war – and 'new war' is no exception – is long-term struggle organised for political ends, commonly but not always using violence. Neither the means nor the ends can be understood without reference to a specific social context. Our definition includes international terrorism, and the activities of ethnic militias in Rwanda or Bosnia, or insurgent or separatist forces in, e.g., Colombia or Sierra Leone, irrespective of whether they base their campaigns on drugs and diamonds or the willing support of land-hungry peasants. We would also include non-violence as a way of mobilising for war. In Banerjee's striking example, the 'martial' Pathans of the North-West frontier fought British colonialism in the 1930s through a movement that clothed its troops in uniforms, and drilled them for the struggle ahead, but without resorting to weapons or the use of violence (Banerjee 2001).

We especially object to the notion of 'new war' as some kind of 'mindless' response to stimuli such as population pressure or cultural competition. As is explained more fully later, we are sceptical about 'environmental' factors, 'clash of cultures', or 'trans-boundary' political economy as causes of war. Our reasons for rejecting these arguments is that none of them offers a convincing explanation of why wars happen when and where they do, offering only an explanation how war is intensified or prolonged. These explanations are quite powerless to explain 'peaceful' wars of the kind Banerjee (2001) describes.

Belligerents gravitate towards resources to fight, but there are plenty of cases where wars begin without plentiful resources, and cases where resources are plentiful and no war occurs. In other words, war does not break out because conditions happen to be 'right', but because it is organised. Someone has to resolve to embark on the high-risk strategy of seizing power through mobilisation and violence. The venture has to be planned. Fighters have to be trained, the weapons obtained. Tactics have to be devised and a campaign executed. This is the work of specific groups in society; understanding the character, organization and beliefs of these groups, and their impact on other groups supporting, resisting or victimised by their activities, is an essential task for the analyst. In short, war is inescapably sociological.[6]

The argument applies as much to al-Qaida as to the Viet Cong. The first step towards wisdom is not to highlight 'new war' but to re-integrate war and peace – i.e. to locate war within the precise social contexts from which it springs. Waving a flag over 'new war' is less helpful, we will suggest, than merging it with its 'background'. We make our argument through the examination of specific cases. Our book, in other words, is a set of ethnographic (or contextual) essays on the intertwined nature of war and peace, written on the basis of field-work undertaken in war-affected and war-vulnerable societies. One of our aims is to demonstrate this approach is possible, even in active war zones. If war is 'exempted' from the world of the social – and left to military specialists – this is only because (at first sight) it seems too dangerous to study. We show there are ways round this problem. The ethnography of 'new war' is possible. However, we are writing not only for professional anthropologists, the usual consumers of ethnographic analysis. We hope also to reach a larger audience made up of practitioners dealing with war and its consequences – an audience that includes policy makers, humanitarian fieldworkers, peace keepers, and peace activists in

---

[6] We should add that much the same argument applies to civil violence; ethnic or religious riots, for example, rarely 'just happen'. They tend to be highly organised events.

war zones. We try to establish, *contra* 'broad brush' explanations, why a contextual approach is worth the effort. We suggest such effort is, in fact, essential for practical intervention. The lessons of a number of botched peace-keeping missions or failed peace processes are that a sound grasp of social issues was missing. Our essays serve to exemplify the *range* of social issues practitioners may need to address.

The ethnographic approach advocated in this collection will stress that war is a social project among other social projects. We do the ethnography of war best, we will argue, not by imposing a sharp categorical distinction between 'war' and 'peace', but by thinking in terms of a continuum.[7] This helps us appreciate, for example, that many wars are long periods of (uneasy) peace interrupted by occasional eruptions of violence, that war is often (as Thomas Hobbes [*Leviathan*, 1651] suggested) a state of mind shared among participants, that 'peace' can often be more violent and dangerous than 'war',[8] and that fighting draws upon the social and organisational skills people deploy to sustain peace (Henriques 2002).

A last point before passing on to review some of the literature: in handling something as tricky as war the devil is in the detail. Our book says 'when it comes to war and peace, every case needs its own context'. Of course, we cannot pretend to cover every war in which a reader might be interested, or to provide more than an introduction to the ten conflicts we do cover. But our cases are sufficiently diverse to indicate a range of approaches to the task of contextualising war. The reader will find we run a gamut from the phenomenological (cf. Nordstrom 1997) to the neo-Durkheimian (cf. Sivan 1995). These different approaches converge on common ends – a better grasp of the social dimensions of war, and of the agency of the war-affected in re-inventing peace.

New Wars, Old Explanations: Some Recent Literature

Viewed as human struggle taken to extremes, war inevitably invites superlatives. It is no surprise to find the literature on war and its causes is vast, and begins in ancient times (cf. Sun Tzu, c. 4th century BCE, date and authorship unsettled [trs. Griffith 1963]). Much of it falls into two very broad categories: how to prosecute (or defend against) war, and what we might term 'war as metric'. The purpose of the first kind of literature is to help train soldiers or advise practitioners of statecraft. 'War as metric', in contrast, uses violent conflict as a yardstick for assessing or promoting other concerns. How does war affect children or environment? What do we learn about the theorems of economics or morality when we consider war? Do the facts of violence support or contradict certain aspects of evolutionary theory? Such studies are, of course, often highly valuable, but they may not tell us as much about war (or peace) as they tell us about childhood, rain forests, the economist's vision of the world, or the sociobiological conception of human nature. Rather than attempt a general (but necessarily inadequate) review of this vast literature we will focus here instead on some recent material

---

[7] Cf. Aretxaga (1997: 4) who writes 'Peace and war are not so much two opposed states of being as they are multi-faceted, ambiguous, mutually imbricated areas of struggle.'

[8] The death toll in the 'exceptionally brutal' civil war in Sierra Leone in 11 years (1991-2002) is estimated at c. 150,000 (i.e. < 15,000/year). The current murder rate in South Africa is c. 25,000 victims a year.

that has been of greatest influence in debates about post-Cold War conflict. A critique of this literature helps establish what is different about our ethnographic approach.

Three kinds of explanation of 'new war' emerged during the 1990s. All are rooted deeply in European thought of the 17th and 18th centuries (and herein lies one aspect of the problem of their relevance and international applicability). Here we will label them 'Malthus with guns', 'the new barbarism', and the 'greed not grievance' debates. As 'broad brush' explanatory archetypes they have been vigorously marketed in policy circles, and have played an important role in new thinking about the linkage between security and development in the South. All three approaches feature in what Duffield (2001) considers a major new Northern project for the 21st century – the putting together of a coalition of governments and aid agencies to impose on the South what he terms a 'liberal peace'. We are perhaps less certain than Duffield that this security-and-development debate amounts to a coherent neo-colonialism. But his argument that 'new war' reflects the terms upon which the South is being incorporated into a global economy raises the possibility that current 'broad brush' interpretations of 'new war' in the South are successful not because they are empirically well-grounded but more because they resonate with particular sets of ideological presuppositions entertained by Northern policy makers seeking to manage globalisation. After considering the 'new war' debate we will then offer an account of some anthropological literature supporting the kind of ethnographic or contextual alternative we develop below.

i. Malthus with guns

Are wars caused by competition over resources? In 1991 T. F. Homer-Dixon published a think-piece *cum* research proposal arguing the case for testing a causal connection between environmental scarcity and human conflict, something he supposed was liable to become more important with increasing world population. A good example of post-Cold War resurgence of interest in Malthusian approaches to the causes of war,[9] the original research design considered six types of environmental change: greenhouse-induced climate change, ozone depletion, land degradation, forest destruction, water pollution/depletion, and fisheries depletion. The cases included Nile and Jordan water conflicts, flood-induced migration in Bangladesh/Assam, Miskito Indian opposition to the Sandanista regime in Nicaragua, land-resource-linked economic decline in the Philippines and China, ethnic conflict in the Senegal River valley, and the Andean insurgency of Shining Path.

After examining the data more closely, and review by expert panels, Homer-Dixon arrived at a rather different (or more nuanced) set of conclusions. Homer-Dixon (1994) still claims that the major hypothesis – environmental scarcity causes violent conflict – is supported by the case-study material. But this conclusion is reached only by considering any type of resource competition evidence of environmental scarcity, and yet clearly this is not the case. For example, he concedes that expropriation of Atlantic-coast peasants in Nicaragua may have caused environmental deterioration in the first place (in other words

---

[9] Thomas Robert Malthus [1766–1834], British 19th century political economist, who argued that population increase always outstrips the resource base until reined in by famine, disease, war or voluntary restraint.

the scarcity was not Malthusian but political). In a second case, ethnic violence between Moors and Black Africans in the Senegal River Valley resulted not from environmental scarcity but from a struggle to control land made more productive by river-basin developments. It is an odd kind of Malthusianism in which people start to fight because the resource base is *more productive* than before.

These apparent contradictions are not explained. Homer-Dixon shifts ground instead, arguing that 'resource competition is partly subjective' (ibid.: 10). Adaptation is introduced to save appearances: 'as environmental scarcity becomes more severe, some societies will have a progressively lower capacity to adapt ... of particular concern is the decreasing capacity of the state to create markets and other institutions that promote adaptation' (ibid.: 40). But it remains a supposition; little evidence is offered concerning this alleged low capacity for institutional innovation in poor countries. At the same time the argument remains doggedly materialistic. Homer-Dixon has little time for the possibility that 'resources' have non-material dimensions, such as access to media, political titles or control of clients. Nowhere does the paper address the notion that the problem might be 'scarcity' not of resources but of *justice* (in resource allocation).

A subsequent book appeared seeking a broader audience for these ideas (Homer Dixon 1999). The defects of the analysis remain. The author avoids literature that contradicts his argument, such as conflicts where it can be demonstrated that there is no significant renewable resource scarcity dimension (e.g. Richards 1996). He continues to define 'environmental scarcity' so broadly that the phrase is pretty well meaningless. Since armed conflict almost invariably involves control of terrain then every conflict is in some sense a 'land conflict'. The author claims to focus on civil war and insurgency, but sweeps coups, urban violence, crime and skirmishing into the frame as and when it suits his purposes. There is no attempt ever to explain what an insurgency is, or what it involves (how it is organised, who takes part). For instance, it is claimed – sweepingly – that land shortage was a 'cause' of the Shining Path insurgency in Peru, but without any analysis of how many of the cadres were actually young aspirant farmers. The book further develops a tendency apparent in earlier papers – so to hedge about what is claimed by exceptions and caveats that in effect nothing is claimed, except by vague implication. A quotation from the concluding chapter highlights the difficulty: 'because the relationship between environmental scarcity and contextual factors is interactive, it is impossible to determine the relative weight or power of environmental scarcity as a cause of violence in specific cases' (Homer-Dixon 1999: 179). This seems so weak as to undermine the argument altogether. The author notes at the very outset of his book that the analysis remains 'still in some ways only a preliminary sketch' (ibid.: 4). All he establishes, in fact, is a *prima facie* case – though he calls it his 'key finding' – that 'scarcity of renewable resources ... can contribute to civil violence'. Who would disagree? But this is far from claiming that environmental scarcity causes war. We might want to conclude, in fact, that the main value of the work of Homer-Dixon lies in the way the data refute the initial assumptions – explanation of violence in Malthusian terms (cf. Peluso and Watts 2001).

Malthusian sentiment remains firmly entrenched in the international developmental agencies and among global campaigning groups, for whom 'scarcity' and 'resources' trigger a presumed instinctive human response. This is despite there being a good test of Malthus at hand. If the scarcity thesis was valid – if hunger (for example) was a regular cause of violence – then food aid would help put an end to wars. A wide range of evidence suggests that exactly the opposite is true. Food aid tends to inflame and prolong conflicts (Keen 1994; de Waal 1997). If the dynamic of war outlives the alleged causal scarcity we must look for more comprehensive – and workable – understanding.

ii. New barbarism

The 'new barbarism' thesis claims the Super-Power balance of nuclear terror kept the lid on many local conflicts, but, once Cold War competition ended, endemic hostilities reasserted themselves, notably in the Balkans and Africa. This is to claim that 'culture' and 'ethnicity' are ineradicable 'things-in-themselves'. Robert Kaplan, whose book on the Balkans (1993) is said to have been responsible for some of the Clinton presidency's dithering on Bosnia, analyses former Yugoslavia in terms of such 'ancient hatreds' (Kaplan 1994; 1996). Samuel P. Huntington (1999) – a noted political thinker from the Cold War era – develops a variant on the idea: that global blocks demarcated by the major world religions are separated by a gulf of such ineradicable cultural hostilities that conflict must ensue. Huntington cites anthropologists among his authorities, but few would recognise his attempt to put the clock back on debates about ethnicity and culture (Kuper 1999). Work by Barth (1969) and Cohen (1969) helped establish that ethnic consciousness emerges at the boundary *between* groups, rather than being something intrinsic to the group itself. Secondly, ethnic mobilisation, as Burnham (1996) has more recently emphasised, is a type of cultural work. Whether or not ethnicity or cultural difference is called into play as a mode of organising depends on what other organisational modes are open to agents and competitors, and the costs and benefits associated with these alternatives. If there is current mobilisation around ethnic difference (whether in Africa or Europe) we should look not to 'ancient hatreds' but to the relative feasibility of arranging different kinds of political action, and how economic and political developments (such as globalisation or market liberalisation in eastern Europe) might have reduced the 'transaction costs' associated with ethnic options.

The appeal of the 'new barbarism' thesis is two-fold. In the case of Africa or the Balkans it justifies a non-interventionist stance (these conflicts are too hard to comprehend). But in the case of Islam (a major concern in Huntington's analysis) it suggests that Western Cold War security and intelligence networks might find a new role for themselves by reorganising to meet a threat operating on the same scale as the Cold War challenge from the 'Soviet empire'. Under the stimulus of the 'war against terrorism' it is an idea that attracts strong advocates.

Kaplan's worst-case scenario failed to materialise: 'barbaric' African wars did not spill uncontrollably over borders and create havoc among peaceful and unsuspecting neighbours. If anything the reverse is the case. In much of Africa it is the neighbours who inflame local conflicts by venturing across borders, seeking to control what might otherwise be quite localised fighting. Cases in point are Nigerian and Guinean 'peace keeping' activities in Liberia and Sierra Leone.[10] Ethiopian and Eritrean support for opposing militias in Somalia, and, most obvious of all, the role of six neighbouring countries (including Angola, Uganda

[10] An upsurge of fighting in Guinea (2000-2001) might be considered a 'spill over' from Liberia and Sierra Leone, though one factor seems to be factionalism within the Guinean army.

and Zimbabwe) in the war in the Democratic Republic of Congo. In complex settings, such as those just mentioned, the 'ancient hatreds' approach, and the focus on causes rather than processes and consequences of war, become untenable, and may in fact serve to obscure a clear analysis of the situation (Keen 1999).

Perhaps we should not fuss too much. It seems that new barbarism's moment has passed. In the end the Clinton administration did engage with the Balkans, and the British were drawn into Sierra Leone (Kaplan's chief examples of pointless conflicts based on incomprehensible barbarism). The 'war against terrorism' demands a new interventionism; failed states like Afghanistan are too dangerous to ignore. In any case, American and Western European inward-looking preoccupation with the 'high tech' economy was on the wane. With capital in a more vigorously expansive mood than for some time, a new notion – 'greed not grievance' – has become the global explanatory summary of choice.

iii. Greed, not grievance

Recently, there has been considerable attention to the idea that internal wars are explained as much by economic considerations as by inter-group hatreds (Berdal & Keen 1997; Berdal and Malone 2000; Le Billon 2000; 2001). The argument has been applied, in particular, to three alluvial diamond producing African countries (Angola, Congo and Sierra Leone) which between them produce all the world's so-called 'conflict diamonds' (about 4 per cent of total output). African alluvial diamonds are mined in 'bush' localities and readily smuggled across borders. It has been suggested that wars in all three countries are largely funded by clandestine diamond mining activity (Smillie et al. 1999).[11] Proponents of 'greed, not grievance' do not limit their arguments to 'conflict diamonds' alone, however. They aspire to explain much or all post-Cold War conflict.

Undoubtedly, there is some merit in the argument that economic rivalries greatly complicate and prolong a number of wars (Angola is a clear case in point). Close reading of a representative text (Le Billon 2000) makes clear, however, that proponents of 'greed not grievance' (rather like Homer-Dixon) are careful not to claim too much. Le Billon appears to be about to offer a new theory of war, but nowhere actually says greed causes war. What is argued in the end is that economic factors are necessary but not sufficient conditions for conflicts to occur, and that '*perpetuation* of war can become an end in itself' (Le Billon 2000: 4, my emphasis). As with Homer-Dixon's conclusion that resource scarcity 'can contribute to violence' it would be hard to disagree, since fighting a war without any resources is difficult to imagine (presumably it would be a bare-knuckle fight lasting less than a day). But Le Billon offers no cases where economic free-for-all is the *only* factor behind a war (cf. Le Billon 2001, Fairhead 2001; Peluso and Watts 2001).

We should also note a bias built into the language used. Downgrading political enemies as 'bandits and thieves' has long been stock-in-trade for the parties to

[11] Cynics wonder whether the 'conflict diamond' argument flourishes only as a by-product of major recent changes in the structure of the world diamond trade, where the major player, De Beers, has abandoned its buying cartel and is investing in new 'industrial' mining sites outside Africa, notably in Canada, from where some of the lobbying to outlaw 'conflict diamonds' has been most intense. It helps to 'ditch' alluvial diamonds produced by artisanal methods. Because of difficulties in proving exact provenance, a decision to ban 'blood diamonds' may exclude most African alluvial diamonds from the USA, giving a clear run for 'certificated' product in a most important market.

any conflict. Duffield (2001) charges that this is happening on a global scale. The North, reluctant to engage in a real political debate about the costs and conse- quences of global economic restructuring, determines instead to impose a 'humanitarian' peace on a South apparently over-run by 'criminals', 'bandits' and 'drug barons'. 'Greed not grievance' serves a clear ideological and practical purpose in this regard. If Southern conflict is apolitical it is not diplomacy but international policing that is needed. Closing down bank accounts and supply trails, imposing sanctions regimes, and naming and shaming the diamond merchants, drug dealers and gun runners is better than tedious negotiations with politically illiterate and self-styled 'rebels'.[12]

One of the most widely noticed analyses of 'greed not grievance' is that by Paul Collier (2000). What makes Collier's analysis interesting and different from explanations couched in terms of neo-Malthusianism and neo-barbarism is his emphasis on war as *process*. He approaches his topic through econometric analysis of data sets covering most internal wars since 1960.

First we need note a couple of caveats. Since wars cannot be fought without resources, correlation between war and economic variables is unsurprising. What Collier is unable clearly to demonstrate is whether it is 'war' or 'war economy' that is the independent variable. There are also problems with the way he labels (proxy) variables. What Collier considers 'economic' others might more readily consider political. For example, his analysis shows that internal wars are more likely where mineral wealth combines with poverty, and where there is high unemployment among young men with limited education, but (perversely) he considers neither circumstance grounds for valid political grievance. This seems very odd to anyone with on-the-ground knowledge of youth activism against oil companies in the Niger Delta or rebels facing mercenary-backed kimberlite concession holders in Sierra Leone. Why it is 'greedy' to want a basic education or a job Collier does not explain.

On the other hand, the results themselves are intriguing, and resonate with several findings from several recent on-the-ground ethnographically-oriented studies. Collier concludes that ethnic diversity correlates only weakly with war. Highly ethnically diverse countries such as Tanzania are better at avoiding conflict than countries such as Nigeria or Rwanda, where two or three powerful ethnic blocks compete for control. This aligns with anthropological findings concerning the relative costs of ethnically-based forms of political mobilisation, as mentioned above (Burnham 1996). The analysis also reveals that inequality (for example, as measured by access to land), and dictatorship are poor statistical predictors of conflict, though perhaps not surprisingly in the latter case, since it is the business of dictators to crush internal dissent. More interesting is Collier's discovery that having a large US-based diaspora is a major factor disposing towards risk of internal war. This surprising result ties in well with recent work on the ground, granted the reservation that this is by no means, as Collier assumes, always an economic issue (wealthy diaspora elements having the resources to meddle). Work on war in the Horn of Africa and the Mano River conflicts (wars in Liberia, Guinea and Sierra Leone) suggests that diaspora groups

---

[12] It has become clear that it is the interaction of 'greed' and 'grievance' that constitutes a central difficulty in the 'war on terrorism'. The ideologically-driven Shining Path imposed order on the drug districts of the Upper Huallaga valley (Gonzales 1992); the highly ascetic Taleban imposed order on the drugs economy of Afghanistan (Rashid 2000).

– especially based in the USA – are just as likely to be engaging in unfinished political business, or to be acting out pan-Africanist fantasies (Richards 2004), as pursuing economic agenda.

In broad terms Collier's approach is consistent with the general argument we make in this book for a greater emphasis on process and practice when explaining war and peace. Our main disagreement is with his assumption that economic factors necessarily predominate. Part of Collier's argument in this respect is especially dubious. He asserts that discourse-based social science analysis of conflict is *inevitably* undermined by informants hiding their true interests. Rebels will always make their greed more acceptable by talking about grievances, he asserts. The only true measure, he believes, is behaviour – as revealed by econometric analysis. Given that our book seeks to promote the importance of the ethnography of war and peace, this is an argument with which we have to engage.

Collier seems to be basically misinformed about how other social scientists approach their research. Anthropologists and others who take what people say seriously are not as naive as he assumes. Different interests tell untruths in different ways, and it is a standard part of anthropological method to reconstruct a more 'objective' picture through careful cross-referencing of 'versions' and 'interests' (cf. Archibald and Richards 2002; Malkki 1995; Sommers 2001). A second important point about the ethnographic approach is that anthropologists (unlike economists) observe at first hand. They work *in* war zones, even at times writing from the perspective of civilians caught up in the fighting directly (see Maček below). In other words, anthropology wrestles long and hard with the manifold *details* of cases. There are no short cuts. War may be deeply unpleasant, and dangerous, but only by stepping up close will the complex intertwining of multiple motivations become tractable to analysis. Reading a balance sheet from afar is simply no substitute for well-grounded attempts to grasp the inherent complexity of war. But perhaps the main point *contra* Collier in this regard is that anthropologists (and others) have already drawn attention to precisely the factors he claims to have 'discovered' through his econometric analysis (cf. Burnham 1996 on ethnicity; Richards 1996 on youth and education).

We leave Collier to his prejudices about the other social sciences. The real basis of our disagreement is not about numbers, but the labelling of the variables. Once the alienation of the young unemployed, or the millenarian dreams of diaspora groups, are seen for what they are – political variables – Collier's proposed conceptual division between 'greed' and 'grievance' disappears.

iv. The ethnographic perspective

Our own approach is that 'new war' needs to be understood in relation to patterns of violence already embedded within society. The way to tackle this aspect of the subject is through the ethnography of practice.[13] Careful analysis of what people do, and how they do it – for example, in carrying out 'bush' campaigns or organising ethnic killing – may help to establish what conflict is about. Here we cannot adequately review the full range of recent anthropological

---

[13] Stewart and Strathern (2002) advocate a practice orientation as a means to keep a focus on two rather distinctive aspects of the anthropological study of lethal violence – the strategic/instrumental approach (cf. Riches 1986) and an approach which engages with symbolic and expressive/emotional aspects (cf. Kapferer 1998).

literature on violence (the reader is referred to syntheses by Riches 1986 and Stewart and Strathern 2002). But it does seem relevant to reflect, briefly, on what anthropologists have written about so-called 'primitive war' as an (at times) mundane aspect of social life in two regions (Melanasia and sub-Saharan Africa).

This theme has been developed particularly in the Melanesian literature. A very useful survey by Knauft (1990) brings out two of the themes we wish to stress: that war belongs within society, that mono-causal perspectives (whether stressing resource competition, material motivation economics or symbolic aspects of violence) are ultimately unsatisfactory. Knauft's main conclusion is that the careful comparative analysis of ethnographic evidence establishes no single explanation of war. War only makes sense as an aspect of social process. The best analytical approach to war as process is through the ethnography of the actual practices of war and peace.

Knauft first directs attention to a long-lasting Hobbesian bias in anthropological writing on primitive conflict. War was viewed as a state of nature overcome only by social contract. This is the very same bias that motivates the analyses of 'new war' most influential over the Northern policy makers seeking to impose a 'liberal peace' on the South. Once especially strong in British social anthropology, it rests on a circularity of definition of political/ social units in terms of 'their ability to adjudicate internal conflict and cohere in hostility against outsiders' (ibid.: 262). As a result, anthropologists tended to under-report, and thus sanitize, violent conflict. Knauft quotes the auto-critique of Elizabeth Colson, who remarked that Africanist anthropologists: '... downplayed the violence, cruelty and unhappiness existing in areas where we worked ... [thinking] such actions were momentary departures from cultural norms that generated long-term harmony, but ... by doing so we falsified the record' (ibid.: 250–1). In the Melanesian case, a second reason for misrepresentation reflects a culture-clash between the specific values of Western militarism (universalised as 'rules of war') and Melanesian ideas about armed combat, in which 'dirty tricks' (surprise attack, terror tactics and rout) are practically effective and cosmologically significant, a misrepresentation compounded by failure adequately to take interpretive account of the impact of colonial violence against local people.

Knauft then addresses an equal but opposite danger – the over-simplified materialist explanations of war, such as arguments that war is a struggle for land, or response to Malthusian pressure of population. Arguments of the kind revived recently by Homer-Dixon have already been tested to destruction in the Melanesian literature, leading to the conclusion that 'the existence or intensity of warfare in pre-state societies cannot be predicted as a linear function of population density, population pressure, or protein scarcity' (ibid.: 270). Nor are structural-functionalist accounts superior. The data concerning the practice of war, he notes, offer little support for any notion that war is a means of dealing with social tensions. Melanesian studies suggest war and peace are concurrent, and competing, modes of existence, not alternating phases in the maintenance of ordered social relations. The consensus among Melanesian scholars is that war can only be explained by reference to cultural and ideational as well as material factors. This necessarily includes reference to the way fear is constituted within society and the way terror is manipulated by belligerent agents. 'Neither peace nor war are "natural" states ...' but ones constituted in practice, at a historical juncture where 'predisposing cultural orientations and sociomaterial opportunities and constraints' meet. Whether local institutions work, or conflict needs mediation, cannot be assessed 'on the basis of ... *a priori* assumptions', but only by reference to the situation in hand (ibid.: 279). The analysis of conflict, and the possibilities of mediation depend, crucially, not on abstract social theory, but (so Knauft concludes) on absorbing the lessons of modern theories of practice.

Africa was 'pacified' (often brutally) by colonial authorities, so (despite Colson's strictures) Africanists have never had quite so much material on war to work with as anthropologists studying the isolated and warlike groups in interior Papua-New Guinea. But Kopytoff (1987), looking with the eye of an anthropologist at precolonial materials, has developed arguments that complement those of Knauft. Kopytoff's view of pre-colonial African history is that politically marginalised groups – forced migrants, runaway slaves or those who lost wars – were not exceptional cases on the fringes of the mainstream of African historical developments. Rather, he suggests, 'loser' groups often constituted the mainstream. This emphasises an aspect of war easily forgotten in current concern to resolve conflict at all costs, and perhaps even before the social issues at stake are fully understood. Kopytoff's view is that as far as African society was concerned, it was often in the social upheaval created by war that human creativity was let loose, fashioning social innovations, or re-enacting traditional ideals of social perfection (cf. Fardon, 1988).[14] While Kopytoff's essay restricts itself to precolonial African history, we might want to consider whether, to some extent, there is an element of living beyond armed conflict in all societies. As historians of the Dutch Revolts, or the English and American Revolutions might allow, many successful societies make themselves against a background of war-induced devastation or near disaster.

Knauft and Kopytoff challenge us to think about war – including, of course, post-Cold War internal conflicts – as aspects of social process, rather than focusing exclusively on causes. If we are to understand war and peace in processual terms we must first comprehend the practices of war and peace: how people mobilise and organise for war, and the role played by ideational factors in such mobilisation and organisation. In short, in our own essays we will place less emphasis on answering the question 'what triggered war' and more emphasis on exploring how people *make* war and peace.

The War-Peace Continuum: Introducing the Case Studies

We arrange our set of ten ethnographic case studies according to a bell-curve representing the continuum peace-war-peace. We want to bring out how pre-war peace is often more delicate and finely balanced than appreciated, and that the seeds of war are to be seen shooting up in peace; that the shift towards intense

[14] An alternative approach is to see war as an aspect of the expansion of states and empires into peripheral regions ('the tribal zone'). Ferguson and Whitehead (1992) draw on an impressive range of historical materials in making this argument over the *longue duree*. But many 'new wars' seem more associated with the retreat of states than with their expansion. It is ironic that the publisher of a second printing of the Ferguson and Whitehead collection (published 2000) chose a picture of two demobilised young civil defence fighters from the war in Sierra Leone, as a cover illustration, since recent research establishes (Archibald & Richards 2002, cf. Richards 1996) that this war, and young people's engagement in it, is a matter of contesting a weak and retreating state, rather than a consequence of state expansion into the periphery.

armed conflict is a process with many twists and turns (and significant pauses, relevant as opportunities for peace makers); that conflict is sustained by an emergent sociology and economy of war; that turning back towards peace, even beyond a peace agreement, is a rocky path with many pitfalls; that the hidden or silent violence behind conflict has to be addressed if peace is to be sustained (justice matters); that sometimes peace breaks out even without formal peace-making efforts; that war and violence echo in collective and individual memory for generations, and that the institutional fabric to keep armed conflict within bounds over the longer term sometimes emerges from below as well as from above. We also try and make clear that arguments over peace-war-peace are part of the stuff of war as well as peace. Again, a necessary ingredient of this approach lies with its insistence that details matter. In Chapter 10, Tiljander Dahlström talks about the 'small details', like divided families and shattered homes. Every armed conflict is made up of an accumulated mass of such small details and they remain as facts, figures and memories in people's attempts to make social life and a living beyond an armed conflict.

We begin with a study by Jan Ovesen on Cambodia. He reviews the contro-versy over whether the Khmer Rouge terror is to be called a 'genocide'. It was mainly inflicted by Khmers on Khmers. But beyond this definitional point he raises two other major concerns central to the overall purpose of our collection. Bracketing off the four years of the terror 'normalises' (or risks marginalising the significance of) violence associated with the preceding and subsequent peace. Excising Khmer Rouge terror from its broader social context may risk setting up a wild goose chase among incommensurables. If the Nazi holocaust, the Rwanda killings and Khmer Rouge terror are not three instances of some unique and isolated human evil, then we might be better to recognise them as extreme expressions of sets of dangers facing us all. Weaving these events back into their social context may help us see important connections with 'low intensity' violent conflict. This cues a study by Sten Hagberg on Burkina Faso, focusing on exactly this low-level 'background' violence at the left-hand of the peace-war-peace bell curve. Burkina Faso is a country at peace, but potential ethnic violence (at the occupational boundary between farming and herding) risks shooting forth at any moment. Hagberg's issue is how and why local incidents of lethal violence do not get out of hand. He draws attention to a neglected and unfashionable social group: local government officials. Anthropologists sometimes idealise 'their' people. Hagberg makes no heroic claims on behalf of his 'tribe' of officials, but he does point out that a functioning bureaucracy is one of the things that keeps local disputes in check. The regime in Burkina Faso has been accused of involvement in the wars in Liberia and Sierra Leone. How much the country makes from transactions in 'conflict diamonds' is hotly disputed. But it does seem as if the political classes have learnt a lesson from the near collapse of states close by; regular payment for state officials is a vital component of everyday conflict management in rural Burkina Faso.

We then pass to two studies focusing more on the ideational and discursive aspects of war and peace. Ivana Maček describes how civilians lived 'against' war in Sarajevo. As in peace, those who shape war impose social roles, but people have mental and cultural resources to reject or modify those roles. Actively resisting war involves 'fighting' against it, which is to be sucked into a kind of 'combatant' role. Maček explores some less heroic, neglected, but nevertheless valuable ideational stances, especially noteworthy being the stance of the mental 'deserter'. At times, walking away from something proves unexpectedly to be the greater part of valour. Staffan Löfving explores some of the discursive ambiguities associated with the long-term civil war in Guatemala. He approaches his problem via a careful critique of the way certain anthropologists have written about the war, warning against the implicit danger in all our study of (perhaps without realising it) 'taking sides'. His is at heart a methodological concern – how to 'read' silence in war zones. Torture is a weapon of dirty war; silence is a tool of resistance, but also of endurance. At times it may also have a positive meaning – it is the silence of tacit assent. Much anthropology comes from rich countries in which wordiness is a virtue (the worth of academics is judged by the number of words they produce). This sits uneasily with other cultures long devastated by violence, where 'talk half, leave half' (to quote a Sierra Leone proverb), with regard to old quarrels, sometimes helps abate violence. In the space of a half silence Guatamalan Indian peasants have to come to terms with each other (and what others have made them do) while asserting their own agency and collective concerns against a hegemonic colonialism and capitalism. We should not too readily read into silence the idea that now the Cold War has ended an 'authentic' culture of identity bubbles readily to the surface.

In the chapters by Sverker Finnström on northern Uganda, and Fithen and Richards on Sierra Leone we arrive at two armed conflicts viewed by many as somehow representative of new forms of internal warfare in post-Cold War Africa. The Ugandan conflict is viewed largely as 'purposeless' violence fueled by religious or cognitive 'backwardness'. The same view of the Sierra Leone conflict prevailed in the mid-1990s (Kaplan 1994; 1996). That there is something odd about the Sierra Leone case is clear from the fact that it has so quickly graduated, in international understanding, from being an irrational outpouring of primitive instincts to a highly calculated conflict pursued for diamonds, i.e. from 'new barbarism' to 'greed, not grievance' (Le Billon 2001; Smillie et al. 1999). If we take the two cases together we note some features unaccounted for by either neo-barbarism or the greed-not-grievance thesis. In both instances, a processual emphasis is more useful in explaining these common elements than a focus on 'causes'. The process in question starts with economic failure and 'downsizing' of state institutions in the 1970s–80s, with knock-on effect on education and regional employment opportunities. A 'mix' of military marginalisation and poor opportunities for youth appears to have fed the Lord's Resistance Movement/ Army (and related insurgencies in northern Uganda, notably the Holy Spirit Movement Forces of Alice Lakwena) that long supplied the Ugandan army with many of its troops. Under Amin and Obote (both northerners) soldiers were more and more despised by civilians. After Yoweri Museveni seized power at the head of an 'anti-army' armed resistance movement – a paradoxical idea also influential on insurgents in Liberia and Sierra Leone – antipathy to northerners as 'martial races' deepened. The LRM/A, drawing on ideas about spiritual forces, sought to transcend this marginalisation by military association, mobilising young people through abduction (somehow a 'baptism of fire') in a cross-border region where insurgency (in southern Sudan) is an American-supported 'way of life'.

In the Sierra Leone case, Fithen and Richards are specifically interested in what happens after young people are seized by the militia factions. Deploying a neo-Durkheimian analytical framework, they argue that groups of young people with similar social backgrounds end up opposing each other for 'ideological' reasons that flow as much from variations in the organisational demands of combat as from the politics of grievance. Both Finnstrom and Fithen and Richards are concerned with the solidarities supporting cultures of violence, and how if these are properly understood they might be reshaped. In both insurgencies, attacks on the authority of elders resulted in atrocity. These atrocities intensified in response to governmental attempts to mobilise 'traditional' civil defence against rebel activists. In Sierra Leone the situation was greatly complicated by the involvement of security companies linked to international diamond mining interests. 'Barbarity' provoked by the involvement of mercenaries in the training of civil defence forces was as much a product of economic 'globalisation' as of anything in the 'traditional' culture.

With Mats Utas' study of Liberia we reach the right-hand down-slope on our bell curve of peace-war-peace, and begin the discussion of how and why peace can be strengthened. An internationally-endorsed democratic transition ended the Liberian war in 1997, even if subsequent unrest continues. Utas follows three groups of young combatants as they attempt to reintegrate within civil society. A group in the capital has undergone training in employment skills, but mainly survives through drug dealing and armed robbery. A second group of local recruits in Sinoe County has quickly resumed its smallholder plantation activities. A third group in the north settled temporarily in 'battle group formation', but switched from guns to making mud bricks, in great demand for local reconstruction. Armed with a small income they were then able to make temporary visits to their home communities to assess chances of being accepted once again. After a year, most had resumed a civilian life. Utas (cf. Fithen and Richards) stresses the importance of knowing as much as possible about the varied social backgrounds of combatants, of understanding and seeking to use solidarities formed under combat conditions for peaceful purposes. Utas' chapter also illustrates the general tenet that it is only by contextualising cases that we can learn something from them. In his case the success of demobilisation is seen to be heavily dependent on the larger structure of opportunities within which it takes place. Practically, this points to the need for agencies to provide training and other demobilisation support carefully related to local social and economic conditions (such as training in mud brick technologies and rural micro-business skills, not activities such as carpentry and/or motor mechanics that imply not rural reintegration but a shift to town life).

The long-term scar tissue of violent dislocation, and the role of religion in the process of forging local social solidarities and healing the wounds of war, but also of keeping alive dreams of recovery and restitution (perhaps also revenge?), are dealt with in the chapters by Björn Lindgren on Zimbabwe and Åsa Tiljander Dahlström on Tibetan exiles in India. Lindgren's chapter on Zimbabwe deals with a paradox. Before the notorious Fifth Brigade was sent into Matebeleland to put down a feared (or imagined) rebellion, ethnicity was not really a good explanation of why there were political tensions and divisions within rural society. But military brutality and atrocity actually created such solidarities. If rebellion were ever to break out again then a rather crude ethnicity – the scar tissue, as it were, of the earlier violence – might well constitute a valid explanation. Lindgren's case helps to highlight that when applying a war-peace continuum as a vantage point for research, what may appear as original 'causes' radically change over time. Lindgren shows how a conflict never really ends, but like scar tissue, has to be accommodated by a (social) body undergoing repair. Tiljander Dahlström, in her chapter on the Tibetan diaspora, spells out the temporal and geographical implications of learning to live with the scars of war. Her case provides a rather particular illustration of our central notion of 'learning to live beyond armed conflict'. Forty years and several generations after Tibetans fled the Chinese occupation, concepts like 'home' have acquired new meanings, and the desired 'peace' is negated by the very existence of a diaspora that cannot realistically ever 'return'. In the meantime new social patterns form, new distinctions and ideas on identity emerge, and even the non-violent ideology of resistance is questioned, but the 'legacy of suffering', transferred from parents to children, perpetuates diaspora status and, indeed, sustains a longer-term possibility of war.

The collection closes with a discussion by Bernhard Helander on whether post-conflict Somalia needs a state. The long and complex war in Somalia is seen as the clearest African instance of the collapse of the state after Cold War subsidies were withdrawn. Somalia seems an especially significant case to political scientists and representatives of the international institutions. Segmented by clanship, it is not polarised by language, religion or ethnicity. The state should have held together. Ensuring the state makes a come-back is, for many commentators and international agencies, a priority. This reflects the modern world's love affair with the concept of the sovereign state. Reviving that provocatively valuable anthropological category – the 'stateless' society – but in a new post-Cold War context, Helander shows the extent to which peace has reasserted itself in the absence of 'peace keeping', demonstrating the perhaps crucial importance of social services in this re-making of the polity 'from below'. Of course, he is aware of the limitations of what can be achieved by a piecemeal approach, but his main worry lies with the international community's apparent determination to regularise a 'marriage' between cohabiting elements. Why is this the priority to trump all others? This encapsulates a central challenge of anthropology to those who see themselves as makers of a new international order.

Re-socialising War and Peace

Since humans relate to each other through social cues, rendering the enemy without (and outwith) society is an essential aspect of setting up a target to be hit. Those who promote war regularly have the job of rendering the enemy 'not like us'. In theories of 'new war' war itself becomes the object of such 'othering'. Theories of 'new war' have stripped violent conflict of its social content.

But with the advent of global terrorism the strategy of rendering war asocial no longer works. Terrorism aims at high levels of demoralisation for limited deployment of tactical resources. By overtly seeking to undermine social cohesion terrorism underlines the true significance of social dimensions in times of war. Social cohesion is the asset that counts above all others. Terrorism skips the battlefield, and cuts to the societal core – it seeks above all to destroy morale. The true threat posed by terrorism as a tool of war becomes fully apparent *only* when we pay due regard how it functions in social terms. In effect, as Zulaika and Douglas (1996) argue, to understand terrorism we have also to understand, and address, the audience for terrorism. 'Surgical strikes' against terrorists fool no one. Challenging terrorism involves recognising, and transcending the social worlds of the terrorists.

But having reinstated the sociological character of war we are left with a basic question. Is the violence necessary? If war is inherently sociological (as we have argued) then waging war and making peace need not involve weapons at all. The view that war and peace are made – ultimately – with social means is not likely to appeal to arms manufacturers; we ask, above their heads, 'who needs the kit?' At the time of the Bosnian conflict *The Economist* magazine reviewed the future of war. At the end of a substantial article exploring the wonders of the electronic battlefield a devastating question was posed: perhaps having agents on the ground speaking local languages would achieve as much?

This is in effect to question the capacity of sophisticated weapons to do anything long-term about conflict that is inherently social. Pulping the enemy into submission is not actually a very efficient way of coping with social rivalries. Repressed social worlds have an uncanny ability to re-make themselves, even after it is thought they have been rooted out. Social facts (as Durkheim might have argued) can only be met with social facts. In the end a 'clash of cultures' implies social accommodation (as the only antidote to genocide). In exploring social accommodation, we pass from understanding to compromise, or where difficulties are deep rooted, and bargaining is not enough, to transcendence. New social worlds – of all the parties – have to be devised. In either case social creativity seems more important than sophisticated equipment. Our essays argue that in denying the irreducible social content of war and peace we risk disabling the 'smartest' of all assets for transcending a state of war.

This is why we believe the anthropology of war and peace to be such a vital contribution. Its practical relevance is clear. Ethnography – as our essays demonstrate – is a tool to probe the social content of war. Through bringing this content to light, we align ourselves with those who seek to render war less dangerous. Note that we are not advocates of social 'harmony', still less the imposition of some kind of social uniformity (an impossible aim). Social worlds will continue to contend much as economies compete. Only through such struggle does it become apparent which ways of organising are viable over the longer term. But violence involves too many unanticipated consequences. Contending in peaceful ways is better, including waging war through non-violent means.

How can conflict be rendered less dangerous? Conflict resolution was once largely a matter of negotiation by leaders and diplomats. Where states have collapsed, or weak leadership is part of the problem, other approaches need to be tried. This has led to so-called Track Two negotiation processes, i.e. addressing wider aspects of a conflict at the same time as leaders negotiate a political deal. The aim of this work is not conflict 'resolution', but conflict transformation, such as re-directing the social energies deployed in war to problem-solving ventures on a cooperative basis. We believe that the anthropology of war and peace has a place in the 'problem solving' approach to conflict transformation (Mitchell and Banks 1996; Dukes 1996).

As anthropologists we have some reservations, however, about the assumptions on which some of these problem solving approaches currently rest. Often, the frameworks adopted derive from some theory of human needs, or are adaptations of game theory, e.g. 'win-win' bargaining (cf. Burton 1990). The difficulty is, that as Douglas et al. (1999) make clear, needs can hardly be separately defined from wants, and that both presume a social context. The worst wars are between groups whose basic social assumptions lead them to define quite incompatible – indeed incommensurable – needs and desires. Stakeholders can bargain, but first they need to agree they hold stakes in common.

The Durkheimian tradition in anthropology, by contrast, makes us aware people hold ideas about morality and the ultimate good that reflect the way they are organised in society, and transcending this functional loop is no easy task. It is illusory to imagine that beyond the Cold War people simply 'wake up' to the idea that 'Western' values – open markets, and rights defined in individual terms – are best. Imposing such values through force of arms, or aid conditionalities, is liable to reinforce the very solidarities they seek to replace. Bombing a 'rogue state', or imposing financial restructuring in such a way that it bears down heaviest upon the poor, may entrench not respect for markets and human rights but the values through which the poorest of the poor presently survive (for example, reliance on powerful patrons). This is where the search for transcendence comes in. Rich and poor have to find common bonds based on mutual respect, not force and need. Bargaining cannot be enough. People will have to grow together.

It is one of our conclusions, based on our studies, that there is more scope for this 'growing together' than is regularly recognised. Scope for sociological solutions to conflict is foundational in human existence: we became human through developing the potential of our species for the social. Among war makers, much effort is devoted to masking this fact. Conflict has to be organised, and one of the first organisational tasks is to try and limit the tendency of ordinary folk to get on with their lives as they see fit, cooperating across battle lines as necessary. Terrorists know this. Those who fight them know it. Unless the sides are thoroughly differentiated there is always a risk (from the warmonger's perspective) of peace breaking out, inconveniently, and by accident.

One of anthropology's tasks, as we view it, is to keep on emphasising this local potential for spontaneous peace. It amounts to arguing for more radical options than conflict resolution. Might not wars sometimes be ended soonest by knowing how and when *not* to intervene? Foreign governments demand the reinstitution of 'failed' states. Without officials and binding agreements donors are lost. But it is much less clear that war-affected people have any such need. Their interests might be served better by reform of *local* governance and justice than a reconstruction of the state. Last (2002) argues that demand for *shari'a* law in northern Nigeria, at recurrent intervals over 200 years, is just such a project in 'grass roots' social reconstruction, despite being pilloried as 'obscurantist' and backward looking. Anthropology may at times be called upon to assist the peace makers, but at times, also, it has a duty to ring-fence the space in which local social creativity flourishes. If 'new war' is the problem it is as yet far from clear that imposition of 'liberal peace' is the answer. Imposed solutions to problems of social transformation have a poor track record. A 'war on terrorism' may produce even poorer results. In the end, people have to decide whether they build on or reject terrorism, and make and re-make social worlds accordingly. This is as true in Ireland as in Afghanistan. Is it not strikingly odd that international advocates of 'democracy' seem at times so to distrust capacity for, and dislike the products of, local social self-organisation?

As politicians and security experts encourage us to believe that rogue states and terrorist networks are causes rather than symptoms of the dangerous world in which we live, never has the anthropology of war and peace been more urgently needed.

References

An-Naim, Abdullahi A. 1998a, 'Expanding the limits of imagination: human rights from a participatory approach to new multilateralism', in M.Schechter, ed., *Innovation in multilateralism* Tokyo, New York, London: United Nations University Press

An-Naim, Abdullahi A. 1998b, 'Human rights and the challenge of relevance: the case of collective rights', in M. Castermans-Holleman, Fr. Van Hoof, and J. Smith, eds, *The role of the nation-state in the 21st century: human rights, international organizations and foreign policy: essays in honour of Peter Baehr* Dordrecht: Kluwer

Archibald, S. and Richards, P. 2002, 'Conversion to human rights? Popular debate about war and justice in rural central Sierra Leone'. *Africa* 72 (3): 339–67

Aretxaga, B. 1997, *Shattering silence: women, nationalism and political subjectivity in Northern Ireland* Princeton, NJ: Princeton University Press

Banerjee, M. 2001, *The Pathan unarmed* Oxford: James Currey

Barth, F. ed. 1969, *Ethnic groups and boundaries: the social organization of cultural difference* Oslo: Univeritetsforlaget

Berdal, M. and Keen, D. 1997, 'Violence and economic agendas in civil wars: some policy implications' *Millennium: Journal of International Studies* 26 (3): 795–818

Berdal, M. and Malone, D. eds. 2000, *Greed and grievance; economic agendas in civil wars* Boulder, CO: Lynne Rienner

Burnham, P. 1996, *The politics of cultural difference in northern Cameroon* Edinburgh University Press for the International African Institute

Burton. J. ed. 1990, *Conflict: human needs theory* New York: St Martin's Press

Cohen, A. 1969, *Custom and politics in urban Africa: a study of Hausa migrants in Yoruba towns* Berkeley: University of California Press

Collier, P. 2000, *Economic causes of civil conflict and their implications for policy* Washington, DC: The World Bank

Creveld, M. van 1992, *On future war* London: Brasseys

Daniel, E. V. 1996, *Charred lullabies: chapters in an anthropography of violence* Princeton, NJ: Princeton University Press

Das, V. and Kleinman, A. 2000, 'Introduction', in Das, V. et al. eds, *Violence and subjectivity* Berkeley: University of California Press

de Waal, A. 1997, *Famine crimes: politics and the disaster relief industry in Africa* Oxford: James Currey:

Douglas, M., Gasper, D., Ney S., and Thompson, M. 1999, 'Human needs and wants', in Rayner, S. and Malone, E. eds, *Human choice and climate change, (Vol. 1. The Societal Framework)* Columbus, OH: Battelle Press, pp. 195–264

Duffield, M. 2001, *Global governance and the new wars: the merging of development and security* London: Zed Books

Dukes, E. Franklin 1996, *Resolving public conflict: transforming community and governance* Manchester: Manchester University Press

Fairhead, J. 2001, 'International dimensions of conflict over natural and environmental resources', in Peluso, N. and Watts, M. eds, *Violent environments* Ithaca, NY: Cornell University Press

Fardon, R. 1988, *Raiders and refugees: trends in Chamba political development, 1750–1950* Washington, DC: Smithsonian Institution Press

Ferguson, R. B. and Whitehead, N. L., eds, 1992, *War in the tribal zone: expanding states and indigenous warfare* Santa Fe: School of American Research

Gluckman, M. 1956, *Custom and conflict in Africa* Oxford: Basil Blackwell

Gonzales, J. E. 1992, 'Guerrillas and coca in the Upper Huallaga valley', in Palmer, D.S. ed., *Shining Path of Peru*, London: C. Hurst

Griffith, S. B. (trs. and ed.) 1963, *Sun tzu: the art of war* Oxford: Oxford University Press

Henriques, P. 2002, 'Peace without reconciliation: war, peace and experience among the Iteso of East Uganda' PhD thesis, Institute of Anthropology, University of Copenhagen

Homer-Dixon, T. F. 1991, 'On the threshold: environmental changes as causes of acute conflict' *International Security* 16 (2): 76–116

—— 1994, 'Environmental scarcities and violent conflict: evidence from cases' *International Security* 19 (1):5–40

—— 1999, *Environment, scarcity and violence* Princeton, NJ & Oxford: Princeton University Press

Huntington, S. P. 1997, *The clash of civilizations and the remaking of the world order* New York: Simon and Schuster

Kapferer, B. 1998, *Legends of people, myths of State: violence, intolerance and political culture in Sri-Lanka and Australia* Washington, DC: Smithsonian Institution Press (first published 1988)

Kaplan, R. D. 1993, *Balkan ghosts: a journey through history* London: Macmillan

—— 1994, 'The coming anarchy: how scarcity, crime, overpopulation, and disease are rapidly destroying the social fabric of our planet' *Atlantic Monthly* February, 44–76

—— 1996, *The ends of the earth: a journey at the dawn of the 21st century* New York: Random House

Keen, D. 1994, *The benefits of famine: a political economy of famine and relief in south-western Sudan, 1983–1989* Princeton, NJ: Princeton University Press

—— 1999, 'Who's it between? "Ethnic war" and rational violence', in Allen, T. and Seaton, J. eds, *The media of conflict: war reporting and the representations of ethnic violence* London: Zed Books

Knauft, B. M. 1990, 'Melanesian warfare: a theoretical history' *Oceania* 60: 250–311

Kopytoff, I. 1987, 'The internal African frontier', in Kopytoff, I. ed., *The African frontier: the reproduction of traditional African societies* Bloomington: Indiana University Press

Kuper, A. 1999, *Culture: the anthropologists' account* Cambridge, MA: Harvard University Press

Last, M. 2002, 'The Shari'a in context: people's quest for justice today and the role of courts in pre- and early-colonial northern Nigeria' unpublished typescript, Department of Anthropology, University College London

Le Billon, P. 2000, *The political economy of war: what relief agencies need to know* Humanitarian Practice Network, Network Paper 33, London: Overseas Development Institute

—— 2001, 'The political ecology of war: natural resources and armed conflicts' *Political Geography* 20, 561–84

Malkki, L. 1995. *Purity and exile: violence, memory, and national cosmology among Hutu refugees in Tanzania* Chicago: Chicago University Press

Mitchell, C. and Banks, M. 1996, *Handbook of conflict resolution: the analytical problem-solving approach* London: Pinter

Nordstrom, C. 1997, *A different kind of war story* Philadelphia: University of Pennsylvania Press

Peluso, N. and Watts, M. eds, 2001, *Violent environments* Ithaca, NY: Cornell University Press

Peters, K. and Richards, P. 1998, 'Why we fight: voices of youth ex-combatants in Sierra Leone' *Africa*, v. 68 (1): 183–210

Rashid, A. 2000, *Taliban: the story of the Afghan war lords* London: I. B. Tauris

Riches, D. ed. 1986, *The anthropology of violence* Blackwell: Oxford

Richards, P. 1996, *Fighting for the rain forest: war, youth and resources in Sierra Leone* Oxford: James Currey (reprinted with additional material 1998)

—— 2004, 'Green Book millenarians? The Sierra Leone war from the perspective of an anthropology of religion', in Kastfelt, Niels, ed. *Religion and civil war in Africa* London: C. Hurst

Salemink, O. 2003, *The ethnography of Vietnam's central highlanders; a historical contextualization, 1850–1990*. London: Routledge Curzon

Sivan, E. 1995, 'The enclave culture', in M. Marty, ed., *Fundamentalisms comprehended*. Chicago: Chicago University Press

Smillie, I., Gberie, L., Hazleton, R. 2000, *The heart of the matter: Sierra Leone, diamonds and human security* Ottawa: Partnership Africa Canada

Sommers, M. 2001, *Fear in Bongoland: Burundi refugees in urban Tanzania* New York: Berghahn Books

Stewart, P. J. and Strathern, A. 2002, *Violence: theory and ethnography* London: Continuum Books

Talbott, S. and Chanda, N. eds, 2001, *The age of terror: America and the world after September 11th* Oxford: Perseus Press

Zulaika, J. and Douglas, W. A. 1996, *Terror and taboo: the follies, fables and faces of terrorism* London: Routledge

2

Political Violence in Cambodia
& the Khmer Rouge 'Genocide'
JAN OVESEN

The Khmer Rouge regime in Cambodia (1975–79), led by Pol Pot and officially known as Democratic Kampuchea (DK), was responsible for probably the most intensive and terrifying atrocities committed by any political regime against any domestic or foreign group since the Second World War. During the nearly four years that the Khmer Rouge held power, between one and three million people were killed, directly by execution, or indirectly by being put to slave labour with insufficient food and inadequate health care. These atrocities are routinely referred to as genocide. The exact number of victims is impossible to determine, even for demographers (Heuveline 2001:106). But even if we choose the rather modest estimate of just over one million (Banister and Johnson 1993), this amounts to an average of almost 800 'excess' deaths per day during Khmer Rouge rule. Unfortunately, this staggering number has all too often helped to create the false impression that an abrupt shift from peace to violence, or 'genocide' took place upon the Khmer Rouge assumption of power, on 17 April 1975, and that a reverse shift, from violence to peace, happened when Vietnamese troops invaded Cambodia and toppled the DK regime on 7 January 1979.

In this paper[1] I argue that the crimes against humanity committed by the DK regime, horrendous as they were in their own right, may be understood as conforming, in principle, if not in magnitude, to a pattern of abuse of political power that runs through most of Cambodia's recorded history. To portray the violence of the DK regime as unprecedented and unique, a genocidal four-year interlude in the history of an otherwise peaceful country, is part of the historiography of the victors which mainly serves the political interests of the current power elite.

Cambodian History

Since my argument is that both contemporary political events and those of the Khmer Rouge regime should be seen in a longer-term historical context I shall

---

[1] For comments on earlier drafts of this paper I am indebted to David Chandler, Henri Locard and Michael Vickery. None of them, however, should be held responsible for any of my arguments or conclusions.

begin with a thumbnail sketch of that context. (For a proper overview of the history of Cambodia, see for example Chandler 1992.)

Cambodia's history is conventionally thought to begin with the Angkor empire in the ninth century. The orientalist fantasy of this polity as a grand 'hydraulic civilization' based on large scale irrigation systems has lately been dispelled (van Liere 1980; Stott 1992; Higham 2001). The Thai overthrew Angkor in the mid-fifteenth century, and the Khmer capital was moved south of the great lake (Tonle Sap), eventually to its present location (Phnom Penh). Trade became an important complement to the traditional domestic agricultural production as the base for the significantly reduced Khmer kingdom. During the period up to the French colonisation (1863), the kingdom's sovereignty was continually threatened by encroachments by its neighbours, the Thai and the Vietnamese.

The French colonial intervention arguably safeguarded the continued existence of the Cambodian monarchy (Osborne 1997:70), but the Khmer population benefited no more than other colonised subjects; modest infrastructural developments were accomplished through a harsh regime of forced labour, and taxation of the rural population was heavy. On the other hand, the French efforts to organise communal elections and establish free medical services for all should not be ignored. The French generally regarded the Khmer as backward, indolent and acquiescent, and fuelled the traditional antagonistic attitude of the Khmer towards the Vietnamese by importing Vietnamese officials to serve in the colonial administration of Cambodia.

At the country's 'independence' in 1953, Prince Norodom Sihanouk attained the position as head of state, and through cleverly manipulating his roles as divine king and ruthless politician, he ruled autocratically until 1970. Apart from effectively crushing all internal political opposition, he managed to withstand Vietnamese pressure (and thereby strengthen the already widespread anti-Vietnamese sentiments among the population) and distance himself from the Americans.

As America's Indochina war escalated during the late 1960s, and bombs fell on Cambodia, the coup that ousted Sihanouk in 1970 and put army general Lon Nol in his place was welcomed (if not directly instigated) by the Americans (see Kiernan 1985:300f). During the Lon Nol regime (1970–75), however, the communist guerrilla movement gained in strength, thanks in large part to the active assistance of Vietnamese forces; already since the 1970 coup the country was in a state of civil war. Lon Nol's hatred of the Vietnamese was of paranoid proportions, and during his rule more than 300,000 ethnic Vietnamese fled or were expelled from the country; the civil war claimed a total of about 600,000 casualties (Banister and Johnson 1993:87).

In April 1975, the revolutionary forces, the 'Khmer Rouge', invaded Phnom Penh and 'evacuated' virtually all of its two million inhabitants (residents and temporary refugees) to the countryside. The revolutionary movement was couched in secrecy. For several years neither the Cambodian population nor the rest of the world knew who the leaders were; reference was made only to angkar, 'the organisation.' The goal of the organisation, inspired to some extent by the model of Mao's cultural revolution, was to establish the perfect communist state, economically self-sufficient, politically self-contained, and diplomatically isolated. The backbone of the revolution was the 'base people', the rural poor, most of whom had supposedly been enlisted prior to 1975. In contrast, the urban population of Phnom Penh and other cities were classified as 'new people,' who had yet to prove their allegiance to the revolution; they were sent out into the country-side and forced to work as agricultural labourers. 'Foreign' influences were seen as the root of most evil. All officers and officials from American lackey Lon Nol's government were immediately targeted (together with all their families and relatives). Urban life was 'foreign' (hence the immediate evacuation of the cities), as was higher education (intellectuals were either sent to work in the fields or executed) and money was abolished (rice and fish were to be restored as the 'traditional' means of exchange, and the National Bank was blown up). Religion was abolished; Buddhist temples were used as warehouses, hospitals or prisons, monks were derobed or executed, and the Catholic cathedral in Phnom Penh was demolished. Total and unwavering loyalty to the organisation was demanded of every individual on pain of death, and family and kinship ties were devalued or negated in favour of the organisation. The most devious and dangerous foreign influence was that emanating from the hated Vietnamese, and it was the regime's repeated and provocative attacks against Vietnamese border areas that finally drove Vietnam to invade the country in 1978–79.

What the Vietnamese 'liberation' army saw in January 1979 should have come as a shock to the rest of the world who had had virtually no information from within the country for four years: a large proportion of the population internally displaced, with almost no material possessions, and on the verge of starvation; and abandoned prisons that showed signs of systematic torture. Within the country the Vietnamese troops were initially welcomed by most of the people, and under the supervision of Vietnamese political advisers they efficiently began to restore the situation: they installed a functioning socialist regime in the country (now named the People's Republic of Kampuchea, PRK), repaired trans-port and communication infrastructure, organised agricultural work and established 'solidarity groups' (krom samaki) in the countryside to ensure the just distribution of the fruits of agricultural labour. For many, however, war fatigue was soon overshadowed by their 'socialism' fatigue, now of the Vietnamese variety, and by 1981 hundreds of thousands of Cambodians had fled towards the Thai border, where they were gathered in refugee camps, some under the auspices of the UNHCR (United Nations High Commission for Refugees). About 300,000 managed to go into permanent exile, primarily in North America, France and Australia. Sihanouk, once more titular head of state, founded the FUNCINPEC party ('Front uni national pour un Cambodge indépendant, neutre, pacifique et coopératif') in 1981, and the following year declared that now it was no longer the Khmer Rouge but the Vietnamese colonisers who were the prime enemy.

Michael Vickery, defensive of the Vietnam-directed PRK government, has claimed that the refugee situation was caused by the luxury problems of a 'bourgeois' urban population who resented the prospect of living like peasants, that none of the refugees were fleeing from political oppression (1990:298), and that the steady flow of refugees to the Thai border was maintained as part of the conspiracy of the UNHCR and the Thai and US governments to discredit the PRK regime (ibid.:309). This view contrasts starkly with the experiences of most ordinary Cambodians inside the country. The Vietnamese 'liberation' forces certainly delivered the Cambodian population from Pol Pot's regime of terror, but they substituted it by a ten-year period of military and political occupation of the country. Steve Heder's 1980 report is a rare testimony from the early days. Soon after the Vietnamese invasion and the general upheaval it entailed, existing stores of rice and other foodstuffs were eagerly sought by everybody.

> In this race for rice, this competition for survival, the Vietnamese army had all the advantages [...] [T]he Vietnamese sent large [...] amounts of rice into Vietnam [...] [they] were also taking factory machinery, rubber, cloth, furniture, spare parts and water pumps out of Kampuchea into Vietnam. (Heder 1980:30–31)

For many Vietnamese officers and men, the Cambodia posting was a lucrative one. 'Surplus' rice could be sold for gold, and those willing to 'engage in private trade of state property, military supplies, economic aid material and war booty' did even better; 'it soon became clear that the net effect was [...] the accumulation of large amounts of gold in the hands of the Vietnamese' (Heder 1980: 21–22).

What remained of the DK military forces and political leadership had retreated mainly to the western provinces along the Thai border, often surrounding themselves by defence lines of landmines, from where they directed the armed resistance against the Vietnamese/PRK government forces. It was not until 1997-98 that their last bastions were given up, and DK, in the eyes of its supporters, ceased to exist. In the meantime, half of the PRK national budget was devoted to war efforts. In a UNESCO report, French anthropologist Fabienne Luco has sketched the situation:

> Although not comparable to the measures of the previous regime, intimidation and coercion kept the population in a state of dread of the authorities. People from villages and towns were forcibly enlisted as soldiers or labourers, put to work along the Thai border for the construction of a long line of defence against the Khmer Rouge, an enterprise that from 1985 onwards was known as 'Plan K5.' In these zones, infested with malaria and landmines, many lost their lives. (Luco 2002:79; my translation)

Two of my research assistants corroborated Luco's description. Being high-school students at the time, they recalled how the Vietnamese conscripted young Khmers to the army, picked them out of high school and sent them as advance guards across the minefields in their campaigns against remaining Khmer Rouge fighting units near the Thai border, while they themselves stayed behind. The dreaded 'Plan K5' (pronounced kor pram in Khmer) was a vast deforestation programme based on the premise that since the Khmer Rouge had taken to the forest, the way to get rid of them would be to cut down the forest. The kor pram had the added 'benefit' of reducing overt everyday conflicts in the villages, since the village and commune chiefs had the authority to recruit people for the programme, and they would primarily send young people who were regarded as troublemakers in the community, so people became very reluctant to take their problems to the local authorities (Luco 2002:82, 88); according to one of Luco's informants, 'it was said that when you left for K5, you left in a truck but returned in a burial urn' (ibid.:90).

As the Soviet empire began dismantling in 1989, Soviet foreign aid to clients such as Vietnam was significantly reduced. Vietnam eventually found its military occupation of Cambodia too costly and decided to withdraw its remaining troops (Chandler 1992:235), even if the civil war was not yet over. Following the Paris Agreement in 1991, parliamentary elections were to be held under the supervision of the UN. The UNTAC (United Nations Transitional Authority in

Cambodia) organised general democratic elections in 1993; the effort involved 20,000 UN personnel and two billion US dollars over 20 months. The result of the elections came as a shock for the ruling pro-Vietnamese Cambodian People's Party (CPP, successor to the CPK, Communist Party of Kampuchea), as FUNCIN-PEC received 68 percent of the votes. But thanks to the manoeuvring of CPP leader Hun Sen and the acquiescence of Sihanouk, the ensuing government became a coalition between these two opposing parties, each one supplying one prime minister; Prince Norodom Ranariddh (son of Sihanouk) of the FUNCINPEC was named First Prime Minister, and Hun Sen of the CPP Second Prime Minister. While this solution was made to look 'democratic', it was politically precarious, and the coalition came to an end in July 1997, when Hun Sen ousted Ranariddh and declared the CPP the sole ruling party. The parliamentary elections the following year (declared free and fair by international observers!) confirmed the position of Hun Sen and the CPP.

'Genocide' and the Cham

Several leading scholars of Cambodia (e.g. Chandler 1993; Locard 1996; Vickery 1984) agree that technically the Khmer Rouge atrocities do not constitute a genocide. Most of the victims – between 80 and 85 percent – were ethnic Khmer, who constituted, and still constitute, about 95 percent of the country's population. Historian Ben Kiernan (1996) dissents from this view and argues that genocide is an apposite term because some non-Khmer groups suffered disproportionately under Pol Pot, and because the regime pursued a deliberately ethnic chauvinist campaign, couched in racialist vocabulary.[2] He argues that closer attention to the plight of the minorities, particularly the Vietnamese and the Cham, reveals that these groups were indeed victims of genocide, and that they were targeted as a consequence of the racist ideology of the regime.

As for the Vietnamese, they were traditionally seen by the Khmer as their hereditary enemy, never to be trusted and always assumed (not always incorrectly) to entertain expansionist schemes for encroaching upon Cambodian territory. The antagonism towards the Vietnamese was exacerbated during the colonial period when the French favoured Vietnamese for official and domestic appointments and used Vietnamese auxiliaries to put down Khmer uprisings (Kiernan 1982:1; Martin 1994:83). So if 'only' about 10,000 Vietnamese perished under Pol Pot, this is because most had already left the country. 150,000 had fled immediately after the Khmer Rouge victory (April–September 1975), and previously more than 300,000 Vietnamese had left to escape persecution under the Lon Nol regime (Kiernan 1996:296). Even after Pol Pot, especially after 1989, resident Vietnamese have been subject to occasional massacres at the hands of the Khmer majority (Jordens 1996). But to argue for DK 'genocide' of the Vietnamese is hardly compelling.

The Cham present a more analytically challenging case. They are a Muslim minority whose permanent presence in Cambodia dates back to the 15th century,

---

[2] Kiernan (2001:83) even cites a legal study that has claimed 'scholarly unanimity concerning the applicability of the term genocide in this case'. Whether one or more persons are found guilty of genocide in the legal sense remains to be determined in a court of law or a tribunal. My concern here is with genocide not as a legal term, but as a concept for social science description and analysis.

and was occasioned by the gradual Vietnamese encroachment and conquest of the Champa kingdoms on the coast of present-day southern Vietnam. The Cham became established as a partially integrated element in Cambodian society in the late 17th century when a significant contingent, including a great proportion of the political elite, fled the Vietnamese troops invading the (Hindu and partially Islamicised) Champa kingdom of Phan Rang and were granted refuge and citizenship by the Cambodian king. There can be no doubt that the Cham suffered disproportionately under Pol Pot, although estimates of the number of Cham victims vary greatly (Vickery 1989; Kiernan 1990; Ysa Osman 2002:2–3); and there can be no doubt that the excessive persecution of the Cham was in some sense related to their 'culture,' or more accurately, to Khmer cultural perceptions of the Cham. Whether this fact makes the label genocide warranted is, among other things, a matter of perspective.

Viewing the situation and events in Cambodia in 1975–79 as a whole, it appears idiosyncratic to argue for a particular allegation of genocide against the Cham. While it is true that the Cham suffered more than average, the sufferings of other ethnic groups, most notably the majority Khmer, are by no means negligible. I believe that the disproportionate number of Cham victims of Khmer Rouge atrocities may be understood as a result of the combination of three characteristics of the regime. One is the Khmer cultural, or ethnic, chauvinism that pervaded the revolutionary movement; the second is the idea of class and the way 'class enemies' were perceived; and the third is the general onslaught on all religious worship.

As for the first element, François Ponchaud has demonstrated that the Cambodian revolution under Pol Pot, even though it was in many respects a frontal attack on core Khmer cultural values, was, paradoxically, also a Khmer (cultural) phenomenon, a 'revolution [that] bears the stamp of Khmer culture' (1989:152). Although it entailed onslaughts on many of the fundamental institutions of Cambodian society, such as the strict hierarchy of elder and younger, parents and children, teacher and pupil, Pol Pot continuously made references to the purity of Khmer culture and to his attempt to restore it by purging it of corrupting foreign influences, such as urban life and the use of money. The foundation of Khmer social life, the household of the extended family, was attacked. It was the ambition of the party, or the angkar ('organisation') to position itself in the place of the family. This was accomplished, among other things, by the establishment of mobile working teams and assigning family members to different teams. Khmer kinship terms were decreed as the proper way of addressing representatives of the angkar, and marriages were arranged by the angkar between young people in the communities. The Khmer-ness of the revolution was emphasised by the prohibition to speak any other language than Khmer. The Cham language was forbidden, and so was for example Chinese and Lao (Kiernan 1991:221).

As for the class element, Steve Heder, in his detailed critique of Kiernan's work, has argued that Marxist ideas of class struggle, rather than racism, were at the root of the atrocities of the Pol Pot regime. The Cham had the misfortune to be depicted as the only ethnic group in the country that included no 'workers'. 'Signs of "Cham-ness" were interpreted as signs of "non-proletarian-ness"' (Heder 1997:112). The discrimination against non-Khmer ethnic groups in general, Heder argues, was based on stereotypes of class rather than of race. '[T]he more an ethnic identity was stereotyped as "upper class", the more died' (ibid.:117). From a socioeconomic point of view, the ethnic stereotyping of the Cham as non-proletarians seems both puzzling and arbitrary; in terms of wealth and livelihood they did not differ systematically from the Khmer. But it may be understood in light of the fact that from the beginning the Khmer Rouge movement was organised, in ideological as well as practical terms, with very heavy assistance from the Vietnamese communists. In order to legitimise the successive Vietnam-ese annexation of the Champa principalities during the fifteenth to eighteenth centuries, the Vietnamese communist historians had depicted them as feudal and construed their conquest as the liberation of the Cham people from feudalism (Dang et al. 1993:187; Nakamura 1999). I suggest the Khmer Rouge view of the class position of the Cham was directly inspired by this self-serving Vietnamese historiography which had been taught to the Khmer revolutionaries by their Vietnamese comrades.

The assumption of total and exclusive authority on the part of the angkar also entailed the abolition of all forms of religion. But while it was a comparatively simple task to desacralise the Buddhist temples and turn them into warehouses or prisons, and to derobe the monks, the traditional belief in the ancestor spirits was less easy to eradicate. Since these spirits (neak ta) were for most Khmer a fact of life rather than a matter of 'belief,' the task became one of depriving them of the power they traditionally held over the life of living people. Thus, Ponchaud cites testimonies by young soldiers having attempted to kill neak ta with AK47s (1989:168–9). The onslaught on religion in general naturally hit the Muslim Cham particularly hard because Islam is not the kind of 'religion' that one can adopt or discard by way of command or instantaneous individual choice; practical Islam is as much a religiously sanctioned set of social, juridical and moral rules as a code for man's relationship to God. And while the efficacy of lethal violence against ancestor spirits may be dubious, it worked unfailingly against humans who did not perceive the possibility of obeying an order to for-swear their doctrines.

From the perspective of the Cham, rather than from that of the total Cambodian situation, it could be argued that this group were victims of genocide. This is the perspective from which Kiernan presents his argument. He has adopted a method somewhat resembling that of anthropological fieldwork, i.e. talking to people on the ground. In the early 1980s, Kiernan conducted a large number of interviews, notably with representatives of various Cham communities. Apart from narra-tives of specific local events, the picture that emerges is that the Cham were forced to eat pork and have the women cut their hair, and that failure to comply with these demands was harshly punished. Such statements have become items of Cham 'collective memory' (a term coined by Maurice Halbwachs 1925) and, indeed, I myself heard them repeatedly during the initial stage of fieldwork in a Cham community.[3] But as I became better acquainted with the local population, a more nuanced picture emerged. During the civil war in the early 1970s, the

[3] Together with Ing-Britt Trankell I have been doing anthropological fieldwork in Cambodia inter-mittently since 1996. A significant part of our work has been with a Cham community in Kampong Chhnang province. Our friends, informants and research assistants – Cham as well as Khmer – who have taken part in our work are too numerous for me to mention all. In connection with the theme of the present paper, I wish particularly to acknowledge the contributions of Ta Riess, *hatep* El, So Socheat, Lath Poch and Heng Kimvan.

area where 'our' village was located was between the national road, controlled by the government, and the railway, controlled by the guerrilla. On the government side there was a steady demand for food supplies, particularly cattle, while the revolutionaries had a constant need of clothes and medicine, and many villagers gained a significant income by trading and smuggling the desired items to one or the other side. The risk of getting caught and killed by either side was considerable, but the business became a way of getting on with a semblance of normal life. Up to and after the Khmer Rouge victory, a few of the villagers were active revolutionaries, but the majority minded their own business and tried to minimise exposure to Khmer Rouge attention. Thus, two of my closest friends and informants, both village religious leaders, would reminisce about the time when one was obliged to assist in demolishing the house of the other. The Khmer Rouge had decreed that everybody should live in small modest houses. The Cham are skilful carpenters and take pride in the quality of their houses; even relatively poor people make considerable efforts to build fairly large and durable houses – something that probably reinforced the Khmer Rouge perception of them as 'feudal'. One of my friends had quite a large house, and it was deemed politic that the villagers 'volunteer' to take it down in order not to incur the violent wrath of the revolutionary forces. My two friends agreed that it was an awkward, unpleasant situation. But the lasting trauma, for them as for most others, was the knowledge and continually resurfacing memory of the ways various people had been involved in atrocities. Even if a different kind of normal life could be lived after the collapse of the Khmer Rouge regime, the knowledge that this or that cousin or neighbour had killed a brother, a son, or a daughter, or that you yourself had acted in ways you wish you hadn't, was the heaviest burden of all. The stereotypes of collective memory, I believe, were mainly resorted to in front of relative strangers as a kind of psychological defence mechanism. Concrete individual memories, on the other hand, were mostly reduced to silence (Trankell 2003).

To make his case for genocide, Kiernan adopts a curiously piecemeal approach to the total situation. Thus, when asserting that the Cham were indeed specially persecuted and therefore victims of genocide, he goes on to argue, 'The fact that other races [sic!] were also persecuted is of no relevance' (1996:461). For whom? one may well ask. Most of the Cham I know find it relevant that all sorts of people, not least among the Khmer majority, were killed by the Khmer Rouge. Contrary to Kiernan (ibid.:462), they also find it relevant that Khmers were forbidden to practice Buddhism. Another part of the argument goes that the Cham were persecuted for being Cham (rather than for not showing sufficient revolutionary fervour), because only they were asked to eat pork. 'There is no record of any members of the majority group, the Khmers, being forced to eat pork' (ibid.). Well, that would hardly have been necessary, since most Khmers love pork! But there were other ways of determining revolutionary zeal in the case of the Khmer, such as asking young people to accuse their parents, or even kill them, for being enemies of the revolution. The Khmer Rouge, it could be said, showed a vicious cultural sensitivity by demanding that people renounce core cultural values as proof of allegiance to the revolutionary cause – such as the food prohibition in the Cham case, and the generational hierarchy in the Khmer case.

Kiernan's work is important for revealing the racialist dimension of the Khmer Rouge regime. But two points need to be made: firstly, Khmer ethnic chauvinism, even though often formulated in racialist terms, is quite different from the kind of racism that has been encountered in Euro-American contexts. Khmer (Rouge) 'racism' was (and still is) fundamentally ethnic rather than biological. In Pol Pot's rhetoric there are repeated references to the need to attain or ensure the purity of the 'Khmer race'. Such concerns for purity were also present in the Nazi ideology, for instance, but the important difference is that in the Khmer Rouge case, membership of a 'race' is not biologically grounded. One of the greatest threats to Khmer purity was to be found not in the physical but in the mental qualities of the people, and many killings of fellow Khmer persons were attributed to them having 'Khmer bodies but Vietnamese minds'. As for the Cham, Kiernan cites Khmer Rouge instructions 'to force Cham people to carry out orders just like *normal Khmers*' (Kiernan 1996:266–7, my emphasis), that 'everybody is to *join* the same, single, Khmer nationality' (ibid., my emphasis), and that 'Chams who eat pork [...] will be spared' (ibid.:271). On the other hand, it would hardly have helped a Jew in Nazi Germany to renounce his or her Jewishness and promise to become a good Aryan.

Secondly, even if the Khmer Rouge measures for promoting Khmer ethnic superiority were extreme, the historical development of nation states (in Southeast Asia and elsewhere) has usually entailed attempts at ethnic homogenisation through the assimilation of minorities into the dominant ethnic group, or, alternatively, through ethnic cleansing; Cambodia is no exception in this respect. In the recent past, the Lon Nol regime (1970–5) rivalled the Khmer Rouge in terms of aggressively promoting Khmer supremacy, which hit the Vietnamese in particular, and the conscious attempt at the 'Khmerisation' of the indigenous upland groups, had been part of the policies of both Sihanouk and Lon Nol (White 1996; Ovesen and Trankell 2003).

'Genocide' in Cambodia – Whose Agenda?

Whether we find Kiernan's arguments for genocide convincing is a matter of opinion. In any case, there are other than academic interests involved in portraying the Khmer Rouge regime as genocidal. Indeed, this has become the 'official' epithet for the events, mainly thanks to the initiative of the Vietnamese communists. After the invasion in January 1979, the Vietnamese not only took political control and began the physical rehabilitation of the country, they also began historical and political investigations of the Khmer Rouge regime. The discovery of Tuol Sleng, a Khmer Rouge interrogation and torture centre in Phnom Penh, known under DK as 'S-21,' yielded important material, and the Vietnamese decided to turn the buildings (a former high-school) into a museum. For this purpose they employed Mai Lam, a Vietnamese army colonel with an interest in military history and museology. Colonel Mai Lam had previously organised the Museum of American War Crimes in Ho Chi Minh City, and for his new task he made a study tour to Europe to visit Holocaust museums and memorials. In 1980, Tuol Sleng was opened to the public as the Museum of Genocidal Crimes. In his book about Tuol Sleng, David Chandler says,

> In turning S-21 into a museum of genocide, Mai Lam wanted to arrange Cambodia's recent past to fit the requirements of the PRK and its Vietnamese mentors [...] Because numbers of the 'Pol Pot–Ieng Sary genocidal clique,' as the Vietnamese labelled them, had been Cambodians themselves, the message that Mai Lam was trying to deliver was

different from the one that he had hoped to convey in the Museum of American War Crimes [...] The history that he constructed in the exhibits at S-21 denied the leaders of the CPK [Communist Party of Kampuchea, the Khmer Rouge revolutionary party] any socialist credentials and encouraged viewers to make connections between the DK regime and Tuol Sleng on the one hand, and Nazi Germany and [...] Auschwitz on the other. (Chandler 1999:5)

The role of Mai Lam, Chandler continues, was deliberately concealed from outsiders, 'creating the impression that the initiatives for the museum and its design had come from the Cambodian victims rather than from the Vietnamese' (ibid.:6). There is thus no doubt that Vietnamese political interests were served by employing the label genocide, thus blaming the failure of the Cambodian socialist revolution not on socialist ideology or practice, but on Pol Pot and his 'genocidal clique'.

But other political interests are served as well. Neither Hun Sen – currently Cambodian Prime Minister and leader of the Cambodian People's Party (successor to the Vietnam-backed Communist Party during PRK) – nor Norodom Sihanouk – present King of Cambodia and de facto political leader of the country, as Prince and as Prime Minister, from independence till 1970 – have had any objections to labelling the Khmer Rouge as genocidal maniacs. Because what is achieved by employing the genocide label is, among other things, that the period of the DK regime is bracketed off, so to speak, as an historical aberration rather than seen, more justly, as a continuation, albeit grotesquely intensified, of the terror-as-usual pattern pursued by all Cambodian post-colonial rulers.

We have already mentioned the brutal and chauvinist regime of Lon Nol (1970–5), which was backed by the USA, politically and militarily, and which resulted, among other things, in the exodus of more than 300,000 Vietnamese. As for the Sihanouk era, Milton Osborne, in his biography of Sihanouk, has summed it up succinctly when he notes that

the horrendous record of the Pol Pot years of tyranny and death has pushed the excesses of Sihanouk's final years of power into the historical background. Added to the horror of the Pol Pot period is the fact that the Lon Nol regime which emerged after Sihanouk's overthrow was characterised by gross incompetence and brutality. [...] Yet the record of Sihanouk's use of the harshest measures against his enemies is clear [...] During 1968 and 1969 [...] the government, with Sihanouk's direct encouragement and explicit orders, waged a campaign of brutal repression. (Osborne 1994:196)

Historically, political terror in Cambodia has not been restricted to the post-colonial period. Writing about the first half of the nineteenth century, David Chandler notes,

it is difficult to overstress the atmosphere of physical danger and the currents of insecurity and random violence that run through [...] so much of Cambodian life in this period. The chronicles are filled with references to public executions, ambushes, torture, village-burning and forced emigrations, (cited by Vickery 1984:7)

and Vickery quotes accounts of torture and executions committed by the Khmer Issarak (a guerrilla movement aimed against the French colonials) in the 1940s that reads just like accounts of those committed by the Khmer Rouge (ibid.:5–6).[4]

To sum up, I find it highly dubious whether 'genocide' as a label for the Khmer

---

[4] Even the much publicised practice of clubbing people to death at the edge of a burial pit turns out not to be an original Khmer Rouge invention, but was practised already by the Khmer Issarak.

Rouge atrocities serves the interests of historians and other social scientists (to say nothing about those of the general public) as well as it does Cambodian, Vietnamese and international political interests. Whatever it conveys about the Pol Pot regime can be (and has been) equally well described in other words. But to the extent that it conveys the impression of a four-year violent interlude in the history of an otherwise peaceful land and gentle people, it contributes to the falsification of that history.

Cultural Models and Cambodian Violence

In a series of articles, anthropologist Alexander Hinton (1996; 1998a; 1998b) has suggested that the Khmer Rouge 'genocide' may be understood, even explained, by a number of Khmer 'cultural models'. First he proposed the concept of 'psychosocial dissonance'. Taking inspiration from Leon Festinger's 1950s notion of cognitive dissonance, he added ideas from American psychological anthropology about the self and embodied emotions and arrived at a definition of psychosocial dissonance which allegedly pertains to situations 'in which an emotionally salient cultural model about the context-dependent self comes into conflict with another emotionally salient cultural model that violates that context-dependent self-concept' (1996:820). The first of these purported cultural models he refers to as the 'gentle ethic', the idea that Cambodians should live a harmonious life of Buddhist non-violence. The second model is labelled the 'violent ethic' and is thought to derive from the legacy of the god-kings of the Angkorian period; it has notably been promoted by Seanglim Bit (1991).[5] Hinton asserts that somehow these two models

> rarely came into conflict in pre-DK. The conditions for [psychosocial dissonance] arose, however, when the violent ethic was legitimated in everyday communal interactions during DK. The unfortunate result was a situation in which acts of extraordinary violence took place. (ibid.:821)

I find this analysis problematic for a number of reasons. To begin with, it reinforces the tendency to bracket off the Pol Pot period as a radical departure from the rest of Cambodian history, which, I have argued, is seriously misleading. Secondly, the whole idea of explaining undesirable social actions in terms of some kind of 'dissonance' implies a rather obsolete view of culture as ideally a well-integrated whole where internal contradictions are the exception rather than the norm. Thirdly, the epistemological status of the 'cultural models' of gentleness and violence is questionable. The 'violent ethic' has been consistently promoted in the propaganda instigated by both Lon Nol and Sihanouk,[6] but we have no real evidence that it had become salient in the minds of ordinary people in the 1970s. The 'gentle ethic', likewise, is mainly a rhetorical construction, in this case of the colonial French orientalist discourse. The picture of the smiling, acquiescent Cambodians could equally well be related, for example, to their desire

---

[5] Seanglim Bit is a former civil servant in Lon Nol's government who was subsequently trained in social psychology in the USA.

[6] 'My people, unfortunately, they have two faces, if I may say so. They are artists. They like singing, making love, etc., on the one hand. And the other face is a warrior. They like war, violence, killing each other. We can smile and we can also kill' (Norodom Sihanouk, in the film The Last God-King, James Garrand 1996).

for staying out of trouble, or, in May Ebihara's words, to their 'distaste for becoming unnecessarily involved in unpleasant situations' (1968:186).

In subsequent articles, Hinton adduces a number of other 'cultural models' as explanatory devices (1998a; 1998b). A major one is that of 'disproportionate revenge.' This implies that some person who bears a grudge against someone else will plot a revenge that by far exceeds the original insult. In order to construe such sentiments as a cultural model, Hinton invokes a sixteenth century popular legend in which King Rama punishes one of his mandarins for disregarding his authority by killing him and his family and relatives seven generations removed, as well as all the members of his political faction (1998a:354). Among the further 'cultural models' of Hinton's explanatory repertoire (1998b) are 'natural inequality' (i.e. hierarchy), 'hierarchical mobility' (the wish to enhance one's status), 'obedience and respect' (of subordinates towards superiors), 'face and shame' (to avoid the shame that derives from the loss of face), 'honour competition', and 'violence against a sociopolitical enemy'. The translation into the Khmer language of the notion of class struggle (tâsou vonnah), Hinton suggests, 'drew on a Cambodian cultural model of warriors (neak tâsou) who 'struggle' [...] against the enemy' (1998a:363).

Terror and Power

It is significant that Hinton's cultural models pertain mostly to interpersonal relations, and that most of them appear rather dissociated from wider structures of economic and political inequality in society. While his work has provided us with valuable insights into how ordinary Khmers relate, and have related to one another, both before, during and after the Pol Pot regime, I believe the concentration on purported cultural models for behaviour in interpersonal relations is not necessarily very well suited to Hinton's declared purpose, i.e. the examination of 'large-scale genocide' (1998b:96). And I am not convinced that posing the question 'Why did you kill?' to individual Khmer Rouge soldiers will necessarily yield the most pertinent insights into the mechanisms behind the killings. While answers to this question will naturally reveal both individual and cultural predispositions, we should bear in mind that, contrary to what Hinton implies (ibid.:112), the DK atrocities were not an instance of ordinary people suddenly starting indiscriminately to kill one another, even if their actions might be motivated or endorsed by cultural models of revenge, hierarchy, face or honour in their interpersonal relations. The killings were part of a systematic and organised state terror.

In his introduction to a collection of essays on state terror, Jeffrey Sluka (2000) has suggested that generally state terror, rather than being a desperate measure of a weak state to hold the polity together, is committed from a position of strength. 'Elites who resort to terror do not do it because the state is weak, but rather because they are strong and can get away with it' (2000:31). I believe this perspective is important, because it invites us to scrutinise the concept of power itself and ask how power is culturally construed, perceived, deployed and executed; we might even want to posit power as a 'cultural model', but, curiously, this is a dimension that Alex Hinton has largely neglected. I believe that a reflection on the nature of power in Khmer society is indispensable for our efforts to understand the political violence committed by Cambodian rulers and would-be-rulers, before, during and after DK.

In the absence of existing analyses of the Khmer concept of power, we may turn, for inspiration and parallels, to Ben Anderson's study, 'The Idea of Power in Javanese Culture' (1990). Anderson suggests that the various elements that make up the Javanese power concept may not all be unique to the Javanese. Indeed it is reasonable to assume that the cosmologies of the various 'Indianised' societies in Southeast Asia have a lot of common ground (cf. Dentan 2002), and in my opinion and experience, several of the traits Anderson has found apply equally well to Khmer culture. The most important contrast between the 'Southeast Asian' (at least Javanese and Khmer) and modern Western ideas of power is that in the former, power is dissociated from social morality and legitimacy (Anderson 1990:21–23). Major power-holders in the West (such as US presidents, for example) can lose their power by disregarding society's moral norms. But in Java (and Cambodia), the source of power is the divine cosmic energy which 'antecedes questions of good and evil' (ibid.:23) and which individuals may tap for political purposes. The power-holder – whether divine king, army general, or chairman of a revolutionary party – does not seek to gain compliance with obligations. If you have power it is irrelevant whether other people comply with your decisions or condone your actions, i.e. whether your use of power may be considered legitimate. You act as you please because this is what power permits you to do. And if you cannot any longer act as you please, it is a sign that you have lost your power. In Cambodia, the prototype of the power-holder is the God-king of Angkorian times. 'The social signs of the concentration of power [in and around his person] were fertility, prosperity, stability, and glory' (ibid.:32); 'all other political actors were condemned to subordinate roles as parts of the system' (ibid.:30). The necessary delegation, for purposes of administration, of power from the monarchic ruler followed the hierarchical structure of patron-client relationships (ibid.:46–7; cf. Osborne 1969: 4–8; Mabbett and Chandler 1995:156–69).

Cambodian rulers' role-model of the semi-divine king has persisted through the ages, including the reign of Sihanouk, and other post-colonial rulers (most notably DK's angkar, and current prime minister Hun Sen) have tried to emulate it. Common to the Cambodian post-colonial regimes has been the exercise of power in accordance with the principles sketched above. The system of patronage, frequently noted as pervading socioeconomic and sociopolitical relationships in Cambodian society, plays an important part. Hierarchical patron-client relations are often described as important functional relationships in peasant societies which cut across, supersede, or take the place of 'official' (kinship or administrative) structures. The role of a patron is to offer physical protection as well as economic assistance and moral support in times of such needs. The obligations of the client are to assure political loyalty and occasionally to supply labour for the patron. In the field of politics, this implies, among other things, that the lines of command are unidirectional, they run down through the hierarchy, from patrons to clients. Formal avenues for 'democratic' critique of those in power by their subordinate clients (or by political outsiders, such as intellectuals) are non-existent; and if critique is nevertheless expressed, it is usually met with violence and terror by those in power. Thus, critique expressed in the independent newspapers that proliferated since the UNTAC period has increasingly been met with violent measures, including bombing of offices and assassination of editors and journalists (Marston 1996:237–9).

In this respect, the Cambodian idea of power seems to differ from the Javanese. In Java, '[b]y doing violence to its powerless critics, the regime confirms their criticism and reinforces the authority of their predictions' ibid.:67). Not so in Cambodia. Generally it seems, critics are construed as enemies. 'Patterns of extreme violence against people defined as enemies, however arbitrarily, have very long roots in Cambodia' (Vickery 1984:7). Milton Osborne noted 'Sihanouk's use of the harshest measures against his enemies' (Osborne 1994:196). The most notable long-term example of such 'enemies' are the Vietnamese. Characteristic of 'enemies' is that they act or behave in ways that are contrary to Khmer cultural values or sociopolitical interests and therefore represent a threat to these values or interests. An 'enemy' is thus a person, or perhaps rather a non-person, whose ultimate fate should be annihilation, as Hinton also noted (1998b:112). One way of behaving like an enemy is to rebel against the prevailing social and cosmological order, for example by showing disregard for established hierarchies. A Khmer Rouge slogan neatly sums up the attitude: 'He who protests is the enemy, he who objects is a corpse' (Locard 1996:170).

As Ponchaud (1989) pointed out, and as Hinton has argued in great detail (1998b), the DK revolution was very much a Khmer cultural phenomenon, and Khmer cultural values were consciously upheld as a basis for the cause. This extended also to the ways the regime exercised its power. Paradoxically, the DK radical revolutionary leadership emulated the ruling style of the traditional Cambodian monarchs. Foremost among the radically revolutionary but culturally grammatical measures adopted by the Khmer Rouge was the reversal of the hierarchy of elder and younger while at the same time establishing the authority of the angkar at the apex of the hierarchical order. This, coupled with the policy of sectarian isolation and extreme secrecy of the Pol Pot movement, induced the lower ranks of the movement to blind obedience towards any person claiming to be closer to the higher echelons. Thus, Henri Locard cites a notebook by the commandant of S-21 to the effect that the interrogators at this prison should be recruited from the youth organisation of the Party, and must come from the poorest classes of society; they must be filled with a 'burning hatred of the enemy' and never be allowed to doubt that the prisoners/enemies are 'cruel people who always devour deeper and deeper into the Party' (1995:26). In other words, the lower one's place in the hierarchy, the more unconditional obeisance could be expected, and the less likely the interrogators would be to rely on their own judgement, since eventual disagreement with superiors would signify doubt about the infallibility of the angkar, something that would define the interrogator himself as an enemy. Small wonder that virtually all inmates of S-21 lost their lives. The obsession with purging the system of enemies had also been characteristic, notably, of the Khmer Issarak as well as of the Sihanouk and Lon Nol governments, although it reached its most paranoid proportions with the Khmer Rouge.

The dimension of revenge in Khmer Rouge atrocities, which Hinton has highlighted should also, I believe, be understood primarily as an expression of the DK leadership's claim to traditional, semi-divine power. Exterminating not only the offender, but also his kin group and clients, was a royal prerogative. 'Like Rama, the Khmer Rouge often attempted to exact revenge in such a manner as to destroy the former supporters of Lon Nol completely' (1998a:361). This is definitely not, I believe, the same, culturally or psychologically, as an ordinary person's wish to exact revenge on a superior or equal who has offended him and/or made him lose face. We cannot, of course, deny the possibility that some low- and mid-level Khmer Rouge cadres occasionally killed people for the latter reason. But Henri Locard, for one, emphatically rejects random, personally motivated killings; 'as always in Pol Pot's Cambodia, every revolutionary had to submit most obediently to the orders from the Centre, and these orders were increasingly to launch the fiercest of attacks against "enemies"'(Locard 1995:30).

My Khmer informants tend to corroborate this view. One of them related how the angkar employed 'messengers' (nearasa) who were sent, on horseback, bicycle or motorbike, to the provinces as envoys and spies to oversee that the revolution was properly conducted. 'When a messenger had visited a place, bad things always happened', he explained. The messengers were much feared locally because they enjoyed the full support of the angkar, and when they decided that someone should be executed, the local leaders were bound to carry out the order. Even if they might sometimes act on a whim or a 'need to assert undue authority' when condemning people to death, the fact that they were outsiders in the local communities would preclude personal grudges as motivation.

The systematic extermination of suspected counter-revolutionaries, which was characteristic of the internal purges from 1976 onwards, seems to me a clear indication of the leaders' assumption of royal power; once a person was suspected of having betrayed the revolution, all his or her associates and political clients were rounded up and accused, and frequently tortured and killed.

Conclusion

Political violence has been an integral part of Cambodian society throughout the time for which historical records exist. In the most recent period, i.e. since UNTAC supervised the general elections in 1993, the political scene has changed from the show of overt tyrannical repression to Mafia-style manoeuvring among the political parties, with occasional outbursts of violence. In spite of massive UN presence during the preparations of the 1993 elections, more than a hundred opposition party members were murdered by police teams directed by the national police chief, directly or indirectly under orders from the CPP government under Hun Sen (Shawcross 2002:42–3). A particularly atrocious instance of contemporary political violence that hit innocent bystanders was the grenade throwing at a political rally of the KNP (Khmer Nation Party, later renamed, after its leader, the Sam Rainsy Party) in Phnom Penh in March 1997 which killed twenty people and maimed about a hundred. The July 1997 coup that estab- lished the CPP under Hun Sen as the sole governing party involved the murder of at least 41 members of the opposition (Brown and Timberman 1998:23), and both the parliamentary elections of 1998 and the municipal elections of 2002 were occasions of political murders. In February 2003, when voter registration for the July parliamentary elections was underway, the secretary of the FUNCINPEC party was gunned down in broad daylight in a restaurant in Phnom Penh. Violence and politics are intimately connected in the minds of the Cambodian people, and violent acts committed with impunity by politicians or their hired hands come as no surprise to anybody.

In the above I have argued that the application of the notion of genocide – as a concept of social science analysis, rather than as a legal term– is inappropriate in the case of the Khmer Rouge regime in Cambodia. Its use as a label for the Khmer Rouge mass murder tends to obscure the important fact that political violence, perpetrated mainly by those in power, has been the order of the day both before and after DK. It is understandable that the Khmer Rouge terror regime, which existed for less than four years, has attracted a fair amount of scholarly attention, but this attention should not obscure or make us ignore the wider historical context, in which any analysis of political culture in Cambodia should be placed. Particularly, if we want to argue for cultural explanations, we need to bridge the gap between timeless 'cultural models' and the specific period between April 1975 and January 1979. This is what I have attempted in this paper. I have suggested that attention to Khmer ideas of political power enables us to better understand the violence perpetrated by the various rulers of the country, from the Angkorian kings to Hun Sen, including the DK leadership.

References

Anderson, Ben, 1990 [1972], 'The Idea of Power in Javanese Culture', in Anderson, Ben, *Language and Power. Exploring Political Cultures in Indonesia* Ithaca, NY: Cornell University Press

Ang Choulean, 1986. *Les Êtres surnaturels dans la religion populaire Khmère* Paris: Cedoreck

Banister, Judith and Paige Johnson, 1993, 'After the Nightmare: The Population of Cambodia', in Kiernan, B., ed. *Genocide and Democracy in Cambodia* New Haven, CT: Yale University Southeast Asian Studies, Monograph No. 41

Bit, Seanglim, 1991, *The Warrior Heritage: A Psychological Perspective of Cambodian Trauma* El Cerrito, CA: Seanglim Bit

Brown, Frederick and David Timberman, 1998, 'Introduction: Peace, Development, and Democracy in Cambodia – Shattered Hopes', in Brown, F. and Timberman D., eds, *Cambodia and the International Community. The Quest for Peace, Development, and Democracy* Singapore: Institute of Southeast Asian Studies

Chandler, David, 1991, *The Tragedy of Cambodian History* New Haven, CT: Yale University Press

—— 1992, *A History of Cambodia* (2nd ed.) Boulder, CO: Westview Press

—— 1993, *Brother Number One. A Political Biography of Pol Pot* Thailand and Indochina Edition, Bangkok: Silkworm Books

—— 1996, *Facing the Cambodian Past* Chiang Mai: Silkworm Books

—— 1999, *Voices from S-21. Terror and History in Pol Pot's Secret Prison* Berkeley: University of California Press

Dang Nghiem Van et al., 1993, *Ethnic Minorities in Vietnam.* Hanoi: Thé Giói Publishers

Dentan, Robert Knox, 2002, '"Disreputable Magicians", the Dark Destroyer, and the Trickster Lord: Reflections on Semai Religion and a Possible Common Religious Base in South and Southeast Asia' *Asian Anthropology*, 1:153–94

Ebihara, May Mayko, 1968, 'Svay, a Khmer Village in Cambodia' Unpublished Ph.D. Thesis, Columbia University

Garrand, James, 1996, *The Last God-King* TV Documentary, Film Australia Distribution

Halbwachs, Maurice, 1925 [1992], *On Collective Memory* (trs. L. Coser) Chicago: Chicago University Press

Heder, Steve, 1980, *Kampuchean Occupation and Resistance* Asian Studies Monographs No 27. Bangkok: Institute of Asian Studies, Chulalongkorn University

—— 1997, 'Racism, Marxism, labelling and genocide in Ben Kiernan's 'The Pol Pot Regime' *South East Asia Research* 5(2): 101–53

Heuveline, Patrick, 2001, 'Approaches to measuring Genocide: Excess Mortality during the Khmer Rouge Period', in Chirot, D. and Seligman, M., eds, *Ethnopolitical Warfare. Causes, Consequences, and Possible Solutions* Washington, DC: American Psychological Association

Higham, Charles, 2001, *The Civilization of Angkor* Berkeley: University of California Press

Hinton, Alexander L., 1996, 'Agents of Death. Explaining the Cambodian Genocide in Terms of

Psychosocial Dissonance' *American Anthropologist* 98 (4): 818–31

—— 1998a 'A Head for an Eye: Revenge in the Cambodian Genocide' *American Ethnologist* 25 (3): 352–77

—— 1998b 'Why Did You Kill?: The Cambodian Genocide and the Dark Side of Face and Honor' *Journal of Asian Studies* 57 (1): 93–122

Jordens, Jay, 1996, 'Persecution of Cambodia's Ethnic Vietnamese Communities During and Since the UNTAC Period', in Heder, S. and Ledgerwood, J. eds, *Propaganda, Politics, and Violence in Cambodia. Democratic Transition under United Nations Peace-keeping* New York: M.E. Sharpe

Kiernan, Ben, 1982, 'Introduction', in Kiernan, B. and Boua, C. eds, *Peasants and Politics in Kampuchea, 1942– 1981* London: Zed Books

—— 1985, *How Pol Pot Came to Power* London: Verso

—— 1990, 'The Genocide in Cambodia 1975–9' *Bulletin of Concerned Asian Scholars* 22 (2): 35–40

—— 1991, 'Genocidal Targeting: Two Groups of Victims in Pol Pot's Cambodia', in Bushnell, T. et al., eds, *State Organized Terror. The Case of Violent Internal Repression* Boulder, CO: Westview Press

—— 1996, *The Pol Pot Regime. Race, Power and Genocide in Cambodia under the Khmer Rouge, 1975–79* New Haven, CT: Yale University Press

—— 2001, 'The Ethnic Element in the Cambodian Genocide', in Chirot, D. and Seligman, M., eds, *Ethnopolitical Warfare. Causes, Consequences, and Possible Solutions* Washington, DC: American Psychological Association

—— ed., 1994, *Genocide and Democracy: The Khmer Rouge, the United Nations and the International Community* New Haven, CT: Yale University Southeast Asia Studies, Monograph No. 41

Kiernan, Ben and Chantou Boua, eds, 1982, *Peasants and Politics in Kampuchea, 1942–1981* London: Zed Books

van Liere, W. J., 1980, 'Traditional Water Management in the Lower Mekong Basin' *World Archaeology* 11 (3): 265–80

Locard, Henri, 1995, 'The Khmer Rouge Gulag' Paris, Canberra, Phnom Penh (mimeo)

—— 1996, *Le 'Petit Livre Rouge' de Pol Pot* Paris: L'Harmattan

Luco, Fabienne, 2002, *Entre le tigre et le crocodile. Approche anthropologique sur les pratiques traditionelles et nouvelles de traitement des conflits au Cambodge* Phnom Penh: UNESCO

Mabbett, Ian and David Chandler, 1995, *The Khmers.* Oxford: Blackwell

Marston, John, 1996, 'Cambodian News Media in the UNTAC Period and After', in Heder, S. and Ledgerwood, J., eds, *Propaganda, Politics, and Violence in Cambodia. Democratic Transition under United Nations Peace-keeping* New York: M.E. Sharpe

Martin, Marie Alexandrine, 1994, *Cambodia. A Shattered Society* Berkeley: University of California Press

Nakamura, Rie, 1999, 'Cham in Vietnam. Dynamics of Ethnicity' Unpublished PhD thesis, University of Washington

Osborne, Milton, 1969, *The French Presence in Cochinchina and Cambodia. Rule and Response (1859– 1905)* Ithaca, NY: Cornell University Press

—— 1994, *Sihanouk. Prince of Light, Prince of Darkness* Chiang Mai: Silkworm Books

—— 1997, *Southeast Asia. An Introductory History* (7th edn), Chiang Mai: Silkworm Books

Ovesen, Jan and Ing-Britt Trankell, 2003, 'Foreigners and Honorary Khmers. Ethnic Minorities in Cambodia', in Duncan, C. ed., *Legislating Modernity among the Marginalized: Southeast Asian Government Programs for Developing Minority Ethnic Groups* Ithaca, NY: Cornell University Press

Ponchaud, François, 1989, 'Social Change in the Vortex of Revolution', in Jackson, K. D. ed., *Cambodia 1975–1978: Rendezvous with Death* Princeton, NJ: Princeton University Press

Shawcross, William, 2002, 'Lessons of Cambodia', in Mills, N. and Brunner, K. eds, *The New Killing Fields. Massacre and the Politics of Intervention* New York: Basic Books

Sluka, Jeffrey, 2000, 'Introduction: State Terror and Anthropology', in Sluka, J. ed., *Death Squad. The Anthropology of State Terror* Philadelphia: University of Pennsylvania Press

Stott, Philip, 1992, 'Angkor: Shifting the Hydraulic Paradigm', in Rigg, J. ed., *The Gift of Water. Water Management, Cosmology and the State in South East Asia* London: School of Oriental and African Studies

Trankell, Ing-Britt, 2003, 'Songs of Our Spirits. Possession and Historical Imagination among the Cham in Cambodia' *Asian Ethnicity* 4 (1): 31–46

Trankell, Ing-Britt and Jan Ovesen, 1998, 'Introduction', in Trankell, I.-B. and Summers, L. eds, *Facets of Power and Its Limitations. Political Culture in Southeast Asia* Uppsala: Uppsala Studies in Cultural Anthropology 24

Vickery, Michael, 1984, *Cambodia 1975–1982* Boston, MA: South End Press

—— 1989, 'Comments on Cham Population Figures' *Bulletin of Concerned Asian Scholars* 21 (1):

31–33

—— 1990, 'Refugee Politics: The Khmer Camp System in Thailand', in Albin, D.A. and Hood, *The Cambodian Agony* New York: M.E. Sharpe

White, Joanna, 1996, 'The Indigenous Highlanders of the Northeast: An Uncertain Futuᴜ. *Interdisciplinary Research on Ethnic Groups in Cambodia* Phnom Penh: Center for Advanced Studɣ (mimeo)

Ysa, Osman, 2002, *Oukoubah. Justice for the Cham Muslims under the Democratic Kampuchea Regime* Phnom Penh: Documentation Center of Cambodia

lemmas
Pastoralist Conflicts in Burkina Faso

STEN HAGBERG

In February 1995 a violent conflict broke out in villages in the Mangodara district in Burkina Faso. People of the farming population attacked pastoral Fulbe, accusing them of letting their cattle cause crop damage and spoil water points reserved for humans. Local farmers even 'arrested' some herders. Their firearms were confiscated and brought to the police station to ensure that the Fulbe herders would financially compensate field-owners. Tensions were strained in the whole area and when the farmers saw that the Police Officer delayed the case, they 'rebelled' against what they saw as unjust treatment and corrupt behaviour. A group of Karaboro farmers took their arms and ran out into the local marketplace and started to shoot at any Fulbe encountered. They then left the market and entered the bush to shoot at 'all that moved and was Fulbe'. Between five and ten Fulbe men were killed that day. The Police Officer escaped and later also the préfet (the administrative head of the Mangodara district). Army units in the provincial town Banfora were alerted and arrived in Mangodara at sunset. A Fulbe man stated: 'the gendarmes arrived when we had started to gather the dead corpses.' The arrival of army units did not end the conflict, but its escalation was hindered. During the coming days and weeks attempts were made to 'cool' down the conflict. Many actors were involved in the work to re-establish a sense of normality, and those accused of murder were arrested (though never judged). Local politicians organised sensitisation tours to try to 'solve' the conflict. On these occasions strong anti-Fulbe sentiments were aired and the politicians played in this game. Some even supported local demands to release those accused of murder. The scapegoats were local government officials who were represented as corrupt. They were said to have closed their eyes to crop damage caused by Fulbe cattle (against all sorts of 'gifts' including money) and thus left farmers without compensation. But Fulbe held they were without any support whatsoever. According to them, the government supported the farmers and only God supported the Fulbe.

This chapter explores the processes by which violent conflicts between farmers and pastoralists are handled in Burkina Faso. It sets out to analyse the involvement of local government officials in dispute settlement between Fulbe agro-pastoralists and Karaboro farmers in the Sidéradougou district (*département*) in the Comoé Province in Western Burkina. First, I approach local government officials as a specific social category of agents in between the State and the local community. Secondly, the social identity of these officials is explored as 'la culture des fonctionnaires'. Thirdly, I make a detailed analysis of how local government officials cope with crop and/or animal damage through administrative dispute settlement procedures. Fourthly, a brief account of outbreaks of violence between Karaboro farmers and Fulbe agro-pastoralists highlights what might happen when things go wrong. The underlying question of the chapter is how local government officials are dealing with the dilemma of maintaining social peace, on the one hand, and making justice, on the other. While the categorisation of 'peace' and 'conflict' is central to the practice of local government officials, most activities carried out by these officials could hardly be defined as resolving conflicts once-and-for-all. The peaceful everyday behaviour of administrative procedures hides the germ of violence and killings. But even in the heat of violence locally based peace processes are at work.[1]

Policy and Politics

The growing interest in the anthropology of development organisations is due to the fact that development has become a main force in shaping the relations between 'developers' and 'those to-be-developed' (Arce and Long 2000; Blundo 1995; Dahl and Hjort 1984; Dahl and Rabo 1992; Escobar 1991; Grillo and Stirrat 1997; Hagberg 2001b; Hedlund 1984; Hobart 1993a; Olivier de Sardan 1995; Robertson 1984). The relationship between these two categories is, in Hobart's words, 'constituted by the developers' knowledge and categories' (Hobart 1993b: 2). Today development represents a universal discourse, linking the world economically and politically. But 'development' is by no means 'neutral or value-free but rather, because of its nature as a moral imperative, is part and parcel of a world-wide order of ranking and power' (Rabo 1992:2). To understand how 'development' takes shape in specific local contexts it is necessary to reflect upon the 'bureaucratic culture' of development organisations. This 'culture' demonstrates many similarities across the world with respect to organisational set-up, approach and discourse, even though the mastery of development discourse varies between state agents operating within the development context in a given country. The variation is due to a wide range of factors, such as position in the organisational hierarchy, level of education, gender, personal assets and status. Catchwords used by central planners tend rapidly to trickle down to local government officials and project staff implementing development projects. While central planners are based in the capital to formulate plans, projects and policies, local government officials are mandated to translate these plans, projects and policies into specific development operations. Hence, local government officials are not merely planners tied to the bureaucratic culture of development, but are first of all implementing agents. They are those who should practically translate both the form and content of the plans, projects and policies into specific actions. However, local implementation of laws or policies often differs considerably from the way they were conceived in the central Ministry (von Benda-Beckmann 1993). In this chapter I use the term 'local government officials' to include any government employed field staff, based in a given village or rural town. In Dyula – the *lingua franca* used in Western Burkina – all government staff are generally referred to as *faama* ('government') or *faama mogo* ('government people'). But the

[1] Since 1988 fieldwork has been carried out in Western Burkina for a total of five years. I am grateful for comments on earlier drafts by the late Bernhard Helander, Jan Ovesen and Paul Richards.

State is multifarious in its organisations and actions (cf. Degnbol 2001), and in this chapter it is the agents of general state administration (*préfets*) and security (police agents and gendarmes) that are the main actors.

There are two main reasons to investigate the processes by which national policy enter local politics in dispute settlement. The first reason is that the official policy defines what should be done in case of crop damage and/or animal losses, according to which the Agricultural Extension Officer, the *préfet* and the Veterinary officer have, each of them, specific roles to play. They have received general instructions on how to proceed in such situations, that is how to measure damages and how to establish administrative dossiers. But policy is also implemented according to what the individual *imagines* are the procedures (cf. Hagberg 2000a). There is often no copy of legal documents in local offices of various line ministries. Moreover, government officials may intentionally ignore the policy and exploit their relative authority for personal gains. They intervene as agents in a social space, shaped by contradictory interests, structures and actions. A second reason to investigate national policy in local politics is that in everyday conversations many local government officials complain that 'people in Ouagadougou' – that is, their superiors in the ministerial hierarchy – do not know anything about 'field realities', and are 'too theoretical'. They are said to formulate documents, salted with the latest catch-words and development jargon, but are far from actual work done by local government officials. Local government officials are therefore situated between planners and local people and their core task is, at least officially, to fit a given policy into the context of a specific local setting.

Internationally promoted development discourse coexists, however, with other, more nationally oriented development discourses. In Burkina Faso the national development discourse falls within two different frames: first, the discourse originating from the French colonial administration; and, second, the specific national political discourse ('revolutionary' in the 1980s and 'democratic' in the 1990s). The first frame of official, national discourse is present in Burkinabe administration and is strongly connected to the French language. Legislation originates from French jurisdiction, even though there has been a conscious struggle to adapt legislation to Burkinabe realities (Blanc et al. 1991). This is the language of the state administration, representing continuity throughout different political periods in Burkina Faso.

The second frame within which official national discourse may be located is the use of language and power in the event commonly referred to as the Revolution, i.e. the *coup d'état* led by Captain Thomas Sankara in August 1983 (Dubuch 1985; Labazée 1989). Revolutionary discourse was accompanied by a wave of slogans and expressions. Individual and geographical names were modified in the framework of being 'authentic', new styles of dressing were 'authorised', national hymn and flag were changed and a stereotyped language was used (Dubuch 1985:46). Even a new country name, Burkina Faso,[2] was adopted to replace the former Haute-Volta. In October 1987, Thomas Sankara

---

[2] The new name of the country is essentially composed of the Mooré term Burkina, signifying men of honour, of dignity, and the Dyula term Faso for fatherhouse (fatherland), giving 'Fatherland of Dignified Men'. Fulfulde, the third national language, is employed to designate citizens of Burkina Faso (Burkinabe), *be* signifying children or persons. The name Burkina Faso could thus be regarded as an attempt symbolically to unite the country.

was assassinated in a *coup d'état* that brought Captain Blaise Compaoré to power, arguing that the Revolution was to be 'rectified'. At the end of 1980s, President Compaoré and his government initiated a democratisation process and the revolutionary language gave way to discourses of democracy. In December 1991 President Compaoré was elected in a presidential ballot, but he was the only candidate, since the other candidates boycotted the elections. In November 1998 he was re-elected for a second seven-year period. The radical opposition also boycotted these elections. While power is still in the hands of Blaise Compaoré, the official, national discourse is today located in the language of democracy (Otayek et al. 1996b). The assassination of the journalist Norbert Zongo in December 1998 increased tensions between those in power and the sociopolitical opposition. Independent survey commissions indicated that Zongo's murderers are to be found in the inner-circle of the president's security forces. The struggle against impunity and for justice has become the main slogan mobilising both political parties and civil society organisations (Hagberg 2002a; Ouédraogo 1999).

Burkina Faso has a continuous experience of socio-political crisis, and political violence has increased in the last 20 years. From strong anti-corruption policies in the 1980s, corruption has become a major blight on society, even though Otayek et al. (1996a:19) argue that corruption and nepotism have remained circumscribed within 'acceptable limits' in Burkina. One important reason keeping these factors within limits is that in Burkina Faso government officials are always regularly paid. A popular saying among officials is that the government has to pay people regularly, otherwise it cannot stay in power. In the *coups d'état* of 1966 and 1980, trades unions played important political roles; this is a constituent part of the self-image expressed by many government officials (Hagberg 2002a).

Local government officials are both 'messengers' and 'messages' (Hedlund 1984; see also Chambers 1979; Poluha 1989) in that they are individuals of various origin, who are mandated to work in a locality for some years and become members of it. They are 'messengers', because they represent the government and its intentions. In contrast to the majority of rural inhabitants, they are French-speaking and educated at least to secondary level. They are messengers carrying information about legal, administrative and financial affairs to local people. But local government officials are simultaneously 'messages' in their adherence to an urban ideology, representing *tubabubaara* (the work of the white men). Although many originate from rural or semi-urban communities, they embody messages of 'progress' and 'development'.

Continuity and Discontinuity in Sidéradougou

There are about 50 government officials in the Sidéradougou district, mostly men. The district covers 33 officially recognised villages and is administratively dependent on the High-Commissioner (*Haut-Commissaire*) of the Comoé Province in Banfora. Sidéradougou is located 65 km east of Banfora on the National Road 11, which connects Banfora and Gaoua. It is situated off the principal road (N7) linking Burkina Faso and Côte d'Ivoire. Government officials in Sidéradougou reside relatively far from the provincial centre, but close to rural producers. Many of them have acquired fields themselves on which they mainly grow food crops. Some also raise cattle. Frequent transfers diminish their integration in the locality; on the other hand, as their explicit mandate is to work for 'development', they often get involved in local politics. Local government officials are modern nomads, though not dependent on rains and pasture but on decisions taken higher up in their ministerial hierarchies.

At the top of the Sidéradougou district is the *préfet* who belongs to the Ministry of Territorial Administration. Since the creation of the Subdivision of Sidéradougou in 1954, this administrative entity has, up to 2003, had 36 heads; the average time-span for each *préfet* is slightly more than 16 months. Any government official may be transferred to another post in the state adminis-tration; the higher up in hierarchy the more likely it is that he will be transferred.

The *préfet* is superior to all other government officials serving in the district and any outside mission is expected to render him a courtesy visit on arrival. Each *service* – that is the common label for decentralised offices of different line ministries – has its own chief, who administratively responds to the *préfet*. The *préfet* is in contact with all different *chefs de service*, who are expected to collabo-rate and be present on various occasions, e.g. inauguration of new constructions, public festivities, development projects, etc. If a *chef de service* is leaving the district for any reason, he needs an *Ordre de Mission* delivered by the *préfet*.

There is an informal hierarchy among the services within the district. The heads of the *gendarmerie* and the police are important *chefs de service*. The Director of the secondary school is another dignitary. There is also a medical centre, headed by a medic (*Infirmier de l'Etat*). A female agent works with social affairs. The Agriculture office has two staff and the Animal Husbandry office two Veterinary Officers. The Agriculture office has a number of extension workers residing in villages outside the centre. This informal hierarchy between different services also depends upon access to external funding; those that host develop-ment projects are envied.

Government officials working in different districts are supposed to work through actors at the lowest administrative level, that is, the villages. Today, there is a Village Administrative Representative in each village. He is still called *délégué* by most villagers,[3] and is heir to the former village chief, an institution formerly promoted by French colonial administration, with the important difference that since the beginning of the 1980s he is not financially compensated by the state administration. Although the roles and functions of today's village chief have undergone crucial transformations, in almost every village I have visited he belongs to the family of the Master of the Earth (or Earth-Priest), supposedly the oldest living agnatic male descendant of the first settler of the site (Hagberg 1998:86–94).

Few officials or functionaries (French *fonctionnaires*) residing in districts such as Sidéradougou originate from within the Comoé Province, especially those in a senior position (*chef de service*). They are regarded as 'strangers' (*dunaw*), and, indeed, many are Mossi, the largest ethnic group of Burkina Faso. A commonly

---

[3] The village head used to be called the Delegate of the Committee for the Defence of the Revolution 1983–87, the Delegate of the Revolutionary Committee 1987–91 and since 1991 the Village Administrative Representative (*Responsable Administratif du Village, RAV*). Although the *délégué* position is officially open to all, I have never heard of a woman *délégué* and rarely encountered *délégués* from latecomer groups.

held opinion is that the Mossi have 'long arms' (*bras longues*), signifying that they have easy access to the state administration, both as employees and as citizens.[4] In disputes related to crop damage and wounded animals etc., government officials of Mossi origin sometimes argue that the outbreaks of violence are particular to the region. On several occasions, I have heard civil servants state that 'it is not like that among us [i.e. the Mossi]'. Such statements suggest that 'people of Banfora' (*Banforakanw*) do not like 'strangers'. Yet despite the dominance of Mossi among government employees, local government officials do not first and foremost express a Mossi identity but an identity proper to their social standing. It is highly valued to become a government employee. For a rural household it is a socioeconomic asset to have a son in state administration.

'La culture des fonctionnaires'

The identity of government officials is linked to status, and they present themselves as 'intellectuals'. This notion does not apply to government officials alone, but to many others with secondary school graduation and university exams working within the private sector or unemployed (Hagberg 2002b). Politicians are a kind of 'intellectual' in the local setting, but many of them simultaneously uphold employment in state administration. The dominant discourse of 'intellectuals' is to a large extent shaped by strong bonds to the state, and represents the local version of the national development discourse. Therefore it is appropriate to explore the social identity of 'the culture of functionaries' (*la culture des fonctionnaires*). In using the case of the Sidéradougou district, I describe five main aspects of this social identity: Office; Language; Boundaries; Alliances; and Status of Wives.

Office

The office is the principal setting for interaction with local people. The case of the *préfet*'s office (*préfecture*) is certainly the most clear cut, but the description is partly valid for other services as well. The préfecture of Sidéradougou is a small complex constructed in the 1950s when the Subdivision (present-day district or *département*) was created. It is composed of two buildings. The office building hosts the *préfet*'s office and that of his secretary. It also includes the administrative archives, some of which have been destroyed by termites. A residential building is the home of the *préfet* and his family.

The office could be seen as a symbol of the state and modernity. It is located at some distance from the village, reflecting the colonial idea of the commander governing at a distance. During working hours the office is frequented by a wide range of people asking for specific services, such as help with birth certificates and other administrative documents, sessions of the District Court, cases of crop damage etc. But the residence of the *préfet* is also to a large extent used for public matters. It is not uncommon that cases of divorce and matrimonial compensation are discussed at length in the shadow of the neem trees in front of it. Family disputes may, in practice, be settled there, and the official administrative dossier

---

[4] It is often stated that the Mossi are over-represented among government employees. Whether this may be proved by statistics lies far beyond the scope of this study, but it should be underlined that Mossi are estimated to represent 50% of the country's total population.

is only established when the parties enter the office to sign, to pay, or to undertake whatever official action is agreed. The use of the residence for public matters could, of course, open up possibilities for bribing, but this is not necessarily the case. It would be more appropriate to understand the role of the residence in office matters as an intermediate space between the formal state institution (the Office) and local politics (the Village). It domesticates disputes, where the office makes them official.

Language

The prevalence of a culture of functionaries is reflected in language. All government officials speak French, which is the official language in Burkina Faso. Some speak Dyula, the *lingua franca* of the region, but many do not, at least not on their arrival in the region. Dyula may be accepted as the language employed by people coming to the Office, but all documents are written in French. Even a Dyula-speaking government official has to translate what has been said into French, which is a language that most local people neither speak nor read and write (Hagberg 2002b). Although discussions are often held in Dyula, notes are taken in French.

The problem of language emphasises the position of government officials as 'strangers'. The French language is used when government officials want to communicate on matters among themselves. In everyday conversation between officials in Sidéradougou, e.g. in bars, the Fulbe are often referred to as *les palestiniens* ('Palestinians'), because they are seen as 'people without land'. The Veterinary officer may be asked by other officials 'what about your Palestinians' while a group of Fulbe youth are sitting next to them. The use of the term 'Palestinians' represents a kind of secret, coded language used among government officials. But the 'secrecy' of this coded language is relative. Once a Fulbe informant with rudimentary understanding of French commented on this to me. 'They think that we do not understand what they say, but often I do.'

Boundaries

Being a government official is a matter of continuously maintaining and crossing boundaries. Frequent transfers from one district and/or province to another discourage durable contacts and integration into the social life of the district. Identity as a government employee, to some extent detached from the local setting, is thereby favoured. The idea that government officials should be integrated into village life is rhetorically strong, but reveals an ambiguity. It is repeatedly stressed that officials should work for the best interest of the population, and for 'development', and that this is only possible by interacting with the population. But if integration goes too far it is assumed that the individual official will be able to build up a personal power base, be open to bribery and develop other loyalties than those to the state administration. Thus government officials are transferred every few years. A *préfet* told me that after three years at a duty station it is impossible to maintain authority over the population. One tends to become too much involved in local social life.

Government officials maintain and cross boundaries in their social position in local settings. Boundaries are also maintained between central and local government officials. Centrally based functionaries tend to refer to their colleagues working in districts as 'bush functionaries' (*fonctionnaires de brousse*). They are simultaneously disregarded and envied. They are people who, according to centrally based colleagues, are incapable or unwilling to do their job, but who benefit from cheap agricultural produce.

Alliances

Continuous transfers from one duty station to another shape the social life of most government officials and of their families. It is therefore part of the deal – or better contract – with the government that they will leave one day. These processes of integration and detachment put local government officials in an ambiguous position. Although the 'culture of functionaries' is made up of boundaries, there is a need to establish alliances with key individuals, or brokers, in the local setting. These persons may be 'sons of the village', who have acquired an influential position in local politics. They speak French and may have been to school for some years, but they also have a certain local political legitimacy. These individuals may belong to the family of a traditional authority, e.g. Masters of the Earth or Village Chiefs. Other 'sons of the village' have gained influence through the Revolution of 1983 or more recently through the president's political party *Congrès pour la Démocratie et le Progrès* (CDP). Most often the legitimacy of these 'sons of the village' is multiple and grounded both in tradition (e.g. as firstcomers) and modernity (e.g. the ability to read and write). The 'sons of the village' are distinguished from traditional authorities in the village in that they are brokers between 'people' and 'the state'. They are well-informed men, who serve as guides when specific missions and visits are to be carried out. These individuals are not officially recognised by the state administration, but ensure continuity in situations where discontinuity is apparent. While *préfets* are transferred to another district after a year or two, and other heads of district offices normally do not stay more than three years, 'sons of the village' remain. For example, most government officials in Sidéradougou when I left in July 1996 had been transferred to other duty stations by early 1998.

Yet the influence acquired by the 'sons of the village' is permanently threatened by the arrival of a new *préfet* or other government officials. These newcomers may choose other advisers, and an individual 'son of the village' will lose influence. The position of these 'sons of the village' is particularly important in times of social crisis; conflicts are the moments during which their use of power becomes evident. Administratively, they have no formal position and cannot act in the name of the government, but as brokers they have significant influence over decisions taken by the state administration.

The 'sons of the village' confirm the 'culture of functionaries'. They have at least some basic knowledge of French and are well aware of how problems should be addressed within the state administration (e.g. *dégât*, *divagation*, *sensibilisation*). For instance, while in local settings people refer to Fulbe agro-pastoralists as *peul* or *fula*, in official national discourse ethnicity should not be stressed, and the accepted term is *éleveurs* (graziers).

Status of wives

The 'culture of functionaries' includes a gendered division of labour that differs from the one prevailing in the local setting. Most often, government officials are men, especially in high positions. In 1996, there was one woman working for the Ministry of Social Action and another for the Ministry of Animal Husbandry.

The secretary of the *préfecture* is a woman employed by the municipality. But the overwhelming majority are men: *préfets*, gendarmes, extension workers, teachers etc. The wives of these male government officials often represent the urban ideology of the housewife. They do not undertake many of the tasks rural women carry out. They do domestic tasks at home, but generally neither farm land nor raise animals.

In 1996 I witnessed the creation of two women's associations, *Association des femmes des gendarmes de Sidéradougou* and *Les Soeurs Unies*. The first concerned the wives of gendarmes (at that time seven at the duty station) and the second was an association for the wives of all government officials in Sidéradougou. Both associations organised festivities such as football and volleyball matches, the symbolic planting of trees and a dance evening (*soirée dansante*). The objectives of the two associations include the strengthening of all women in Sidéradougou, but their members in particular. These associations confirm the prevalence of a functionaries' culture. The wives do important social work, but often they do not refer to their tasks as work. If asked, these 'housewives' may say, '*je suis à la maison seulement, je ne fais rien*'.[5] Instead, men's work is rewarded by the state administration, and in urban settings men are supposed to provide the wives daily with *nasongo*, i.e. relish money for cooking.

To sum up this section, the 'culture of functionaries' is a label that covers a specific social identity forged in the interplay between the state administration, and local life. It is maintained by drawing and crossing boundaries. Both practically and symbolically this social identity is articulated in the key relationship between government officials and 'sons of the village'.

Coping with Damages and Dilemmas

Local government officials have to deal daily with dilemmas grounded in law and policy propositions, whose contradictions are articulated in the local setting. They should pursue procedures of dispute settlement as a means to cope with damage and decide on compensation for the aggrieved party. Laws and policies need to be modified in local contexts. In this process, the alliance between government officials and 'sons of the village' is particularly important.

In 1961, the newly independent state adopted a law to regulate straying of domestic animals.[6] Straying (*divagation*) of domestic animals was defined as illegal. I once asked a retired African administrator, who had served in the French colonial administration, about how they handled cases of crop damage and straying prior to the 1961 law.

> There was not any problem with straying. The herder was whipped if there was a case of straying. The herders were only children. But there was no law.

This indicates that before the 1961 law, straying was a problem of bad behaviour by the attendant (i.e. the herder). The owner of the animals was not held to have

---

[5] The fact that these women argue that they do not work does not necessarily say much about how they perceive their tasks. Domestic work is a female task and to carry it out is part of being a woman. Yet I would still argue that these wives, who state that they do not do anything, are reproducing a view on work that dominates in the 'culture of functionaries'.

[6] Law 40/61/AN, 25 July 1961.

any responsibility. The 1961 law established the responsibility of the owner. Although the herder could be accused of neglecting his duties in cases of crop damage, the owner of the cattle must pay.

There has been another major change in cases of straying since the 1960s. The 23 records of animals causing damage between 1962 and 1965 almost exclusively concerned animals belonging to people of local origin in the region (Tiefo, Dogossié, Dyula and Karaboro ethnic groups). Today, however, Fulbe agro-pastoralists are involved in almost all cases of straying in Sidéradougou district. Crop damage caused by animals of people of the same ethnic group (e.g. Karaboro cattle damaging crops of another Karaboro) rarely involve the state administration. Most cases of crop damage were solved, and are still solved, directly between the cattle-owner and the field-owner. Such settlement may include the payment in money or kind to compensate the field-owner. Social relations prevailing between the parties overcome potential disputes that never come to the *préfet*'s knowledge. The cattle-owner may ask the field-owner to forgive him, and farmers generally hold that they may forgive once or twice, but then they start to claim financial compensation.

Government officials – particularly the *préfets* – advise people to solve 'problems' themselves instead of bringing them to the state administration. At the same time, it is often recommended that the agricultural extension worker and the veterinary officer should assess even minor crop damage and/or wounded animals. If the damage is measured, the difference may still be settled out of court, but the case may possibly be reintroduced into court later if payment is delayed.

The administrative procedure starts when the farmer addresses the *préfet*, either directly or by passing through the Village Administrative Representative. The complaining party (in case of crop damage) is asked whether he (most field-owners and graziers involved in these cases are men) can identify the cattle-owner or not. Perhaps he knows, or says something like 'I have followed the tracks to the cattle enclosure of so and so...'. The farmer is asked to pay a small administrative fee required for initiating proceedings to establish the facts of damage (a *constat*). The *préfet* sends a requisition to the Agriculture Office asking its chief to send someone to the site to evaluate the damage. The Village Administrative Representative, the field-owner and the cattle-owner participate in the *constat* carried out by the agricultural extension worker. Gendarmes or police agents also participate to ensure the security. The veterinary surgeon takes part in the *constat* only if animals have been wounded or killed. It is not uncommon that farmers beat animals entering the field or shoot at them, wounding or, in worst cases, killing them. Such situations often lead to long and complicated processes, in which the farmer may eventually find himself the net loser.[7]

The complaining farmer, who brought the case to the *préfet*, bears all costs until the case is settled; the total costs for transport, crop damage, and straying taxes will ultimately be paid by the cattle-owner. Later, the parties are convened by the *préfet*. If the parties accept the outcome, the dispute is settled. The cattle-owner is generally given a one month period of grace to make payment, but delayed payment often leads to frustrations. The case becomes more complicated if the farmer has wounded animals. If fields are located close to a water-course,

---

[7] The agricultural extension worker estimates the damage by counting the stalks destroyed and those spared within a 10 m^2 surface to be extrapolated to the entire field. He then establishes the proceeding (PV) to be signed by the disputing parties.

where cattle are watered, crop damage is likely to occur frequently. Fulbe agro-pastoralists often accuse farmers of 'sabotage', by farming too close to cattle tracks and water-courses, hindering cattle from passing. Recurrent crop damage would, the argument goes, give them a legitimate reason to chase the Fulbe agro-pastoralists from the village.

It is important to understand the ways in which social problems are translated into administrative dossiers in the dispute settlement process. While the French legal language might give the impression of a timeless and impersonal state administration, people are well aware of the social and political stakes involved. Four frequent problems are often evoked in relation to the administrative procedure of compensation: 1) how to identify the cattle-owner; 2) how to evaluate damage; 3) how to enforce payment; and 4) accusations of corruption.

Firstly, farmers complain about the difficulty of identifying the cattle-owner, especially as crop damage generally occurs at night. They may follow the tracks of the cattle, but the cattle-owner may deny that his cattle have caused damage. It can then be hard to prove the origin of the cattle. Sometimes farmers accuse herders of letting the cattle cross the tracks of another herd in order to escape. Many agriculturalists say that they are cheated by the cattle-owner, inciting them to 'make justice' if they chance to encounter cattle causing damage.

Secondly, many debates concern the measuring of crop and/or cattle damage. Farmers often complain that compensation for crop damage does not correspond to the actual work invested. Compensation is based on current prices on the local market. A government official strongly supportive of the farmers' cause told me that many officials do not consider *la sueur du paysan* – that is, the sufferings of the peasant – but only the results of the work. This, he argued, was not fair, because farmers suffer a lot in farming but are only compensated at local market price levels, i.e. the bare costs of substituting the damage caused by the cattle, and not their trauma or stress. The logic of this reasoning alludes to the frustra-tions of many farmers. An agricultural officer in Sidéradougou once admitted that the methods for estimating crop damage are not very reliable. It is easier to measure damage to crops later when the field has been harvested (e.g. stacked on the fringe on the field) than to measure it in a growing field. But according to him, it is socially impossible to wait until the harvest is finished because the malice between the parties would increase. Some farmers object to the way animal damage is estimated; if a cow is killed, not only is the meat valued, but also any expected offspring (calves).

The disputing parties present claims and counterclaims first on the spot and then at the *préfecture* in case no agreement is reached in the village. The specific circumstances within which crop and/or animal damage took place are elaborated in the negotiation at the *préfet*'s office in Sidéradougou. In a specific case that I followed in 1996, cattle had caused crop damage, and a group of agriculturalists captured the animals and brought them to an enclosure to oblige the cattle-owner to be recognised. The cattle remained in the enclosure for three days, even though the cattle-owner had been identified. However, one animal was wounded and later slaughtered by the veterinary officer. The agriculturalists contested being responsible for this. However, the District Court judged that the farmer had to pay 80,000 FCFA[8] to the cattle-owner for the loss of the animal

[8] 520 Euro.

and the cattle-owner 43,500 FCFA[9] to the farmer for the crop damage. The farmer who was the net losing party contested this and said that he was not responsible for wounding the animal: 'Even if we use the jo ('fetish') to find out who is responsible, I will argue.' He threatened the court, but was warned by one of its assessors (an influential 'son of the village'), to pay within one month. I do not know whether the farmer ever paid the cattle-owner or not, but it did not seem likely that he would.

Thirdly, there is a problem of delayed payments, frequent among both field-owners and cattle-owners. The decision taken by the *préfet* is not respected, and sometimes people do not even show up to settle the dispute. Delayed payments contribute to increased tensions between the parties and consequently between their communities. The *préfet* does not possess the legal competence to enforce the court's judgement. If it becomes a judicial matter (e.g. a criminal case) the dispute has to be transferred to the Regional Tribune in Bobo-Dioulasso. But to bring a case of crop/animal damage to Bobo-Dioulasso means that the individual must posses enough money for his stay there. Even in cases of non-payment by the cattle-owner and/or the field-owner, the complaining party tends to drop the case at district level.

Fourthly, farmers often accuse local government officials of corruption. Farmers conceive of Fulbe as being rich and able to sell off some cattle to get money to bribe government officials. Fulbe, in return, consider that nobody is working for their cause or understanding their problems. A Fulbe agro-pastoralist expressed himself thus, 'all the government is supporting the farmers, and only God is supporting the Fulbe'. The issue of corruption and accusations of corruption is extremely difficult to deal with. Bribery is not an activity spoken of by most people involved, but often assumed. To define what is bribe and what not is also a tricky issue. When does a gift move from being a gesture of respect and kindness towards being an act of corruption? Accusations of corruption reflect doubts about the administrative procedures involved, but do not constitute proof of the practice of corruption.

The four problems discussed here could be understood as mere technicalities to be solved, but all the procedures of dispute settlement prevail in a context of tensions and threatening violence. References are often made to the outbreaks of violence that are commonly called the 'Sidéradougou conflict'. There is a sense of living on the edge, and of war lurking within peace.

Lost Local Legitimacy.

Violent clashes occurred between Karaboro agriculturalists and Fulbe agro-pastoralists in the Sidéradougou district in December 1986. In February 1995 violence broke out again between these groups, but this time in the Mangodara district further south. And in 2001 another violent conflict broke out in the village of Kankounadéni, some 25 km southeast of Banfora. At each event between 5 and 10 people were killed. With few exceptions (one person in each instance) the dead and wounded people have been Fulbe. Threats of violence have occurred on several occasions in between these outbreaks of violence. Here

---

[9] 280 Euro.

I describe some of these incidents to illustrate the role and involvement of local government officials.[10]

The violent conflict in December 1986 was started by a quarrel related to 'crop damage' between a young Karaboro farmer (the son of the field-owner) and a young Fulbe herder in a small village outside Sidéradougou. The argument between the two men concerned whether the cattle had caused damage or not. In the heat of discussion the Fulbe herder was shot dead by the Karaboro farmer. The young Karaboro left the site, but later he and his father went to the *gendarmerie* in Sidéradougou. Gendarmes and security guards immediately went to the site, and the field-owner and his son were put under arrest. The following day, the Agricultural Extension Worker was to carry out the *constat* in the presence of the field-owner. But when they arrived at the field, a group of Fulbe had gathered to bury the young herder. After a heated discussion, a cry was heard. All Fulbe ran towards the field-owner, who tried to escape in the bush. The gendarmes and security guards were unable to protect him. The Karaboro field-owner was soon caught and killed by the Fulbe crowd. These and subsequent events led to outbreaks of violence in the entire area. Karaboro 'rebels' went out and killed any Fulbe encountered. The peak of the violence occurred on a Friday market-day. Army units came from Banfora and Bobo-Dioulasso, and they soon took the Sidéradougou district in their hands. Curfew was installed and two markets (normally taking place every five days) were suspended. The intervention of military and paramilitary units seems to have been an efficient means to gain control of a situation threatening war. A 'refugee camp' was urgently established at the gendarmerie in Sidéradougou, where Fulbe could hide. Others took refuge wherever they could find protection. Two Fulbe informants were in Sidéradougou to participate in a meeting the very day the 'war' broke out, but they were able to hide with a Dyula family. It was not until a couple of days later that they could return to their village. There were many problems and tensions in the area for a long time. A 'son of the village' told me that there were cases of vengeance everywhere.

This brief description of the outbreaks of violence in December 1986 highlights the involvement of the state administration. This was of various significance according to different actors. Local government officials did not, to say the least, play the ideal, depersonalised and politically neutral role, but many seem to have been deeply and personally involved in critical stages of the violent conflict. The gendarmes and the agricultural extension worker brought the Karaboro field-owner to the site to allow him to participate in the *constat*. It is not established whether it was the Karaboro field-owner himself who demanded participation; the gendarmes could in any case legitimately have refused such a request.

The intervention of military and paramilitary units from Banfora and Bobo-Dioulasso appears to have been important, because the violence stopped more or less rapidly. This is at least the official version. It is the winner's version of a series of apparently contradictory events. Accordingly, the 'solution' to the conflict was something 'brought in' by actors external to the Sidéradougou district. To limit the burning crisis prevailing in the Sidéradougou district, 'people from Banfora and Bobo-Dioulasso' came and reinstalled order. Those 'people from

---

[10] For elaborated case studies of these violent conflicts (see Hagberg 1998, 2000, 2001a, forthcoming; Ouédraogo 1997).

Banfora' were regarded as somewhat external to the conflict, but the external intervention of 'armed forces' is described in a way that overshadows actions undertaken by local actors. For instance, one Karaboro elder played a critical role in convincing the Karaboro 'rebels' to lay down weapons. An old blacksmith opened his house for Fulbe 'refugees' during the crucial days of violence. Other local actors were instrumental in stopping bloodshed. But the official version holds that 'people from Banfora and Bobo-Dioulasso' ended the conflict. These actors represented state administration, and preserved its legitimacy during the 'Sidéradougou conflict' in 1986. Instead, it was the legitimacy of *local* government officials that was lost.

Today, past outbreaks of violence and threats of more violence continue to influence decisions taken by local government officials in the Sidéradougou district. The individual government official can act neither only in accordance with his own vision or interest nor strictly according to policies, but needs to take the maintenance of social peace into account. A gendarme said: 'We are sitting on a powder-magazine.' Moreover, the 'Sidéradougou conflict' in 1986 and the 'Mangodara conflict' in 1995 have important connections with each other; some of the main actors, notably among Karaboro farmers, participated actively in both conflicts. In 1995 the violence in Mangodara was also about to spread to Sidéradougou, but important local actors (government officials and 'sons of the village' alike) succeeded in avoiding violence there.

It is in the light of violent conflicts that an attempt to recreate a District Court is revealing. It was reinstalled in the Sidéradougou district between 1995 and 1997 to cope better with crop damage and wounded animals. Such a court had existed in one or another form since colonial times, when it was called *Tribunal indigène*. In the 1980s the District Court (during this period called *Tribunal Populaire Départemental*) was composed of elected members and presided over by a figure connected to the Revolution's local popular structures. In 1995 the court was once again headed by the *préfet*, backed up by four assessors, who were important personalities in the district. The District Court in Sidéradougou started to function in October 1995, but in 1997, with the departure of the *préfet* who reinstalled it, it ceased functioning. Since then *préfets* have 'judged' cases themselves without any court or committee.

The use of the District Court between 1995 and 1997 illustrates how government officials seek to employ a legal language to solve disputes, while in reality the court had no judicial status or power whatsoever. If a dispute turns into a criminal case, the dossier must be transferred to the Regional Tribune in Bobo-Dioulasso. The same goes for any of the *préfet*'s decisions. Although the District Court functioned within a legal vacuum, the *préfet* considered that the court helped him in dispute settlement. But the court stood powerless when the parties refused to accept the judgement. The District Court was a local solution to immediate problems. There was no time to wait for the law to be adopted, because social peace must be promoted. Despite the legal language, local government officials have neither the power nor the legal competence to settle violent conflicts. While the court was mandated to settle disputes by means of negotiation rather than adjudication, its 'judgements' were expressed in a language of adjudication. And the exercise of state functions and that of legal control were vested in the same government official: the *préfet*.

Discussion

Outbreaks of violence and the attempt to reinstall the District Court bring the ambiguous social identity of local government officials to the fore. They are faced with dilemmas of handling the interplay between the State and the local community. The point is that local government officials are forced to deal with these dilemmas and many also exploit them in their own interest. One such is the lack of resources to assign a legally competent and independent official of the Ministry of Justice to every district of the country. Even the provincial court (*Cour d'Appel*) in Banfora did not function in 1996. A second dilemma is the mixing up of legal and administrative functions. This is difficult even in an ideal type of situation, where government officials are committed to their job and bribing is minimal. But it is particularly problematic in dispute settlement between Fulbe agro-pastoralists and groups of farmers. In outbreaks of violence government officials are often part of the conflict. In the 'Sidéradougou conflict' in 1986 (and in the 'Mangodara conflict' in 1995 as well), local government officials were accused of having acted in a way that led to bloodshed.

The dilemmas to be dealt with by government officials may be exploited in their own favour, ignored or settled more or less arbitrarily. Whatever types of actions they choose, dealing with conflicts is at the core of the practice of local government officials. It is important to make 'justice', on the one hand, and to maintain 'social peace' in the local community, on the other. It is a balancing of frustrations, demands and struggles. If a person pushes a case too far, he is likely to lose support even from his allies. People would say that he is exaggerating. A government official who only uses his power and resources to serve his own interests will, in the long run, be supported neither locally by his allied 'sons of the village' nor centrally by his 'protectors' at the central ministry in Ouagadougou.

This dealing with dilemmas clearly demonstrates that law is not only an instrument for enforcing rules, but also interacts with other normative orders, e.g. notions of social peace and forgiveness. The alliance between local government officials and 'sons of the village' articulates different normative orders and fuses them together. On the one hand, government officials recognise a certain influence on the part of the 'sons of the village' in defining and intervening in particular disputes. But, on the other hand, the 'sons of the village' modify local politics to fit into the national legal discourse, thereby confirming the legitimacy of state administration. Together, local government officials and 'sons of the village' create and recreate the specific system of meaning that I here label the 'culture of functionaries'. They are acting within a social space between the State and the local community, where the agency of the individual government official is crucial. While a committed official may be successful in making justice and building peace, another may worsen or even fuel conflict. The alliance that they establish and maintain with individuals belonging to the category of social brokers here called 'sons of the village' is of utmost importance. Continuity is ensured through the alliance between government officials and 'sons of the village', whose legitimacy tends to be based on traditional chieftaincy, political activism and personal dynamism. In their role as brokers, these 'sons of the village' confirm the 'culture of functionaries'.

To conclude, local government officials constitute a specific social category in dispute settlement between farmers and pastoralists. I have particularly described situations in which administrative procedures for implementing policy and coping with damage work more or less smoothly. The seemingly innocent administrative procedure of carrying out a *constat* has in some contexts led to violence and killings. Conversely, in the heat of violence, peace making is at work. But local actors who intervene to 'cool' conflicts are not recognised when 'people from the outside' come to end the conflict. And the memories of the Sidéradougou and Mangodara conflicts continue to influence decision making in the region. While local government officials work in contexts in which violence threatens to break out between farmers and pastoralists, central bureaucrats tend to regard them as *fonctionnaires de brousse*. In outbreaks of violence local government officials are represented as incapable, lazy and corrupt. Although outbreaks of violence tend to draw much attention to the dynamics of a specific locality, it is in the everyday dealing with dilemmas that we must ground our understanding of the dispute settlement practices of local government officials in Burkina Faso. Studies of larger, more damaging war in other parts of West Africa are beginning to reveal the part played by the breakdown of local administration and the corruption of local dispute-resolution procedures (Archibald and Richards 2002). The fact that Burkina Faso has not yet succumbed to widespread civil war owes something to the fact that the administration still functions, and that local officials and village brokers continue to elaborate their roles creatively.

References

Arce, A. and Long, N. 2000, 'Reconfiguring Modernity and Development from an Anthropological Perspective', in Arce, A. and Long. N., eds, *Anthropology, Development and Modernities: Exploring discourses, counter-tendencies and violence* London & New York: Routledge

Archibald, S. and Richards, P. 2002, 'Conversion to Human Rights? Popular debate about war and justice in rural central Sierra Leone' *Africa* 72(3): 339–67

von Benda-Beckmann, F. 1993, 'Scapegoat and Magic Charm: Law in Development Theory and Practice', in Hobart, M. ed., *An Anthropological Critique of Development: The Growth of Ignorance* London and New York: Routledge

Blanc, F.-P., Lourde, A., Saint-Girons, B. and Sandaogo, M., eds, 1991, *Administration et Société au Burkina Faso* Perpignan and Toulouse: Publication des Cahiers de l'Université de Perpignan and Presses de l'Institut d'études politiques de Toulouse

Blundo, G. 1995, 'Les courtiers du développement en milieu rural sénégalais' *Cahiers d'Etudes africaines* 35: 73–99

Chambers, R. 1979, 'Administrators: A Neglected Factor in Pastoral Development in East Africa'. *Journal of Overseas Administration* 18: 84–94

Dahl, G. and Hjort, A. 1984, 'Development as Message and Meaning' *Ethnos* 49: 165–85

Dahl, G. and Rabo, A. eds, 1992, *Kam-Ap or Take-Off: Local Notions of Development* 29. Stockholm: Department of Social Anthropology, Stockholm Studies in Social Anthropology

Degnbol, T. 2001, 'Inside Government Extension Agencies: A Comparison of Four Agencies in the Sikasso Region of Mali', in Benjaminsen, T.A. and Lund, C., eds, *Politics, Property and Production in the West African Sahel* Uppsala: Nordiska Afrikainstitutet

Dubuch, C. 1985, 'Langage du pouvoir, pouvoir du langage' *Politique africaine* 20: 44–53

Escobar, A. 1991, 'Anthropology and the Development Encounter: The Making and Marketing of Development Anthropology' *American Ethnologist* 18: 658–82

Grillo, R.D. 1997, 'Discourses of Development: The View from Anthropology', in Grillo, R.D. and Stirrat, R.L. eds, *Discourses of Development: Anthropological Perspectives* Oxford and New York: Berg

Grillo, R.D. and Stirrat R.L. eds 1997, *Discourses of Development: Anthropological Perspectives* Oxford and New York: Berg

Hagberg, S. 1998, 'Between Peace and Justice: Dispute Settlement between Karaboro agriculturalists and Fulbe agro-pastoralists in Burkina Faso' *Uppsala Studies in Cultural Anthropology* 25. Uppsala: Acta Universitatis Upsaliensis

—— 2000a, 'Droits à la terre, pratiques d'aménagement: le cas de la forêt de Tiogo au Burkina Faso', *Environnement et Société* 24, 63–71

—— 2000b, 'Strangers, Citizens, Friends: Fulbe Agro-pastoralists in Western Burkina Faso', in Hagberg, S. and Tengen, A.B. eds, *Bonds and Boundaries in Northern Ghana and Southern Burkina Faso* Uppsala Studies in Cultural Anthropology 30. Uppsala: Acta Universitatis Upsaliensis

—— 2001a, 'A l'ombre du conflit violent: processus de règlement et de gestion des conflits entre agriculteurs karaboro et agro-pasteurs peul au Burkina Faso' *Cahiers d'Etudes africaines* 161 (XLI-1): 45–72

—— 2001b, 'Poverty in Burkina Faso: Representations and Realities' ULRiCA 1. Uppsala: Department of Cultural Anthropology and Ethnology, Uppsala University

—— 2002a. '"Enough is enough": An Ethnography of the Struggle against Impunity in Burkina Faso' *Journal of Modern African Studies* 40 (2), June: 217–46

—— 2002b, 'Learning to Live or to Leave? Education and Identity in Burkina Faso' *African Sociological Review* 6 (2): 28–46

—— forthcoming, '"Each bird is sitting in its own tree": Authority and Violence of a Hunters' Association in Burkina Faso (typescript)

Hedlund, H. 1984, 'Development in Action: The Experience of the Zambian Extension Worker' *Ethnos* 49: 226–49

Hobart, M. ed. 1993a, *An Anthropological Critique of Development: The Growth of Ignorance* London and New York: Routledge

Hobart, M. 1993b, 'Introduction: The Growth of Ignorance?', in Hobart, M., ed., *An Anthropological Critique of Development: The Growth of Ignorance* London and New York: Routledge

Labazée, P. 1989. 'Discours et contrôle politique: Les avatars du sankarisme' *Politique africaine* 30: 11–26

Olivier de Sardan, J.-P. 1995, *Anthropologie et développement: Essai en socio-anthropologie du changement social*. Paris: Editions Karthala

Otayek, R., Sawadogo, F.M. and Guingané, J.-P., eds, 1996a, 'Introduction: Du Burkina, du changement social et de la démocratie', in Otayek, R., Sawadogo, F.M. and Guingané., J-P. *Le Burkina entre révolution et démocratie (1983-1993): Ordre politique et changement social en Afrique subsaharienne* Paris: Editions Karthala

Otayek, R., Sawadogo, F.M. and Guingané J.-P., eds, 1996b, *Le Burkina entre révolution et démocratie (1983-1993): Ordre politique et changement social en Afrique subsaharienne* Paris: Editions Karthala

Ouédraogo, J.-B. 1997, *Violences et communautés en Afrique Noire: La région Comoé entre règles de concurrence et logiques de destruction (Burkina Faso)* Paris and Montreal: L'Harmattan

Ouédraogo, J. 1999, 'Burkina Faso: Autour de l'affaire Zongo' *Politique africaine* 74: 163–83

Poluha, E. 1989, *Central Planning and Local Reality: The Case of a Producers Cooperative in Ethiopia* Stockholm Studies in Social Anthropology 23. Stockholm: Department of Social Anthropology.

Rabo, A. 1992, 'Introduction', in Dahl, G. and Rabo, A. eds, *Kam-Ap or Take-Off: Local Notions of Development* Stockholm Studies in Social Anthropology 29. Stockholm: Department of Social Anthropology

Robertson, A.F. 1984, *People and the State: An Anthropology of Planned Development* Cambridge: Cambridge University Press

4

Sarajevan Soldier Story
Perceptions of War & Morality in Bosnia

IVANA MAČEK

The Ideal War and the Ideal Soldier

Born and raised in the former Yugoslavia (Zagreb, Croatia), I had initial images of soldiers and combatants formed mainly through fiction and history classes during childhood. I saw many a film and television series about brave and righteous Communists and Partisans and evil and stupid German soldiers. From the beginning of my education, history lessons were teaching me the same, as well as some of the books in our literature curriculum. I also saw foreign – mostly North American and British – films about anglophone war-heroes[1] and German, Italian or Japanese villains. In my child's imagination, when alone or with my playmates, I created various scenarios in which I/we would play the hero role, the proverbial 'good guy' – young, healthy, strong, honourable, gifted, loved by everyone, and willing to offer his[2] life for the right cause and justice, but, of course, always surviving. Apart from 'playing war', we also played 'Star Trek' and 'Cowboys and Indians', so Doctor Spock, Winetou, Old Shatterhand, a Communist resistance activist under German occupation (*ilegalac*) or a small boy who was a Partisan message-bearer (*kurir*) in the Second World War were all interchangeable hero characters. I believe that this sort of early moral imagination, in which I am certain that the reader can recognise at least a part of her/his own childhood, is largely underestimated when it comes to its influence on our grown-up images of soldiers and judgements of what is right or wrong. The principles forwarded in such games were similar to the guiding principles in the writing of one of greatest fathers of modern war theory, Carl von Clausewitz:

---

[1] I use the term 'war', not in an analytical way, which I believe is non-productive, but rather as a term which is most widely used locally and internationally to demarcate the events I am referring to. I am fully aware that the labelling of these events is a highly politicised act, which positions even the most earnest researcher's attempt at being as impartial as possible within one of the political fractions of the very conflict she or he wishes to analyse. These are the pitfalls of this kind of work and I believe that the best we can do is to be as clear as possible about our own positions in the field, and consequently also our choices of terminology.

[2] The heroes were always male, so at the time it did not make any sense to try to put a female into such a role.

57

If we take a general view of the four elements composing the atmosphere in which war moves, of *danger, physical effort, uncertainty*, and *chance*, it is easy to conceive that a great force of mind and understanding is requisite to be able to make way with safety and success ... a force which ... we find termed by military writers and annalists as *energy, firmness, staunchness, strength of mind and character*. (Clausewitz 1997:46)

What Clausewitz described, thus, was an ideal soldier character, and not the soldiers he had met during his military carrier. Aware of the realities of wars he had experienced as a Prussian officer (see Keegan 1994), he designed the desirable qualities of a soldier which would conquer the unpredictability and chaotic nature of war, and thus make war an ordered sociopolitical event under control of the participants. This great military theoretician admittedly described a fictive state of affairs. Nevertheless, we can find the ideas about the ideal war and the ideal soldier, such as portrayed by Clausewitz, as well as in the fiction of my childhood, existing in our grown-up perceptions of reality, and consequently also influencing our actions and moral judgements in the wars we face today. To illustrate this, I shall draw on examples and my own observations from the war in Bosnia and Hercegovina, as this is the recent 'case' with which I am most familiar.[3]

Both local and international commentators on the war in Bosnia and Hercegovina demonstrated some shared presumptions about wars and soldiers. In the opening pages of his *Slaughterhouse: Bosnia and the failure of the West*, David Rieff, a journalist living in New York, wrote:

In reality, war, for all its bestiality, has its dignity and its laws, and soldiers, at least when they are faithful to their codes, rightly claim theirs to be an honorable as well as a terrible calling. (1996:17)

Rieff, thus, sees war as an ordered and controlled event, the bloodshed terrible but acceptable, and soldiers as honourable although they conduct terrible deeds. Alija Isaković, a Sarajevan writer, commented in a similar manner on the early shelling of Sarajevo:

I do not know whether this is war. War is not an encompassing word. War has some rules of war. This is something unseen, unseen and [until now] not experienced forms of evildoing and dirtiness of these evildoings. These savages are bereft of any kind of style. (Isaković 1994:13, my translation)

In Isakovic''s comment one more important dimension of this way of perceiving war comes to light, namely, the ideas of 'the other', 'the enemy', the 'bad guys' of my childhood, necessarily pictured as 'the inhuman', 'savage', the immoral ones (see also Levi 1999:22ff). However, the 'enemy' emerges not only as a moral opposite to a 'we'-group, 'our/good guys', the morally righteous ones, but additionally, both of these groups are of a homogenous character. Elaine Scarry, in her bench-mark analysis of torture and war language, points to this phenomenon:

[I]n the opening moments of war [there are] no longer the diffuse five hundred million persons, projects, and concerns that existed immediately prior to war's opening, because those five hundred million separate identities have suddenly crystallised into *two* discrete identities. ... The distinction between 'friend' and 'enemy' – identified by Carl Schmitt as the fundamental distinction in politics equivalent to good and evil in

---

[3] I conducted my fieldwork in Sarajevo for a duration of six months intermittently between 1994 and 1996, which resulted in my PhD thesis (Maček 2000, also Maček forthcoming).

moral philosophy and beautiful and ugly in aesthetics[4] – is in war converted to an absolute polarity ... registered in some version of us-them idiom. (Scarry 1985:88)

A modern nation-state, writes Hobsbawm (1990:83), needs to convince its citizens that their individual sacrifice is worth the 'nation' or any other centre of loyalty that the state bases its legitimacy and sovereignty upon. In the following passage from a book for secondary schools, issued by the Muslim-dominated government in Sarajevo during the war, we can see how the above identified elements in structuring an explanation of war – an ordered and controllable image of war – were components in the government's interpretation:

> Bosnia and Hercegovina ... had never experienced what Serbo-Montenegrin aggressors and domestic Chetniks did to them in the war that they started in the spring of 1992. ...The attack was prepared over a long period organised by the former Yugoslav People's Army and carried out with the help of the former *JNA*. The extreme part of the Bosnian Serbs was also included. Their intent was to attach Bosnia and Hercegovina to Serbia, in order to accomplish the ancient dream of the Serbian nationalists to make a so-called Greater Serbia.
>
> The reason for the attack was easy to find. They made use of the political circumstances which followed the disintegration of Yugoslavia, when Bosnian and Hercegovian people decided to become independent and to live in a state of their own...
>
> The attack started on the 6th of April 1992. The former Yugoslav People's Army and domestic Chetniks armed to the teeth started to attack the unprotected settlements and the unarmed people with the most lethal weapons. ...Although the people were unarmed, they showed a fierce resistance. With hunting guns and hand-made weapons Bosnian and Hercegovinian fighters confronted the tanks, cannons, and aeroplanes of the aggressor. ...During the early days of the aggression the people showed resistance by organising into Territorial Defence and other defence formations, and then the Army of Bosnia and Hercegovina was formed. In a short time it became an organised power which took a stand before its people in order to protect them from the crimes of Serbo-Montenegrin aggressors and domestic Chetniks.
>
> ...The intention of the aggressor was to clear the Bosnian and Hercegovinian territories of the non Serbian people, in the first place of Bosniaks, in order to create an ethnically cleansed Serbian territory. ...The unseen crimes followed. Women, children and old people were slaughtered, there were rapes, plundering and burning. Villages, schools, factories, mosques, old monuments, all that was Bosniak and Muslim, were disappearing in flames. (Imamović and Bošnjak 1994:17–18, my translation)

The 'people', identified as unarmed and unprotected (i.e. 'victims'), righteously showed resistance, heroically raising their almost bare hands against the military machinery of the enemy, in order to defend their lives. Eventually, grown out of the people, righteous, proud, and heroic, the Army of Bosnia and Hercegovina (ABiH) raised itself, carrying all the characteristics of 'our/good guys'. The enemy group was identified as nationalistic Bosnian, Serbian and Montenegrin Serbs (i.e. Chetniks), who not only planned and initiated the war, but who were also the inhuman cowards committing crimes against the weakest segments of society: children, women, and old people. It is interesting to note that the exact same image of the Partisan uprising against the Italian and German forces during the Second World War was used during the 50 years or so of the former Yugoslavia. So the image not only had all the desirable moral quality but was also something people were used to from their earlier (ideological) experiences of talking about war and perceiving it. The Muslim (i.e. Bosniak) nation was promoted as a

[4] Carl Schmitt, *The Concept of the Political* (1928:26ff)

homogenous entity, since the attack on the innocent and unprotected people was equated with the attack on Muslim culture, and with the attack on the state of Bosnia and Hercegovina.

In my conversations and informal interviews with Sarajevans during my field-work, I found that this image of war was indeed used to explain and justify their own choices and actions during the war. A woman in her forties, of a secular-ised Muslim family background, used the images promoted by the government's text book – unarmed people, inhuman crimes, extremist Serbian perpetrators, people's heroic and righteous revolt, resistance against evil, defence without weapons, identification of an individual with the Muslim nation – when she explained why she forced her husband to join the ABiH at the beginning of the war in Sarajevo:

> Serbs made a mistake when they went into Bjeljina, and made a bloody fight, because it was Arkan's troops (*Arkanovci*)[5] who found the unprepared, unarmed folk. And they made bloody slaughter. And in the people a tremendous obstinacy, defiance and the wish to survive were awakened, and they realised on the basis of this event that we were something different. There, I never knew that I was a Muslim, but now I know that I am something different [from the Serbs] because somebody is slaughtering me. Somebody slaughters me and I am something different. And then the people somehow arrayed themselves without weapons, without anything they defended themselves. (My translation)

Of course, Arkan's troops committed bloodshed against unarmed people in Bjeljina, and many people world-wide were revolted by this event. These are the facts about war that most of us would agree upon. But why did the woman assume that the people who were killed in Bjeljina were killed because they were 'Muslims'? And why did she assume that the same destiny was also awaiting her if she 'never knew that [she] was a Muslim'? The answer is very simple, and characteristic of the role of ideology in war. Because the woman felt that her life was threatened – 'somebody was killing her' – she identified herself as belonging to the same group as the innocent people in Bjeljina. The rest of us, who watched the war in Bosnia from our TV-sofas, could empathise with people in Bjeljina, and even be enraged, but since we did not perceive our lives to be threatened at that time, we did not identify ourselves as the same-sort-of-people as those in Bjeljina. That the threatened group was identified as 'Muslim' was something, as we have seen in the above example from the school book, that was promoted by the power-holders. The war was talked about, structured and understood, as a conflict between Bosnian nationalities. The ultimate moral justification of taking to arms was finally achieved as a consequence of this sort of reasoning – if somebody was killing unprotected people, it was morally only right that these people should defend themselves.

Characteristic of the above type of interpretation of war is a clear definition of the causes of the war and the aims of the enemy. In the school book quoted above the aim of the war was presented as the extermination of non-Serbian people in the first place Muslims, from Bosnia and Hercegovina in order to achieve Greater Serbia. The picture of war is even easier to grasp if the dates of

---

[5] The paramilitary troops from Serbia, known for their extreme brutality and Serbian nationalism. The leader himself, Željko Ražnjatović (alias Arkan), was wanted by international police for his criminal activities even before the war. He was killed in Belgrade in early 2000, in what seemed to be a gang attack.

its beginning and end are exactly identified. The perception of war as a clearly limited period of time makes it also more easy to accept the atrocities, and the people that commit the atrocities (i.e. the soldiers), because it is understood that the atrocities will end at the end of the war, and the soldiers will go back to being normal citizens respecting the lives and integrity of other fellow humans. In the case of Bosnia and Hercegovina the beginning of the war was identified by the Muslim dominated government as well as by international analysts as the spring of 1992, and more exactly as the 6 April 1992.[6] On this day, Suada Dilberović, a nineteen-year-old student, was killed in firing from the Holiday Inn hotel directed at people demonstrating on Vrbanja Bridge. The killers were identified as Serbian snipers and only a week after her death, Suada Dilberović was referred to as 'the first heroine of Sarajevo's defence' (*Preporod*, 15 April 1992). In the place where she was killed, renamed Suada Dilberović's Bridge sometime towards the end of the war, there is now a commemorative plaque. Fairly soon, in the spring of 1996, when there were practically no more new victims of the war in Sarajevo, it became clear that the death of this girl was going to symbolise all deaths and losses that happened during the war – especially among the civilians of Sarajevo killed by random shelling or sniper fire. That the 'first victim of the war' was a young woman, a student and bearing a Muslim name, was hardly coincidental. A man would have been a potential soldier, and an old person would not have had her entire future life destroyed. A student symbolises intelligence and civilisation and the future of the nation. Muslims were considered to be *the* victims in this war, especially in the official Sarajevan government interpretation, although the same interpretation generally accepted that other groups in the conflict also had their share of suffering and losses. Hedetoft defined a 'hero' as a 'cluster of national meanings' (1993:281–300, cited in Jabri 1996:140) and this definition applies well in this case, as the heroisation of Suada Dilberović's death was part of the constitution of a Muslim national identity which took place during the war.

The character of the war was defined also through other important dates, such as 2 May 1992 and 7 July 1992. On the former day, Sarajevo was heavily shelled for the first time, particularly the centre. In 1996, the scenes from the town on that day were played and replayed on television, and people often reflected on the day's events. It became a symbol of Serbian barbarism, mercilessly imprinted on the body of the destroyed town and a constant reminder of the nature of the enemy and the character of the war. On the latter date, the first bread-queue massacre happened on the pedestrian street Vase Miskina (now Ferhadija). A chronicler wrote in *Sarajevan War Drama* :

[6] The critique that can be aimed at the analysts of war is that through taking part in pinpointing the date and the event with which the war started, they are reifying the picture of war as ordered sociopolitical activity, in this way ignoring the experience of war, which is rather opaque. In the first place, the beginning of the war is a process of accelerating disruptive events which in the end makes the idea of peace-time normality unsustainable. Thus, it was no surprise that when I asked people in Sarajevo to tell me about their experiences from the beginning of the war, the phrase they would use was 'in the beginning' rather than 'at the beginning'. For the people in Sarajevo, the war started invariably on the day that they experienced their first heavy shelling of their part of the town, and they were very much aware that this day was different for different people. This awareness was only a part of their general awareness of the complexity of war as experience, and the impossibility of a homogenous and clear story of the war. For more see Maček (2000:242ff).

7th of July. Shock! Stress! Spit fastened in the throat! Stupor. TV cameras informed the civilised world about the massacre in Vaso Miskin Street. Serbian medieval Forest-people aimed at and hit the people waiting in the queue for their daily bread. Body parts thrown around, blood, dead, wounded, tears, cries. God, is there a proper punishment for these crimes? Shelling innocent people.

Are Serbian and Montenegrin strings going to sing about this? Is this their courage and humanity? Yes. This is Serbian courage. This is Montenegrin humanity/manhood. Great-Serbian ideology is based on defeat, on glorifying the Kosovo-defeat. ...To base one's life's credo on defeat and the past means to take rights over the other, to take their lives whenever, to massacre a citizen who simply wants to live. To survive. To provide bread.

To celebrate defeat as victory means to celebrate death instead of life. 'Serbian people show by their conduct that they do not belong to civilisation' proclaimed American statesman John [sic] Baker. (Miličević 1993:15–16, my translation)

That the symbolism of these events was meaningful not only to the local Sarajevan population but also for the broader international public was obvious after the pictures of the two Markale marketplace massacres were broadcast worldwide. The first one, on 5 February 1994, led to an international intervention which forced the Bosnian Serb Army to withdraw heavy artillery 20 kilometres from the centre of the town, and marked the start of the first long cease-fire. The second one, on 28 August 1995, triggered the long awaited NATO bombing of Bosnian Serb artillery positions on the mountains surrounding the town, and eventually led to the signing of the Dayton Peace Agreement in November of the same year.

The definition of the character of war and of the sides in it – brutal aggression by immoral and uncivilised Serbian nationalists and a righteous defence by innocent, unarmed, and heroic Muslim people – already defined the most morally loaded question, namely, who was to blame for the war.

Why is this way of perceiving war so resilient, despite lessons from all wars telling us that experienced war realities are very different, and escape this sort of rationalisation and order? In my doctoral thesis (Maček 2000) I have argued that it is because of our psycho-cultural need to understand events, to explain our experiences and to create a sense of control over our life situation (see also Levi 1999:23). This process is most urgent for people experiencing war on a daily basis, but also for those who experience war indirectly through the media or fiction. In other words, there is a need to adapt perceptions of normality so that they can also include the shocking, illogical and chaotic experiences of war. In these cognitive processes of clarification, it is easy for various simplifications to become life-sustaining strategies. This opens the space for ideological manipulation, and, as Scarry (1985) argued, it is those who hold the power (political or military) who also define the truths and the normality.

The 'Messy' War and the Volunteers – Denying the War

Let me take us back to my own past again, in order to present yet another very common view of war and soldiers, namely, the complete refusal to accept wars, the violent destruction they imply, and the threat to the way of life that we consider to be normal. When I came of age, the meaning of soldiering changed as all of my male classmates were obliged to do army service, something which they hated even as an idea; they saw it basically as a loss of one year of their lives.[7] At this stage in our lives, when we were graduating from our secondary school, deciding upon a future profession and applying for various university courses, war seemed something very distant, and to be a soldier a completely meaningless activity. Along with my friends, I was more interested in the world than frightened by it; unknown people and cultures were a source of excitement rather than a potential threat. We were belated children of 'flower-power' ideals, reggae and rastafarianism. We sang the Beatles, Bob Dylan, Bob Marley, Benjamin Zephaniah, and Linton Kwesi Johnson. We loved *Hair*, *The Deer Hunter*, *Taxi Driver*, and *Apocalypse Now*. War was a matter of history, and an impossibility in our world.

This kind of background influenced very much the ideas I developed at the outbreak of war in the former Yugoslavia in 1991. Although I was born and raised in the former Yugoslavia, my picture of soldiers in this war was initially formed by media in Sweden (where I lived at the time, and still do). The war was portrayed in Swedish media as a 'messy' enterprise and the soldiers who participated in it were neither the above described ideal hero-types, nor the orderly figures I was used to seeing in peacetime parades. In the first place, they were volunteers. I remember television pictures of young armed men in black and camouflage clothes, half military-half civilian, with black bands around their heads. Someone called Crni Marko (Black Marko) was giving an interview. He was obviously very pleased with himself. He was the unit leader in the new Croatian Army, and as he saw it, they were fighting for the long-awaited sovereignty of Croatia and freedom from Serbian hegemony over the Croatian people. In the end, with a wide grin, he sent greetings to all the lovely Swedish girls.[8] It was strange to see these big boys, who mostly appeared interested in resembling Rambo, standing there as representatives of one's own people and country. Then I heard that one of my best friends had volunteered for the Croatian Army. It came as a shock. This young man was a genuine pacifist if ever I knew one. The year he did his obligatory army service he developed a nervous gastric ulcer, not only because of the meaninglessness of his duties, but also because he was a genuine individualist with a dislike for any form of authoritarianism. He spoke four European languages, loved travelling, mountain climbing, speleology and skiing in loose clothes, which would flutter in the wind, giving him a sense of freedom. He was the one who introduced me to Bob Dylan and Jimi Hendrix, Friedrich Nietzsche and Erich Fromm. I just could not put these things together. I could not believe that he was now like Crni Marko; yet that was the information I had received.

As I continued to work with war, it became clearer and clearer that the war did not come as a shock only to me. I found that it was a rather characteristic reaction to the first encounter with war. Many of my informants, as well as other written accounts of war, described it as 'unimaginable' (Morokvasić 1998:66), never before experienced (Bruchfeld and Levine 1998:77, Levi 1999:23, Vuković 1993:14–15, Imamović and Bošnjak 1994:17, Isaković 1994:13), and/or as the

---

[7] One of the most popular ex-Yugoslav pop-singers, Đorđe Balašević, expressed it in 1993 during a concert in Belgrade, in his poem 'Fuck off, JNA' (*Odjebi JNA*): 'I gave you one year of my life, perhaps the best one'.

[8] See also Mattijs van de Port's description of volunteers in militia brigades in a Serbian Gypsy bar in 1991 (1998:3ff).

most cruel war in human history (Kubert 1996:141, Vuković 1993:14-15, Imamović and Bošnjak 1994:17). The supposed uniqueness of the experience of one particular war, though, points to a common characteristic in these accounts; the incapacity of people to let go of their perceptions of the normal peace-time order of things. This, in its turn, explains why the experience of war seems always to be unexpected and shocking.

Moreover, no one seems to expect to become involved in a war. Wars happen elsewhere, to other people. No matter how near, no matter how interconnected, as long as the war stays outside of our everyday lives, we find it impossible to imagine ourselves involved in it. The best examples here are the repeated accounts of Sarajevans telling how they watched the war going on in neighbouring Croatia, and were still taken aback when Sarajevo was hit.[9] A young woman told me in 1994:

> War in Dubrovnik. We watched it on the television, they said that there was no water for seven days. That was incomprehensible to us, that you could live without water. Or that there was nothing to be bought in the stores. I couldn't understand that. But, when the war started here, when I experienced it, then everything became clear to me. When we survived the worst winter cold without water, without electricity, without gas, without bread, without everything, when it was impossible to go out of the house, only then you understood what you had been watching on the TV. Really, until you experience it, you can't understand what's going on. We had no picture of what grenades and splinters were. What their [destructive] capacity was. (My translation)

With these words, the young woman pointed to one of the major methodological problems of the anthropology of war, namely, how to communicate experiences of war (Taussig 1992:10, Green 1994, and Maček 2000:28ff), or how to express the existential threat and pain, as Scarry puts it, in the opening paragraphs of *The Body in Pain*. As many others whose everyday lives became informed by war, the young woman settled for the explanation that such experiences were impossible to communicate to someone who did not have them. In Scarry's words 'physical pain has no voice' (Scarry 1985:3). But Scarry also suggests that the human creative capacity is capable of communicating existential threat and pain, and that such a language questions the political and perceptual order of things.

> Although this book has only a single subject, this subject can itself be divided into three different subjects: *first*, the difficulty of expressing physical pain; *second*, the political and perceptual complications that arise as a result of that difficulty; and *third*, the nature of both material and verbal expressibility, or, more simply, the nature of human creation. ...Physical pain has no voice, but when it at last finds a voice, it begins to tell a story, and the story that it tells is about the inseparability of these three subjects, their embeddedness in one another. (1985:3)

I believe the insight about the political and perceptual consequences of finding a way to communicate the experiences of war is the key to understanding why the language of war is so highly morally charged. In the final part of this article, where I discuss the necessity of changing our perceptions of war in order to change our inability to influence and avoid wars, I will also come back to the role of human creativity for these changes.

The ordering of war seems to start taking place at a point in time when it is no longer possible to deny the existence of either war or soldiers. As I have argued

[9] See for instance Softić (1994:6).

earlier in this essay, this is where we start to use our moral judgements. If the existence of combatants cannot be denied, then we can label them and define them as essentially different from us. Thus, for me the Croatian soldier volunteers became a symbol of horror; they were immoral criminals, homicidal and destructive, in short 'the other'. Each one of us, depending on our position in the war and our experiences of violence, forms a suitable perception of 'the other' – the combatants responsible for our pain and fear. We can tackle the immorality (i.e. moral unacceptability) of war by referring to it as unseen and unique in human history, as indescribable, as a 'slaughter', as a 'genocide' or an 'aggression' which will put the blame on one side, the 'other', or as a 'civil war' which will put the responsibility on all the involved parties. Whichever way we choose to describe a war, it seems to be a common trait to ascribe blame to a group of people we do not consider ourselves to belong to. Such an 'othering' of war and our responsibility for it, enables the ideal perception of war and soldiers to continue to exist parallel to our firsthand experiences of war as inhuman and terrible. The inhuman and terrible are ascribed to 'the other' while 'our guys' are still perceived as the ideal type of soldier and the war we fight as a righteous one.

Sarajevo War and Sarajevo Soldier

During the years following the outbreak of war in Croatia, Hercegovina and Bosnia I continued travelling to the war zones, and I developed a new understanding of soldiers and combatants, namely, that they were ordinary people like me, and that however pacifist my life-philosophy was, given certain circumstances, I could also become a soldier.[10] Carolyn Nordstrom has nicely expressed the heterogeneity of the soldier-role, albeit referring to a different war:

> A soldier is a member in a fighting group, and as well a member of an ethnic group, a language group, a gender group, a cultural group, a community, and a family group. All these alliances variously cross-cut the alliances of the fighting group. A soldier is also a child with parents, possibly a parent as well, a lover, a spouse, a person embedded in a network of friendships and economic pursuits. A soldier is a composite history projected onto the present, imbued with variously negotiated meanings, myths, emotions. And all these interwoven identities come to bear on each soldier's actions. (Nordstrom 1997:48)

By the time I got to Sarajevo and met Emir[11] I was not surprised to find out that he had been a volunteer in the Army of Bosnia and Hercegovina (ABiH) between 1992 and 1994. We easily found a common language of interests and a sense of humour, and I spent quite a few late evenings with him and his wife at their apartment, eating, drinking and chatting – socialising, as Sarajevans would say. Although they knew about my research, in this private context we never really discussed it. Similarly, we never really discussed their experiences of the first years of war, nor the changes they felt had occurred in their lives. At one point

---

[10] In recent years, there has been an upsurge of books taking up a similar discovery, for instance Agrell (2000), Bourke (1999), Browning (1992), Chandler (2000), and Goldhagen (1997). The phenomenon is, naturally, also tackled by psychologists (e.g. Zimbardo 2000).

[11] I use this pseudonym in order to protect the identity of this man. Suffice it just to say that he was in his forties, married, a father of two, a computer programmer, and from a secularised Muslim family background.

I asked Emir whether he was willing to talk to me about his soldier experiences, and if I could tape that conversation, to which he agreed.[12] He described his war experiences and the choices he made: from a civilian turning into a soldier, and from a soldier finding ways of avoiding the armed service. To better understand Emir's story, it is useful to know about the war-context between 1992 and 1994 during which it took shape, so I shall intertwine his story with the more generally shared perception of war events that emerged during my fieldwork.

When Sarajevans talked about their experiences of war, they usually referred to several significantly different periods (c.f. Maček 2000:283ff). 'The beginning' was characterised by notions of chaos and unbelief, and first experiences of shelling and snipers. The former Yugoslav People's Army (JNA) was retreating from barracks in the city and positioning its weapons in the surrounding mountains. The frontlines, which eventually defined the siege of Sarajevo, were being formed, although people did not yet know which politico-military force was to establish itself as the authority in the town. It could have been the Serb-led former JNA, it could have been extremist Serbian nationalists, it could have been some religious or nationalist Muslim regime, or some successor of the former Yugoslav multi-national authorities. In the parts of the town formally under the Muslim dominated Sarajevan government, from which the former JNA had retreated, some armed units were being formed. Green Barrettes became one of the best known. The members of Green Barrettes had participated already in fighting in Croatia in 1991 and were seen by the official discourse in Sarajevo as the basis out of which the ABiH was eventually formed. The other most important armed groups were perceived as somewhere between local militias and street gangs. As the centralised authorities were powerless at this time, the local armed units and their leaders had complete control over the population, property and goods in the parts of the town they controlled. At the same time they also fought to preserve the frontlines forming around the town. During the war their moral status was ambivalent – they were perceived as protectors of the town as well as a terror to the population. They kidnapped people and took them to the frontlines, they plundered stores and searched apartments, at the same time as they were sung about as Sarajevan heroes in many a war-song. During this time social networks were falling apart, as people were leaving the town. Everyone tried to decide whether to go, send only a part of the family abroad, or to stay together. The summer was approaching, so the weather was not so harsh. People had some food reserves, as well as money reserves with which they could buy the most essential supplies. Most of those who left thought that they would come back by the end of the summer, and so did those who stayed.

For Emir, 'the beginning' was confusing, and the normality of his life was disrupted by the impossibility to move freely, by the lack of work at his firm, and by the obvious inefficacy and powerlessness of the pre-war ideology of 'brother-hood and unity' between all nationalities.

> It came like a thunder from bright skies. You know that we had a small private business, so we drove to Tuzla to fetch some goods. With enthusiasm and optimism, we filled the car. Of course, there were some things going on: suddenly you couldn't

[12] Sarajevan men and women were reluctant to talk about their experiences as soldiers unless they knew me well enough, which always took time, and Emir was one of the few who was willing to do it.

go to Grbavica,[13] then they put up some containers and ramps so that you couldn't pass through to Koševsko Brdo,[14] in the middle of the day, suddenly. Or you couldn't get back if you passed, so you gave up. There were some things going on, but when I think of it, I had no idea [pause], I couldn't even imagine this sort of war happening.

So we fetched the goods, thinking that we were to work for some more time. I continued going to my firm, but you didn't really know whether to go or not. Trams were not working, and some people came while others didn't. You came to work, but you didn't have anything to do. Total chaos.

I worked for the Social Accounting and Auditing Service (*SDK*), an institution on the Republic level, good conditions, nice salary, nice work, nice people. Highly educated people. A nice and healthy surrounding. At least I thought so until there was a rumour that a Serb branch had been formed. You only heard about it, but nothing official, nothing formal. So who is in it? And you hear one, two, three, all the people you wouldn't expect it of, how could they be destroying? This new branch had some Serbian prefix, you know, something totally unknown.

In the beginning we even had secret meetings, younger people, we wanted to pursue our own line, we wouldn't allow the division, we were against national firms. Today you see how all that was naive. You thought you could do something, but you could do absolutely nothing. The centres of power where decisions were made were detached from our institution, and we were totally out of touch with those centres.

In the end I stopped going to work. There was a local call for all men of a certain age who wanted to volunteer and join units for defence. I was primarily thinking, like everyone else, whether I should leave. But whichever route I would choose, it was uncertain whether I could get out of town. I planned to move the family, my wife and children, but we voted and they wouldn't leave.

So I answered the call to join the units for defence. Of course, I still didn't understand the situation. I asked whether all [nationalities] were represented in these units. They showed me the list and I saw that there were Croats, Serbs and Muslims on it. Naturally, since we lived in a mixed part of the town. So I volunteered and we made a sort of military formation. We met in a room, 50 souls, we had 3 guns, everybody was talking, no one understanding anyone. It was actually a huge chaos. There was nobody who could stand out by his qualities as a leader. This was in our Municipal Centre.

It was the beginning of May. Shells were already falling, bullets whistling, frontlines were established. It was more or less already known which territory belonged to whom. Some of the people had already left the town. The [normal, Sarajevan, pre-war] surroundings were already falling apart. Every day someone was leaving, in the office as well as in the neighbourhood.

We sometimes went to the lines of separation [frontlines], although these lines were protected in the first place by the people living there. They protected their hearths. There was as yet no consciousness formed in people, they were asking why should they go [to the lines of separation] when there were people who lived there. But we went as additional help, here and there, messing around. There was already real shelling, they [Serbs] had artillery and all. (Emir, Sarajevo, February 1996, my translation)

After this period, 'the first winter' came, characterised by scarcity of food and fuel. Mobilisation into ABiH and Croatian Defence Council (HVO) was going on in an attempt by the Muslim dominated Bosnian government to gain military, political and economic control of the besieged city. The fear of starvation and malnutrition forced Sarajevans to fetch water and gather wood and grass, under

---

[13] Grbavica is a fairly central part of Sarajevo, held by Bosnian Serbs during the war, reintegrated in March 1996.

[14] A part of Sarajevo on a hill. He lived nearby.

shelling and sniper fire. The continuous reporting of the bestialities of 'ethnic cleansing' and the arrival of the first 'ethnically cleansed' refugees from Eastern Bosnia with their terrible stories added to already existing fears for the future. Even more people decided to leave the town, while others started to turn to their national groups' organisations for help and protection.[15]

> Then the state managed to establish itself, and an army was formed, so we were dispersed into larger units, it was Battalion Centre (*Odred Centar*). There was a lot of stupidities: while the town was shelled and destroyed, we were running and getting fit. Then they took us to a location, the first encounter, with a real front. You came and saw bloody uniforms, thrown around. The people you met were retelling the stories, how someone was wounded, how someone got killed. Where the others went, and where they were stopped.
>
> Only then did you understand the situation and what was going on. And you saw yourself in a situation of real danger. Danger to one's life. You understood how serious and how risky all this was. But you didn't have any other choice. My decision to join was not in the first place because of national feelings. I told you that it was difficult and risky to leave the town, so what next? Your own decision became simply imposed on you, the decision to defend yourself, and nothing else.
>
> As time went by, more and more Serbs were leaving. Suddenly someone would not come for several days. When you sent men to see what was going on – it turned out that he had left. You know, it was war. You went with them [Serbs] to the frontline and you asked yourself who you were actually with. How safe were you, from that same fellow-soldier. So I went over to a unit with mostly people from Vratnik,[16] where I was born, supposing that there were people I would know. Our [local] Serbs from the Muslim quarters of town (*mahale*) were also here. And it is interesting that there were no cases of someone turning his back on you or running away. It might be because they knew who they were with, and were not feeling threatened, afraid. Because those who ran away must have been as scared of me as I was scared of them. It was because we didn't know each other. But here [in the new unit] the situation was different. If you had a Serb with you, you knew for sure who he was. (Emir, Sarajevo, February 1996, my translation)

During a period of roughly a year between spring 1993 and 1994, people got used to the new life circumstances and new daily routines were established. Many found war-jobs, and managed to plant some vegetables in the gardens that occupied the place of the pre-war town lawns. New social relations were consolidated between the remaining members of the family now increasingly moving together into one single household,[17] as well as newly formed war-friend-ships (for more see Maček 2000:105ff). The frontlines around the town were fairly stable, but the mistrust between different national military formations in Sarajevo grew. The Muslim-dominated Bosnian government in Sarajevo managed

[15] Croats turned mostly to Caritas for additional humanitarian aid, for work in order to escape the mobilisation, or in the hope that they would be able to leave town through this organisation. Muslims turned to IGASA for work and financial help to soldier families, and to their local mosques for additional food. Serb organisations were very weak so there was not much for Sarajevan Serbs to gain from them, while Jewish Benevolencia was helping with the exit from town and free meals for those who stayed. All national/religious communities were providing Sarajevans with a sense of (national) belonging and spiritual peace.

[16] Vratnik is an old part of Sarajevo with a predominant Muslim population and a Muslim town-character.

[17] In the situation of harsh subsistence resources, it was easier to survive in a larger household were the chores could be divided. It was also mentally and emotionally easier to have the people one cared most about close on a daily basis, which would have been difficult if they lived somewhere else.

to establish itself as the central authority, also in command of the ABiH. The local armed groups and their leaders became subordinate through more or less violent episodes. Also the Sarajevan HVO was disarmed and integrated as a brigade into ABiH. Now it was not only Serbs who were perceived as a threat to non-Serbs, but also Croats and Muslims started to perceive each other as a source of threat.

For Emir, the experience of being a soldier was intertwined with his experiences as a civilian, and the expected ideal perception of the two roles became confused. For example, ideally, a soldier would experience a larger threat to his life while the civilian could more easily satisfy his needs to socialise. For Emir it was exactly the opposite:

> We went to the lines of separation [frontlines] in shifts – 5 days on the line and 10 days rest [at home]. There were no significant changes of lines, so in comparison with other fronts in the town this was a relatively peaceful one. ...Coming home was chaos. You came from terrible unhygienic conditions, sleeping for 5 days in a half-destroyed, deserted and filthy house, making fire in ovens that were falling apart, digging trenches but not being able to wash yourself. The interesting thing is that no-one got head lice, although people were switching beds, and you never got to lie down in the same place. So, when you came home your first thought was to take a bath. And what that bath looked like! There was no electricity, and no gas to warm the water. You had a bit of wood. My wife would somehow warm up some water. I always took off all my clothes immediately in the hall, and went into the bathroom which was freezing in winter time. You washed yourself quickly. Then all the domestic activities would wait for you. Physically heavy tasks that are not suited for women, like fetching the water. The first thing I would do after coming from the front was to fetch water. I needed a whole day for this. And the same before leaving for the front. There was a reservoir 300–400 metres up the hill. There were terrible queues, you'd wait for hours and then it could be that the water was out when your turn came. Because everything was working without any rule, without any order. Then you had to go to Brewery (*Pivara*) which had an old well. This was a rescue for the town. There was always a crowd waiting for water. People were nervous, there was shelling. It was interesting when a shell would fall, you didn't leave the queue, because if you had already waited for two hours, what then? You had to have water. Well, obviously not if you got hit by a shell, but [pause]. It was interesting how people got used to it all. A shell falls, explodes, there is smoke, and cries, but you don't leave the queue. ...That was really the worst, bringing water from the Brewery. ...I didn't go to the neighbour's [where mostly women gathered] for coffee and chat. I was tired of all the talking. All our stories came down to the same. Where did a shell fall, whom did it kill, how did it kill, who left from the neighbourhood, where did they go? I was tired of all that. I got the social component [of needs] satisfied on the line. In 5 days you had time to talk enough, to change the flow of thoughts in your head. So I'd stay at home and listen to the news, meditate in the dark, pointlessly. You strained your head thinking of what to do, but you couldn't do anything. You sat and waited for your destiny. You heard a shell falling and you only wondered whether it would hit or miss you. (Emir, Sarajevo, February 1996, my translation)

During the initial phase of the war the significant events for Sarajevans were negotiation dates and ceasefires. After some time these dates, however, lost their meaning as people realised that they did not result in better living conditions. During the second half of the war the escalation and diminishing of fighting was significant because it directly affected the closing and opening of the UN controlled 'blue lines', which in turn regulated the amount of goods coming into the town and the prices – when fighting escalated, the roads and airport were closed, less food was coming in and the prices would increase drastically so that daily survival could be difficult.

After the February 1994 ceasefire came the period of slightly better living conditions, with more food and fuel at lower prices, less shelling, and some of the peacetime symbols being re-established, such as the first tram since the beginning of the war. As the ABiH was now an established military force, and the frontlines around Sarajevo were stable, the police units gradually took over the military responsibility for the town, while the Army units were moved to other Bosnian frontlines. As a result, many soldiers of the ABiH tried to get a transfer into police units, to get backline duty, to find work and demobilise, or to leave the town (i.e. to desert). This indicated that Sarajevans had difficulties to identify with the common Bosnian state and its military aims. While they were willing to risk their lives in order to defend their town, to defend a country that they could not perceive of as really existing was definitely not worth their lives. The disappointments of national solidarity and the purpose of armed combat (i.e. 'defence') were characteristic of this period.[18]

> People were getting killed. I can tell you one case. In my old unit there was a boy from the orphanage which was near our headquarters. In the orphanage he also had a younger brother and sister. A fine boy. Good person. Scared and young. He had just turned eighteen years of age. After I changed units I heard that he got killed, somewhere in Vogošća.[19] They were going, naively, across a field, and an anti-aircraft cannon (*PAT*) was shooting at them. He got hit in the groin. They couldn't evacuate him so they hid for some time, and he bled to death. There was a colleague with him who tried to help him, they had bread with them so the colleague tried to stop the bleeding by pressing the bread against the wound. But he died. What hurts is that the brother and sister he was taking care of – he was their mother and father – they lost him. ...Until 1994 I was on these lines of separation. After that I continued in the same unit but not in the fighting formation. I went over to the command, to finances, as an accountant, I did some programming. Basically I saved my ass. I got myself out of the way. (Emir, Sarajevo, February 1996, my translation)

The Big Blur

'...their experience of the world being meagre, they do not like ambiguity', wrote Primo Levi (1999:23) about the newcomers to the Lagers (camps). I could easily substitute 'the world' for 'the war', in order to formulate one of the most interesting discoveries I made during my work in Sarajevo. The richer the

---

[18] This is where Emir's soldier story ends chronologically. The summer of 1995 was a period of heavy shelling, once again, and it ended after NATO's bombings of Bosnian Serb positions in August 1995. The period between September 1995 and March 1996 was characterised by hopes of seeing an end to the war. The Dayton Peace Agreement was reached in November 1995, and the slow implementation of its resolutions eventually led to reintegration of Sarajevo and finally to the lifting of the siege. The lifting of the siege, however, was by no means the end of the everyday realities of war, but rather a slow process into a different kind of life, characterised by lack of shelling and sniping, but otherwise full of disappointments with the supposedly 'peacetime' living conditions and a constant threat that the 'peace process' would turn into a longlasting violent story such as the Palestinian-Israeli 'peace process' or the one in Northern Ireland.

[19] Vogošća is a Sarajevan municipality slightly out of town, held by Bosnian Serbs throughout the war, re-integrated in March 1996.

firsthand experiences of war, the more ambivalent the moral positioning of the people that I met. And vice versa. Those who had a meagre firsthand experience were more prone to simplifications of the type I described as idealised perceptions of soldiers and war. The confusion, similar to the one that Primo Levi describes at the entrance into the 'indecipherable' world of the Lager (1999:23), was characteristic of the majority of war stories I heard in Sarajevo between 1994 and 1996, i.e. after more than two years of direct war experiences. The categories of 'us' and 'them' were blurred, the clear distinction between civilian, soldier and deserter characteristics, the aims and causes of the war were not clear any more, the justification of killing and destruction was not convincing, and consequently also the judgements of right and wrong were difficult and ambiguous. Emir's attempt to evaluate the decision of some neighbours who left in 1992 clearly demonstrates this moral ambiguity:

> Smart people, really. Smart, not smart, I don't know. Yes, they are smart, now. From today's perspective, when you add all things up, when you see that most of the politicians talk about one thing, and do something else. All the politicians hid their sons or placed them abroad, or had them employed somewhere where they were far away from, from [pause], dangers. So it was not only characteristic of Serbs. The majority, well not a majority but a large number of people, tried to avoid the gun [armed service], of course, in order to protect themselves. Especially in the beginning, because they couldn't grasp the whole of the situation. Because what happens if you wait, rely on someone else? Who is that 'someone'? I mean, if you don't join the forces and resist, your destiny is clear. He'll come to your house, into your apartment. [This is] aside from all the moral dilemmas. (Emir, Sarajevo, February 1996, my translation)

It seems that after a longer period of feeling existential hopelessness and chaos,[20] during which time people discover that none of the explanations of war seems to be able to rightfully capture its full complexity, people start looking for their own explanations. In this fight for the meaning of their lives, they combine freely all the moral norms they come into contact with – from the pre-war ones to the wartime propaganda and the gossip of neighbours. The pre-war and wartime moral norms start to coexist. That was why Emir could fully understand and trust his Serbian neighbour, despite the fact that the neighbour refused to join the ABiH and that Emir considered such Serbs to be unreliable and a potential threat to his life.

> The man simply didn't want to go into the army, so they said, very well, you won't carry a gun but then you'll dig trenches. He probably didn't like it so he left. ...The digging of trenches was worst for people who were not soldiers. Why? Because they came to a totally unknown terrain. When I was on the 'line-of-responsibility' I knew when I was sheltered and when I was visible. I knew where the machine-gun was firing from, where the sniper was shooting from. But these people came from outside and they didn't know the terrain. The ones guarding the line didn't tell them what they needed to know. You know, they exposed themselves, and got hit by a sniper or a grenade. There were really many accidents, mostly with those people who were on work-duty brought in by trucks [collected on the streets by gangs]. There were these units of Civilian Defence that came to dig trenches for us. But their digging of trenches was meaningless. They caused more damage than use. But, I understand them. They just wanted to get through that day, they came for one day to dig. Mostly, we soldiers dug too, all of us. You got your part for digging. OK. We dug trenches for ourselves.

[20] The collapse of infrastructure, of social relations, of the political ideology and of everything that people considered to be their everyday normality.

The deeper and better you dug, the better it was for yourself.

When an anti-tank shell hit [flew through] my apartment, this Serb neighbour was the first one to come and help to clean it up. A fine man. Not because he helped me, I also thought the same earlier. He was a man who knew how to fix many things, he was an electrical engineer. He had tools, so when I needed something I went to him, and if I didn't know how to do it he would show me. And he was always ready to help. (Emir, Sarajevo, February 1996, my translation)

The neighbour was judged through Emir's own combination of pre-war and wartime norms. This can cause the above-mentioned ambiguity and the apparent lack of logic, but for the people experiencing the war the ambiguity is a matter of sociocultural competence.

Of course, there are soldiers and soldiers, as there are wars and wars. Had the war events been different, perhaps the story of this man would have been, too – his insights, his moral dilemmas, and eventually his acts. The changing circumstances of the war in Sarajevo were important in order to understand why and how this 'soldier story' took shape. At the same time, this was also a 'kind of war story' that exposed some elements that I found common also to other war stories, from different wars and different peaces. Most importantly, I found three essentially different ways of perceiving events in a war – the time, the notions of order and norms, moral legitimisation of individual choices, and notions of group belonging. In an earlier article, I have labelled these three modes of perception as 'civilian'[21], 'soldier'[22] and 'deserter'[23] modes of perceiving war. Because of their legitimising nature – on a collective as well as the individual level – these modes present three utterly different moralities that I found coexisting in Sarajevan stories of war between 1994 and 1996. At the same time, I started noticing these modes of perception and war moralities and not only among people I met in Sarajevo but also in media and war reports, and not only in the local ones, but also internationally.

This is why I hope that this article can be a contribution to bridging the rift that seems to be appearing among the anthropological community of war researchers.

[21] 'The "civilian" mode of thinking about war is characterised by perception of war as opposite to peace, where peace is considered to be the normal way of living, civilised, moral, with juridical routines of dealing with unacceptable destruction and manslaughter leading to a punishment. War is a disruption, an interval of time which is abnormal, and generally impossible to happen to "us". War is something that the "others" experience, whether it is 'others' in time, or "others" in space' (Maček 2001:198).

[22] 'Accepting war as a social phenomenon controlled by human beings is characteristic of the "soldier" mode of thinking. In this perspective, wars have their rules which are different from peacetime rules. These rules legitimate what would otherwise be socially and morally unacceptable (for instance, killing fellow humans and material destruction). There is always a reason for a war, its legitimate cause and aims. The knowledge that it is war makes unacceptable events and acts acceptable - it implies that this would never have happened in normal (peacetime) circumstances, so what one did (or does) does not make one a different person. It is understood that this mode of living shall end with the ending of the war' (Maček 2001:190).

[23] 'The "deserter" mode of thinking is characterised by a realisation that the violent life-circumstances are a part of life. Every deserter has to come to terms with changes that happened in his or her life: the means of survival, the social relations, the existential threat, the religious changes, and the political changes. Deserters feel personally and morally responsible for their acts and deeds, no matter whether in peace or war. In an earlier article I have described this socio-cultural process taking place in Sarajevo during 1992–1995 as "negotiation of normality" (Maček 1997). It is a process in which all individuals, faced with inexplicably violent disruptions of their lives, constantly engage in making sense out of their situation. In this mode of thinking, the differences and borders between war and peace become blurred – they increasingly start to resemble each other' (Maček 2001:200f).

While some researchers promote the detailed ethnographic knowledge of a concrete violent conflict, and consequently also the local meaning of various war symbols and terminology, others seem to be more dedicated to finding general human phenomena connected to experience of massive violence in everyday life. I hope that the use of detailed information and a full respect for local meanings in this article can show a way to use ethnographic knowledge in order to escape the boundedness of a specific field of war and discover similarities of experiences and perceptions across other wars, and other peaces.

Beyond Desertion

What then, are the possibilities that moral ambiguity – caused by a long first-hand experience of war – arises when it comes to understanding and acting in concrete wars in the world of today and tomorrow?

As Scarry (1985:3) has suggested, the change in perception of war and soldiers has its political implications. If the war is no longer unambiguously perceived as evildoings by 'the other', if the division of combatants into two homogenous opposing sides is not always a clearcut one, if the roles of civilians, soldiers and deserters intertwine, and the justification of killing and explanations of war are not always convincing, then the political power of the elites based on the control of the means of violence[24] can be questioned. The use of weapons can no longer be justified if there is no unambiguously defined 'other' – inhuman, responsible for the catastrophe of war, and immoral – which the weapons have to be used against in 'defence'. As homicide and destruction become criminal and unacceptable in the individual judgement based on personal experiences, the use of weapons becomes unjustifiable. Consequently also the grand war narratives – with heroes and villains, civilian victims and criminal psychopathic perpetrators, with exact chronologies, limited in time and thus understandable and acceptable – come into question. What emerges, instead, is an understanding of war, of its diversity, of its ambiguous nature, of the relativity of morality and the need to take responsibility for one's own decisions and actions. This demands a constant sociocultural-emotional engagement from everyone in contact with a war. The process calls upon all our creativity to find new ways of understanding each other, new ways of communicating the most important aspects of our experiences.

Thus the understanding and communication of experiences of war emerges as a main challenge, as the main antidote to the existing political, social, cultural and perceptual institutions and models which make war as we know it today possible. I suggest that an institutionalisation of knowledge – of the ambiguous ways of perceiving war and soldiers – that I found to be specific for people who had a longer direct experience of war, might be a way to move towards a world inflicting less harm upon all of us who live in it.

However, talking about war experiences is an extremely difficult enterprise. An easy way out of it is to refuse to talk about it at all, explaining one's choice by the 'fact' that only those who experience a war can really understand it anyway. After having worked with a war for a decade, I am convinced that it is possible

---

[24] Let me just remind the reader of 'Max Weber's celebrated definition of [the state], as that agency within society which possesses the monopoly of legitimate violence' (Gellner 1992:3).

to find a language to communicate war experiences, and that in order to start forming this language we are going to need all our creativity – just as Scarry (1985:3) has suggested. The apparent uniqueness of war experiences might seem to be a problem at first, but we know that there are other experiences that are just as unique and as intense in their capacity completely to overthrow the perceptions we have of our world and reality.[25] We know, also, that to talk about such overwhelming experiences means also to start to organise them and to gain control over them, and over one's own life (cf. Scarry 1985, Suárez-Orozco 1992, Green 1994). This is why, as I have argued above, the idealising perceptions of war and soldiers (or at least, the ideal perception of 'our' role in the war and 'our' soldiers) gain ground, and the people involved in war are more easily manipulated by the power-holders. If instead of institutionalising idealised perceptions we could institutionalise the perception of war as morally ambiguous the knowledge of war that nowadays seems to be unique only to those of us who have experienced a war would have a chance of becoming common knowledge about war. In order to establish such a new perception, of course, the existing political structures would also have to be challenged. In the first place the control and legitimate use of violence has to be discussed and changed. Existing power elites, whether states or other institutions or groups, have to be challenged in their persistent belief that there can be war that is *not* morally ambiguous.

Naturally, there is no universal recipe, and my point in this article is in the first place to introduce an alternative way of perceiving war and soldiers. If I have succeeded, readers involved in war situations will hopefully have some new tools to tackle the practical problems and moral dilemmas, in a never-ending process demanding all their creative capacity. Let me end by giving some indications of the kind of creative understanding of processes that I have just suggested as a possible way out of wars (whether via 'desertion' or 'reconciliation'). South Africa's Truth and Reconciliation Commission has tried to get people to recognise responsibility for their deeds, 'to confess their guilt'. Through this act, the suffering of the 'victims' is publicly recognised, put in words and shared, which is the first step to a long-lasting healing and recovery. In turn, the 'victims' are required to 'forgive' the 'perpetrators', which is the first step for the 'perpetrators' to long-lasting recovery from the destructive acts they have committed.[26] A similar act of mutual 'confession', 'understanding' of the position of both sides, and both sides taking the responsibility for their reactions, is described by Thich Nhat Hanh, as evolved among Tibetan monks during the last 2500 years (1996:74–79). Only when both monks involved in conflict have understood each other, apologised ('repented') and accepted apologies from the other ('forgiven'), and accepted the verdict, are they dismissed from the meeting where the elders are the mediators and the whole community the witnesses.[27]

---

[25] As an example we can take the individual or group crisis connected with sudden deaths or large accidents. For such situations cultural and institutional knowledge and methods exist, for people to talk about such experiences, and to overcome their paralysing and even destructive consequences.

[26] From psychological practice and literature we know that a prison sentence works as a short-term compensation for the 'victims', and does not generally lead to 'repentance' and taking of responsibility by the 'perpetrator'. In the long run, the 'compensation' is insufficient, the 'victim' continues to feel victimised and no long-lasting reconciliation is possible.

[27] The seven 'practices of reconciliation' are: 'Face-to-Face Sitting', 'Remembrance', 'Non-stubbornness', 'Covering Mud with Straw', 'Voluntary Confession', 'Decision by Consensus' and 'Accepting the Verdict' (ibid.).

Traditional African models of conflict resolution also have some of these components. Finally, there is also a psychological model of 'Nonviolent Communication' (Fisher and Rosenberg 1999, and Widstrand et. al. 1999), which describes the communicative forms for expressing a moral reconciliatory intent, without falling into the emotional and psychological traps of short-term compensation through hurting the other.

Hopefully, understanding and raised communicative capabilities might then open up the possibility that one's suffering may really be recognised as fully as possible, and that deeds causing suffering to the others will be forgiven. The only real reconciliation must, thus, come from the ground, and not from above, as in the Dayton Agreement for Bosnia and Hercegovina. It is bound to involve much more energy and creative force than the bureaucratic implementation of a number of signed paragraphs. In the new wars of the 21st century it is people, and their relationships, not treaties, that will count.

References

Agrell, Wilhelm 2000, *Ökenvägen* Stockholm: Carlssons Bokförlag

Bourke, J. 1999, *An Intimate History of Killing: Face to Face Killing in 20th Century Warfare* London: Granta Books

Browning, Christopher R. 1992, *Ordinary Men: Reserve Police Battalion 101 and the Final Solution in Poland* New York: Harper Collins

Bruchfeld, Stéphane and Levine, Paul A., 1998, *...om detta må ni berätta... En bok om Förintelsen i Europa 1993-1945* Stockholm: Regeringskansliet

Chandler, David P. 2000, *Voices from S-21: Terror and History in Pol Pot's Secret Prison* Berkeley: University of California Press

Clausewitz, Carl von, 1997 [1832], *On War* trs. J. J. Graham. London: Wordsworth Classics of World Literature

Fisher, Maylin H. and Rosenberg, Marshall, 1999, *Nonviolent Communication: A Language of Compassion* Encinitas: PuddleDancer Press

Gellner, Ernest, 1992 [1983], *Nations and Nationalism* Oxford and Cambridge, MA: Blackwell

Goldhagen, Daniel Jonah, 1997 [1996], *Hitler's Willing Executioners: Ordinary Germans and the Holocaust* New York: Vintage Books

Green, Linda, 1994, 'Fear as a Way of Life' *Cultural Anthropology* 9 (2): 227–56

——, 1999, *Fear as a Way of Life: Mayan Widows in Rural Guatemala* New York: Columbia University Press

Hedetoft, U., 1993, 'National Identity and Mentalities of War in Three EC Countries' *Journal of Peace Research* 30 (3): 281–300

Hobsbawm, Eric, 1990, *Nations and Nationalism since 1789: Programme, myth, reality* Cambridge: Cambridge University Press

Imamović, Enver and Bošnjak, Jozo, 1994, *Poznavanje društva 4. razred osnovne škole.* Sarajevo: Ministarstvo obrazovanja, nauke, kulture i sporta

Isaković, Alija, 1994, *Antologija zla* Sarajevo: Ljiljan

Jabri, Vivienne, 1996, *Discourses on Violence: Conflict Analysis Reconsidered* Manchester and New York: Manchester University Press

Keegan, John, 1994 [1993], *A History of Warfare* London: Pimlico

Kubert, Joe, 1996, *Fax from Sarajevo: A Story of Survival* Milwaukee: Dark Horse Books

Levi, Primo, 1999, *The Drowned and the Saved* London: Abacus

Maček, Ivana, 1997, 'Negotiating Normality in Sarajevo during the 1992–1995 War' *Narodna umjetnost* 34/1, 25–58. Zagreb

—— 2000, *War Within: Everyday Life in Sarajevo under Siege* Uppsala Studies in Cultural Anthropology 29. Uppsala: Acta Universitatis Upsaliensis

—— 2001, 'Predicament of War: Sarajevo Experiences and Ethics of War', in Schmidt, Bettina E. and Schröder, Ingo W. eds, *Anthropology of Violence and Conflict* London: Routledge

—— forthcoming, *War Within: Everyday Life in Sarajevo under Siege* Oxford and New York: Berghahn Books

Miličević, Hrvoje, 1993, *Sarajevska ratna drama* Sarajevo

Morokvasić, Mirjana, 1998, 'The Logics of Exclusion: Nationalism, Sexism and the Yugoslav War', in Charles, N. and Hintjens, H. eds, *Gender, Ethnicity and Political Ideologies* London: Routledge

Nhat Hanh, Thich, 1996 [1987], *Being Peace* Berkeley, CA: Parallax Press

Nordstrom, Carolyn, 1997, *A Different Kind of War Story* Philadelphia: University of Pennsylvania Press

Port, Mattijs van de, 1998, *Gypsies, Wars and Other Instances of the Wild: Civilisation and Its Discontents in a Serbian Town* Amsterdam: Amsterdam University Press

Preporod, 1992, 'Sarajevo: Mešihat Islamske zajednice Bosne i Hercegovine, 15 April

Rieff, David, 1996, *Slaughterhouse: Bosnia and the Failure of the West* New York: Touchstone

Scarry, Elaine, 1985, *The Body in Pain: The Making and Unmaking of the World* New York & Oxford: Oxford University Press

Schmitt, Carl, 1976 [1928], *The Concept of the Political* New Brunswick, NJ: Rutgers University Press

Softić, Elma, 1994, *Sarajevski dani, sarajevske no?i: dnevnik i pisma 1992–'94* Zagreb:V.B.Z

Suárez-Orozco, Marcelo, 1992, 'A Grammar of Terror: Psychocultural Responses to State Terrorism in Dirty War and Post-Dirty War Argentina', in Nordstrom, Carolyn and Martin, JoAnn eds, *The Paths to Domination, Resistance, and Terror*. Berkeley, Los Angeles, Oxford: University of California Press

Taussig, Michael, 1992, *The Nervous System* London: Routledge

Vuković, Željko, 1993, *Ubijanje Sarajeva* Podgorica: Kron

Widstrand, Towe, Göthlin, Marianne and Rönnström, Niclas, 1999, *Nonviolent Communication för att inspirera till ömsesidig respekt i skolan: Vad kan en "giraff" göra i skolan?* Stockholm: The Centre for Nonviolent Communication

Zimbardo, Phil, 2000, 'Transforming Ordinary People into perpetrators of Evil', paper presented at the XXVII International Congress of Psychology, Stockholm, July

5

Silence & the Politics of Representing Rebellion
On the Emergence of the Neutral Maya in Guatemala

STAFFAN LÖFVING

The notion that the indigenous majority of Guatemala was, and always had been, 'neutral' in the civil war that ravaged the country from the early 1960s to the signing of the peace accord in December 1996, emerged in two inter-connected spheres of analysis and activism during the peace process of the 1990s. One was the Pan-Maya movement, its policies and practices. The other was a body of post-modern ethnographic representation of indigenous peoples and politics. This chapter focuses on the latter, and on the ways in which neutrality conceptually separates rebels from allegedly true Mayas and thereby contributes to clearing the ground for a political separation in post-war reality. The voices presented here[1] contradict the view of Mayanness as an all-encompassing strategy beyond or between Cold War dichotomies – a view adhering to what I have previously called *the neutrality paradigm* (Löfving 2002). It is a Latin American mirror image of the New Barbarism, as outlined by Richards (1996). The Cold War was not that cold in countries like Chile, Argentina, El Salvador, Nicara-gua, and Guatemala. It put fuel and not lids on local conflicts. However, the New Barbarism's presumption that culture and ethnicity are 'things-in-them-selves' also counts for much of the discourse on neutrality. The Central American equivalent to the notion of African chaos (when the lid came off) is a post-(cold)war discourse on Amerindian (cultures-in-themselves) peace-loving neutrals.

The current fame, outside the narrow community of Guatemalanist academics, of American anthropologist David Stoll is due to a book on the dubious factuality of the testimony of Nobel peace laureate, Rigoberta Menchú. Published in 1998, Stoll's allegations induced a revaluation of loyalties among many of those who had supported the work and resistance of grassroot organisations throughout Latin America during the years of military dictatorships. In a recent volume on the Menchú controversy, edited by Arturio Arias (2001), Stoll repeats that his aim, when questioning Menchú, was the same as when he published on the Guate-malan war in 1993, i.e. it was a critique of what he refers to as a widespread

---

[1] The essay is based on twelve months of fieldwork between 1996 and 1998 among (primarily) displaced Ixil Mayas in the *municipio* of Chajul, Quiché.

notion of vast indigenous support for the rebels during the seventies and early eighties. He then stated: '[R]evolution [in the Ixil area of Guatemala] came from outside, with less reference to Ixil experience and aspirations than has often been assumed, and [...] the local population became involved mainly because of the polarizing effect of guerrilla actions and government reprisals' (Stoll 1993: 313).

In the Arias collection, Mary Louise Pratt suggests: 'It is up to Guatemala specialists to assess the empirical precision of Stoll's conclusions and research methods' (2001:44). In this chapter I take both Stoll and Pratt seriously by going back to the work that laid the foundation of the discrediting of Menchú – the book on Maya Ixil neutrality in 1993. From the same field, but at a later stage in the war and from the other side of the frontline, I challenge Stoll on both empirical and conceptual grounds.

> ## The Neutrality Paradigm

Experience is the guiding light for the recent anthropology of violent conflict. However, from the 1960s and up through the 1980s it was rather reason, motif, and structure that caught the attention in social research (see Sluka 1992, Warren 1993, Green 1994). Samuel Popkin (1979) wrote about peasant rationality in joining rebellions. Theda Skocpol (1979) identified those most prone to revolution by structural means alone. Eric Wolf (1969) and Jeffrey Paige (1975, 1983) provided analyses in accord with this rationalist structuralist emphasis. James Scott (1976) brought it closer to anthropology by showing how people revolt in response to the capitalist penetration of what he coined their moral economies. Implicit in this school of thought was a view of violence as a legitimate response to injustice and social inequality. War itself was just, as long as it aimed at ending the other more subtle war of poverty and exploitation. *Structural violence* was regarded as the key to successful understanding of human conflict (Galtung 1969).

In principle I align myself with those who now oppose these models on the grounds that peasants cannot be expected to react collectively in such a predestined way. However, I will dwell on a certain scepticism towards analyses that substitute one essentialised social category (peasants) with another (indigenous people). Today, David Stoll's notion of the mutual exclusiveness of 'rebel' and 'Maya', the anti-thesis to the revolutionary potentiality of the poor, is paralleled, if not so much in local communities, then, at least, on the level of national politics in Guatemala. The contemporary Mayan movement portrays itself as a third way, a neutral political alternative between or beyond the country's militant left and militant right (see Cojtí Cuxil 1994, 1995, Esquit Choy and Gálvez Borell 1997). And even though he is an outspoken critic of Stoll, Charles Hale characterises Stoll's analysis of the process that preceded revolutionary alignment as 'a pioneering example of a new genre of social science research on Guatemala's failed revolution' (1997a:820). In an attempt to define the rupture between the old and the recent anthropological view of resistance and revolution I choose to build on Hale's identification of a new genre, and go so far as to suggest that a new paradigm has emerged – *the neutrality paradigm*. What follows is an assessment divided into three aspects.

From resisting to coping

The first aspect of the neutrality paradigm is the assumption that strategies to *cope* with constraints of reality, rather than to oppose or resist them, are the most relevant focus of anthropological attention. This position rests on giving voice to war-torn communities and to the claim that the reasons for war have little or nothing to do with the inhabitants of such communities. On the contrary, every form of participation in atrocities is forced upon innocent civilians. It is the alien agents of war that are threatening native culture. War *experiences* are approached at the expense of war *reasons*. Anthropologists are thus looking for answers to the question of *how* war is being experienced, not *why* it is being fought (see Simons 1999, Ferguson 2001).

Analysts of language highlight the conceptual dichotomy in which violence (read destruction) is seen as the opposite of culture (read creation) (Scarry 1985). From this coalesces an anti-essentialist view of ethnic conflicts emphasising the process that leads from violence to culture, not from cultural divides to violence (Warren 1993, Bowman 2001). The clash of cultures in civil war is thus always preceded by a violence that caused the combatants to construct meaning and formulate identities as opposites and in conflict with each other. Some scholars argue that resistance is inherent in chaotic perceptions (e.g., Nordstrom 1995, 1997). By persistently denying the reason for war, the war-affected civilians refuse to be part of it. It is argued that you become an agent of war the moment you ascribe meaning to it. Then war and violence become culture (Green 1994). Let us not deny the benefits of this new approach. By abandoning Cold War models, an emergent anthropology of war has proved able to grasp the complexities of local constructions of alliances, enmities, and power previously reduced to a binary scheme of oppressor and oppressed.

Yet, the anti-thesis to resistance has reached extremes too rapidly, and it has obscured disturbing facts on its way to paradigm status. In what follows I will examine the question of whether the Mayas supported the revolution in Guatemala or not, by focusing on that which defines 'Maya' and 'revolutionary'. Those whose voices are represented below acted militantly during the Guatemalan war. They thereby constitute the dark force of perpetrators who are anonymous in accounts of neutral victims. The major obstacle in my inquiry is that the denial of the *reason* for war in the Ixil area of Guatemala would mean – so my material suggests – an abuse of the memory of the displaced.

The second aspect of the neutrality paradigm is a portrayal of indigenous political thinking and agency that resonates with *essentialist* perspectives on the persistence of Mayan peoples in Mexico and Guatemala (see Watanabe 1992, Wilson 1995). Contrary to the view of traditions and ethnic identities as expressions of a *false consciousness* created by a continuum of exploitation and oppression since the Spanish conquest (Martínez Peláez 1971, Friedlander 1975), the essentialist perspective emphasises the *content* of culture, independent of the social setting that surrounds the locality. In Fischer and Brown (1996) the identity that grounds political alignment is believed to be ethnic or cultural in character. 'Maya activists', writes Fischer, 'are taking advantage of decreased tensions in current world politics to revive and strengthen their cultural heritage' (ibid.:14). About the Protestant converts in Nebaj, Stoll states that 'politically their limited goals and avoidance of confrontation are in line with traditional Mayan practice' (Stoll 1993:311).

Political dimensions of the paradigm shift

If the two aspects of the neutrality paradigm above relate to theory, the third concerns its political dimensions in present-day Guatemala; that is, the rejection of the claims of the guerrilla movement, even in cases of previous membership. We are moving here towards a refashioning of the nation-state, brought about by geopolitical and discursive changes in the wake of 1989, the collapse of communism as utopia, and new interpretative frames to fit a political setting that grew out of the Guatemalan peace process of the 1990s. An American anthropologist in the forefront of post-modern theory-making, Edward Fischer, writes, '[In] Guatemala, as in much of the world, native peoples were unwillingly pulled into an ideological battle between two competing Western political philosophies' (1996:63).

By paradigm is generally understood a general theory which has assumed a dominant role; the paradigm serves to define a scientific field and, within it, issues and topics in need of investigation (Kuhn 1970, Kurtz 2001). When I suggest that neutrality has reached such a status I evoke yet another quality inherent in a paradigm, namely its appearance after the decline of a preceding one. The new paradigm comes into existence due to its capacity to account for anomalous phenomena, and because it attracts a large number of adherents. Popper emphasised the sociological nature of paradigmatic shifts (1959). They are hence not to be understood as scientific progress in an objective sense; the change occurs within the culture and discourse of academia, and is not necessarily related to the external world.

Organised Resistance

For anthropology, the US-backed Guatemalan counter-insurgency project that aimed at draining the sea (meaning the people) in order to kill the fish (meaning the guerrillas) represents one of the most analysed wars of the 20th century (see e.g., Carmack 1988, Stoll 1993, Wilson 1995, Green 1999, Zur 1998, Schirmer 1998). But the gradual surrender of the displaced populations to the militarily controlled regions of the Ixil townships in the 1980s did not lead to the final defeat of the rebels, nor to the end of community support for the guerrilla movement. The Communities of Populations in Resistance (henceforth the CPR) presented itself to the world in 1990. For the first time in almost ten years, a couple of representatives had managed to break the military encirclement in the Guatemalan jungles and mountains and reached the capital. They revealed that some thirty thousand civilians inhabited their regions – areas that the Guatemalan military claimed to be guerrilla bases (i.e., the Ixcán jungle of northern Quiché and the Sierra in the mountainous Ixil area). Back then the delegates denied any relation to the insurgency. They established a political representation in the capital and invited representatives of the international community. The attention had the expected effect; the bombardments and civil patrol raids came to a halt, even though armed clashes continued until 1993. Confrontations between the army-engineered civil patrols and the rebels lasted at least until October of 1996.[2]

---

[2] Until April 1998, the villages in the CPR of the Sierra were divided into three administrative areas, with one political authority, referred to as *the local committee*, in each. The northern area consisted of ten communities. It was called Santa Clara and was ethnically the most heterogeneous.

Among the displaced, the very being of a resister was not viewed as an opposition to local culture and custom. Instead, it corresponded to both the epistemological aspects of identity, and to the ontological (see Daniel 1996). First, it was a repeated claim that 'we resisted militarisation, recruitment into the civil patrols and reintegration into national society', accordingly, resistance was what separated 'us' from 'them', the non-resisters. Second, the resistance was existential. It was the very reason for survival. It blended with ideas of divine blessing and it covered the very ontology of identity for this group. The concept of displacement directs our attention to the issues of 'loss', 'uprootedness' and illegitimate existences in the national and 'placed' order of things (Malkki 1995). Even though the displaced would attest to being out of place, the place they currently inhabited, cultivated and defended was invested with cultural and political meaning. This whole struggle came together under the heading of resistance. To leave the area was to *leave resistance*; to turn oneself in. To go the other way was to *enter resistance*; to let oneself be mobilised in a struggle for a new world. To remain, finally, was phrased as *being in resistance*. Given the importance of this language for the people in displacement I have found it difficult to follow the post-modern trend in anthropology which substitutes 'resisting' with catch-words like 'coping' and 'negotiating'.

Mobilisation and Agency

The time limits of war, its beginning and end, are political constructs and thus always controversial. According to the neutrality argument, the Ixils suddenly found themselves trapped between both promising and threatening guerrillas on the one side, and by ruthless reprisals of the Guatemalan army on the other (see Le Bot 1995, Stoll 1993). Such a representation of war, and of the normality of peace that precedes it, is part of a discourse on culture and politics in which political legitimacy is related to the coherence, or the 'group-ness' of social categories. The strong emphasis on a war-peace rupture cuts insurgency off from history (see below) and people, and it thereby makes rebellion illegitimate.

The guerrilla movement in Guatemala used the same rhetoric, but for the opposite purpose. In response to my questions in the field it was emphasised that, in the mid 1970s, an Ixil peasant went with his mule down the Kuchumatan to the Ixcán to look for the Guerrilla Army of the Poor (henceforth the EGP[3]) and ask them for help against state and landowner oppression. The guerrillas thus emphasised the 'Ixil *invitation*', while the protagonists of neutrality emphasised the 'EGP *infiltration*' or 'coercion' (Stoll 1993:117–28, 132–33). The location of the initiative and the revolutionary attempts, and thereby the time of the beginning of war, is at the core of both arguments.

---

[2] (cont.) The central area, where I was based in 1996 and 1997 and to which I returned in 1998, was called Cabá. It consisted almost exclusively of eighteen communities of Ixils from the municipality of Nebaj. Further to the south-east was the area of Xeputúl, the size of Santa Clara with a mixed population of Ixils from Nebaj and Quichés from Uspantán and Chiul. The men elected to the local assemblies held each year formed the local committee. The Central Coordinating Committee (CDC, *La Coordinadora Central*) was located in Cabá, with the task of coordinating the work of the distinct communities. It was formed in 1990 in an effort secretly to maintain the contact between the Guerrilla Army of the Poor – the EGP (*Ejercito Guerrillero de los Pobres*) – and the local committees
[3] *Ejercito Guerrillero de los Pobres.*

Instead, the recruitment of guerrilla soldiers in the Ixil area in the 1970s depended on a) the ability of local literate Ixils in Nebaj to make common cause with the guerrilla against discriminating employers, b) the experience of mobile villagers who achieved political training in radical trade unions active on coastal plantations, and c) the experience of violence, once 'the war' was in motion, which forced people by means of fear into militant resistance.

Xal 'the literate'

Xal, an Ixil-speaking former resident of Nebaj, was head of education in the CPR at the time of my fieldwork. He was different from most people in more than one way. Apart from his openness he was rather robust. This, he explained, stemmed from the fact that he was not a *campesino* back in Nebaj, but was working as secretary at the *Juzgado*, the local court.

Xal had vast rebel credentials and revealed past and important positions within the EGP, such as being the leader of the regional intelligence of the organisation. As early as 1975 he participated in the killing of infamous *fincero* Luis Arenas (see Payeras 1985:71-77, Stoll 1993:71-74, 80), and maintained that a broader guerrilla base was already developed among the Ixils of Nebaj at the time of the Guatemalan earthquake in February 1976. Up till then, the task of people from town had been to supply the *compañeros* in the mountains with food and water. Now Xal took on new responsibilities.

The EGP siege of Nebaj in 1979 required detailed planning. The guerrillas depended on local nuclei of support groups for the infiltration of police forces and *hacienda* guards. Xal became central to that process. He knew both the policemen and the guards personally and invited himself for beer and chats a couple of evenings prior to the EGP arrival. 'As we got a little drunk they relaxed and permitted me to move freely in their offices. I could check where the beds were, and the location of the weapon supplies. I memorised and reported it.' The infiltration of the *hacienda* police was even easier. They were illiterate, so Xal offered them his help in the form of typewriting. When the EGP arrived at 4 a.m. on Sunday 21 January 1979, the guerrilla did not have to fire one shot, and Xal credited himself for a take-over in which the lives of local policemen were spared.

In his analysis of the EGP siege of Nebaj, David Stoll relies on three different sources in an attempt to uncover the origin of the one hundred rebels who marched into Nebaj that Sunday morning. One is *Polémica*, a rebel-oriented journal that states that they were mainly Indians, while a Christian journal argues that they were university students from the capital (in Stoll 1993:61). The third source is a fellow North American eyewitness whose statement leads Stoll to the conclusion that the accounts 'point to a very special social group that has provided the first recruits for more than one guerrilla movement in recent years: urbanized, educated youth from indigenous backgrounds who return to the country-side to make the revolution' (ibid.). The complexities of loyalty and of an insurgency of the magnitude of the one in Nebaj in 1979 are concealed by this alleged divide between the guerrillas and the local population.

The argument is not irrelevant, however, in the sense that people within the geographical and cultural boundaries of Nebaj by the mid-1970s possessed the same characteristics as student rebels – educated, and, if not urbanised, then at least mobile with political experiences from outside of the community. During the last years of that decade Xal worked at the municipality, as third and second secretary of the civil registry. In our talks he argued that all the literate Ixils in communal offices supported the rebels, and that the political divide followed the ethnic.

Xal came to function as a messenger between local civil committees in resistance and the guerrilla leadership until 1985. Then he got sick, infected by the rubber mosquito. He was transferred to the Ixcán jungle and then taken to Mexico, where the guerrillas had access to medical treatment. Cured and back in Ixcán, Xal turned from *trabajador de masa* ('worker of the masses') to an armed combatant in the EGP. He stayed in the Ixcán, however, and did not return to the Ixil region until the mid-1990s.

Tec and Nil 'the migrants'

The ideological grounds for Xal's commitment were never an issue in his story. Instead he stuck to the technicalities and was very generous when it came to the details of his revolutionary career (see Löfving 2002). Tec, whose storytelling is presented in an edited but more direct way below, was more keen on explaining the reasons behind his stance. He took me back to the early seventies, to the migratory pendulum of the Ixils and their experiences of trade union activities on the coastal plantations and on the *fincas* (large estates) back home:

> I first fought on the coasts with the trade unions. I participated in demonstrations, and in manifestations in demand of better salaries. I started to think about how to fight and all that. But unfortunately, I did not know how to read and there I was – always with this idea to fight with the people. I participated in three strikes of the workers on the coast, over in Mazatenango. But after that, in 1977, I had the first contact – in the month of October – with the member of the EGP. We met when we were both alone and when I was walking on the road from Nebaj. So he stopped me. And he asked me whether I knew what the guerrilla was. I told him that I didn't. So for a moment I got a little nervous. But soon ... talking to him inspired me. He told me that if I wanted we could keep company along the road, chatting so that we wouldn't frighten the people. 'We won't scare them if we talk while we're walking', he told me, so 'Let's go', I said. I reckon we talked for more than half an hour, walking like that. He gave me the contacts, told me what I had to do, how to do it. Three days later I went to see him and the contact he had given me. It was about ten o'clock in the evening. You see, they were moving at night, not in the light of the day. [...] I began to talk to them and they asked me to invite them to my house. I told my wife to prepare something for them, something good to eat. Then we had animals like now. I killed two chickens and prepared them. They arrived at exactly two o'clock in the night. My wife was still awake, waiting. But when they entered the house, she got scared. We could not recognise them with their olive-green uniforms and with their weapons. In an attempt to calm her down they started to explain. They explained to us everything that their work entailed. So, after their explanations, we were all given food, and after that they gave me... like a mission. They trusted me because I gave them well-prepared food. That's why. They told me: 'Today you're a guerrilla. Today you're a *compañero*. Our *compañero*, you'll have to work here in your community. We don't know exactly how. It depends on how you get along with your friends, your relatives. But we will pass by every second week'. They stayed for three days, teaching me how to work. This was in 1977. Then I started to work on my own.

Tec was soon a dedicated guerrilla. Eventually he became a member of the political cadres (*cuadros politicos*) of the EGP. The role of the cadres entailed the continuous recruitment of EGP supporters in the hamlets surrounding town centres and, as the tensions increased, sustaining the contact between the armed soldiers and the organised civil populations.

Nil, a forty-year-old woman, lived in Cabá during the first half of my fieldwork. She was politically active in the women's organisation, and it was later revealed to me that she had served for many years in the guerrilla, first as combatant and later as educator and spokesperson within the political cadres. In contrast to Tec, Nil never talked about her guerrilla affiliation. It was as hidden in her stories as the ties between the civil communities of the CPR and the EGP. But she was eager to inform me about how it had all started.

Nil's first memories of coastal migration are from when she was about five years old. Her father had always gone south to find extra income working in the sugar-cane production, but at the age of five Nil went along. This had to do with the fact that Nil's mother was able to earn some extra by working as a kitchen maid. At the age of five, Nil could make herself useful in the kitchen, and the whole family migrated. 'As I grew older I began helping my brother picking coffee and gradually our father managed to work less and less. We made him happy when we earned some 50 Quetzals. That money we invested in corn, sowed it back home, cultivated, and when the corn was finished we returned to the coast.' At a later stage, Nil was given the responsibilities of her mother and began preparing food for the workers.

Nil remembered certain things clearly: the undrinkable water, the heat, and the long working days. The most painful memory was the death of her elder brother. The loss made the family choose less lucrative work on the *fincas* around Nebaj, but the salaries were lower and so coastal migration resumed after a couple of years. The suffering they endured did have a purpose and logic to it, since the family managed to allocate a sum of money to land purchase back home. Nil did not find the savings worth the suffering, however; 'I was afraid of the men on the coast, they did not treat women respectfully, and I always stayed by my father's side; he always helped me.' Not until she married at the age of seventeen did the migration end. This was in 1974.

Nil never revealed her commitment to the guerrilla, but when she had moved back to Nebaj I was told that she had served within the political cadres during the 1990s and occasionally as an armed combatant during the 1980s. I interpreted her life story, and the prominent place of suffering in it, as a rationalisation of her commitment to the guerrilla and the revolution.

Nil and Las 'the terrified'

Dual violence did indeed have the effect of forcing people into opposing armed sides, as claimed by David Stoll. For most people, however, violence is better captured by the epithet of singularity. To the large majority of survivors, war arose as an attack from only one side. The scorched-earth campaign of the army did scare people both away from and into military control. In the population as a whole the absence of ideology and the presence of violence at the time loyalties were decided upon existed parallel to the presence of a defined cause in politically active circles. Violence as determinant was perhaps most obvious for those too young to have acquired a political experience when war broke out. For them, the violence of the late seventies and early eighties arose as a reality that divided neighbours in ways previously unheard of. Nil said:

I was captured on December 11, at 8 p.m. Soldiers entered our house and stayed until December 12. They enquired about the guerrilla, where they got food and where they were hiding. I told that I was very busy taking care of my own relatives, but they kept asking. The family was very frightened by all the bombs and shooting. They kept asking and tied me to a pole. We are going to kill you they said and they started to beat me. Perhaps they beat me twenty times. I began to bleed heavily. It was my brother at that time only six years old, who got me off the hook. He was in the house, but the army did not care since he was so young. At two or three in the morning, when the soldiers slept he began untying the knot behind my back. I tried to make him stop. Our grandmother was in the house as well, and I thought that if we disappear they would certainly kill her. But my brother kept going, and all of a sudden I felt that I could move my hands. We went quietly across the room, but could not leave easily since the soldiers were lying in the doorways. I had to let go of my skirt, and once we were out we ran. By dawn we reached the house of my aunt. She could not believe our story and sent her daughter to check. When she returned she confirmed that the soldiers were occupying our village. If it had not been for my brother... I never saw my grandmother again. Sometimes I do not think about it, but I will never, never forget.

Las, health worker and former guerrilla soldier in the CPR village of Pal, remembered his first encounter with the army. 'I was about ten', he said, 'when the military came to our school in Nebaj. They grabbed all the children and brought us to the house of Diego Lux'. One soldier asked Las for his age and refused to believe him when he responded. 'You must be much older', the soldier yelled and continued, 'Tell us where you hide your gun! We know that everyone from Pulay is mobilised by the guerrilla.' Las was beaten up, and then placed in line for registration.

'We discovered that age did not matter to them. Child or elder, the army killed everyone. That's why we left, and gradually approached Pal, where we found refuge.' The escape from Pulay turned out to be just the beginning of horror. At the age of twelve, Las was to be captured while looking for food close to his old home, taken to the military barracks, tortured, and held for forty-five days before he managed to escape. Two months later, still at the age of twelve, and still an unarmed displaced person, he was on his way from Pal to Cabá with a sack of corn on his back when he was stopped by a soldier who turned up behind the bushes. Las dropped the sack and ran, as he says, 'like a dog' all the way back to Pal. He heard the shots behind him but was never hit. Ten days later, he heard the rumours about the butchering of a goat in the community, and he went to see if he could get some meat. An army helicopter that turned up from nowhere spotted him. Again he ran but the helicopter kept track of him and soldiers tried to kill him with machine-gun fire from the air. Finally, he managed to hide. Fifteen years later, he showed me the scars. 'They never hit me, but my legs were all torn up from tumbling and falling.' Las concluded:

> I was twelve at the time, and joined the guerrillas much later. I joined because of all the bad things the army did to me, but also because they killed my uncle, my grand-father, and my cousin. My uncle got the bullet in his head. His brain splashed out beside my father and my grandfather, who witnessed the killing. I saw it because I was sent there to clean up.

Of the three examples presented above, it is only 'the terrified' that fits the neutrality paradigm's model of Ixil behaviour, mentality, and culture.

Mobilisation and Structure

If the examples above were used to emphasise individual agency as opposed to the 'destiny approach' of the neutrality paradigm, a view of national and global political structure is crucial for a fuller understanding of the unfolding events. The epithets 'literate', 'migrant', and 'terrified' do indeed position them in a structure defined by powers beyond their own control.

The development of trade-union organising during the democratic period in Guatemala's twentieth-century history ended with the *coup d'état* of 1954. The unions' close connection with the communist party exposed them to severe repression on the part of the anti-communist regimes from 1954 onwards (Le Bot 1995:153–60). During the twenty years up until the mid-1970s only a few demonstrations were considered legal, and less than five percent of the national workforce, it is estimated, was organised. Le Bot identifies two strands of union activity that started to expand again in the seventies. The first was the militant FASGUA (*Federación Autonoma Sindical de Guatemala*). The other, more relevant to this discussion, was a result of an attempt by the main political opposition at the time, the Christian Democrats (DC), to consolidate its support in rural areas. They grouped their peasant leagues and trade unions into the CNT (*Central Nacional de Trabajadores*). The Ixil municipio of Cotzal was one of the few areas where fragmented organising took root.

The notorious massacre in Panzos in 1978 of ninety-eight Quiché peasants who had been organised by FASGUA marks the beginning of escalating tensions, as military authorities sought to limit the political space of civil political opposition. The massacre set a new scene for political organisations. It resulted in a break between CNT and its Christian Democrat network on a Latin American level. Several other unions divided along the line separating militant revolution and moderate protests within the frames of national law (ibid.:155). At that time the EGP was already absorbing the various radical alternatives that existed in two of the three Ixil municipalities.

One of the many among the displaced who remembered the pre-war interconnections between local and national politics was Nicolas Toma, dedicated Catholic from Cotzal and former politician. Now at the age of seventy, he attributed the facility with which people identified with the claims of the rebels to three causes. The first was the presence of a radicalised *Acción Catolica*. From being a renewal movement within the church in the 1950s and 1960s that employed fundamentalist strategies to purify the Catholic religion from pagan ingredients (Warren 1978, Falla 1980), it became politicised in the seventies, emphasising social and economic equality in the spirit of liberation theology. The second was the peasant league with headquarters in Quiché and an active branch in Cotzal. The third was the trade union of *Finca* San Fransisco. Nicolas Toma supported, joined, and thereby embodied all three of these modernist forces. As he described it,

> The plan of the peasant league was to put pressure on the government to make roads, drainage [...] to make faucets and arrange for potable water and electricity in the houses. The league had a branch in Cotzal of approximately two thousand members. Based on that work, we organised the unions of Finca San Fransisco.

The union encompassed all the workers not living on the *finca*. Nicolas Toma calculated that the leadership consisted of twenty Cotzaleños. The campaigns of the union included proposals for days off for the elders and for higher salaries. But it also went as far as demanding the right of the people to the land regarded as occupied by the owner of the *finca*. This resulted in legal disputes in which the *finceros* – the Brol family – easily produced legal documents from the national registry. The protests in the mid-1970s escalated into demonstrations, and the workers built up camps in the streets of Cotzal and refused to be enlisted as labour:

> But since the Brols are very much friends of the mayor of Cotzal, he helped them and went to get rid of the people and the camp. People refused since we were advising them to remain in the streets. So they stayed until the mayor burned their camp to the ground. At this time the guerrilla was rising and spreading its propaganda. So many people of Finca San Fransisco left with the guerrilla. That was because neither the government, nor the employer at the *finca* accepted their demands.

Among the twenty leaders of the union, everyone signed up for the EGP. In the interview Nicolas could only recall one of them surviving the war.[4]

Padre Axel, Catholic priest in the Quiché community of Chichicastenango, started his career within the Church in the Ixil community of Cotzal in 1973. He testified to the impact of peasant leagues in the Ixil region from the mid-1960s to the mid-1970s and emphasised the unionist character of the leagues, as they demanded higher salaries for the *colonos*, i.e., for those who lived on the *fincas* and worked permanently. According to Stoll (1993) it was primarily the *colonos* who rejected the coming of the rebels and who feared that the killing of their patron would undermine previously guaranteed subsistence. Stoll challenges Mario Payeras' claim that the people on the *finca* cheered the killing of their *patrón* (Payeras 1985:76). Stoll writes:

> Whatever the true feelings of La Perla's dependents, they were not gladdened by the subsequent bankruptcy of their only source of wages. In contrast to Ixils from surrounding villages, *colonos* are more likely to recall Don Luis with nostalgia, if only because during his time they did not live in the middle of a war zone and their purchasing power was higher. (1993:73)

Padre Axel's view of the relationship between the *finceros* and their permanent workforce is more gloomy. Since the leagues attracted the *colonos*, the administrators on the *fincas* began sacking the most active people on orders from the landlords. So the people turned to their poorly constructed huts and tried to

---

[4] Others behind the establishment of peasant leagues in Nebaj were still living with the CPR at the time of my fieldwork. They told how they grouped together in the 1970s prior to the arrival of the guerrillas. The first step was the creation of cooperatives for the poor. They organised a *Cooperativa de Consumo* around 1970. Around 1973 they continued with a *Cooperativa de Apicultura* [bee-keeping]. The members collected honey, which they tried to sell for the benefit of those who lacked other means of income. As the economic foundation of these efforts grew stronger, they were able to join forces outside the community. The first large-scale project was called *Ahorro y Credito* [savings and credit] in Nebaj, and it was a member of the nationwide FENACOAC (*Federación Nacional de Cooperativas de Guatemala*). The cooperative attracted between two and three hundred peasants, and a fund was established from which the most needy could take loans at low interest. In those days similar initiatives were nonexistent, and it was customary to take loans from the rich. The names that usually came up in these talks were the Brol family and the Samayoa *finceros* with land in Zona Reina (on which the Vizan military quarter was built) and most of the land around Nebaj. According to the memories in Cabá, most of the Samayoa lands had been acquired through debts that Ixil families had been unable to pay. The interest was between 10 and 20 percent, and the police were said always to have assisted in the collection.

survive on small fruit plantations. For those who did not migrate to the coast, the leagues offered a frame within which to organise and push their demands forward. The *finceros* responded by burning down their fruit trees. After continuing protests, the landlords stepped up the heat further by burning the houses. Axel said that about two hundred families left, some for the coast, and some, presumably, to the now growing rebel movement.

When I confronted the priest with Stoll's argument, he agreed to the complexity of the issue and invoked a topic known to all Ixils: The *finceros* at *finca* San Fransisco have traditionally taken advantage of their power and used the women among the residing *colonos* as concubines. This 'tradition' has survived from father to son, and has created over the years a large number of light-skinned offspring, regarded as bastards, or else regarded as biological children of the Ixil families in attempts to forget the sexual abuse of their bosses. The most common response among people on the *fincas*, according to Padre Axel, is an acceptance of the situation – rape, through the means of what Bourdieu has termed symbolic violence, is seen as a normal thing. There are even families who expressed what could be interpreted as a kind of pride, due to the fact that the rich patron is biological, if not social, kin.[5] So the many families with biological ties to the *finceros* generally did not support the uprising initiated by the peasant leagues, but the rest generally welcomed it. And that 'rest' was driven away before the coming of the rebels and the execution of the La Perla owner, Luis Arenas.

The influence of the leagues was waning when Padre Axel began working in Cotzal in 1973. The leaders had faced severe repression. They had escaped or been killed. The church now resumed the work abandoned by the suppressed leagues, but on a smaller scale. The *finceros* responded by banning people from Cotzal from going to the *finca* on Saturdays to sell their goods as they customarily did. The landlord was afraid that the Cotzaleños would bring revolutionary ideas to his workforce. Axel continued to go to the *finca* to hold mass, but now he discovered how people from the administration monitored every word that was said. Even though he himself was spared from threats and hostility, he observed how the people he stayed with at the *finca* were subsequently sacked and expelled after his visits.

The analysis of many in Cabá also added a commercial aspect to the explanation of Ixil-guerrilla contacts in the mid-1970s. An increasing number of Cotzaleños went to the Ixcán to sell goods to the guerrillas. This business had ideological side effects, and the opposition between people in Cotzal and the Brol

[5] Colby and van den Berghe (1969) comment on this: 'A number of Indian children look phenotypically more European than Indian. Some of these are rumoured to be children of Catholic priests, brought up by their mothers since they could not be acknowledged by their fathers. [...] To be genetically a Mestizo does not necessarily imply acceptance as a Ladino, and a good many of those children are brought up as Indians and are regarded as such' (pp. 162–3). They explain: '[A]mong Ladino men, who stress the value of *machismo* (masculinity) and adhere to a dual standard of sexual morality, affairs with Indian women are regarded with amused tolerance. Several men are famous in the region for the number of their illegitimate progeny by Indian mistresses. Some Ladinos keep several households in the same town, or in town and elsewhere, and reside alternatively with their wife and mistresses according to a system somewhat analogous to "hut polygyny" in African societies' (ibid.:161–2). It should be mentioned that infidelity and the 'possession' of concubines are not phenomena exclusive to non-Ixil residents in the area. This has a history as well among the Ixils themselves, which is documented and analysed by anthropologist Palimo Ojeda (1972). Indeed, people in the CPR, even though accused by others of infidelity, bragged in interviews about the number of women they 'had'.

family at the *finca* grew ever more radical. As the majority in the Ixil towns got a revolutionary organisation together, they found it increasingly difficult to get contracted for plantation work on the coasts. The landowners responded to the reputation of vigilantism by refusing to employ Ixils, which in turn made it even more difficult for people in Nebaj, Chajul, and Cotzal to pursue life as they were accustomed to. This indicates that without the possibility of earning extra from seasonal work on the coast they were driven by their enemies closer to the militant side of political opposition. The easy access to labour on the coasts made the protests of the Ixils ineffective. There was always someone else within the unorganised workforce who could step in and complete the task for the employer.

In his effort to argue against the guerrilla and its international supporters, Stoll has covered up the 1970 level of political organisation in the Ixil area that is kept vivid in the memory and stories of the ex-rebels. He, and the notion of neutrality that he propagates, thus draw upon a misinformed notion of social isolation. As claimed by Foucault, and maintained by a number of anthropologists (e.g., Aretxaga 1997, Daniel 1996, Feldman 1991), history is the maker of truth. Therefore, all attempts to de-legitimise the EGP must emanate from its separation from history.

Narration and the Predicament of Trust

Lying, misinformation and direct silence adhere to the communicative tool kit of people in politically unstable circumstances. This is partly the reason why 'the truth' is so contested in war and why the successful interpretation of storytelling requires a sensitive ethnographic approach. In what remains of this essay I will discuss three interrelated themes in an attempt at presenting such an ethnography. The first concerns the role of rumours when facts are difficult to come by, and the second the role and identity of the listener. The third theme has to do with lying, conceptualised here as silence in the context of distrust.

The paradox of not knowing

The tendency to cover up what really happened with mysterious and highly manipulative misinformation was not reserved for inter-group communication. Within the CPR, and even within families, conflicts seemed to be nourished by the suspicion of not getting proper information. People's explanation for withholding the truth was the repeated reference to their war experiences and the need to control sensitive issues. To portray oneself as a sufferer, and thereby enjoy the privilege of silence, worked even if the root of the dispute concerned unfaithfulness (in the case of the family) or corruption (in the case of a political office).

It could indeed be claimed that violence fragments the social body of a community (Warren 1993, Green 1994). That means that information in war is shared in diminishing social circles. It is not controversial to claim that the displaced communities in Guatemala have been subjected to such a process. But the armed threats to people's lives came to an end in the early 1990s. At that time it is likely that broken norms of conduct had been replaced by a wartime behavioral pattern in which the 'selectiveness' of truth did not depend any longer on raids and shelling. The effect of violence in Cabá was a change in the collective demand for the veracity of information. An example may serve to clarify this point.

The need to know exactly what is happening seems to grow in relation to the impossibility of achieving that very knowledge. This is the case in an isolated condition characterised by fear and uncertainty. A prominent feature in responses to my questions and in more extensive narration was the expression, 'Así dicen' – that's what *they* say. Occasionally, the narrative itself specified who 'they' were, when 'así dicen' was used. But most often it referred to an unspecified and anonymous source of knowledge that people viewed with ambivalence. On the one hand, it was used when something crucial was discussed, something that profoundly affected peoples lives. On the other hand, the information was measured against an experience when what 'they' had said had proved to be wrong. People were thus dealing with an important but vague piece of information.

The very day after the disarming of the guerrillas – the first day that the villagers were without armed protection – assailants dressed in the black uniforms of the army's elite unit G2 showed up, threatening and robbing people on their way to the market in neighbouring Chel. Immediately the event was on everybody's lips. Fear of a continuation of military repression in spite of the peace accord and its implementations (the disarming of the rebels) united the themes of the discussions. But the details varied on how many the assailants had been, on the type of weaponry they had carried, and on how many they had robbed or just threatened. I had the 'luck' of being close to an eyewitness, since Baltazar, my host, had spotted the four men when he was approaching Chel on his horse. He hid and watched them for a few minutes. Then he turned back on the three-hour ride to Cabá, warning everyone he met on the trail. I could thus compare the narrated versions of this event with Baltazar's over-excited record. No one – except Baltazar – ever claimed to know the details. Everyone – except Baltazar – included the reference 'they' in their accounts. 'Asi dicen' was thus a rhetorical device employed to neutralise the paradoxical relation between telling and not knowing.

The Identity of the Listener

James Scott (1992) teaches that what subordinates tell those in power differs from what they tell each other. By studying gossip, rumours, jokes, and informal communication, he argues that an understanding of social tensions could be acquired before the outbreak of open hostilities and revolutions. This model guides a large number of Maya studies. The general conclusion reads: what they say among themselves is different from what they tell foreign researchers and those in power. That assumption is also central to the neutrality paradigm since it can be claimed that guerrillas and foreign solidarity activists (as well as anthropologists) only get access to formal, public discourses. Cil, an Ixil woman in her early forties and an active guerrilla fighter, contested that assumption.

Cil's testimony contained the horror of surviving two massacres and a capture from which she managed to escape with the help of her six-year-old brother, whom the army had neglected to tie up. After having given me her story, which served as a focal reference to the preceding narration on mental and physical disorders, she spoke about the frequent and sudden outbursts of crying. She referred to them as attacks, even if her crying was silent.

The CPR had institutionalised efforts to promote the work of women and the participation of women in the political spheres of the community. Cil was very actively involved in politics, but the women's group constituted a place where gossip and slander flourished. She said that she felt bullied especially by three other women, and that this added to her problems. They focused their attack on the issue of Cil's childlessness, but she interpreted the hostility as envy. I did not know about her affiliation with local political power, in fact, her central position within the guerrilla leadership at the moment of the interview, so the envy was left unexplained in her narrative. To my question about whether she shared her troubles with a great number of other women, she answered that she didn't know. I turned to Juan, the health worker and interpreter, and he explained. 'People don't talk about their health. They tell us because we interrogate them. To admit your problems would mean that you admit that you are weak.' Later Juan and his colleagues put me in contact with a great number of their patients. Just as their illness narratives appeared similar to me, so they all seemed similarly unaware of the fact that many shared their suffering. Sanctioned by the religious leaders and Maya traditionalists was the notion that health-related problems (and indeed war) represented a just punishment.

Neither Cil nor her husband ever mentioned their commitment to the armed resistance. Like almost everyone else, they kept quiet before the signing of the peace agreement, and they did not utter a word afterwards, even when it was obvious to them that others had been telling me about their central positions within the very leadership of the Ho Chi Minh front of the EGP. I was not in Cabá when the Guerrilla Army of the Poor was disarmed in March 1997. Instead I visited Xeputúl, the CPR area closest to the guerrilla base. I concluded, a couple of weeks later, when leaving Xeputúl and passing the empty house of Cil and her husband in Cabá, that both of them had gone for a three-month stay at the guerrilla reintegration camp in the village of Tzalbál near Nebaj. They had left with 250 others from Cabá. As far as military identity was concerned, and in line with Scott, there was thus a clear line separating those within the group of resisters and the group of 'others' to which I belonged.

However, the guerrillas and ex-guerrillas willingly narrated their nightmares, apathy, and seemingly unmotivated outbursts of crying and mourning and their willingness to talk to me about this; the secrecy of their rebel identity represented two seemingly contradictory ways of expressing memories, two informative strategies that revealed the complexities involved in studying violent memories. As an interviewer (interrogator, according to health worker Juan) I posed a threat to the security of the villagers since my status as an alien newcomer hid potential connections to military power and state security. I had not lived through the hardships – something that was explicitly mentioned in talks about trust. Hence I could not count on any kind of military information. But the same alienated position made me a 'good listener' for narratives of suffering. The patients of Juan and his colleagues knew that my lack of social anchorage within the villages prevented me from exposing their weakness to the evil powers of community gossip.

This implies a call for a critical reconsideration of the relevance of Scott's 'hidden transcripts' (1992), at least in a setting silenced by war. It seems that the anthropologist can easily use the ethnographic representation of *the* covert story in her/his attempt to legitimise a newly acquired knowledge. The stories of

Cil and her fellow revolutionaries have led me to reject the notion that the hidden transcript is available for objective study. Instead, truth telling must always be contextualised, and the position of voice *and* ear considered, no matter how intimate the communicative sphere appears to be.

Lying as Silence in the Context of Distrust

The hard-liners among the rebels – that is, those with a clear political agenda – emphasised purpose and meaning in the discussions of both suffering and the organisation of the resistance communities. They also delivered what I gradually came to understand as false statements in descriptions of past events. The more I learned about the history of the communities the more dubious some of the stories of the guerrillas appeared. But rather than dismissing these discrepancies as 'lies' I will develop an argument below about 'two realities', which I depict as a legacy of war and the revolutionary project mediated by Ixil history and culture.

Once a guerrilla affiliation had been openly admitted it seemed that the most committed were proud when relating past events. They were the heroes of their own accounts, while people less involved seemed more troubled, and more divided between their loyalties to neighbours and the civil community on the one hand and to the guerrilla leadership on the other. But far from everyone spoke about armed activity after the signing of the peace. Most kept quiet even after the disarmament of the rebels in the spring of 1997, and those who refused to talk were often those whom I thought I knew best. What they all had in common was a sense of political powerlessness, even within the local setting. It was obvious that they had not been in the forefront of mobilisation campaigns, nor active as speakers in the revolutionary meetings. Ironically, it seemed that the state and military machinery of blame got to them with much more strength than it got to the dedicated rebels. I would argue that the two categories of people possessed two different conceptions of resistance. Everyone defined themselves as resisters, but to the non-militants resistance was existential, it was a way of life created through years of incomprehensible suffering. The accusations from parts of national society, the conscious propaganda, and its counterpart – a receptive cultural setting that transforms accusations not into protests but into guilt (Zur 1998, Löfving 2002) – had created a silence among most people in Cabá. Resistance was thus psychologically positioned on the same level of consciousness as guilt, and the two constituted a highly ambivalent state of being, a contradiction that language and the spoken word could not resolve; hence silence.

Since the analytical tool provided by Scott initially appeared particularly apt in the controlled CPR setting, I began wondering *how* the public transcript – the official way of treating the inside and the outside of sociality – was being taught and withheld. One day I ran into one of the more experienced European volunteers as he was putting a poster on the wall of the community library. It depicted a fully armed Guatemalan guerrilla soldier, camouflaged with leaves and branches and with an AK47 in hand. When he saw the scepticism of my reaction, he said that this kind of open support for the armed left was now 'allowed', thanks to the advanced stage of the national negotiations.

The same day a few kids passed the open door of the library and stayed with me a while. They laughed and played. All of a sudden, the youngest, a girl of approximately five, stopped and pointed at the poster on the wall. Overjoyed, she said a name in Ixil and then waited for the happy reaction of the others. But they said nothing. Instead they stared at the poster, and then at me, and then the eldest girl, of about ten, grabbed the youngest by her arm and the whole group ran away.

The boy on the poster was most likely recognised as a family member. At the age of ten a CPR member knew that the guerrilla identity of the social surrounding was banned from official talk. At the age of five this was still not known, but through events like the one described, the youngest was taught a lesson: the playing in the library was abruptly interrupted. I hypothesise that language aided people's control of public and hidden transcripts. When Spanish was spoken, an official atmosphere emerged that implicitly sanctioned a public transcript. People were safe from spies in the language of Ixil. The Guatemalan term for spy – *oreja* [ear] – seems particularly functional here. It was the ability to listen that threatened the great secret of the CPR.

The double life of the Ixils who had been affiliated with the guerrilla required a double terminology. The villages and the areas of the region were renamed and given certain codes.[6] The names chosen for this clandestine version of geography were drawn from various sources: fallen heroes, communist or 'liberated' areas and countries, Guatemalan places important to the symbolism of the nation, like Sololá and San Marcos, and finally the Bible. The rebel-affiliated individuals were renamed in a similar way.

This dual system resonated with the Ixil tradition of double names: one in Spanish and one in Ixil. All the Baltazars are called Xal in Ixil; Margarita is Kit, Diego is Tek, Cecilia is Cil, Petrona is Nil, Domingo is Ku, and so on. It is likely that this facilitated the Ixil adoption of guerrilla ways of doing things. But it also had implications for the ways in which the people affiliated with the guerrilla told their stories. It was as if the world consisted of two realities, and while one was narrating within the discourse of one of them it was not regarded as immoral or false to keep the other totally out of the discussion. 'Lying' was thus an inappropriate term for not telling the whole story, in the same way that 'truth' was a highly relative concept. At least two truths were believed to exist simultaneously – one for each reality.

This argument is partly at odds with the influential psycho-philosophical argument of Elaine Scarry (1985) and her interpreters within anthropology (e.g., Nordstrom and Martin 1992, Green 1994). Whereas they refer to the legacy of war and/or pain in terms of silence as a proof of the diminishing effects of violence on individual and cultural worlds, the discussion here concludes that the silence of the guerrilla – maintained through misinformation, lying, and direct silence – was highly instrumental; that is, the 'silences' were conscious strategies aimed at controlling the actions and reactions of the listeners. If one were to criticise what has been described here as a typical guerrilla way of storytelling, one would, of course, direct attention to the potential power of this control and

---

[6] Salquil Grande was called Monte Rey, Vicalamá was Sololá, and Tzalbál was Sierra Maestra. The village of Sumal Chiquito was San Carlos, Cheucalwitz was Sovietico, a hamlet not specified to me was called Israelito, and Nebaj together with Acul was known as Liano. The area code Namibia was given the villages of Acul, Tzalbál, Salquil Grande, Vicalama, and Cheucalvitz. The area between the river and closer to Cabá was called Herera after a member of EGP's DR (*dirección regional*) killed in action.

the use of the knowledge about the two realities in exercises of power within the non-secret reality (see Löfving 2002). Important to note would then also be that the disappearance of the secret reality through the peace process, and the dissolution of the guerrilla, undermined the possibilities and powers of the now ex-rebels to control the turn of events.

In a context marked by a violent repression that had been justified throughout the last two decades by references to the knowledge of the secret reality of the guerrilla, it should also be said here that many among the displaced refrained from asking sensitive questions, which leads to my claim that those who possessed a vast knowledge about the two realities indeed saved many from trouble by talking about just one of them. The occasional alleged immorality of lying and secrecy could therefore be questioned from two fronts.

Conclusion

In this chapter I have argued that the war–peace rupture is a political construct that conceals the nature of human agency in contexts marked by the violence of poverty and exploitation. In search of the cultural and political mechanisms needed to create a state of 'no war' it should thus be crucial to reconceptualise normality in terms of 'no peace', and to keep a window open for the possibility that the emergence and endurance of rebel movements might depend on the consent and agency of local populations rather than on demonic powers to manipulate and control.

With a sigh of resignation I finally have to admit the political power of representation. When I returned to Guatemala in February of 1998 for a last visit to the field, the CPR was in the middle of a final displacement. According to the peace agreement the government was required to find practical solutions to the crisis of land tenure among the displaced. In the case of the CPR of the Sierra this had resulted in an extended process of negotiations, with a final offer to the villagers of resettling in four different areas.[7] More than a year after the signing of the agreement the families were now leaving the huts and cornfields of the resistance, with pigs, dogs, chickens and the few things that they could carry. The migration resembled a slow and peaceful version of how they must have fled almost twenty years ago. I joined them, and to leave Cabá for the last time, walking, eating and sleeping together along the two day path to Nebaj was for me an epic experience. Tired and dusty but seemingly relieved, the families reached Nebaj. For good or for worse, peace, not war, had finally crushed the resistance. I met with old friends, and after the initial success stories, one of them slowly began to tell me about the present stream of members leaving the popular resistance to be integrated in culture-oriented organisations. One of those was Ojlaju Ajpop, a unity of Mayan spiritual guides, all of whom were guerrilla dissidents. Discontented with the leadership of their former organisation, they

---

[7] Two grand estates had been bought for the relocation of about 400 families on each. Due to the delays in the search for purchaseable estates the number of 100 families that chose to return to their original land in Nebaj had increased to nearly 400 in April of 1998. The need to sow in the beginning of the year forced people to return without guarantees of available land in Nebaj. The fourth option was to remain in the municipio of Chajul, provided agreements could be reached with former landowners.

had left one year earlier to create something of their own. Among the Mayan groups represented and analysed by a new cadre of American anthropologists, CPR and other popular Mayan organisations are seen as being too close to the insurgency to fully comprehend the Mayan cause (see Fischer and Brown 1996). I noted the irony of my own views of Maya neutrality. My sense of having read biased accounts from the Stoll publication in 1993 was now challenged by my most recent field observations. In the violent peace of contemporary Guatemala, reality was adjusting to the power and politics of representation.

References

Aretxaga, B. 1997, *Shattering Silence: Women, Nationalism and Political Subjectivity in Northern Ireland* Princeton, NJ; Princeton University Press

Arias A. ed. 2001, *The Rigoberta Menchú Controversy* Minneapolis & London: University of Minnesota Press

Bowman, G. 2001, 'The Violence in Identity', in Schmidt, B.E. and Schröder, I.W. eds, *Anthropology of Violence and Conflict* London: Routledge

Carmack, R. ed. 1988, *Harvest of Violence* Norman, OK: Oklahoma University Press.

Cojtí Cuxil, D. 1994, *Politicas para la reivindicación de los Mayas de hoy: fundamento de los Derechos Específicos del Pueblo Maya* Guatemala: SPEM y Editorial Cholsamaj

—— 1995, *Configuración del Pensamiento Político del Pueblo Maya* Guatemala: SPEM, Cholsamaj

Colby, B. and van den Berghe, P.L. 1969, *Ixil Country: A Plural Society in Highland Guatemala* Berkeley: University of California Press

Colby, B. and Colby, L. 1981, *The Daykeeper. Life and Discourse of an Ixil Diviner* Austin, TA: Texas University Press

COMG 1995, *Construyendo un futuro para nuestro pasado: Derechos del pueblo maya y el proceso de paz* Guatemala: COMG/Editorial Cholsamaj

Daniel, V.E. 1996, *Charred Lullabies: Chapters in an Anthropography of Violence* Princeton, NJ: Princeton University Press

Dunkerley, J. 1988, *Power in the Isthmus: A Political History of Modern Central America* London and New York: Verso

Esquit Choy, A. and Gálvez Borell, V. eds, 1997, *The Mayan Movement Today: Issues of Indigenous Culture and Development in Guatemala* Guatemala: FLACSO

Falla, R., 1980, *Quiché Rebelde: Estudio de un Movimiento de Conversión Religiosa, Rebelde a las Creencias Tradicionales, en San Antonio Ilotenango, Quiché 1948–1970* Guatemala: Editorial Universitaria

Feldman, A. 1991, *Formations of Violence: The Narrative of the Body and Political Terror in Northern Ireland* Chicago: University of Chicago Press

Ferguson, B.R. 2001, 'Materialist, Cultural and Biological Theories on why Yanomomi make War' *Anthropological Theory* 1 (1): 99–116

Fischer, E.F. and Brown, R. M. eds, 1996, *Maya Cultural Activism in Guatemala* Austin, TA: University of Texas Press

Fischer, E.F. 1999, 'Cultural Logic and Maya Identity: Rethinking Constructivism and Essentialism' *Current Anthropology* 40 (4)

Friedlander, J. 1975, *Being Indian in Hueyapan: a Study of Forced Identity in Contemporary Mexico* New York: St Martin's Press

Galtung, J. 1969, 'Violence, Peace, and Peace Research' *Journal of Peace Research* 6 (3): 167–91

Green, L. 1994, 'Fear as a Way of Life' *Cultural Anthropology* 9 (2): 227–56

—— 1999, *Fear as a Way of Life: Mayan Widows in Rural Guatemala* New York: Columbia University Press

Hale, C. 1994, 'Between Ché Guevara and the Pachamama: Mestizos, Indians and Identity Politics in the Anti-quincentenary Campaign', *Critique of Anthropology* 4 (1): 9–39

—— 1997a, 'Consciousness, Violence, and the Politics of Memory in Guatemala' *Current Anthropology* 38 (5) December: 817–38

—— 1997b, 'Cultural Politics of Identity in Latin America' *Annual Review of Anthropology* 26: 567–90

Kuhn, T., 1970, *The Structure of Scientific Revolutions* Chicago: University of Chicago Press

Kurtz, D.V. 2001, *Political Anthropology: Paradigms and Power* Boulder, CO: Westview Press

Le Bot, Y. 1995, *La guerra en tierras mayas: Comunidad, violencia y modernidad en Guatemala (1970–1992)* Mexico D.F.: Fondo de Cultura Económica

Löfving, S. 1998, 'On the Veracity of Ixil War Memories' *Acta Americana* 6 (2): 59–68, Uppsala: Uppsala University

—— 2000, 'Traditional Blame: Rigoberta Menchú as a Noble Savage', in Löfving S. and Maček I. eds, 'On War – Revisited' *Antropologiska Studier* Stockholm: University of Stockholm, 66–67

—— 2002, 'An Unpredictable Past: Guerrillas, Mayas, and the Location of Oblivion in War-Torn Guatemala', Dissertation, Uppsala University

Maček, I. 2000, *War Within: Everyday Life in Sarajevo under Siege* Uppsala: Acta Universitatis Upsaliensis, Uppsala Studies in Cultural Anthropology 29

Malkki, L. H. 1995, *Purity and Exile: Violence, Memory, and National Cosmology among Hutu Refugees in Tanzania* Chicago & London: University of Chicago Press

Martínez Peláez, S. 1971, *La Patria del criollo: Ensayo de interpretación de la realidad colonial guatemalteca* (6th ed. 1979) San José, Costa Rica: Editorial Universitaria Centroamericana

Montejo, V. 1999, *Voices from Exile: Violence and Survival in Modern Maya History* Norman, OK: University of Oklahoma Press

Nordstrom, C. and Martin J-A. eds, 1992, *The Paths to Domination, Resistance and Terror* Berkeley: University of California Press

—— 1995, 'War on the Front Lines' in Nordstrom, C. and Robben, A.C.G.M. eds, *Fieldwork Under Fire: Contemporary Studies of Violence and Survival* Berkeley, Los Angeles and London: University of California Press

—— 1997, *A Different Kind of War Story.* Philadelphia: University of Pennsylvania Press

Paige, J. 1975, *Agrarian Revolution: Social Movements and Export Agriculture in the Underdeveloped World.* New York: Free Press

—— 1983, 'Social Theory and Peasant Revolution in Vietnam and Guatemala' *Theory and Society* 12 (6): 699–737

Payeras, M. 1985, *Days of the Jungle* New York: Monthly Review Press

Popkin, S. 1979, *The Rational Peasant: The Political Economy of Rural Society in Vietnam* Berkeley: University of California Press

Popper, K., 1959, *The Logic of Scientific Discovery* London: Hutchinson

Pratt, M. L. 2001, '*I, Rigoberta Menchú* and the 'Culture Wars'' in Arias, A. ed. *The Rigoberta Menchú Controversy* Minneapolis & London: University of Minnesota Press

Richards, P. 1996, *Fighting for the Rainforest: War, Youth and Resources in Sierra Leone* Oxford: James Currey

Scarry, E. 1985. *The Body in Pain: The Making and Unmaking of the World* Oxford: Oxford University Press

Schirmer, J. 1998, *A Violence Called Democracy: The Guatemalan Military Project 1982–92* Philadelphia: University of Pennsylvania Press

Scott, J. 1976, *The Moral Economy of the Peasant: Rebellion and Subsistence in Southeast Asia* New Haven, CT: Yale University Press

—— 1992. *Domination and the Arts of Resistance: Hidden Transcripts* New Haven, CT & London: Yale University Press

Simons, A. 1999, 'War: Back to the Future' *Annual Review of Anthropology.* 29: 73–108

Skocpol, T. 1979. *States and Social Revolutions* Cambridge: Cambridge University Press

—— 1982. 'What Makes Peasants Revoultionary?' *Comparative Politics* 14 (3): 351–75

Sluka, J. 1992, 'The Anthropology of Conflict' in Nordstrom, C. and Martin J. eds, *The Paths to Domination, Resistance and Terror.* Berkeley and Los Angeles: University of California Press

Sluka, J. ed. 2000, *Death Squad: The Anthropology of State Terror* Philadelphia: University of Pennsylvania Press

Smith, C.A. ed. 1990, *Guatemalan Indians and the State, 1540–1988* Austin, TA: University of Texas Press

Stoll, D. 1993, *Between two Armies in the Ixil Towns of Guatemala* New York: Columbia University Press

—— 1997, 'To Whom Should We Listen? Human Rights Activism in Two Guatemalan Land Disputes' in Wilson, Richard A. ed., *Human Rights, Culture & Context: Anthropological Perspectives* London: Pluto Press

—— 1998, *Rigoberta Menchú and the Story of all Poor Guatemalans* Boulder, CO: Westview Press

Warren, K.B., 1978. *The Symbolism of Subordination: Indian Identity in a Guatemalan Town.* (Expanded edition 1989) Austin, TA: University of Texas Press

—— ed. 1993, *The Violence Within: Cultural and Political Opposition in Divided Nations* Boulder, CO: Westview Press

—— 1998, *Indigenous Movements and their Critics: Pan-Maya Activism in Guatemala* Princeton, NJ: Princeton University Press

Watanabe, J., 1992, *Maya Saints and Souls in a Changing World* Austin, TA: University of Texas Press

Wilson, R.A., 1995, *Maya Resurgence in Guatemala: Q'eqchi Experiences* Norman, OK: Oklahoma University Press

Wolf, E., 1957, 'Closed Corporate Peasant Communities in Mesoamerica and Central Java' *Southwestern Journal of Anthropology* 13 (1): 1–18

Wolf, E., 1969, *Peasant Wars of the Twentieth Century* New York: Harper Torchbooks

Zur, J., 1998, *Violent Memories: Quiché War Widows in Guatemala* Boulder, CO: Westview Press

6

'For God & My Life'
War & Cosmology in Northern Uganda

SVERKER FINNSTRÖM

Introduction

In this chapter I hold that today's conflict in northern Uganda, although fought on local grounds, is international and even global in character. The Ugandan army, led by Lieutenant General Yoweri Museveni, who also is the president of the country, is fighting the Lord's Resistance Movement/Army rebels (henceforth the LRM/A). Joseph Kony, a self-proclaimed Major General, fronts the LRM/A. Worldwide flows of imagery, weaponry and humanitarian aid entangle with local sociopolitical realities, in a way typical for most small-scale and low-intensity wars at the turn of the millennium. Alliances on the regional level add to the complexity of local battle scenes. In the local discontent my informants articulated these complexities. 'The surroundings are bad', they often said. In discussing important aspects of a life with bad surroundings my chapter focuses on the local lifeworld, and on actions, interpretations and explanations that are essential to any understanding – academic or popular – of the conflict. In pursuing this aim I investigate how non-combatant people in the war zone understand and explain the rebels' violent practices on the ground, but also how they relate to the fact that the international community has become increasingly and inescapably entangled with the politics and practices of war. On the existential level, I propose people actively practise a kind of knowing by engagement. To be able to highlight this I put emphasis on *meanings in use*. Such meanings are never fixed but negotiated in an interactive sociocultural and political process of interpretation and counter-interpretation, including not only the most influential agents, like the rebel movement, the Ugandan government or international relief organisations, but also the ordinary people with direct experience of the war.

Evolving Conflict in Acholiland, Northern Uganda

Like a foreign body in your eye – that is the situation [of] the Acholi people. (Clan elder, Gulu town, December 1997)

We are told by Museveni that the Lord's Resistance Army belongs to past governments.

But the Lord's Resistance Army children are born under Museveni's rule. (Middle-aged woman from Acholiland, London, July 1998)

Yoweri Museveni and the National Resistance Movement/Army (NRM/A) seized power in 1986. For some five years, Museveni had been leading a guerrilla insurgency in central Uganda, with the objective of replacing Milton Obote's second government (1981–85) and Tito Okello's succeeding but short-lived government (1985–86). A quotation from Ngoga (1998) expresses a common view among scholars doing research on war and conflict. The end of war is erroneously equated with the capture of a capital, or the signing of a peace agreement. As Ngoga states, 'On 26 January 1986, it [the NRM/A] captured Kampala and *the war was effectively over*'. He continues that the NRM/A was 'one of the most effective guerrilla insurgencies in Africa, and the first to defeat an incumbent regime and replace it by a successful *post-insurgency government*' (Ngoga 1998:104, emphases added). Woodward puts forward an equally common conclusion, writing that Museveni 'had a remarkable army that had come from the bush to overthrow the existing regime in the capital by a popular guerrilla campaign, a rare success in Africa for all its internal wars' (Woodward 1991:180). Hansen and Twaddle (1994:3), on their side, argue that Museveni's takeover was a military success, 'pacifying the greater part of Uganda and leaving only a small strip of land bordering the southern Sudan prone to millenarian protest and external disruption'. Similar conclusions often find their way into comparative studies on post-colonial Africa. In one such study, Uganda is mentioned only briefly. In very general terms the authors conclude that Uganda is one of the African countries 'where a logic of violence has been replaced by a political process of negotiation and rebuilding' (Bayart et al. 1999:5).

With regard to the insurgency in central Uganda, launched militarily by Museveni in 1981, some of these conclusions on Museveni's takeover may be correct. From a wider national perspective, however – most often neglected when Uganda's recent political development is discussed internationally – it is important to observe that the 1986 capture of Kampala also marks the starting point of several armed conflicts in Uganda (see Finnström 2003:103ff). Below, however, I will limit the discussion to the northern region.

As Museveni captured Kampala, soldiers and supporters of the previous governments left Kampala and fled northwards, towards Acholiland (Gulu, Kitgum and Pader districts) bordering the Sudan. Museveni's army followed hard on the heels of the fleeing soldiers, crossing the symbolically significant border of the Nile. Soon thereafter the conduct of Museveni's former guerrillas, often said to be members of a well-disciplined army controlled and educated by its political wing, deteriorated. Killings, rape and other forms of physical abuse aimed at the non-combatant population became the order of the day when they reached Acholiland, which was foreign territory to them (see notably Amnesty International 1992). From within the Sudan, opposition elements regrouped and launched the Uganda People's Democratic Movement/Army (UPDM/A), simultaneously called *cilil* (report our presence to the government) and *olum olum* (people of the bush) by the Acholi people, whose homeland soon turned into a violent battlefield (see Lamwaka 1998). Other insurgency movements were also formed, of which the most well known is Alice Lakwena's Holy Spirit Movement (see Behrend 1999). As war evolved, people in the war-torn region came to differentiate between two dimensions of armed resistance, the first called 'the army of the earth' (*mony me ngom*) and the second 'the army of the heaven' (*mony me polo*).

At the initial stage, the uprisings had considerable support among people who found their homes, belongings and cattle herds destroyed and looted *en masse* by the intruding soldiers. In their view, Acholiland was under occupation, something they resisted. Others did not explicitly support the uprising, but according to a kind of standardised version I often encountered, informants claimed that they saw no alternative survival than to join in one way or the other. They joined the rebel ranks as a direct response to the military brutality they experienced (see also Brett 1995:146ff).

The evolving war has caused an enormous humanitarian catastrophe in northern Uganda, the home of the Acholi people. Some 800,000, or 70 per cent of the Acholi population, are displaced, the great majority forcefully to large camps cynically called 'protected villages' (Gulu Archdiocese 2003a:3; Human Rights Watch 2003:5). The LRM/A rebels have abducted thousands of minors into their fighting ranks (Amnesty International 1997; Human Rights Watch 1997), which eventually alienated them from the local population. Until today, no overall or lasting cease-fire has been reached, and no peace agreement is visible in the near future.

Cosmology in crisis

To hell
With your Pumpkins
And your Old Homesteads,
To hell
With the husks
Of old traditions
And meaningless customs,

We will smash
The taboos
One by one,
Explode the basis
Of every superstition,
We will uproot
Every sacred tree
And demolish every ancestral shrine.
(from *Song of Ocol* by Okot p'Bitek,
first published by EAPH 1967)

Listen Ocol, my old friend,
The ways of your ancestors
Are good,
Their customs are solid
And not hollow
They are not thin, not easily breakable
They cannot be blown away
By the winds
Because their roots reach deep into the soil.

Listen, my husband,
You are the son of a Chief.
The pumpkin in the old homestead
Must not be uprooted!
(from *Song of Lawino* by Okot p'Bitek,
first published by EAPH 1966)

In comparative studies, researchers try to quantify and thus define the phenomenon of war. For example, according to Wallensteen and Sollenberg's (2001) definitions, the conflicts in Uganda oscillate between 'war', 'intermediate armed conflict', 'minor conflict', and even 'peace', based on the number of people alleged to have been killed annually in 'battle-related deaths'. Doom and Vlassenroot (1999: 20), citing northern Uganda as case study, define peace as 'the absence of open and widespread violence rather than a situation where all disputes are settled by procedural methods'. However, as Galtung (1969) and Sponsel (1994:6) point out, research on war and conflict often characterises peace by negation only.

Peace is then nothing but the absence of war, which contrasts with the most common standpoint I encountered in the field. In late 1999 – by coincidence only some few days before the rebels launched new attacks that brutally replaced two years of lull in the fighting – an informant put it rather poetically, 'The silence of guns does not mean peace.'

Commonly using the Acholi phrase *piny rac*, people described their lived surroundings as seriously bad. 'Annoyance is commonplace', even 'everywhere', I was often told. According to the late Acholi writer and scholar, Okot p'Bitek, *piny rac* is when 'the whole thing is out of hand, that the entire apparatus of the culture cannot cope with the menace any more' (Okot p'Bitek 1986:27). In other words, the conflict is beyond immediate and local control. Sickness is abundant, children are malnourished, cattle are gone, young people do not marry, education is too expensive, crops fail, bad spirits roam the surroundings, and people are killed or die at an early age and in large numbers.

The lack of control in quotidian life naturally frustrates people in northern Uganda, but they still tried to grasp and master their fate. For example, male clan elders (*ludito kaka*, sing: *ladit kaka*) and diviners (*ajwaki*, sing: *ajwaka*) – the latter mostly women – framed the state of affairs in the context of their local moral world and cultural knowledge. What is happening in Acholiland is not only bad. It is also something beyond Acholi tradition and culture, these senior members of society said. A clan elder in a displacement camp smiled at me as I asked my naive question – could not the spiritual world and the ancestors counter the potent but violent spiritual powers of the rebel movement and especially Joseph Kony? 'Acholi spirits can only confront other Acholi spirits', he then explained. Most Acholi regard the many spiritual powers (*jogi*, singular: *jok*) of the greater world as ambivalent manifestations, potentially with both healing and harming powers and actively evoked in the everyday interpretation and diagnosing of misfortune, illness and the like. The man suggested, however, that the very spirits that present themselves through Joseph Kony, the rebel leader, are alien and even evil, 'not Acholi' and therefore beyond immediate comprehension. Other informants argued that although Kony is an Acholi, the violent rebel spirits could not be of Acholi origin because there are no such violent and militant spirits or powers in the Acholi cosmological order of things. There never were. Rather the contrary, the LRM/A rebels sometimes explicitly target elders, healers and other arbitrators of the local moral world, as was the case already with Alice Lakwena's movement in the 1980s. As then, the LRM/A rebels claim that they want to establish a new moral order, with the objective to break with the violent postcolonial history of Uganda (cf. Behrend 1999:48f).

Some informants argued that Joseph Kony claims to have 'taken over' Alice Lakwena's Holy Spirit (*Tipu maleng*) when the latter fled Uganda in October 1987. One could perhaps suggest that he claims to have done so to be able to legitimise his own spiritual and political authority. According to most informants, however, Kony cannot have taken over Alice Lakwena's Holy Spirit, because there are important differences between the Holy Spirit of Alice Lakwena in the 1980s and the spirits of Joseph Kony in the late 1990s. The clan elder quoted above told me the following:

> The evil spirits of Kony are something new. They are beyond Acholi spirit mandate; Acholi spirits can't cope with them. During Alice's time, there were few [unlawful] killings, even though she failed [in her mission]. She failed, but then there was not as

much suffering as now, with Kony. Kony is worse. Alice was fair, at least. Kony kills people who perform the spirits of Acholi. Kony's spirits are not Acholi. Kony is the root of the evils. (Amuru displacement camp, December 1997)

Tonny, my friend and co-worker in the field, explained that Kony cannot possible have the Holy Spirit, because '*Tipu maleng* cannot kill anybody'. Tonny's mother, a retired healer, once well known over most of west Acholiland because of her ability to deal and negotiate with the extra-human world, agreed with her son. The old woman argued that even if it is most likely that Joseph Kony and Alice Lakwena once were presented with the Holy Spirit of God, they have both misused it to the extent that it has now been replaced by, or even transformed into, a spirit of darkness (*tipu macol*). Both Joseph Kony and Alice Lakwena are responsible for unlawful killings of innocent people and can only be regarded as evildoers and witches (*lujok*, sing: *lajok*), she concluded. In a kind of boomerang effect, then, Joseph Kony, who claims to be fighting for a new moral order, purified from corruption, sorcery, witchcraft and past evils, has turned into a witch himself. Behrend writes of Alice Lakwena:

> In a situation of existential crisis, the [the Holy Spirit called] Lakwena ordered Alice to heal society and to cleanse the whole of Uganda from witchcraft and sorcery. But to heal society she had to use violence, the power to kill. In doing so she, like the *ajwaka* [healer], used the means she pretended to fight. Although she was fighting witchcraft and sorcery she used the means of a witch, because she used her power to kill. And this explains why she was accused of being a witch. (Behrend 1991:176)

Influential and powerful people may summon potent powers to harm and even kill enemies from afar, outside Acholiland, to incorporate them into the lived Acholi cosmological order of things, p'Bitek (1971: 140, 142) once noted. However, if these powers are misused, they can easily turn against their user and eventually also against the wider surroundings. Accordingly, most of my Acholi informants questioned the legitimacy of Kony's spiritual objectives and military methods. Still, many were convinced that he possesses powerful but dangerous spiritual powers that indeed can harm society. Among Pentecostals, for example, rebel spirituality was equated with the devil and evil forces, in the same manner that all kinds of Acholi spiritual powers are equated with evil forces that must be fought in the name of Jesus Christ. James, a lay Pentecostal in his late thirties, argued with reference to the rebel spirituality, 'Jesus is the only good spirit. Others exist, oh yeah, but they are evil. All of them.' When I discussed the matter with my friend Komakech, an unmarried man in his mid twenties, Komakech confirmed this, even though he is neither a Pentecostal himself nor a frequent churchgoer: 'The devil exists. The devil is in the Bible. It is true as far as I am concerned.' However, Komakech expressed his ambivalence about the rebel spirituality more clearly on another occasion:

> The rebels have some kind of spirit, you know, some kind of supernatural power. Because sometimes the bullets [aimed at the rebels] will turn around and hit [the rebels'] enemy. ... But I don't know, I haven't seen it. (Gulu town, December 1997)

Alternatively, as an elderly man, once involved in efforts to mediate between rebels and government,'commented upon Kony's spiritual powers, 'If that power is to destroy Acholi, then let that power go away.' He did not deny the spiritual power of the rebel leader Joseph Kony, but he argued, in a similar vein to Tonny's old mother, that Kony is losing his spiritual power bit by bit, 'because he has misused it'. A young man in a rural displacement camp placed the rebel spirituality in relation to his own frustrations. Neither he nor his relatives could possibly raise the money needed for school fees, and as long as there is war, he can only forget his dreams of secondary school education. But rather than questioning the existence of Kony's spiritual powers, he questioned their spiritual legitimacy. He countered my queries with a question, 'Does this spirit develop the world and our schools?'

Escalating Spiral of Violence

Recent years have been characterised by an increasing number of brutal rebel activities, such as child abductions, atrocities and terrorist acts aimed at civilians. Yet to conclude that the complex pattern of increased violence is solely the responsibility of Joseph Kony and his spirit possession and alleged religious fanaticism – only a too common trend in the media – would hardly be analytically satisfactory. This was not how informants primarily interpreted the situation and their lived surroundings, although they argued that the spirit of a killed person (*cen*, or ghostly vengeance) most often would return to disturb its killer. If healers do not assist in settling this problem, the result is that the killer, whether rebel or a government soldier, will behave to an increasing degree in asocial and violent, even self-destructive, ways. People who merely witness or otherwise experience the violence of war can be equally disturbed, with repeated nightmares and other daily flashbacks that assail their memories, thus posing a continuous and destructive challenge to ordinary, quotidian life. Perhaps if a term of Western psychiatry is used one can talk about post-traumatic stress disorder (PTSD), although always framed and articulated, however, in locally informed terms.

Military violence will obviously assail the memory of its victims, but such violence, my informants held, also assails the victims' local moral world, which they share with friends and relatives. Consequently, the exorcism of ghostly vengeance (*cen*) has to be a public and social event rather than one of individual dealing with traumatic memories only (see Finnström 2001). Violence is not limited to the battlefield, or to the individual perpetrators and their victims, I was told, but will increasingly infest the wider surroundings of the living and the dead, and even future generations. Yet, more frequently, informants mentioned the Ugandan army's bad conduct and inability to protect civilians, and the government's official reluctance to promote peace talks, as factors in the escalation of violence. Informants also brought up the issue of anti-personnel landmines, a steadily increasing problem in war-torn northern Uganda. The Sudanese government has provided the rebels with landmines. Some of the landmines are marked with Arabic writing, as some that have been confiscated reveal. Other mines that the Ugandan army has captured from the rebels are manufactured in Belgium and Italy, the Ugandan army claims (see *The Monitor*, 5 February 2000). But also the Ugandan army is planting landmines in Acholiland, especially in the Agoro Hills bordering the Sudan in Kitgum district. The objective is to seal the border to make it more difficult for the rebels to enter Uganda from their bases in southern Sudan. Ugandan military authorities regard the Agoro Hills as a notorious point of entry for the rebels when they cross between Sudan and Uganda.

Ironically enough, the Ugandan army planted the mines in Agoro Hills in late 1998 and early 1999, around the same time Uganda officially ratified the international treaty banning the manufacture and use of landmines (see Landmine Monitor 2001). In early 1999, after twelve people had died in landmine blasts, and several others lost legs as they tried to collect food from their gardens and granaries, the army ordered residents of Agoro Hills to assemble in a camp set up by the UN's World Food Programme. Victims had stepped on landmines on the paths to the gardens, below their granaries, on the doorsteps to their own huts, I was told in Agoro. Even indoors, under the beds, mattresses and in the cooking hearths, the Ugandan army had planted landmines, some victims claimed. Again, the battlefield entered the most private and central domains of Acholi life.

In the perspective of my informants, the landmines planted in Acholiland are lethal weapons without any sense of direction. The mines destroy, maim and kill indiscriminately. Like corruption, they are said 'to be eating people'. In the context of local distress, the mines are powerful symbols that capture the global character of the war. As with the machine gun, the landmine is originally a Western invention and product (cf. Hutchinson 1996: 103, n.1). Obviously, the landmines are not manufactured in Acholiland.[1] On the contrary, informants often stressed, the landmines are of foreign origin, with a foreign character, imported to Acholiland and planted in gardens, on rural roads or even in homesteads. This is also a common interpretation of the conflict that I encountered – today it gets its fuel from elsewhere than Acholiland, adding to the feeling of life with bad surroundings.

'The stump of a pumpkin plant should not be uprooted' *(te okono pe kiputu)* is a proverb with multifarious interpretations, well-known in Acholiland. Some commonly expressed aspects of the proverb are that one should not destroy Acholi traditions; one ought to respect the clan, relatives, elders, ancestors and their shrines. Furthermore, one should not forget about one's old friends when meeting new ones. Then one can always go back, if one were to meet problems in a new place. As is the case with the roots of the pumpkin, so too the roots of culture *(tekwaro pa Acholi)* ought be nourished. Yet the rebels seem to target precisely these traditional values. Clan elders, spirit functionaries, diviners and healers are killed, and ancestor shrines are burnt along with whole villages.

The more than thirty-year-old poems by p'Bitek quoted above, describing the encounters of development and modernisation with the local moral world, seem strikingly up to date regarding the present understanding among informants about the situation in Acholiland.

Arthur, a former rebel, told me more. He is a former religious functionary of the rebels, a so-called *controller.* He was eighteen years old when abducted in 1989, twenty-five when interviewed. He stayed with the rebels for more than one year, the first time very willingly and with great excitement. Right from the initial abduction from his rural home in the middle of the night, the rebels made a great impression on Arthur, with their weapons and military clothes, rugged but well-trained bodies, and dreadlocks hair. In addition, the rites of initiation and the religious observances impressed Arthur. Like many young men around

---

[1] Informants claimed that landmines that the Ugandan army uses are manufactured in government-run facilities in Nakasongola in Luwero in central Uganda, something that is suggested also by Landmine Monitor (2001).

the world, Arthur found it exciting to learn how to crawl in the bush, fight, and handle different types of high technology weapons. At the time, the rebel training camps were located inside Murchison Falls National Park, in the southwest of Acholiland. Thus, this was also the first time for him to see big game such as hippos, elephants and giraffes. He liked it, and he accepted further training to be a *controller*. In the beginning, most battles were easily fought and victorious. It was only later on, when things became tougher and many non-combatants were killed in the fighting, that he decided to defect.

Arthur told me about his experiences as a rebel *controller* in the early 1990s. There may be one to three controllers in each rebel brigade, unarmed, and their function is to protect fellow rebels with holy water, which is kept in small jerry cans and sprinkled from calabashes. As a *controller*, Arthur had been engaged in destroying ancestor shrines. Elders and sprit mediums were also killed. However, some of the ancestor shrines in a particular area were so powerful that it was impossible to burn them down. In one case, his rebel unit tried for three days but they finally had to send for Joseph Kony, the rebel leader, who came and set the shrines on fire. 'It was easily done for him', Arthur said about Kony. 'He is a man with the spirit. He has it.'

When I asked if Joseph Kony does not know the pumpkin proverb, informants argued the contrary. For example, a farmer in his early thirties commented upon a discussion I held with two older men in a compound a few kilometres outside Gulu town, a major town in northern Uganda:

> He knows! Because he is an Acholi, he knows. Why he doesn't follow it, we don't know. He is not following that proverb, because he now has his [own] proverbs, different from Acholi [ones]. And even the pig, the rebels don't eat it. They don't smoke; they don't drink alcohol [like we Acholi do]. (December 1997)

Evidently, according to local understandings, the rebels are not behaving the way Acholi people ought to behave. In my informants' understanding, the seemingly alien behaviour of the LRM/A rebels connects to the military support coming from the Sudanese government, in a deeper sense influenced by Arabic or even Islamic culture. References were drawn to the rebels' policy of not eating pork, to their praying practice of kneeling on mats or plastic coverings, to their strict ban on narcotics, tobacco and alcohol, and to their strategy of killing people who work in their gardens on Fridays. According to the rebels, Fridays as well as Sundays are to be respected as the day of rest and prayers. Informants also claimed the parallel to the mass killings of civilians in Algeria, at the time of my first fieldwork, commonly reported on in Ugandan newspapers. The rebels are behaving just the way the Arabs in Algeria are behaving, informants often rationalised, as they tried to comprehend the present situation in which the vast majority of people killed are unarmed non-combatants. The consequence seems to be the same in northern Uganda as in Algeria, informants imagined.[2]

Parallel to this, but earlier in Acholi history, experiences of slavery, epidemics, diseases and social change have sometimes been interpreted as the coming of powers from outside Acholiland. Examples are *Jok Ala*, the spiritual power of Arab influence, *Jok Omarari/Marin*, the powers of the King's African Rifles (the British

---

[2] Already in the 1980s, Alice Lakwena and the Holy Spirit Movement introduced some of these regulations, e.g. the ban on pork, alcohol and cigarettes, for which they found inspiration in the Bible (see Behrend 1991:168f).

colonial army), and *Jok Rumba* and *Jok Muno*, the powers of European influence (p'Bitek 1971:114ff; Behrend 1999:109f). In retrospect, and in line with the phenomenological anthropology proposed by Jackson (1998:45ff, 108ff), this can be interpreted in existential terms. By engaging and incorporating the unknown, foreign or other, or by framing the alien within the existing cosmological order, one can bring it under control. Eventually, its menace can be disarmed. Yet, in the context of an ongoing crisis, this sense of control is not easily achieved. In the words of a young Gulu man in his mid twenties, 'Earlier in Acholi history foreign spirits have come and created problems and social unrest. But elders usually gathered and found ways to cope with and handle these spirits.' The young man then related this to the present crisis in Acholiland, 'But this time, the militant spirits [of Joseph Kony] came when our society was already disintegrated by war.'

Even though there is no immediate or easy solution to the many years of conflict in northern Uganda, people living there still have to cope with the situation. And life does go on. My informants' description of the situation as one of bad surroundings should not primarily be interpreted as if the local people are without agency, or that Acholi culture is doomed to ruin. Rather, I argue, when they described the bad surroundings, they very vividly defined a moral order against violence and atrocity. It is an effort to act upon the immediate surroundings in order to change them for the better, exemplifying the creation and recreation of the cosmological order in a situation of lived uncertainty and existential crisis. In conceptualising the wider surroundings of the living and the dead and of nature and culture as seriously bad, my informants attempted existentially to comprehend the phenomena of fratricide and cultural and social breakdown, where the outside world tended, however, to blame the local culture. They furthermore aired the hope that the international community would properly address the international dimensions of the conflict. 'Why do your countries in the West send us all these modern weapons?' was the rhetorical question that informants often wanted me to bring back to Sweden. The land-mine, so frequently commented upon and planted almost everywhere in their surroundings, has become a symbol of these wider dimensions. Below I will elaborate upon the international dimension.

A Global War but a Local Battlefield

As mentioned above, the rebel leader Joseph Kony is an Acholi, as are most of his high commanders. However, among the fighters there are also individuals from several other ethnic groups of Uganda. The rebel political wing claims wide co-operation and contacts with 'liberation movements in Karamoja, Soroti, Iganga, Mukono, Mpigi, Bushenyi, Hoima, Kisoro, Kasese (ADF) and now Mbarara, as well as the West Nile Bank Front (WNBF)'. The political wing continues, 'It is the usual ... lie that the LRA is only a remote and insignificant Acholi affair' (Lord's Resistance Movement/Army 1997: 4). According to media reports, former LRM/A commanders verify co-operation with Mengistu's former government of Ethiopia as well as the government of Angola to fight UNITA. As indicated by these alliances, real or imagined, it is difficult to dismiss the conflict in northern Uganda as one of those many African wars essentially localised on unknown peripheries.

Richards argues that the Revolutionary United Front of Sierra Leone was moulded by initiation and creolisation. It was a 'multi-ethnic rather than "tribal" movement' (Richards 1996:84). The same must be said about the LRM/A. Thus, the violent practices of the LRM/A are more likely to be a result of cultural contacts than of ethnic isolation. In mid 2002, Tonny and I encountered displaced people from the camps whose reports suggested that the number of non-Acholi commanders in LRM/A had increased. Over the years, the conflict in northern Uganda has evolved to be increasingly international, even global, in character. In the town of Juba, southern Sudan, the LRM/A has been buying machine guns from Britons, military advice from Americans, anti-tank weapons from Iraq, and landmines from the Sudanese. And as mentioned above, the rebels are also said to possess mines of Italian and Belgian origin, and base camps have been located in southern Sudan. Rebel manifestos can be found on the Internet as well as in the bush, and tapes and videos with the rebel leader's speeches find their way to the Ugandan diaspora.

In another but equally global network, young men displaced to the camps sometimes hire guns from local Ugandan army personnel, guns that have been captured from the rebels but kept hidden from the military authorities in Gulu town. Taking the full risk themselves, the young men then go to the nearby national park to hunt wild game, if successful, a welcome addition to the relief diet. The meat is divided, half the share given to the army as the gun is returned. Westerners working with some of the most acclaimed organisations occasionally buy the meat from the soldiers in the camp. Sometimes the wild game is ferried in NGO vehicles all the way to interested buyers in Kampala, who know little about the jeopardy the young displaced men had put themselves in in the first place. If caught, the young men will be taken for rebels, while the providers of the guns will deny any knowledge about the whole affair.

Inspired by Appadurai's (1991) concept of deterritorialised and globalised 'ethnoscapes', Nordstrom describes the situation in war-torn Mozambique as a 'warscape'. This is accurate also for northern Uganda:

> Foreign strategists, arms, supplies, soldiers, mercenaries, power brokers, and development and interest groups move into a country. Guerrillas and soldiers travel to other countries for training and strategic planning. Refugees and displaced people flow across borders. An international cast of businesspeople and blackmarketeers provides goods and profit from the upheavals of conflict. As these many groups act and interact, local and transnational concerns are enmeshed in the cultural construction of conflict that is continually reconfigured across time and space. Each person, each group brings a history that informs action and is negotiated vis-à-vis the various other histories of those with whom they interact. (Nordstrom 1997:37)

The point here is to acknowledge that 'warscape' realities indeed are global but still violently emplaced in local war zones, as is the case in northern Uganda. In 'warscapes' contemporary experiences meet and intermingle, locality meets and fuses with translocality, the global is manifested in the local, exiles and diaspora groups are involved for political and/or humanitarian reasons, as are Western agents and foreign interest groups, and the character of the particular conflicts constantly evolve, and change, over time. Consequently, I have to conclude that the LRM/A finds inspiration in a global and cross-cultural future rather than in an essentially localised, bounded and primordial ethnic identity or a tribal past (see also Richards 1996:111).

The international dimension of the conflict in Acholiland relates to local understandings, here exemplified by the words of an elderly Acholi man:

> Now, what is taking place now, I think it is well known through the whole world, that Sudan is being fought, and the route is through Uganda. In particular, what one can say, the Government of Uganda and other foreign forces like the Americans are fighting Sudan. And what do you think can stop Sudan from giving dangerous things to Kony, huh? The weapons that the rebels have are of international standard. That is why you can find that even ten rebels can terrorise the army. (Gulu town, January 1998)

Until recently, the Sudanese government has openly supported the LRM/A with logistics and military equipment, and the LRM/A had its base camps in southern Sudan, located close to military installations of the army of the Sudanese government. Former rebels witnessed that the LRM/A camps, located on the very war frontier in Sudan, have functioned as a buffer between the Sudanese army and the rebels of the Sudan People's Liberation Movement/Army (SPLM/A). In return for this support, the LRM/A has been fighting alongside the Sudanese army against rebels in southern Sudan. Child combatants, abducted in their thousands, are used in the front line by the LRM/A, both when fighting in Sudan and in northern Uganda.

The Uganda government for their part have long supported the rebels in southern Sudan. In Ofcansky's (2000:196) words, Uganda and Sudan have been 'engaged in a war of proxies by providing aid and havens to each other's enemies'. In late 1999, the US-based Carter Center facilitated the signing of an agreement between Uganda and Sudan to ease their frosty diplomatic relations, after which most Sudanese support for the LRM/A ceased. The Ugandan government, it seems to me, continues to support the rebels in southern Sudan, by allowing Sudanese rebels to ferry and repair their war machinery on Ugandan soil, or, for example, by facilitating US training and equipping of the Ugandan army and Sudanese rebels on location in northern Uganda (Twaddle & Hansen 1998:6). In early 2000, when talking to one of my co-workers, a Ugandan army officer described it 'like an exchange now', Sudanese rebels coming to Gulu army barracks for 'refreshments courses' and 'our young boys are taken to that side, to take up the positions and maintain the positions [of the Sudanese rebels].' This support is these days officially labelled as 'moral support' only. In December 2001, the global war against terrorism reached Uganda, as the US government included the LRM/A on its list of terrorist groups.

Most of my informants, who saw the US involvement as a great obstacle to peace, dismissed it as yet another variant of Western imperialism. They reacted to the fact that travellers in rural northern Uganda are stopped frequently and forced to unload their entire luggage at military roadblocks, while vehicles of the Sudanese rebels are free to travel on these roads with weaponry and uniformed soldiers. Tonny and I frequently encountered people in the camps and rural trading centres who commented upon the international dimensions of the conflict. With their own eyes, they had seen Sudanese rebels travelling in their home areas and they indeed had explanations as to why the LRM/A has its bases in the Sudan. They knew that the LRM/A is but one among many actors in the violent drama of regional alliances, terrorism and global politics of war. I do not agree with Doom and Vlassenroot (1999:30), therefore, who hold that '[t]he Acholi people at grassroots level can easily identify the dog that bites, but cannot see its master'.

In the late 1980s, the rebels could move freely in the countryside, and also along the main roads. Arthur, the former rebel *controller* introduced above, testified that by then the rebels had a well-established network and supply system in Acholiland, and an intelligence system in the villages making it possible for them to know about the movements of the Ugandan army. However, the increase in brutal atrocities committed by the rebels since the beginning of the 1990s has alienated the movement from the local population. Yet to separate cause from effect is not always an easy task. Suspicion and lack of confidence in the Ugandan army remains, as its passivity and misconduct continues. The increase of violence towards the civil population also relates to local government officials' attempt to set up home guard troops and local defence units (LDUs) in the rural areas in the early 1990s. Even today, rural young men and minors aged as low as ten years are recruited into the local defence, particularly former rebel abductees, who seldom find meaningful positions or assignments in civil society after their return from the bush. Instead of a life of uncertainty and idleness in displacement camps, they are offered, as members of the local defence, a uniform, a weapon and a small salary (less than that of the Ugandan army private, however). Some are recruited by force. The local defence personnel operate in close co-operation with the Ugandan army and are expected to engage rebels, which they do.

The home guards and the local defence units were initially armed with bows, arrows and spears. In the early 1990s this was a compulsory order of the government's local representatives, and all men had to carry *pangas*, spears, or bows and arrows, while every woman was forced to carry at least a knife. Around Gulu municipality, roadblocks were set up, and people who ignored the order were not allowed to pass. Sometimes the authorities closed the market in Gulu town, and forced people to join demonstrations and chant slogans against the rebels. As suggested by Richards (2000), in the perspective of fighting rebels, people in such home guard units or forced demonstrations may easily be seen as government supporters, which consequently turns them into legitimate targets of rebel military violence (see also Behrend 1998:117; Gersony 1997:31). Even villagers who happen to have a spear or only a knife in the hut are now and then accused of having joined the government. To handle the tricky situation, as informants let me know, people generally do not keep such items of everyday use at home but hide them in the nearby bush.

Encampment, Relief and the Rebels' Share

For God and My Life.
(Writing on a hut in Palaro camp, Gulu district)

The writing on the wall in one of the many huts in Palaro camp for the internally displaced is immediately graspable by every Ugandan who happens to read it. It is a direct and remarkable rephrasing of Uganda's national hymn, 'For God and My Country'. Perhaps, it may be suggested, the writer wanted to emphasise a feeling of disconnection or expulsion from the rest of Uganda and its acclaimed developments.

The Ugandan government has responded to insecurity in northern Uganda by forcefully resettling a large number of Acholi in 'protected villages', more accurately described as enormous camps for displaced people. As already mentioned, recent reports estimate the number of internally displaced in Acholiland as some 800,000, or 70 per cent of the Acholi population (Gulu Archdiocese 2003a:3; Human Rights Watch 2003:5). The forced mass movement of people to camps can partly be understood in terms of a military strategy. Locating people in bounded areas with strict curfews made it difficult for the rebels to get intelligence information and move freely in the countryside, but the Ugandan army also took the opportunity to loot foodstuff and other things from the deserted villages. Now and then, the army announces that it will consider people found in the countryside as 'rebels', and thus legitimate targets of military violence by, for example, the feared helicopter gunships. Sometimes, when increased fighting replaces temporary lulls, people are given a 48-hour deadline to move to the camps before the gunships join the rural counterinsurgency. As with landmines, the helicopters kill indiscriminately (see also Gulu Archdiocese 2003b:2ff).

Officially, the camps were created to protect civilians against rebel attacks. In practice, the situation is rather the contrary. 'It is the people protecting the army', camp inhabitants complained, with reference to the most common geographical structure of the 'protected villages'. An army detachment is most often located in the centre of the camp. From this privileged position the army is supposed to protect the thousands of people surrounding it. People found themselves being used as a human 'shield', or *kwot* as they said in Acholi. If a camp comes under rebel attack, the army frequently withdraws and launches grenades from a distance, right into the camp. Still, for the population of the camps there is no easy solution to the situation. Even though they want to leave the camps, they also fear leaving them for the uncertain situation in their home villages deep in the rural areas. A common desire in the camps therefore was that the international community should intervene, arrange and guarantee everyone's safe repatriation (cf. Allen & Turton 1996:1ff; Barrett 1998:36ff). But ironically enough, the UN and other representatives of the international community partly uphold the camp structures. Any international relief is distributed exclusively to camps that are recognised by the Ugandan government (cf. Keen 1998:58ff).

In rural northern Uganda, people often told me that 'you can't plan your life. It is impossible to plan beyond the very day of today. You don't know anything about the coming days.' Any long-term planning is extremely difficult. To arrange social gatherings around the compound or village fire (*wang oo*), children and youth listening to the stories of the seniors, nourishing the roots of culture, is unthinkable. Such gatherings will attract rebels or wartime bandits, people suggested. The bandits are often connected with unscrupulous Ugandan army personnel, it is believed, who provide the weapons, and take advantage of the juridical vacuum that has followed the war.[3]

If people hear noises, shooting and screaming during the night, indicating that rebels or wartime thugs are arriving, they will run into hiding in the bush. 'If you are asleep and you hear people running, you just take off with them', a young man in a displacement camp said. In 2002, as war intensified, I recorded several cases of what people called 'rebel scares'. All the time suspecting rebel attacks, people experienced lessened control over the lived situation. Even the

---

[3] In Acholi, wartime bandits are called *boo kec*, '[the vegetable] boo is bitter', which indicates that such people prefer to loot nice food like meat rather than work hard for an honest living. The insurgency is their cover-up. For the same reasons, they are sometimes called *pit kumi*, 'developing the body'.

most mundane happenings, which people who live in peace may not even reflect upon, can result in rebel scares. In one such case, in the middle of the night, as a thunderstorm was approaching, lightning struck a building in a camp near Gulu town. Some people took it for a rebel attack and fled. As these people fled, more fled with them and some ran all the way to Gulu town. Soldiers from a nearby Ugandan army detachment, on the other side, started to fire into the night, increasing the panic. It was only in the morning hours that people realised that lightning, not rebels, had struck the camp.

In most camps people will hide during the days that follow the relief distributions of the International Red Cross, the Norwegian Refugee Council, the World Food Programme or some other well-known international agency working in the region. The rebels have eyes, camp inhabitants said, and they know when the relief agencies have been in the camps with their big lorries. It will be little more than three days after a distribution before rebels arrive to loot, people argued, with experience in mind.

In my introductory field endeavour in 1997–98, when I had no means of transport of my own, I was given the opportunity to visit several camps together with the International Red Cross. I asked people living there if they thought that rebels would be coming the following night. 'They will not', people responded if I had arrived in a Toyota Land Cruiser but not a loaded lorry, as I did when the organisation was to take the census of the population in the camps. Quite naturally, in taking the census the Red Cross did not use its lorries. However, people in the camps knew that the rebels registered such movements. The rebels would then wait until any of the organisations involved in northern Uganda came back with lorries for an actual distribution of aid.

In a strategy to handle the situation, people in the camps would leave some of the distributed goods in their huts, hide some of it in the bush, and themselves sleep in the bush during the nights following the distribution. If people did not leave something 'on display', as they said, the rebels would search for camp inhabitants and most likely beat them until they found the goods. If the rebels found a cooking pot with remains of newly prepared food they forced camp inhabitants to tell where they had stored the rest of the food. 'We are only coming to take our share', rebels told people. 'To obey is essential', some young male informants in displacement camps told me. Yet, if camp inhabitants hid the goods they had received in several places they hoped that the rebels would loot from one place only.

That rebels are coming for their share is as simple as it is sad. If there were no rebels, there would be no relief distributions. Cynically speaking, the distributions exist because of forced resettlement in camps that have made it difficult for people to grow the food themselves. The camps, in turn, are the consequence of rebel activity, and consequently some of the distributed goods and food belong to the rebels. So rebels say to the people in the camps when they come to loot, and so people in the camps said to me, the anthropologist (cf. Richards 1996:156ff).

Clashes of Interpretation: the Rebels and the Relief

Das and Kleinman (2000) point out that power relations on national and global levels will influence the subjective experience of violence as negotiated in the local moral world. Subjectivity, in this context, is 'the felt interior experience of the person that includes his or her positions in a field of relational power' and it 'is produced through the experience of violence and the manner in which global flows involving images, capital, and people become entangled with local logics in identity formation' (Das and Kleinman 2000:1). In other words, a particular political subjectivity takes form. Complementary to this conclusion, Englund (2002) points out that global power flows, often regarded as disconnected and non-local, imagined by many academics to have a kind of life of their own, actually are concrete and very real, always situated and interpreted in specific contexts, always with an involvement with people's lifeworlds. Actual social networks and exchanges, as well as specific historical circumstances, provide the inescapable 'emplacement' of global forces, to use Englund's (2002) terminology.

A most unfortunate case from northern Uganda illustrates the point. In November 1997 a group of rebels attacked the outskirts of Pabo, which is a trading centre located some twenty-two kilometres north of Gulu town that has been turned into a congested camp with over 47,000 displaced individuals. During the attack, which went unnoticed by the local army personnel supposed to protect the population, rebels stabbed fourteen people to death. Elderly women and men, as well as children and babies, were among the victims. The attack in Pabo seems to be extraordinary in its brutality, without apparent logic or rationality.

However, most often the rebels' violent strategies contain messages to the local people. Rebels had been in Pabo earlier, to loot foodstuff. They had stolen a sack and filled it with beans. When arriving in a rebel camp, the beans were cooked and eaten. However, I was told that eight rebels died after eating the looted food. Surviving rebel commanders then assumed that the stolen sack, in which the beans had been carried, was bewitched and therefore poisonous. The rebel commandant sent a unit of six rebels to Pabo to take revenge on the people responsible for the witchcraft, hence the massacre.

Even if not bewitched, according to Western logic the beans were somehow made poisonous. They were distributed as relief to the people in Pabo, as seeds to be planted. As seeds they were chemically treated, something that might have made the people eating them sick or even to die. Beans are vulnerable to insect pests and so are often treated with insecticide. Beans might also contain high levels of cyanide, which makes it important to prepare them carefully, with long cooking. However, looted food is often prepared in haste, and it is indeed possible that people under pressure, such as rebels in a hurry, unintentionally poisoned themselves.

To observe that the rebels often have their own explanations and interpretations for their actions is not to excuse their terror. But the observation highlights that international relief, most often said to be neutral and humanitarian only, immediately becomes entangled with the practices and politics of war. This obviously happens in northern Uganda as well as in southern Sudan, to mention a close-by but better-known example. As one commentator notes, 'In Northern Uganda and Southern Sudan voluntary aid organisations have virtually operated as local administrators, co-ordinating and planning activities' (Hulme quoted in Riehl 2001:4). But as these organisations have taken over many of the functions of the government, they will also be perceived, as the government is, as a parallel partner to the Ugandan army. Seldom, therefore, can aid and humanitarian efforts by the international community be neutral in the eyes of the locals (see Richards 1996:157). For example, when a truck from the United Nations World Food Programme, drove through Gulu town loaded with armed and uniformed government troops, people in the town just shrugged their shoulders. The incident was not without implications. When I asked about the lorry, people related it to the wider international context, where the UN and the international community are said to be allied with the Ugandan government, but also with political actors such as the United States and the rebels of southern Sudan. The objective of such an alliance, informants along the street argued, is to counter the alleged expanding Islamism of the Arabs, and more recently, global terrorism. This is done with Uganda and more particularly Acholiland as the necessary stepping-stone. Standing in opposition to this political body are not only the LRM/A and the Sudanese government, but also the sufferings of the Acholi people, who have found their homeland turned into a battlefield and an arena of international politics. The LRM/A rebels, for their part, do not hesitate to ambush the United Nations, the World Food Programme, UNICEF or the various NGOs working in the area. In an Internet press release the rebels accuse the UN and UNICEF of providing 'poison food aid to the northern population...' (Lord's Resistance Movement/Army 2001).

For God and My Life? A Conclusion

'No change' is the political slogan of President Museveni, well known all over Uganda. At the beginning of this chapter, I note that Museveni's capture of Kampala in 1986 marked the starting point of several armed conflicts in Uganda, also in the northern region. Ever since, Museveni's uncompromising dismissal of the LRM/A rebels, and the rebels' equally militant determination to continue the war, never seem to change, my informants often concluded. And, as Doom and Vlassenroot (1999:28) write, 'Each attack by the LRA is undermining the president's position, because it is seen as a demonstration of his lack of power or his unwillingness to turn Acholi-land into a safe haven.' As a Ugandan friend once put it, dryly paraphrasing Museveni's slogan, 'People are tired. We are voting and voting, but nothing happens. There will never be any change.' Or as a young man said, again with an ironic reference to the slogan of the incumbent, 'People have no change from their problems.'

In northern Uganda, as in many other war-torn settings, lasting peace will not simply equal the signing of any agreement. Peace – a life without pressure as some informants described it – remains to be established also in the most mundane routines of everyday life. Only then may the bad surroundings (*piny marac*) develop toward good, fertile and prosperous surroundings (*piny maber*). To the Acholi, good surroundings are not only the *absence* of war. More importantly, they manifest balance in societal, cultural and economic life. Balance, in this understanding, does not imply any golden tradition of static harmony, but an ongoing intersubjective dialectic so that fate and even the future may be controlled or governed (cf. Jackson 1998:18ff). Peaceful life can be infested with conflicts and frustrations, but in the peaceful order of things, problems are handled, strategies beyond mere survival are developed, life is continuously constituted and reconstituted. It is as in war, as I illustrate above, only with less difficulty. As Okot p'Bitek (1986:27) writes, good surroundings refer to 'when things are normal, the society thriving, facing and overcoming crises'. This is a realisation of the human condition. Going from bad to good surroundings, from war to peace, is a long process, a continuum – rather than involving an essential or even illusory break between two absolute, defined and definite conditions of human life.

Eventually, when the surroundings change for the better, people will leave the desperate congestion of the camps and be better able to face the problems of quotidian life. By then the displaced family's version of the Ugandan national hymn, 'For God and My Life', may again be expressed as the more all-embracing original, 'For God and My Country'. In facilitating this, I suggest, we need to investigate how people in war-torn Uganda act upon their immediate and wider surroundings, as they try to understand not only violent rebel practices, but also international involvement. Rather than suggest that '[t]he Acholi people at grassroots level can easily identify the dog that bites, but cannot see its master' (Doom & Vlassenroot 1999:30), I propose that we seriously ask people at the grassroots levels who they identify as the masters of the dog, and why.

References

Allen, Tim and Turton, David. 1996, 'Introduction: In search of cool ground' in Allen, Tim ed., *In search of cool ground: War, flight and homecoming in northeast Africa* London: UNRISD/James Currey

Amnesty International. 1992, *Uganda: The failure to safeguard human rights* London: Amnesty International

Amnesty International. 1997, 'Breaking God's Commands': The destruction of childhood by the Lord's Resistance Army'. Amnesty International Country Report, AFR 59/01/97 (PDF version downloaded 10 Sept. 2002). Available online: <http://www.web.amnesty.org/ai.nsf/index/AFR590011997> Email: <amnestyis@amnesty.org>

Appadurai, Arjun. 1991, 'Global ethnoscapes: Notes and queries for a transnational anthropology' in Fox, Richard G. ed., *Recapturing anthropology: Working in the present* Santa Fe, NM: School of American Research Press

Barrett, Michael. 1998, 'Tuvosena: "Let's go everybody." Identity and ambition among Angolan refugees in Zambia' Uppsala: Department of Cultural Anthropology, Uppsala University (Working Papers in Cultural Anthropology No 8)

Bayart, Jean-François, Ellis, Stephen & Hibou, Béatrice. 1999, *The criminalization of the state in Africa* Oxford & Bloomington: International African Institute/James Currey/Indiana University Press

Behrend, Heike. 1991, 'Is Alice Lakwena a witch? The Holy Spirit Movement and its fight against evil in the north of Uganda' in Hansen, Holger Bernt and Twaddle, Michael eds *Changing Uganda: The dilemmas of structural adjustment and revolutionary change* London, Kampala, Athens, OH & Nairobi: James Currey/Fountain Press/Ohio University Press/Heinemann Kenya

—— 1998, 'War in northern Uganda: The Holy Spirit Movements of Alice Lakwena, Severino Lukoya & Joseph Kony (1986–1997)' in Clapham, Christopher ed. *African guerrillas* Oxford, Kampala & Bloomington: James Currey/Fountain Press/Indiana University Press

—— 1999. *Alice Lakwena & the holy spirits: War in northern Uganda, 1985–97* Oxford, Kampala, Nairobi & Athens, OH: James Currey/Fountain Publishers/E.A.E.P./Ohio University Press

Brett, E. A. 1995, 'Neutralising the use of force in Uganda: The role of the military in politics' *Journal of Modern African Studies* 33 (1): 129–52

Das, Veena and Kleinman, A. 2000, 'Introduction' in Das, V. et al. eds *Violence and subjectivity* Berkeley: University of California Press

Doom, Ruddy and Vlassenroot, Koen 1999, 'Kony's message: A new Koine? The Lord's Resistance Army in northern Uganda' *African Affairs* 98 (390): 5–36.

Englund, Harri. 2002. 'Ethnography after globalism: Migration and emplacement in Malawi' *American Ethnologist* 29 (2): 261–86

Finnström, Sverker. 2001, 'In and out of culture: Fieldwork in war-torn Uganda' *Critique of Anthropology* 21 (3): 247–58

—— 2003, 'Living with bad surroundings: War and existential uncertainty in Acholiland, northern Uganda' Uppsala: Acta Universitatis Upsaliensis/Uppsala Studies in Cultural Anthropology, vol. 35

Galtung, Johan. 1969, 'Violence, peace and peace research' *Journal of Peace Research* 6 (3): 167–91

Gersony, Robert. 1997, 'The anguish of northern Uganda: Results of a field-based assessment of the civil conflict in northern Uganda' Kampala: Report submitted to United States Embassy, Kampala, and USAID, Kampala

Gulu Archdiocese. 2003a, 'Justice and peace news February 2003' *Justice and Peace News. A monthly newsletter of the Justice and Peace Commission of Gulu Archdiocese*. 2 (8)

Gulu Archdiocese. 2003b, 'Justice and peace news March 2003' *Justice and Peace News. A monthly newsletter of the Justice and Peace Commission of Gulu Archdiocese*. 2 (10)

Hansen, Holger Bernt and Twaddle, M. 1994. 'The issues' in Hansen, Holger Bernt and Twaddle, M. eds *From chaos to order: The politics of constitution-making in Uganda* Kampala & London: Fountain Publishers/James Currey

Human Rights Watch. 1997. *The scars of death: Children abducted by the Lord's Resistance Army in Uganda* New York: Human Rights Watch

Human Rights Watch. 2003, 'Stolen children: Abduction and recruitment in northern Uganda' (PDF version downloaded 31 March 2003). Available online: <http://hrw.org/reports/2003/uganda0303/> Email: <hrwnyc@hrw.org>

Hutchinson, Sharon Elaine. 1996, *Nuer dilemmas: Coping with money, war, and the state* Berkeley: University of California Press

Jackson, Michael. 1998, *Minima ethnographica: Intersubjectivity and the anthropological project* Chicago & London: University of Chicago Press

Keen, David. 1998. *The economic functions of violence in civil wars* Oxford & New York: Oxford University Press (The International Institute for Strategic Studies, Adelphi Paper 320)

Lamwaka, Caroline. 1998, 'Civil war and the peace process in Uganda, 1986–1997' *East African Journal of Peace and Human Rights* 4 (2): 139–69

Landmine Monitor. 2001, 'Landmine Monitor report 2001: Toward a mine-free world. Uganda' (downloaded February 26, 2002). Available online: <http://www.icbl.org/lm/2001/uganda/> Email: <lm@icbl.org>

Lord's Resistance Movement/Army. 1997, 'A case for national reconciliation, peace, democracy and economic prosperity for all Ugandans: The official presentation of the Lord's Resistance Movement/Army (LRM/A), by Dr. James Alfred Obita, secretary for external affairs and mobilisation, and leader of delegation' (paper presented at Kacoke Madit, London 5–6 April 1997, PDF version downloaded 15 April 2002). Available online: <http://www.c-r.org/km/> Email: <km@c-r.org>

Lord's Resistance Movement/Army. 2001. 'Unicef determined to finish the people of northern Uganda' Press release May 2001 (downloaded 12 June 2001). Available online: <http://www.spacegroove.com/joesphkony/> Email: <aoloya@hotmail.com>

Ngoga, Pascal. 1998, 'Uganda: The National Resistance Army' in Clapham, Christopher ed.. *African guerrillas* Oxford, Kampala & Bloomington: James Currey/Fountain Press/Indiana University Press

Nordstrom, Carolyn. 1997, *A different kind of war story*. Philadelphia: University of Pennsylvania Press

Ofcansky, Thomas P. 2000, 'Warfare and instability along the Sudan-Uganda border: A look at the 20th century' in Spaulding, Jay and Beswick, Stephanie eds *White Nile, black blood: War, leadership, and ethnicity from Khartoum to Kampala* Asmara: The Red Sea Press, Inc

p'Bitek, Okot. 1966, *Song of Lawino* Nairobi: East African Publishing House

—— 1970, *Song of Ocol* Nairobi: East African Publishing House

—— 1971, *Religion of the central Luo* Nairobi: East African Literature Bureau

—— 1986, *Artist, the ruler: Essays on art, culture, and values* Nairobi: Heinemann Kenya

Richards, Paul. 1996, *Fighting for the rain forest: War, youth & resources in Sierra Leone* Oxford & Portsmouth, NH: James Currey and Heinemann for The International African Institute

Richards, Paul. 2000, 'Rain-forest resource conflicts: would stakeholder analysis help pacify labouring casuals in Sierra Leone?' in Wiersum, K.F. ed. *Tropical forest resource dynamics and conservation: from local to global issues* Tropical Resource Management Paper, no. 33. Wageningen: Wageningen University

Riehl, Volker. 2001, *Who is ruling in south Sudan? The role of NGOs in rebuilding socio-political order* Uppsala: Nordic Africa Institute (Studies on emergencies and disaster relief, report no 9)

Sponsel, Leslie E. 1994, 'The mutual relevance of anthropology and peace studies' in Sponsel, Leslie E. and Thomas, Gregor eds. *The anthropology of peace and nonviolence* Boulder: Lynne Rienner Publishers

Twaddle, Michael and Hansen, Holger Bernt. 1998, 'The changing state of Uganda' in Hansen, H. B. and Twaddle, M. eds *Developing Uganda* Oxford, Kampala, Athens, OH & Nairobi: James Currey/

Fountain Publishers/Ohio University Press/E.A.E.P

Wallensteen, Peter and Sollenberg, Margareta. 2001. 'Armed conflict, 1989–2000' *Journal of Peace Research*. 38 (5): 629–44

Woodward, Peter. 1991, 'Uganda and southern Sudan 1986–9: New regimes and peripheral politics' in Hansen, H. B. and Twaddle, M. eds. *Changing Uganda: The dilemmas of structural adjustment and revolutionary change* London, Kampala, Athens, OH & Nairobi: James Currey/Fountain Press/Ohio University Press/Heinemann Kenya

Acknowledgements

Fieldwork was conducted in northern Uganda in 1997–98, 1999–2000 and 2002, a total of 12 months. In the fieldwork endeavour, I worked in close co-operation with Anthony Odiya Labol. Without Tonny, nothing. *Omera madit, apwoyo matek!* I also want to thank Helena Edin for never-ending support. The research was financed by the Swedish International Development Cooperation Agency, the Swedish Council for Research in the Humanities and Social Sciences, Olof Palme's Memorial Trust for International Understanding and Mutual Security, Lars Hierta's Memorial Trust, and Helge Axson Johnson's Trust.

7

Making War, Crafting Peace
Militia Solidarities & Demobilisation in Sierra Leone

CASPAR FITHEN & PAUL RICHARDS

Introduction

Viewed conventionally, war is a period in which organised, socially-sanctioned, violence is used by opposing sides for specific strategic ends. Peace arrives when one side attains its objectives, or compromise is reached. Social normality is then re-asserted. The displaced resume their place in a society recognisably continuous with that disrupted by war. Disarmament, demobilisation and reintegration (henceforth DDR) prepares ex-combatants (in some way or other) to return home. The processual view of war (and peace) developed in this book offers a different perspective. If the roots of conflict are to be found in pre-war society, sending ex-combatants home risks rekindling hostility. Bearing such a possibility in mind, two questions become important. Is post-war society changing in ways amenable to the peaceful absorption of ex-combatants? Second, do ex-combatants have social skills or knowledge (perhaps formed in war itself) to contribute to the shaping of a new, more stable post-war society. In short, a 'no peace, no war' perspective is less concerned with reintegration than with societal trans-formations embracing ex-combatants and civilians alike.

The civil war in Sierra Leone (1991–2002) mobilised young people margin-alised by poverty, educational disadvantage, and injustice (Richards 1996). If social exclusion was a cause of war then peace requires society to be reformed along more inclusive lines. Civilian recognition that reintegration of ex-combatants into unreformed communities risks reproducing conditions causing war has been discussed elsewhere (Archibald and Richards 2002). The present essay focuses on the fighting factions, and asks what social lessons combatants may have learnt during armed conflict, and whether any of this constitutes 'social capital' relevant to the making of post-war society.

Analytically, we probe variations in combat task group cultures (McFeat 1972). Specifically, links are traced between organisation, cooperation and solidarity in two militia groups. A specific interest is what happens when group solidarities are threatened by operational failure. Here our interpretation draws on a neo-Durkheimian typology of forms of social solidarity (Douglas and Ney 1998). Much of the pattern of violence in this war, we argue, can be related, functionally, to the formation of, and changes in, group values under various combat contingencies. Lack of understanding of the fragile and peculiar solidarities of the rebel Revolutionary United Front (henceforth RUF) was one of the reasons an initial (1996) peace process failed, plunging the country into a vicious cycle of atrocity and revenge killing (1997-99). We question the conclusion of Shearer (1997) that pressure from international private security companies reinforced momentum towards peace. Such pressure, we argue, plunged the egalitarian RUF into a crisis of a kind more normally associated with slave revolts, or the last days of failing millenarian sects. Our analysis points to ways in which descent into fatalist violence might have been avoided. A negotiated end to hostilities was agreed in November 2000, and since that date there has been extensive DDR, involving both the RUF and the pro-government Civil Defence Forces (henceforth CDF). A postscript (May 2003) reflects on the extent to which, through DDR, militia solidarities have been transformed into resources for peace.

Task-group Solidarities (a neo-Durkheimian Perspective)

How can we grasp the 'mutually supportive relationship between a structure of organisation and a set of values and beliefs'? (Hood 1998). Neo-Durkheimian theorists (e.g. Douglas 1996) propose a helpful schematic, the grid-group diagram, to capture a range of possible associations between organisation and group values. *Grid* is the extent to which people see themselves as 'locked in' by rules and undertakings. *Group* refers to the intensity of social bonding. The grid-group scheme helps chart a mid-course between post-modernism, where there can be as many solidarities as people choose, since nothing is real, and the world as conceived by neo-liberals, for whom there is a stark choice between only two realities – hierarchy (authoritarianism) and individual freedom (or states and markets). The grid-group scheme offers a four-dimensional world of social solidarities, with many specific compromises and trade-offs between the four main positions.[1]

In grid-group terms *individualistic (entrepreneurial) cultures* are low in both authority and bonding, and *hierarchical cultures* are both strongly constrained and strongly bonded. What happens where there is low constraint but high bonding? This is the sector of the grid in which *sectarian* organisations tend to cluster. A useful term is *enclave*, to avoid the implication that sectarian organisations of this sort are somehow exclusively religious phenomena (Douglas 1993; Sivan 1995). Enclavists espouse egalitarian notions about distribution of social as well as material goods (e.g. offices may be rotated or assets held in common). Lacking internal status differentiation and clear executive leadership, enclave groups tend to depend on some kind of 'wall' to defend themselves against the world, and crossing this barrier incurs high entry and exit costs.[2] The fourth sector of the grid – high authority, low bonding – is a neglected area, but important for our analysis. Its value set has been labelled *isolate*, or *fatalist*. People are joined in a kind of anti-solidarity – a shoulder-shrugging acceptance that 'nothing can be

---

[1] The schematic derives from Durkheim (1956 [1897]), hence neo-Durkheimian analysis. On the significance of Durkheim for the stand-off between post-modern and neo-liberal perspectives see Mestrovic (1992), Stedman-Jones (2001).

[2] Enclavists worry about defection of members and being undermined through penetration of the enclave by non-members.

done'. One response is to knuckle down and endure. Another is to hasten the end of an unendurable world (perhaps in the hope of forcing divine intervention). Extreme (suicidal) violence ensues (Bromley 1997, Sundquist 1993).

Neo-Durkheimian analysts sometimes remark on an apparent 'opposition' of diagonal elements in the grid-group diagram. It is as if individualism was the special enemy of hierarchy, and fatalism the nemesis of egalitarianism. The army has no use for soldiers who think for themselves, only those who jump to command. But equally the enclavists appear to realise that the peculiar energy animating the commune is especially problematic where the strongly-bonded begin to lose their faith. Collapse into collective despondency seems a greater risk than dissidence and the multiplication of viewpoints. Perhaps we should view the spaces of the grid-group diagram as unequal. There is – as Douglas (2001) implies – something special about hierarchy. It is necessary in extreme circumstances, and none is more extreme than the need to manage military violence. The enclave, by contrast, is often a particular response to prior experience of social exclusion. It appeals to those most oppressed by dysfunctional hierarchy. There is an ever present danger, however, of the vision perishing, and collapse into inchoate rage. On this account, individualism is a kind of default condition – the freedom of action we enjoy when things go well. It is perhaps unsurprising that some social theorists elevate it to normative status. The problem is how to ensure things go well.

Our chapter outlines specific circumstances in which enclave solidarities in Sierra Leone gave way to isolate attitudes and patterns of violence. We contrast the collapse of the rebel RUF into group fatalism with the break-up of the (weak) hierarchy of the CDF into individualistic, entrepreneurial forms of violence. The challenge for DDR is to find effective ways of dealing with ex-combatants who have experienced these rather different kinds of task-group dynamics, and to ensure alignment with a civil society undergoing its own major changes of organisation and values as a result of more than a decade of dislocation and conflict.

The Failure of Patrimonial Solidarity

One of the predominant notions of social solidarity and social reproduction in Sierra Leone is that of patrimonialism. Its roots lie in the pre-colonial period. Warrior chiefs controlling rival trade networks built up large followings of retainers and protected clients, many first acquired as slaves in war. British colonialism nearly foundered when chiefs in the interior of the south and east of the country suspected that colonial law (The Protectorate Ordinance of 1896) was about to deprive them of slaves whose labour power was the basis of their wealth. Anxious to avoid any recurrence of a chiefly rebellion in 1898 the British hesitated to abolish domestic slavery until pressured by the League of Nations in 1927. At the point they were declared free by law (1 January 1928) up to 50 per cent of rural populations in districts bordering Liberia were slaves (Grace 1977). Grace notes that slavery cases (e.g. reclaiming runaways) were still vigorously pursued in chiefdom courts in Pujehun District in the 1920s. Many slaves laboured on farms and plantations stimulated by the building of a government railway. It is perhaps not accidental that the RUF rebellion was most intense in those districts (i.e. the chiefdoms bordering Liberia) where domestic slavery lasted longest.

The Sierra Leone War, 1991–2002

*   *Origins of the Revolutionary United Front (RUF).* Rebellion emerges from West African radical debate over Museveni's 'people's army' in Uganda (Yeebo 1991). Crushing of student movement by the All People's Congress (APC) regime of Siaka Stevens (1977, 1986). Leaders exiled. Some 35–50 reach Libya for guerrilla training (Abdullah 1997). A handful reappear as RUF activists in 1991.

*   *RUF incursion (March-September 1991).* President Momoh slow to deploy army against rebel movement he suspects is in league with banned Sierra Leone People's Party (SLPP), still strongly supported in south and east of country. Ill-supplied government forces, reinforced by Guinean troops and local irregulars, secure a strategic axis from Daru to Joru in mid-1991, and prevent RUF from linking across south and east. Officers fighting war plan a coup, contact RUF about sharing power.

*   *NPRC coup (April 1992).* Momoh regime collapses, after junior officers from the war front, protesting pay and conditions, take control of Freetown, to wide popular acclaim. National Provisional Ruling Council is formed, and repudiates RUF. RUF vows to continue war, but is dislodged from strongholds, except for an enclave in the Gola Forest, by enlarged and better supplied RSLMF, 1992–3.

*   *RUF Phase Two offensive (1994–95).* RUF builds forest camps to train teenage cadres and abductees. Re-supplied from raids on army stores starts new offensive mid-1994. Far-flung raids disguised as work of disloyal army units, spreading panic in capital and countryside. Offensive has mixed results. Many assume violence the work of army dissidents. NPRC chairman offers ceasefire, initiates peace talks, agrees elections, but RUF is excluded from elections.

*   *Democratic transition & Abidjan peace accord (1996):* election won by Ahmad Tejan-Kabbah, leader of SLPP. Kabbah renews ceasefire, begins peace talks with RUF in Abidjan. Army is stood down, but enlarged civil defence attacks RUF bases, assisted by Executive Outcomes (EO), during peace talks. RUF signs Abidjan accords (30 November 1996), but leadership is unable to reach field commanders, scattered by CDF attacks.

*   *Army revolt (May 1998).* Distrusting an army (RSLMF) still dominated by officers loyal to Momoh, SLPP prefers CDF under the leadership of the deputy minister of defence. Sidelined from peace process, elements in the regular army mount a coup, drive the government into exile, and invite the RUF to join power sharing regime (Armed Forces Revolutionary Council). AFRC shunned internationally.

- *Restoration of Kabbah (February–March 1998).* Nigerian-led (ECOMOG) peace keepers drive AFRC from power, February 1998. RUF and AFRC retreat, regain strongholds in Kailahun District. Restocked during AFRC rule, Buedu base serves as refuge, with supply lines to Liberia.

- *RUF/AFRC bush war (1998–99).* RUF/AFRC fighters receive arms and training from international mineral and arms supply consortium (East European, Israeli and South African) modelled after EO, aided by lax regional arms and air traffic control (UN experts 2000). RUF/AFRC attack Freetown January 1999, repulsed by Nigerian troops. Nigerian president-elect vows to withdraw ECOMOG contingent. Scandal erupts in UK over private security support for Kabbah government by British company (Sandline) succeeding EO. New peace process begun by a Kabbah regime short of options.

- *Lomé peace accords (July 1999).* RUF offered role in a short-lived power-sharing government (1999-2000). Sankoh becomes chairman of a national minerals authority. Poor initial terms offered to AFRC, but junta leader (Johnny-Paul Koroma) brought into agreement October 1999.

- *Collapse of Lomé accords (May 2000).* ECOMOG withdraws April 2000, RUF abducts UN replacements. Government jails RUF leaders. RUF guns down demonstrators. Johnny-Paul Koroma backs elected government against RUF. Britain deploys troops to reinforce UN positions. Abuja agreements (late 2000) lead to full UN deployment in RUF territory.

- *UN confidence building (February–March 2001)* Fear of extermination once fuelled RUF intransigence. Better advice now prevails. UN troops undertake proper confidence building measures, leading to commencement of DDR process in 2001. Disarmament begins. About 70,000 combatants disarmed by end of year and await skills training.

- *Peace finally declared (January 2002).* Peace is accompanied by acceptance that war had social causes. A Freetown commentator remarks 'ours is not just a history of a few crack-heads taking guns... shooting and amputating...; ours embodies a history of long years of injustice in a highly impoverished society...' ('Still groping in the dark.' *Concord Times*, 2 May 2001)

British-supervised 'Indirect Rule' (rule by chiefs) fostered a variety of arrangements through which 'domestic slavery' became benign, but these arrangements did little to encourage former slaves to develop a wider national or civic outlook.[3] The British view was that slavery was dying a natural death. But slave-owners were ingenious in tying their former slaves to the land, to counteract the attraction of paid work. One instance was a system of imposing fines on young men (who could not afford to marry) for interfering with the wives of chiefly polygynists ('woman damage'). These fines were often commuted into labour service, with the result that many young men found themselves continuing to work without wages on the farms of chiefs, even though nominally free (cf. Holsoe 1977). In recent discussions many villagers cite heavy fines – for various torts, including 'woman damage', originally sanctioned by the British as part of 'native law' (Fenton 1948), but inflated arbitrarily in the post-colonial period – as being among the main reasons why young men became 'outlaws' in the diamond fields, some later enrolling in the RUF (Archibald and Richards 2002, Richards and Vlassenroot 2002).

A discourse continues to resonate among the propertied classes about these youths. The RUF is widely condemned as a movement of 'rarrays' (footloose youth) or 'lumpens' (Abdullah 1997). Migrants to the diamond districts are typical 'rarrays' according to stereotype, feckless proto-criminals in search of quick wealth, hence an international perception the war is more about 'greed' than 'grievance' (Collier 2000, Smillie et al. 2000). In their own eyes, however, these footloose youths are simply trying to find waged work, where to remain in a rural community risks the arbitrary labour demands of the chiefly classes.[4]

Patrimonialism tried to provide a (post-slavery) framework for the incorporation of young people less inclined to challenge the values of chiefly rule. The basic idea is that of forming an orderly queue for emancipatory resources. Under patrimonial notions of solidarity a 'big man' or 'chief' looks after and protects the 'little' people on a personalised basis. Followers look up to their patron as to a father, treating his duty to protect as a moral or familial obligation. The 'big man' in turn expects 'family' loyalty from clients. To let down clients or switch patrons is like failing to provide for a child or attempting to 'divorce' a parent (it happens, but is a 'sin'). Patrons are linked vertically. As Mende people say 'no one stands by him or herself, everyone is behind someone' (i.e. every local patron enjoys the protection of a patron higher in the system). A loose vertically-integrated hierarchy results. The main branches of this (inverted) 'tree' at times take on 'ethnic' colourings.

In broad terms, our argument is that the war in Sierra Leone was a product of the failure of patrimonial hierarchy (Richards 1996; 2003). Patrimonialism promises inter-generational transfer of capacity through 'sponsorship'. But sponsorship – for education and jobs – is particularistic. It does not combine well with the demands of modern technological society for advancement according to ability. In contemporary Africa, it also runs into a logistical problem. Systems of sponsorship are bankrupted by sheer numbers of applicants. In a continent where more than half the population is under the age of eighteen, militia mobilisation

---

[3] In general, British colonialism in Africa created 'subjects' not 'citizens' (Mamdani 1996).

[4] For detailed evidence see Archibald and Richards (2002). It is clear, in fact, that diamond pit labourers, far from bettering their position, are among the most exploited artisanal workers in the country (OTI 2000; Zack-Williams 1995).

mops up young people lacking other jobs. But it is only a temporary solution, unless it triggers far-reaching political change (as in Museveni's Uganda), because the predation is unsustainable. As will be indicated, the RUF was never able to turn its vision of a fairer system for young people without patrimonial support into political gains. To some extent DDR – through an emphasis on skills – has succeeded where war failed. It buys time for political reforms (de-emphasis of 'vertical' solidarities, and support for stronger 'horizontal' linkages based on common livelihoods-based interests) needed to consolidate a just peace and break cycles of social exclusion and enclavisation.[5]

The RUF – the rise and fall of a secular sect

The RUF represents a paradox. It claimed to have ambitions for a more just society, and yet ended up a random and arbitrary killing machine. The armed sect is an inherently dangerous mechanism. Neo-Durkheimian theory predicts a fundamental incompatibility between attempts at an egalitarian mode of organ-isation and the need for strong (central) control of military means. Collapse into fatalistic violence and random killing is a development which might have been foreseen by opponents of the RUF, had they been less busy denying the move-ment's reasons to exist. Thus we will argue that the violent paranoia of the RUF was also a product of inappropriate strategies adopted against it.

The political ambitions of the RUF were real. In particular, the movement identified the problems of Sierra Leone as those of failing patrimonial hierarchy. Foday Sankoh, in charge of ideological training, Pendembu Base 1991, stated the problem to be 'a country in which those with qualifications have no jobs, and those with jobs have no qualifications' (Richards et al. 1997). The contradictions between patrimonialism and meritocracy could be put no more clearly. The movement appealed to those upon whom the brunt of patrimonial failure fell: young people in the diamond pits and failing schools of the eastern forests. The children of a political elite, fed by diamond wealth, enjoyed superior education overseas, while local schools fell apart and teachers remained unpaid. Cadres dreamed of a fairer, more inclusive, system where hard work and ability would determine success.

Recent accounts (Peters 2002) make clear the extent these were (for RUF ex-combatants) real reasons to fight. One male rebel fighter joined 'to overthrow the APC government because they exploited the people and were taking all the money to Europe to build mighty houses or buy luxurious cars and forgetting about the youth...'. A 23-year old woman 'joined the rebels purposely because of difficulties we were having; we were suffering too much; the RUF was encouraging us to help ... so that later we could enjoy a proper life'. She also noted there were seven girls and 13 boys in her village who joined the RUF willingly. 'The main reason', she added, 'was the lack of job facilities and lack of encouragement for the youth.' Civilians and CDF equally firmly believe young people joined the RUF because of lack of jobs and social marginalisation (Archi-bald and Richards 2002, cf. Peters and Richards 1998, Peters 2002). Some CDF

---

[5] Vertical and horizontal is, in effect, the distinction Durkheim (1964 [1893]) draws between 'mechanical' and 'organic' solidarities.

fighters imply it was largely chance they, themselves, ended up fighting for the other side.

The initial approach of the RUF to the social exclusion of marginalised young Sierra Leoneans was guided by the Green Book of Col. Gaddafi.[6] This text of egalitarian populism was widely known among students and school children in Sierra Leone. Foday Sankoh, a photographer with a clientele among young diamond miners, joined a Green Book study group while plying his trade in Bo in the 1980s. In early contacts with the international media Sankoh made clear he spoke on behalf of a (Green Book-inspired) leadership collective. In this early stage of the military campaign the RUF was dependent on Liberian and Burkinabe 'special forces'. Some may have been Green Book ideologues. Others, however, were soldiers of fortune, battle-hardened by periods of service in the Liberian war (from 1989). Atrocities against villagers with whom the mercenaries had few if any ties (not even language – some of the fighters spoke more French than Krio) shocked even the RUF leadership (RUF/SL 1995). This element was dismissed by the movement in March 1992, but not before losing the RUF much potential support in the countryside. (Along the Liberian border the RUF initially had been welcomed by populations deeply alienated from the APC regime.) Thereafter, the hard core of the RUF comprised mainly young volunteers from the more remote parts of Kailahun and Pujehun Districts, many of whom had been encouraged by parents to join. But expanding nationally, as stories of atrocities spread, the movement quickly ran out of willing adherents, and was forced to recruit mainly by capture. Many of the captives (including children of primary school age) responded to the movement's ideological instruction. Those who remained unconvinced were mainly used as labourers. Branded as belonging to the RUF, persistent absconders were killed, either by the movement, or by government troops.[7] Adults were harder to convince than children. Even so, Sankoh and the leadership set great store that they would 'convert' captured government troops and civilians held as hostages (Peters and Richards 1998).

RUF egalitarianism intensified during its self-declared Phase Two campaign (1993–96). Dislodged from Pendembu and other settlements in Kailahun District by RSLMF troops in 1992–3, the leadership, sheltering in the forests of Nomo Chiefdom (Gola North and East Forest Reserves), reinvented the RUF as a survivalist movement with the help of cadres trained as teachers at Bunumbu College (Kailahun District). A UN-aided programme at Bunumbu in the 1980s had prepared primary school teachers to use the forest as a source of lesson materials when other facilities were unavailable. Taking these lessons to heart, the RUF established a network of 'self-sufficient' forest camps centred on the 'Zogoda', a secure locale in the southern extremity of the Kambui West Forest Reserve (Barri Chiefdom). The camps became vast outdoor schools-cum-military training facilities for increasing numbers of captive children.

Operating along bush tracks hardly known to the army, the cadres secured Bunumbu itself, and a swathe of territory behind Segbwema, which became RUF

---

[6] This extended to considerable gender equality in training of fighters. RUF fighting forces were, at maximum, about 25–30,000 of which as many as 5000 may have been women. The question of why so many female combatants seem to be missing from DDR is briefly examined in a discussion of gender aspects of demobilisation in the postscript.

[7] Summary execution of abductees suspected of collaborating with the RUF by government forces (Amnesty International 1992) made it easier for the movement to motivate its captives.

heartland for the duration of the war. Bunumbu controls routes from Kailahun District and the Liberian border to the diamond fields, and RUF units were soon raiding diamond-rich Lower Bambara Chiefdom from a forward camp (Peyeima) located between Bunumbu and Tongo Field. This in turn gave access to the extensive forested hilly terrain linking the Kono diamond fields and the diamond mining country around Boajibu and Tungie, from where Camp Bokor was established in the Kangari Hills more or less in the exact centre of the country. This became a major camp threatening both the town of Bo, and the main motorable route from Freetown to the Kono diamond fields along which much of the country's diamond wealth flowed.

Camp life developed a number of classic features of the enclave or closed sect (Douglas 1993, Richards 2004). Movements were strictly controlled, and harsh punishments (including death) meted out to would-be 'free movers'. Distribution of goods – notably basic medical supplies – was free according to need (all such supplies were acquired by raiding, but cadres were forbidden to keep looted items as private property). Collective leadership was strongly maintained. This became a problem for the Abidjan negotiations, where the 'War Council' (the RUF's team of most highly educated negotiators, including former staff from Bunumbu College) evidently lacked authority to conclude a deal without conferring with the young military commanders in charge of the movement in the field. RUF command was a meritocracy, and juniors could move ahead of seniors according to the boldness of their exploits, directly challenging the strict birth or entry-order ranking of the patrimonial hierarchy in wider society. The leadership potential of the most junior fighters was tested under a system of rotating command ('commander for the day'), recalling aspects of Latin American guerrilla movements, notably Shining Path (Palmer 1992). Cadres had some access to Cuban and Sandanista training materials (Peters personal communication, 2003).

Sankoh – a cashiered former army corporal, and in some accounts less a Green Book convert than an opportunist looking to settle grudges associated with the coup attempt of Brigadier John Bangura in 1969 – had become the 'leader' of the movement after purging student radicals in 1992 (Richards et al. 1997), but in sectarian style (Douglas 1993) maintained his position only because of remoteness from daily affairs. Cadres in the scattered bush camps entered his presence only after rare, and traumatic, journeys to the Zogoda (Peters and Richards 1998). These treks of many days along hazardous bush tracks must have seemed like pilgrimages. Many never met him at all. To them, Sankoh was a disembodied, god-like figure, supervising the movement's activities only via intermittent radio messages.

In short, while possessing considerable charismatic authority Sankoh lacked operational control. Practical security decisions lay with the young camp commanders (a factor which explains some of the variation in patterns of violence). Having signed the Abidjan deal Sankoh was nervous about his reception in delivering it. This was no exaggerated fear. CDF actions, backed by international security forces, destroyed the Zogoda and other camps in the south in September-October 1996, while peace negotiations were still current. Sankoh was helicoptered to his movement in the field, to sell the deal he had signed. After only the briefest of visits the deal was apparently spurned by the secure camps in northern Kailahun. In the south there was nothing left to visit. The scattered survivors of the CDF/EO raids must have been even less interested in an agreement that seemed only a smokescreen for their intended elimination. The sect lost its solidarity. Large parts of the movement veered in the direction of paranoid and vengeful fatalism.

Sankoh never rejoined the RUF in the bush. He was detained in Nigeria in 1997, apparently searching for weapons supply. In 1998, the government requested the Nigerian authorities to return Sankoh to Freetown to help the search for peace, but placed him on trial for treason. Jailed, and sentenced to death, Sankoh had even less practical control over his movement than when ensconced in the Zogoda, but remained a powerful symbol of the plight of cadres hunted down in the bush. Were he to escape hope lived. Prophecies of eventual success based on the justice of the cause might yet prove true. But not without daring rescue measures. The scene was thus set for RUF commitment to the destructive (AFRC-led) attack on Freetown of 6 January 1999.[8]

Later, living a life of ease in Freetown as a member of the government (1999-2000), Sankoh lost much of his appeal. After a violent incident at his house on Spur Road (8 May 2000) the RUF leader fled to the forests above Freetown. His younger companions escaped along bush tracks, and reached Makeni within a matter of days, but after some time in the hills Sankoh tamely surrendered to the authorities, unable to withstand the rigours of the bush. Evidently, the lion was old and toothless. Finally convinced by UN troops that they were not walking into a trap, as in 1996, the RUF bush commanders called their struggle off.[9]

Before that point was reached, however, Sierra Leone lived through a three-year period of intermittent and at times very violent conflict, triggered by the army mutiny in May, 1997. In the chaos RUF units regrouped but never achieved former levels of coherence or discipline. Driven into the bush by Nigerian ECOMOG forces in 1998, the RUF took no steps to re-open the forest camps, apart from Buedu base, controlling a vital supply route from Liberia. Due to firm control by the CDF of the Liberian border south of the Gola Forest, the RUF was unable to recover old haunts in Pujehun and Kenema Districts, being constrained instead to a more northerly (Kailahun-Kono-Makeni) axis. This gave it access to diamond and gold mining opportunities, and international backers, rivalling Executive Outcomes and Sandline, became interested in the movement's potential as a minerals mining venture. The RUF now took control of villages and towns, with little pretence of being anything other than an occupying power. Its mode of production was the coercion of local labour.[10]

Where it had no secure control, levels of terror violence reached new heights, notably in the form of a 'lottery of life' (randomised executions and amputations of civilians). It may not be coincidental that some of the worst violence was in Sankoh's home area, Tonkolili District. After seven years of struggle the Kailahun volunteers were no closer to going home, on ground where they might have expected a better welcome (one of Sankoh's brothers ruled locally as a Paramount

---

[8] During that attack one cadre was overheard urging another, looting a kiosk in West Street, to focus instead on reaching nearby Pademba Road jail. The jail was sacked and many prisoners escaped (some to join the irregular force known as the West Side Boys). The government spirited Sankoh away to a more secure address.

[9] Foday Sankoh died (apparently of a stroke) in August 2003, while awaiting trial for war crimes by the UN-sponsored International Special Court for Sierra Leone.

[10] In northern Tane chiefdom (2001) we were told that able bodied male villagers had been forced to labour in alluvial gold mine workings for two days every week.

Chief). But a prophet is not without honour, save in his own country. One part of the southern part of Tonkolili, directly bordering Sankoh's home, was particularly adamant in rejecting the RUF. Encouraged by the same international security advisers backing the CDF attacks on the RUF southern camps in 1996, the Paramount Chief of Bonkolenken Chiefdom, a former mining company engineer – organised one of the strongest civil defence forces in the north, using Mende initiators (from Ribbi in the south). This must have been as severe a jolt to the Mende-dominated RUF's sense of security as losing the southern camps in 1996. A Temne-speaking CDF force now threatened to push the RUF into alien territory north of the Makeni-Kono axis using magic supplied by Mende initiators.

In this world turned upside-down it is not hard to envisage that the movement's sense of social dislocation peaked. Shifted on to socially remote terrain, and threatened with annihilation by the ever-strengthening CDF, the ideologically-motivated cadres who might have disciplined and held the movement together were swept aside in a wild orgy of revenge. Prime targets included the defenceless villagers reckoned by disillusioned cadres to be among the (failed) prophet's kith and kin. The RUF had become the embodiment of the anti-social values it had set out to change.

The CDF – Sorcerers' Apprentices

The first stirring of village civil defence took place in the context of the national army's failure to protect villagers in the east and south of the country against the initial excesses of RUF 'special forces'. Various hunters were drawn into counter-attacks against the RUF on a more or less freelance basis. A Fula hunter in the Gola Forest singlehandedly drove off a small group of 15 or so RUF attackers in June 1991 by stalking them as he would animals (Richards 1996). Waiting until early evening when the RUF party was settling down to eat he shot the leader dead, escaped into the dusk, and shot and wounded two others. The rest of the group fled back to the village on the Liberian border from which they had come. No RUF unit dared approach the hunter's village for the next 18 months. The hunter acted on his own initiative; he had a large plantation to defend.

By 1992–3, the NPRC forces were deploying *tamaboro* (Koranko professional hunters from the north of the country) as guides to Gola Forest terrain. These hunters live as strangers, one or two to a village, around the forest edge, and before the war made their living mainly from supplying the market for bush meat in Kenema and Monrovia. The RUF was sufficiently troubled by *tamaboro* to mount a strike on Kabala, a Koranko town in the north of the country, to destroy the residence of a famed master of the craft. This same strike led to the abduction of the RUF's first international hostages (two British volunteer aid workers) in November 1994.

If war finds new uses for the technology of the hunter it also challenges social innovation. NPRC-loyalist army officers from border-zone communities, analysing RUF tactics, quickly realised that local recruits would be effective agents of bush combat, since in a war largely dependent on raids and ambushes knowledge of local terrain was the most important military skill of all. Desire to defend homes was also a powerful motivating factor, especially given the atrocities committed by RUF special forces. Border zone irregulars with basic weapons training were thus both more reliable and effective than regular troops softened by many years in Freetown. Lieutenant (posthumously Captain) Prince Ben(jamin)-Hirsch, a Daru-born RSLMF officer, said to be one of the architects of the NPRC coup, experimented with Poro modalities for mobilising young irregulars, as did a university lecturer from Kenema District, Dr. Alfred Lavalie.[11] Poro is the major men's sodality in the border region, and after initiation boys traditionally took on a role in defending their communities. Ben-Hirsch envisaged a militia role for this *hindo-hindo* cohort in contributing to the shaping of the irregular 'border guard'.

Steps towards the militarisation of hunters outside the framework of the army were taking place contemporaneously in the extreme south of the country. According to Muana (1997) an inventive hunter in the Jong Chiefdom (Bonthe District) began (in 1992) to train a local defence militia, drawing on initiation associated with the local hunting tradition in 1992. The innovativeness of this move should be stressed. There is no 'hunter militia' in Mende tradition.

'Special hunters' are common in forest villages. Those of Koranko origins might use the designation *tamaboro*. Others might refer to themselves by the name Mende speakers apply to craft hunting, *kamajoi (kamajoisia*, pl.). Craft hunter technique in the forest involves approaching and shooting an animal at as close range as possible. Cartridges are expensive, generally obtained on credit from Lebanese in return for an agreed number of carcasses. Any hunter who blasts off on the off-chance of hitting an animal is risking very narrow profit margins. The best hunters reckon only to miss a shot or two per box of cartridges. This is a highly individualistic matter. Craft hunters stalk alone, are highly secretive, wander the forest for lengthy periods, and invest heavily in medicine to make themselves invisible. The last thing they desire is to be followed by an excitable group of apprentices. They tackle big animals, such as bush cow, or colobus monkey (and the occasional elephant), and are members of what Muana (1997) appositely terms a 'guild'.

Magic plays a great part in their art, and it would be correct to refer to 'initiation' as part of the process of acquiring the appropriate charms and medicines *(hale)*. Craft hunters are linked by Manding cultural values, and acquire rights to various medicines via specific initiators. Like the village blacksmith (cf. McNaughton 1988), craft hunters tend to be regarded with fear by local populations, because of their knowledge of both magic and the mysteries of the forest. They often trace distant origins within the wider Manding cultural realm. This is distinct from hunting as practised by village farmers. A farmer may have an old gun and shoot the occasional bird or monkey when in possession of some gunpowder and shot. But farmers mainly trap animals in their farms, or join neighbours to hunt with dogs and nets. Thus some ingenuity was needed to get from the mysteries associated with the making of the craft hunter to a mass movement – 'hunter' civil defence. What the initiator from Jong Chiefdom achieved was to marry up the magical technology associated with craft hunting with some of the organisational modalities of youth initiation. The hunter civil defence might thus best be understood not as a pre-existing institution but a syncretic institutional response to the security threat posed by the RUF.

The modality was effective. Many young men volunteered, and initiators

---

[11] Both men were killed in the conflict. Some allege foul play by jealous rivals on their own side.

'processed' them through rituals needed to confer magical protections and capacities. Brimming with confidence as a result of these protections, 'hunter militia' village patrols became increasingly effective in denying mobility to the RUF in its Phase Two campaign (1994–95). Standard 'uniform' was the magic hunter's gown, variously treated to protect against bullets and confer invisibility. Units preferred ambush tactics, or to surround the enemy and engage in hand-to-hand combat. In such close encounters knives tended to be more useful than guns. Some groups reputedly used nets. Such militia were perhaps little different in organisation from the border-zone army-associated irregulars pioneered by Ben-Hirsch, except in owing nothing to NPRC or army patronage. They were supported by and accountable to rural communities increasingly distrustful of the national army motives during a period in which the RUF disguised many of its raids as attacks by soldiers.

The incoming Kabbah government, equally unable to trust an army shaped by the APC regime, quickly spotted potential to scale up these local defence initiatives. Many of the internally displaced rural populations, living in camps in and around Bo, came from Pujehun District, and were anxious to secure rich alluvial diamond mining terrain around Zimmi and valuable plantation resources scattered throughout the district, but were unwilling to return under army protection, fearing government troops as much as the RUF. Meanwhile, the RUF was gaining valuable resources to support its campaign, as a result of being able to roam and raid at will over a huge depopulated zone for valuable resources it then exported via Liberia in return for weapons and supplies.

Under the auspices of the incoming government's deputy minister of defence, a retired (Sandhurst-trained) army captain, Samuel Hinga Norman, regent chief of Telu Bongor, an area south of Bo, resources were found greatly to increase 'hunter militia' training. Some material appears to have come from a Belgian-based arms supplier holding an alluvial diamond mining concession in the Zimmi sector, one of the least depleted alluvial resources in Sierra Leone (Fithen 1999). The Zimmi field would be available to mining interests once the RUF were cleared from the district and the southern sector of the Liberian border sealed.

A first cohort of 1000 or so such fighters passed out from training in Bo in June 1996. Most were deployed in their chiefdom of origin, as scouts with a good local knowledge of the bush tracks used by RUF units on its raiding operations or for inter-camp communications (Peters and Richards 1998). The fighters placed more confidence in their magic gowns, bush knives and secret passwords than guns. Led by aptly named 'ground commanders' their strategic objective was to deny rebel patrols access to bush paths through areas earlier emptied by RUF pin-prick raids. They returned RUF tricks and terror with tricks and terror of their own, and took few if any prisoners. The movement challenged the international community (in an e-mail circulation) to provide the modalities to care for RUF prisoners-of-war.

'Hunter' civil defence was also important for being able to occupy terrain once RUF threats were contained. Returning villagers, too often fooled by 'fake' soldiers, needed a force they could readily identify and trust. But there still remained the threat of the RUF camps, several of which were located adjacent to Potoru, on the border of Pujehun and Kenema Districts. This required a more aggressive – and controversial – approach. Behind the attention-grabbing magic of the 'ground commanders' it seems a second kind of civil defence force was shaped along more conventional counterinsurgency lines, equipped with modern weapons, and, incorporating some RSLMF specialists, capable of taking on well-protected RUF bush camps. Executive Outcomes may have been involved in the training, and in supplying some specialised support services (e.g. radio triangulation and helicopter back-up). Seemingly, a well-equipped force successfully attacked and dislodged the RUF from its camps in Pujehun and Kenema Districts in September and October 1996, during the cease-fire period declared to cover the Abidjan peace negotiation.[12] Advice to deal with the RUF in this way may have reached the government through British and South African security experts interested in promoting the private security 'solutions' to the commercial development of mining in Africa's war zones. Shearer (1997) claims private security was important in getting the RUF to sign the Abidjan accords. 'Stick' was needed when Foday Sankoh reneged on his agreement to sign the peace accord. If Shearer is referring to the actual agreement his timing is awry. Sankoh signed on 30 November 1996, whereas the attacks on the Zogoda and other RUF camps occurred several weeks earlier. The camps were already in ruins when Sankoh attempted to return to the bush, to sell the Abidjan deal to his followers, with destabilising effects on the RUF as already described.

Dissolution of Solidarities: RUF & CDF Compared

There is a striking similarity between the RUF and CDF. Both movements recruited among the marginalised or displaced in the Sierra Leone countryside. Both groups seem to have had problems in command-and-control, and trouble with 'special forces'. Our proposition is that military violence tends to depart furthest from the Rules of War where combatants fight as social isolates. The RUF – an organisation trying to maintain a collective style of leadership – was unable to rein in its alien 'special forces'. But when its camps were destroyed cadres lost the ideological thread, and sank towards a violent fatalism. Despite the suggestion of Muana (1997) that there was a hierarchy among initiators and ground commanders, it seems doubtful the CDF itself was ever under firm *central* command and control, except perhaps for the counterinsurgency 'special forces'.[13] CDF 'ground commanders' we have interviewed talk about pursuing their own (highly local) objectives in the war. They also settled disputes through their own courts. Civilians meeting in Governance Reform Secretariat consultations complained loudly about these kangaroo courts and the CDF being 'a law unto itself' (Archibald and Richards 2002). Elsewhere, civilians grumbled about chaos at roadside checkpoints, where one group of CDF fighters would give a vehicle the command to move, only to be countermanded by a rival group. General Maxwell Khobe, the Nigerian (ECOMOG) commander given the job of restructuring the Sierra Leone armed forces after the RSLMF was disbanded (1998), considered CDF fighters to be too ill-trained to join the new army. There are as many whispers about CDF acts of indiscipline as there are more overt accounts of RUF

[12] But participants in the CDF attack on Bokor Camp in the Kangari Hills at about the same time claim they were armed only with sticks, cutlasses and 'seven shot guns' (fieldnotes, July 2003, Paul Richards).

[13] An explanation, offered by CDF organisers, is that the CDF is a secret society, in which 'overt' command is different from 'covert' commands.

atrocities. Some allegations will be aired in the Truth and Reconciliation Commission and Special War Crimes Court.[14]

How does this then affect our general proposition linking atrocity and social isolation? It seems to us there are important differences in the way social solidarities of the two movements fared (and were transformed) under pressure, with implications for understanding the prospects of the two groups within the DDR process. Briefly put, RUF egalitarianism collapsed under pressure of military reverse into a fatalism comparable to some of the worst violence associated with sectarian sieges (e.g. the latter stages of the siege of the Anabaptists at Muenster in Westphalia in 1535, cf. Cohn 1957) or slave revolts (e.g. the Turner rebellion at Jerusalem, Southampton County, Virginia in 1838, cf. Sundquist 1994). The crisis was one of belief. Unrestrained violence spiralled out of control as Sankoh's prophecies of eventual victory seemed less and less plausible. Indiscipline in the CDF, by contrast, appeared to reflect a weak central command perhaps implicit in the craft hunter tradition, but in this case the expressions of individualism probably represent something more than a breakdown (or lack) of command and control. The swelling of individualism among the CDF was also a marker that the war was coming to an end, that peace was reasserting itself in the midst of war, that (indeed) the combatants were demobilising themselves, even as they fought.[15]

A crucial difference between the RUF and CDF is that the RUF was being pushed towards a corner from which there seemed no escape, whereas the CDF were expanding into areas of livelihood recovery. As 'ground commanders' took back land and property they began to develop other (market-oriented) interests. Improved security meant the return of civilians in increasing numbers. An interesting new 'space' began to appear, in which CDF individualism merged with some of the more general war-induced societal changes in rural communities. At first the CDF fought to restore land and livelihoods under the patronage of their chiefs. But the chiefs – some accused of fostering the injustices against which the RUF rebelled – were late-comers to the resettlement process (even now, some paramount chiefs live in the urban areas, and commute to their rural chiefdoms). Many returnees found they could manage perfectly well settling their own disputes, preferring to keep their earnings in their pockets as the rural economy recovered (chiefly justice is expensive, even when honestly dispensed). People in the villages say they first saw the true value of their produce when congregated in camps for the displaced. Only then did they realise the extent to which they had been fooled by a combination of traders, politicians and the ruling elite. Many are now vocal about the injustices of chiefly patrimonialism. CDF cadres recognise they were the victims of similar injustice. Everywhere it is said that rural deference is dead, and that rulers, when finally they resettle, will have to earn renewed respect on the basis of the good governance they supply (Archibald and Richards 2002). This makes clear the point to which we have been aiming: fatalism (in the presence of opportunities or incentives to violence) is much more

[14] In addition to RUF leaders the war crimes court has also arraigned Samuel Hinga Norman, the leader of the CDF. It remains to be seen how the charges are framed, and whether the defence will implicate foreign policy advisers from the world of private security.

[15] This serves to remind neo-Durkheimians that it is perhaps less the solidarity itself than the dynamic – the direction in which solidarity is being 'pushed' – that matters in understanding violence.

dangerous than individualism. Fatalism stokes and concentrates violence, individualism tends (eventually) to diffuse and deflate it. Individualism is a stable alternative which DDR should aim to reinforce. But to avoid the charge of wishful thinking (making the desirable a norm) we need to know how to defeat fatalism. An answer, explored in the postscript below, is to encourage interdependency of individualism and egalitarianism around creation of livelihood opportunities for ex-combatants through DDR.

Postscript: Crafting a Peace

During 2001 approximately 70,000 combatants from the civil war in Sierra Leone were demobilised (i.e. they surrendered a gun of a specified type, received a bounty and registered for skills training). About 10,000 then disappear from the record. Perhaps they were mainly CDF, effectively self-demobilised upon recovering village land or other livelihood assets. As indicated above, there was only a weak CDF hierarchy of command-and-control, and a 'slide' towards individualism evident even as the movement grew. CDF individualists met and merged with a returning civil society less enamoured (or in awe) of patrimonial authority than before the war. Where chiefs were once the champions and pro-tectors of their people, now everyone was clear it was the ground commanders who had made recovery of chiefdom land a possibility.[16] Two streams – returning civilians and CDF ex-combatants – converged upon a new basis for rural social solidarity; heightened respect for individual expressions of rights (Archibald and Richards 2002).

Of 60,000 or so ex-combatants registered for skills training about 40,000 had received their entitlements by May 2003. About half have found jobs, though many are self-employed. Those still looking for work are positive about their new (mainly artisan) skills, and remain optimistic they will find work soon. Most say their reception within society has been positive or at least trouble-free. They, and the communities within which they have settled, are ready to forget the war. Few ex-combatants seem to suffer unmanageable anger or war trauma. If the war was fought over education and jobs then all factions appear, as a result of DDR, to have emerged victorious.

How this looks from the perspectives of those who never fought is less clear. There may be considerable resentment at the apparent rewards of combat in a country with shortages of skills training and much youth unemployment. Perhaps even more pressing, we do not know much about the 20,000 yet to receive skills training (the donors wound up the DDR phase of the post-war recovery in Sierra Leone at the end of 2003). The statistics do not demarcate ex-combatants by faction (ostensibly to avoid stigmatisation). The RUF may have accounted for about a third of ex-combatants disarmed (leaving aside children, a special category treated by other means). It might be the case that the un-processed group contains a large proportion of RUF. Some parts of Kailahun and Tonkolili District, where the RUF constitutes the main case load, only became fully accessible at a later stage in the DDR process.

---

[16] A few chiefs (despite age) 'led from the front', most notably PC Bai Sunthugba Osara III, architect and commander of the Bonkolenken CDF, resident in Yele for long periods despite his house being destroyed and being wounded in the fighting.

As already noted, a shift across the diagonal from hierarchy to individualism seems positive for the post-war integration of former CDF ex-combatants in a society already becoming more individualistic, and increasingly willing to challenge patrimonial authority. What is less clear is what happened to RUF egalitarianism (did any of it survive?), and the present state of mind of those cadres who experienced the war-induced slide into violent fatalism. This is a topic requiring more investigation.

A second such topic is gender. Gender aspects of DDR are neglected (exceptions in the literature are Shepler 2002 and Arthy 2003). A few women fought as irregulars with the government forces (Peters and Richards 1998), and (as in any war) there were numerous camp followers. The CDF claims to be a male-only militia. But there is particular concern about the much larger number of women mobilised by the RUF. Their documentation is inadequate. A suspicion circulates that fewer women than fought for the RUF turned up for demobilisation. Some women fighters may have been 'disarmed' by their male commanders (i.e. their weapon was assigned to another fighter before the process began). One claim is that women fighters agreed to this – and to 'skip' DDR – to avoid stigmatisation in a civilian society especially hostile to the idea of women as killers. But no one really knows until RUF women have been located and interviewed.

Shepler (2002) points to an even more intractable problem concerning young women mobilised into the RUF but not trained to fight. The RUF practised marriage-by-capture. Many young women were seized and assigned as wives to fighters. In RUF terms, they were 'mobilised',[17] but have not come under the scope of DDR because they had no weapon. There is conflicting information on the extent to which these partners of combatants ('bush wives') are free to move. A range of possibilities is known. Some rallied to the movement spontaneously. Some accepted the husbands to whom they were assigned, and by whom they had children. In rural Sierra Leone women have relatively limited choice over marriage partners, and arranged marriages are common and frequently succeed. But others forced into marriage have been badly treated by a succession of abusive partners. They would like to move on, but face huge obstacles in the way of returning home and gaining social respectability. Many lack confidence that they could find a husband if their history was known. Some suffer the long-term effects of rape and sexually-transmitted disease (including being HIV-positive). Some agencies feel an answer may be for such women to settle with male ex-combatants, or in special ex-combatant communities where stigmatisation would be less of a problem (Arthy 2003).

What is clear is that there are major gaps in information on the reintegration of female ex-combatants and 'bush wives'. Nothing is known about whether or to what extent their sense of social solidarity has been reshaped by the war, or about the ways in which they socialise their children. It is possible to imagine a strongly gendered post-war sub-culture of doubly-oppressed RUF women. On the other hand, we have interviewed female ex-combatants who have been among the most forthright defenders of the RUF struggle and the movement's values. The RUF promised a degree of gender liberation, and the regret of these ex-combatants is that the rebellion failed. Their attitudes to social reform remain in advance of the mainstream rural society.

---

[17] Within a special unit for combat wives (Richards et al. 1997).

We conclude with a few remarks about what the DDR process might yet achieve for the more problematic groups, including RUF 'hard core' egalitarians. Some clues lie in accounts of successful self-demobilisation, involving cooperation between CDF and RUF cadres. One such success concerns the post-war explosion in the use of two-wheeled (motorbike) taxis in the town of Bo. The Bo Town Bike Renters Association was established in March 2000, in part as a response to demobilisation. Fighters were in the process of being disarmed but lacked job opportunities. The union started out with four ex-combatant organisers and a handful of bikes, which they chartered to riders they had trained from among unemployed ex-combatants (all ex-CDF at the outset). There was a gap in the market caused by so many 4-wheel taxis having been destroyed or grounded during the war (especially from 1994). Bike taxis helped revive links between Bo and the surrounding rural and mining districts in the immediate post-war period. The bikes had better accessibility on war-damaged roads, and penetrated rural tracks where no car could go. Users were predominantly traders, often female, bringing in produce from the villages and supplying services in mining camps. Having crossed fighting lines in the war (e.g. trading palm oil) where a man's movements might have aroused suspicion, many women have lost inhibitions about the danger or seemliness of perching on the back of a motorbike on a dusty bush track. A bike spill seems a minor hazard to those who regularly risked ambush during the war. Demand rises all the time, especially from women traders.

The association today has 600-plus members and 350 bikes (each bike is operated by two riders so that it is on the road for potentially up to 24 hours a day, and can be paid for in the first six months of operation, at Le1 million/month). About half the association's executive are ex-combatants, including former RUF. What is striking, in talking to the executive, is the story they tell about political lessons learnt as a result of the war. They have registered their association under commercial law, as a company limited by guarantee, and retain a solicitor as legal representative. This is because they reject 'big men' as political patrons, arguing that they were manipulated by the political classes to fight the war, and found themselves destroying their own environment, whereas the 'big men' had their families safe overseas, and developed 'wings to fly' as soon as conditions became intolerable. The combatants fighting the war had no alternatives to reliance upon local (war-damaged) educational or health systems. For this reason, they vow not to fight each other with guns again. Commercial law is a better tool, they reason, in the struggle for a fairer society. They give a recent example of a strike they organised against police harassment over delays in issuing registration papers by the Road Transport Department. The strike was supported by women traders, and a successful compromise was reached with the police.

There are several striking features about this account. First is that 'reintegration' is not just a matter of 'fitting in', but of spotting and developing new opportunities for self-employment in a changing society (the pattern of interaction between Bo and its surrounding rural and mining districts is intensifying as the diamond mining economy recovers from the war). Finding such opportunities strengthens social acceptability (in this case the support of women traders for the bike taxi riders' strike) as well as providing livelihood opportunities. Social acceptability, in turn, strengthens chances of winning political battles (the strike forced the authorities to pay attention to complaints, and the case with the police was settled by compromise). Most remarkable of all is the sense of common purpose among young men fighting each other only a few years earlier, and their recognition they had been manipulated to fight. Their scepticism about 'big men', and vertically-linked 'ethnic' or locality-based associations is evident. They are part of a new wave of horizontal (or interests-driven) associations of civil society in post-war Sierra Leone, ranging from sports and entertainment to a wide range of artisan and petty-trader livelihood associations. These ex-combatants are not just 'fitting into' such a society – they are helping to forge it.[18] As artisans, they are crafting a peace.

This reflects a new kind of balance between individualism and egalitarianism, and it is around strengthening this trade-off (we suggest) that the two combatant factions will achieve a stable resolution of the differences sustaining the war. The greatest danger seems to be that in dealing with the aftermath of war through physical restitution – i.e. as a problem of *reconstruction* – rather than as a problem of social change, the donors tend unwittingly to inject too much money into the system, and thus strengthen, and over-emphasise, neo-patrimonial linkages precisely at the point in history where this particular form of hierarchical solidarity should be encouraged to assume a less prominent role, if it is not to fade away altogether.

References

Abdullah, I. 1997, 'Bush Path to Destruction: the Origin and Character of the Revolutionary United Front/Sierra Leone' *Africa Development* 22 (3/4), Special Issue: *Lumpen Culture and Political Violence: the Sierra Leone Civil War*

Amnesty International 1992, *The extrajudicial execution of suspected rebels and collaborators* London: International Secretariat of Amnesty International, Index AFR 51/02/92

Archibald, S. and Richards, P. 2002, 'Conversion to human rights? Popular debate about war and justice in rural central Sierra Leone' *Africa* 72 (3), 339–67

Arthy, S. 2003, 'Reintegration lesson learning and impact evaluation: Phase 2 Report' Unpublished report to DfID on reintegration activities in Sierra Leone

Bromley, D. G. 1997, 'Constructing apocalypticism: social and cultural elements of radical organization' in Robbins, T. and Palmer, S. J. eds. *Millennium, messiahs and mayhem: contemporary apocalyptic movements* New York & London: Routledge

Cohn, N. 1957, *The pursuit of the millennium* London: Secker & Warburg

Collier, P. 2000, *Economic causes of civil conflict and their implications for policy* Washington, DC: The World Bank

Douglas, M. 1993, *In the wilderness: the doctrine of defilement in the Book of Numbers* Sheffield: Sheffield Academic Press

—— 1996, *Thought styles: critical essays on good taste* London: Sage Publications

—— 2001, 'A feeling of hierarchy' Unpublished text of a lecture given in the University of Dayton, 9 October 2001

Douglas, M. and Ney, S. 1998, *Missing persons: a critique of the social sciences* Berkeley: University of California Press

Durkheim, E.1964 [1893], *The division of labor in society* trs. G. Simpson, New York: Free Press

—— 1952 [1897], *Suicide: a study in sociology* trs. J. A. Spaulding and G. Simpson, London: Routledge & Kegan Paul

Fenton, J. S. 1948, *Outline of native law in Sierra Leone* Freetown: Government Printer.

Fithen, C. 1999, 'Diamonds and war in Sierra Leone: cultural strategies for commercial adaptation

[18] In the case of the Bo Town Taxi Renters' Association this extends to a new gender consciousness. Encouraged by a speech by President Kabbah stating an ambition for gender equality, and recognising that most of its clients are women, the Association has recruited 45 women members as trainee taxi riders.

to endemic low-intensity conflict' Unpublished PhD thesis, Department of Anthropology, University College London

Grace, J. J. 1977, ' Slavery and emancipation among the Mende in Sierra Leone' in Miers, S. and Kopytoff, I. eds *Slavery in Africa: historical and anthropological perspectives* Madison, WI: University of Wisconsin Press

Holsoe, S. E. 1977, 'Slavery and economic response among the Vai (Liberia and Sierra Leone)' in S. Miers & I. Kopytoff, eds., *Slavery in Africa: historical and anthropological perspectives* Madison, WI: University of Wisconsin Press

Hood, C. 1998, *The art of the state: culture, rhetoric and public management* Oxford: Clarendon Press

McFeat, T. 1972, *Small-group cultures* Oxford & New York: Pergamon

McNaughton, P. R. 1988, *The Mande blacksmith: knowledge, power and art in West Africa* Bloomington, IN: Indiana University Press

Mamdani, M. 1996, *Citizen and subject: contemporary Africa and the legacy of late colonialism* London: James Currey

Mestrovic, S. G. 1992, *Durkheim and post-modern culture* New York: Aldine de Gruyter

Muana, P. K. 1997, 'The kamajoi militia: civil war, internal displacement and the politics of counter-insurgency' *Africa Development* 22 (3/4): 77–100

OTI 2000, *Diamonds and armed conflict in Sierra Leone: proposal for implementation of a new diamond policy and operations,* USAID Office of Transition Initiatives, Washington, Working Paper http://www.usaid.gov/hum_response/oti/country/sleone/diamonds.html. (August)

Palmer, D. S. ed. 1992, *Shining Path of Peru* London: C. Hurst

Peters, K. 2002, 'The storm is not yet over? Interviews with ex-combatants from the war in Sierra Leone' Unpublished typescript, Technology & Agrarian Development Group, Wageningen University & Research Centre, The Netherlands

Peters, K. and Richards, P. 1998a. 'Why we fight: voices of youth ex-combatants in Sierra Leone' *Africa* 68 (1): 183–210

Richards, P. 1996, *Fighting for the rain forest: war, youth and resources in Sierra Leone* Oxford: James Currey (reprinted with additional material 1998)

—— 2003, 'Green Book millenarians? The Sierra Leone war from the perspective of an anthropology of religion', in Kastfelt, Niels ed. *Religion and civil war in Africa* London: C. Hurst

Richards, P., Abdullah, I., Amara, J., Muana, P., Stanley, E., and Vincent, J. 1997. 'Reintegration of war-affected youth and ex-combatants: a study of the social and economic opportunity structure in Sierra Leone' Unpublished report, Freetown: Ministry of Relief Rehabilitation & Reintegration

Richards, P. and Vlassenroot, C. 2002, 'Les guerres africaines du type fleuve Mano' *Politique Africaine* 88: 13–26

RUF/SL. 1995, *Footpaths to democracy: toward a New Sierra Leone* (n.p.) The Revolutionary United Front of Sierra Leone

Salemink, O. 2002, *The ethnography of Vietnam's Central Highlanders: an historical contextualization 1850–1990* London: Routledge

Shearer, D. 1997, 'Exploring the limits of consent: conflict resolution in Sierra Leone'. *Millennium: Journal of International Studies* 26 (3): 845–60

Shepler, S. 2002, 'Les filles-soldats:trajectoires d'apres-guerre en Sierra Leone' *Politique Africaine* 88: 49–62

Sivan, E. 1995, 'The enclave culture', in M. Marty, ed. *Fundamentalism comprehended* Chicago: Chicago University Press

Smillie, I., Gberie, L., Hazleton, R. 2000, *The heart of the matter: Sierra Leone, diamonds and human security* Ottawa: Partnership Africa Canada (January)

Stedman Jones, S. 2001, *Durkheim reconsidered* Cambridge: Polity Press

Sundquist, E. 1993, *To wake the nations: race in the making of American literature* Cambridge MA: The Belknap Press

UN Experts 2000, 'Report of the Panel of Experts appointed pursuant to the UN Security Council Resolution 1306 (2000), para. 19, in relation to Sierra Leone' (mimeo., United Nations Organization, December)

Yeebo, Z. 1991, *Ghana: the struggle for popular power* London & Port of Spain: New Beacon Books.

Zack-Williams, A. B. 1995, *Tributors, supporters and merchant capital: mining and under-development in Sierra Leone* Aldershot: Avebury Press

6, Perri 1999. *Morals for robots and cyborgs: ethics, society and public policy in the age of autonomous intelligent machines.* Brentford: Bull Information Systems

8

Building a Future?
*The Reintegration & Remarginalisation of Youth in Liberia**

MATS UTAS

> In this connection, we are faced with the responsibility of providing assistance to
> former combatants through the repair of schools, clinics, and the provision of jobs, in
> order that they will be gainfully employed. Ex-combatants from all former factions
> remain a serious concern of this government, and legislation will be introduced for the
> creation of a National Veterans Administration Agency, to attend to the needs of our
> injured young men and women nationally. This administration is going to work hard
> to solve the problem of getting our ex-combatants readjusted (President Charles
> Taylor's annual message to the National Legislature, quoted in *Daily Times*, Monrovia,
> 2 February 1998, p. 2).

Quite contrary to the speech of the then Liberian president, once the rebel leader
of the NPFL (National Patriotic Front of Liberia), little or nothing has been done
from the government's side to accommodate young ex-combatants in post-war
Liberia. As compared to many other ex-combatants worldwide, Liberian war
veterans are far from viewed as heroes in their country. For example, Joe was
fighting as a soldier in the NPFL when he was wounded in his foot by a grenade.
After recovering at the Methodist hospital in Ganta he could not return to his
previous trade due to a heavy limp. Even as a veteran of the victorious NPFL
army he did not receive any government aid, as Charles Taylor had promised –
he simply had to take care of himself. Joe, however, fought well for himself.
Where many others would have failed, Joe managed to establish a small shop
in a residential area of Ganta, thus eking out a living for himself and his
girlfriend. In his small shed, sweets, cigarettes, Maggi cubes (soup stock), chilli-
pepper and at times cassava were traded over the counter. But by far the most
attractive part of the shop was the drinking booth. Here, a clientele of
unemployed youth, police, military and night watchmen hid to drink a bottle of
gin (local liquor that had taken a detour around Monrovia to be cleaned, bottled
and labelled), or cane juice (local gin straight from the sugarcane farms outside
Ganta), to smoke dope and play checkers. Ex-combatant status was what most
of the clientele had in common.

In Joe's shop I met up with Adolphus, who had lost a leg in combat, Georgie,
Anthony and a lot of other youths. Complaining about post-war society was a
predominant pastime here, most especially when the police and military were
absent. One day Georgie came and briefed us about a wartime friend who had

chosen to return to his village right after the end of the war. The previous day the friend had come to Ganta and paid him a visit. Georgie said:

> The man is talking about his cassava farm, his rice and palm-nuts. He is living with his two wives and has recently got a child, and all we are doing here in Ganta is just sitting and looking at the coal-tar road.

Georgie expressed this with clear envy in his voice, hesitant about the sweetness of modernity.[1] Another time, Anthony explained to me the problems he had about going home to his people.

> Me, my people rejected me because today I am a wounded man. They all believe that we (ex-combatants) have gunpowder in our heads. Today, the only man I depend on is Charles Taylor. If someone would give me USD 2500 to go fight in Zaire, I would go. I would leave the money with my family and if I die, at least I would have helped them. I fought for Liberia and I 'died' in the war.

His statement is full of contradictions. But it is apparent Anthony feels rejected by everyone, from family to the government of Liberia. His reference to Taylor is chiefly rhetorical, but hints at a frail hope that the president might live up to the abundant promises he made to his men during the war. Anthony is, like Georgie, dragging his feet up and down the tarmac road not knowing where to start or where to go. On the other hand, Georgie's friend back in 'the bush', and Joe in his small shop, through different means and positions in the local opportunity structures, work their way back into respected positions in society. In this chapter I focus on the demobilisation and social reintegration of ex-combatant youth in the aftermath of the Liberian Civil War; focusing on the concerns of youth like Georgie, Anthony, Joe and Adolphus. What happens to the young combatants who fought the war in a post-war world? How does the social reintegration of ex-combatants function? Having in mind that many of these young persons committed terrible atrocities during the war years, even in their home settings, how are they received? Do ex-combatants have possibilities at all to go home? Is there still a place to call 'home'? How are they perceived in the home setting? In this chapter I show that social reintegration of ex-combatant youth differs from setting to setting. In some settings reintegration has hardly been taking place, whilst in other settings it is working remarkably well.

1998, the year of my fieldwork in Liberia, was relatively peaceful, except for a few incidents (of which the 18 September fighting in Monrovia was the most serious). The general view was that Liberia was heading towards peace. Taking an institutional perspective, the time after the election in mid-1997 is generally referred to as the post-war period. I have also chosen to refer to the period as 'post-war', but as peace in Liberia has remained fragile, and as a new rebel faction appeared in late 1999 in Lofa County, it could also be argued that 1997–99 was just an intermediary period in a longer conflict. From a combatant perspective, I argue that their life predicaments, during 1998, were not just products of trying to reintegrate, as promptly as they could, but also a kind of

---

[1] The tarmac road ends right after Ganta town and the continuing main roads leading either to Guinea (via Yekepa), or to Ivory Coast (via Kahnple) are dirt roads. The tarmac road bears heavy symbolism as the main connection between Ganta and the experience of cosmopolitan modernity of Monrovia. Ganta's connection to the larger world was completed by the construction of the road from Monrovia in 1945-46. During the first period only one man, American missionary, Dr. Harley, had a vehicle to ride the road.

post-war stand-by mode, where it was tactically important not only to reintegrate, but also to maintain contacts with commanders as well as rank-and-file within war-networks, in case the war would start all over again.[2] Equally so, when we talk about ex-combatants in a post-war setting, it has become natural to talk about reintegration, but, as I have argued elsewhere (Utas 2003), combatants were mainly youth who already experienced marginalisation, thus in the concluding part of this article I describe alongside a process of reintegration a process of re-marginalisation.

Liberian Civil War as a Continuum

Officially the Liberian Civil War started on Christmas Eve 1989 and ended with general elections in 1997. However, as Paul Richards argues in the introduction to this book, war ought to be seen as a continuum without a clear beginning or a clear end. For a small group of Liberians, the war started much earlier than 1989 as they were drafted for military training in Libya in the first half of the 1980s (Richards 1996a; Ellis 1999).[3] Certainly in the town of Butoe in Nimba County the arrival of NPFL (National Patriotic Front of Liberia) rebels on Christmas Eve 1989 signalled the onset of the civil war. However, other areas were affected much later, or hardly at all. Even during the war, in most areas people experienced long periods of relative peace and normality, suddenly interrupted by fierce battles, or a newfound intensity of skirmishing. As Paul, one of the key informants in this paper, notes: 'You know the war was just in some places while in other places people can be enjoying themselves.' In 1998 Liberians tended to agree that the war started in 1990 (or Christmas Eve 1989, to be precise) and ended in 1997, but in the middle of it no one could tell whether a particular incident marked the end of the war or not. Such uncertainty is clear if one looks at Liberian refugees in the neighbouring countries of Ivory Coast, Guinea and Sierra Leone. Some refugees have stayed behind up to the current day, because they are not sure whether the war has ended or not. Was 1998 just another period of relative peace in the war–peace continuum?

During the first half of 1996, when warlords, and national and international experts, called the war off, many refugees were heading home when the news of renewed fighting in Monrovia met them. Learning from such experiences, refugees have been reluctant to return home (the lack of clear opportunities in Liberia has further deterred refugees from going back).[4] The Liberian Civil War entered a new phase when the former warlord Charles Taylor was elected President in democratic elections on 19 July 1997. But even so, during 1998, parts of what we generally call war activities continued. Renewed fighting took place in pockets of the country. During my stay in Liberia in 1998, I experienced a few battle-like incidents with dissident groups fighting against government

[2] The civil war has dragged on in a low intensity mode. Both the Liberian army, a plethora of pro-government militias and LURD (Liberians United for Reconciliation and Democracy) have recruited from among many ex-combatants willing to pick up arms again. In that sense the stand-by mode can be seen as a sound strategy.

[3] NPFL recruitment started already in 1983 according to my informants in rural Nimba County.

[4] Larger groups of Liberian refugees returned from Guinea and the Ivory Coast during 1999–2000 (Guinea) and 2002–03 (Ivory Coast). This is not because stability has returned to Liberia but rather because of political unrest in the host countries.

soldiers in Monrovia. By far the worst fighting in Monrovia was the so-called 'battle of September 18th' that again turned Monrovia into a war zone and created countrywide repercussions.

It is, however, not only war in its most obvious form that Liberians have been experiencing. They also experience the government's maintenance of a war bureaucracy, with the transformation of the NPFL rebel army into a 'democratic party', the NPP (National Patriotic Party). For instance, the security apparatus is maintained by former NPFL commanders, and as such continues to harass the Liberian citizens. Furthermore, elements within the civil service at all levels of the hierarchy continue to loot private and state property rebel-style. For instance, the SSS (Special Security Service), SSU (Special Security Unit) and the SOD (Special Operations Division) are notoriously known for their 'go-by-chop' raids (go by and get something to eat), emptying whole stores during the night hours. Many ex-combatants are involved in these activities (Utas 2004a).

Youth Participation

It was youth in abundance that fought the Liberian civil war.[5] 'There is no more revolution except in resistance' (Virilio and Lotringer 1997:83), in the minds of youth combatants, participation in the civil war was a revolution – a way of freeing themselves from a heavy workload and parental expectations (Richards 1995; 1996a). It was also a response to lack of opportunities in society (Chingono 1996; Cruise O'Brien 1996). The war served as a means to wrestle power from the hands of 'big men' (Keen 1998) and ease their own precarious economic situation – i.e. using the gun as a credit card (Sesay 1996).[6] In reality, however, youth became subjects of another set of even more unscrupulous 'big men' (Ellis 1998; Reno 1995; 1998).

A feature of Liberian society that has often been omitted in discussions about root causes of male youth participation in the civil war, because of its rather mundane character, is young men's limited access to women and potential wives. Indigent young men are, relatively speaking, excluded from possibilities of establishing long-term relationships with women. Passively they sit and watch older, wealthier men pick up their sisters and cousins, as well as the girl-next-door with whom they innocently played love games just a few years earlier, and who now cuts them dead. The prospect of remaining a bachelor throughout life

[5] Youth is an increasingly studied category in African society (Honwana & De Boeck, forthcoming 2005). I here use youth in a loose sense as a category of young individuals who themselves feel mature enough to become adults, but who are not perceived as such by society in general. In a creolised society (Hannerz 1987; 1996) like Liberia earlier obvious paths from childhood to adulthood have changed, adding to the complexity of becoming adult. Up-front means, such as joining a secret society and/or becoming a warrior protecting the community, that earlier worked as clear markers of the passage between childhood and adulthood, have in present Liberia become blurred with urban, cosmopolitan or Western influences, thus creating a space for a novel category of youth. As social age is important in the Liberian context, aging people without the right social capacities fit well into the category of youth thus making it impossible to put any formal age frame around the youth category. The category is rather created as an opposition to larger society (a subculture, or counter-culture).

[6] As youth in general only participated in very rudimentary forms of the Liberian economy, at the very bottom, the increased economic hardships that affected Liberia during the past three decades have hit this group the hardest (for similar arguments see e.g. Ferguson 1999; Guyer 1995; Mac-Gaffey 1991).

(quite normal in Liberia because of formal and, more often, informal conventions of polygyny)[7] might indeed serve as an important reason to join a rebel force. Obtaining power and wealth as a rebel fighter reverses the scenario, granting young men access to numerous girlfriends and the right to take 'wives' (Utas forthcoming, 2005). As the category of youth is constructed upon notions of social age, social markers such as marriage, or at least a stable relationship with a woman, are requirements for moving out of the youth category and into adulthood. Many older men (approximately 20–45) who participated in the civil war were in effect youth in social terms; i.e. they were mature men lacking the wealth and power required to cross the border between youth and adulthood.

Youth participation in the Liberian Civil War must be seen as a means of strategic upward mobility aiming at obtaining respect and status, by turning society's power structure upside down (taking command, instead of being commanded). Rising from self-perceived (though largely real) victimhood – involving tactics such as foot-dragging, pilfering, and dissimulation (i.e. the infrapolitics of the powerless, Scott 1990: xiii) – to a position of agency is the product of taking up arms. Sure wealth also functions as a principal means of upward mobility; possibilities of looting further entice youth to participate in the rebel trade. However, taking up arms and getting involved in guerrilla warfare might also be regarded as a 'weapon of the weak' (Scott 1985), and thus as tactics (Certeau 1984), it can pay off only in the short run. Once war is over marginal souls are once again deported to the margins.

A Note on the Material

In this chapter I deal with three different cases that I loosely categorise as urban, semi-urban and rural. My first case is from Monrovia, where I did fieldwork for six months during the first part of 1998. My second case is taken from a rural area (Sinoe County), where I toured the countryside for seven days in April 1998 with a team of local Red Cross volunteers conducting 97 qualitative interviews with youth for the Belgian Red Cross. The third case study derives from Ganta in Nimba County, NPFL heartland, where I spent an additional six months during the latter half of 1998. These three cases illustrate three different trajectories of reintegration of youth very much visible in post-war Liberia. However we should bear in mind that urban, rural and semi-urban are only analytical categories constructed to organise the material. The borders are thus in reality blurred, local differences occur, and on an individual basis they are repeatedly transgressed. This fact becomes most clear in the focus on the semi-urban case where it is easy to observe both urban and rural traits in a small enclosure such as Joe's shop, presented in the vignette.

Urban – Monrovia

The Palace is situated right on the beach in central Monrovia. The location would be most attractive, were it not for the fact that the beach is used as a

---

[7] See Bledsoe (1990). However it should be noted that today a majority of Liberians do not see polygynous marriages as viable alternatives.

public latrine (the beach is nicknamed *puhpuh-cana*) and that the land behind is a garbage dump. Even so, some of the houses in the near vicinity are inhabited by expatriate aid-workers and well-to-do Lebanese businessmen. The Palace is a deserted petrochemical factory with only the concrete structure remaining. In early 1998 more than a dozen ex-combatants had settled in the Palace. They originated from all over Liberia, but this was where the latest fighting had discharged them. Their war histories differed a lot and it was something that many kept hidden, due to their dangerous liaisons during the last part of the war. Thus instead of going into detail about their backgrounds I attempt to give a general picture of the origins of ex-combatants currently living in Monrovia.

Those who originated from southern Liberia had primarily joined the NPFL (National Patriotic Front of Liberia) as it moved through the southern part of the country early in the war. Later, if they had remained in the south, they typically changed sides and joined a southern force, of the (ironically-named) LPC (Liberia Peace Council) – see below for details. Those who originated in eastern Liberia typically joined NPFL, or INPFL (Independent National Patriotic Front of Liberia), and remained loyal up until the April 6 war, when some were incorporated in ULIMO-J (United Liberation Movement for Democracy in Liberia/Johnson-wing), or ULIMO-K (United Liberation Movement for Democracy in Liberia/Koromah-wing).[8] Northerners might find themselves included among the ranks of NPFL, ULIMO-K, ULIMO-J, or the regional LDF (Lofa Defence Force). Additionally, some with roots in the south, or from the Mandingo diasporia minority, living in Monrovia as the war started, went into exile in Sierra Leone. There they joined ULIMO (before it split) at its inception in Freetown. Those who remained in Monrovia could have joined any of the factions, including the remnants of the AFL (Armed Forces of Liberia). Once inside the rank-and-file of the various rebel factions, they often moved between the different (and opposed) factions and encountered little ethnic prejudice. During the April 6 war Palace youth, along with many other urban youth, joined the ULIMO-J forces, at the time recruiting heavily among urban footloose youth. Following the April 6 war Palace youth laid down their guns, either spontaneously, or in response to a demobilisation exercise structured by the international community.

In the post-war setting the youth in the Palace were making their living through day-to-day contracts in construction work, making coal pots[9] out of scrap metal, selling sand from the nearby beach, or searching the garbage dump for copper and other valuables for resale. They were also involved in rougher activities. Some of the youth in the Palace sold marijuana – all of them smoked it – and other drugs were traded. Stolen petrol, mainly from the generators sustaining the offices and staff housing of the international NGOs, was traded in the Palace during night hours. Another nocturnal activity involving Palace dwellers was petty thievery in various forms. A feature of post-war Liberia was crime sanctioned by the security apparatus. This was especially so as long as curfew was maintained, as only police and military in various guises had the freedom to pass in the streets during night hours. Loyal youth operated in conjunction with these units. In this activity Palace youth relied on their close connections with the army (AFL). Yet other footloose youth had connections and carried out missions in alliance with the police or other units of the security

---

[8] During the April 6 war ULIMO-K fought alongside NPFL against ULIMO-J.

[9] A small charcoal-fired cooking stove used by most urban dwellers.

block.[10] Certainly the daily struggle of Palace youth and other marginal youth in Monrovia did not differ much from youth in similar settings elsewhere in urban Africa.[11]

There were few indications of Palace youth reintegration in larger society. Palace youth and other footloose youth were parts of a subculture much at odds with the larger society. Even so, Palace youth at times participated in the various reintegration and rehabilitation programmes hosted by international and national NGOs. Obtaining skills in mechanics at Don Bosco (a Catholic relief agency), carpentry at LOIC (the Liberian branch of a US-based NGO, Opportunity and Industrialization Center), and a spell participating in a drama course held at Don Bosco was a fairly normal career path among youth in the Palace.[12] Irrespective of what kind of skills training they took, and whatever trainee position the NGO managed to arrange, very few students were able to get stable work. Well aware of these limitations, participation in reintegration and rehabilitation programmes generally served as means to get away from the daily grind for some time, and enjoy the logistic advantages of the programmes.

From a perspective of reintegration and reconciliation there were no indications of Palace youth prepared to return to the communities they originated from. Generally they had no idea if their parents had survived the war, or of their families' whereabouts. Neither were they in a position to find out. The resettlement programmes that some of the international organisations were offering were not utilised by Palace youth. In fact even those who had parents, or other relatives in Monrovia tended to avoid them. Family networks were instead replaced with informal structures of wartime friends and commanders. Post-war livelihoods made little difference to this, and it was clear that in the Palace the military structure prevailed. The military structure was, for instance, used to maintain discipline. Senior Palace dwellers effectively punished theft inside the Palace, or crime outside the Palace that led to police raids. Inhabitants were also punished if they broke other informal laws.

Palace youth also formed the lowest echelon in larger patron/client networks, mainly populated by former commanders, but often reaching all the way up to government level. Through such vertical links the Palace youth were used by 'big men' in town for boosting political rallies, carrying out illegal activities such as busting business of rivals' stores etc. (cf. Momoh 1999; Rashid 1997, for similar activities in Nigeria and Sierra Leone). Another feature of life in the Palace was the chronic lack of young women. Of the fifteen or more people – the population in the Palace fluctuated considerably during my stay – resident in the Palace, only four were females. Palace youth had few possibilities to have a girlfriend,

---

[10] Palace youth's close contacts with AFL revealed the prevailing connections between part of the AFL and ULIMO-J fighters. Ex-fighters from NPFL lines largely occupied positions in police, special security forces and immigration, agencies that have been thoroughly restructured and reoccupied after Charles Taylor took up office. Former NPFL fighters carried out missions together with these units.

[11] See e.g. (Abdullah 1997; 1998; Abdullah *et al.* 1997; Cruise O'Brien 1996; El-Kenz 1996; La Fontaine 1970; Jensen 2001; Kynoch 1999; Marks 2001; Momoh 1999; Ssewakiriyanga 1999). Resemblance is also observed with youth in similar settings in the western world, see e.g. (Bourgois 1995; Bucholtz 2002; Hall & Montgomery 2000; Hazlehurst 1998; Panter-Brick 2002; Schneider 1999), and elsewhere (Bernat 1999; Sykes 1999; Scheper-Hughes 1992).

[12] For young females the programmes were rather limited at the time, and the NGO community stated that they had a harder time to reach out to them.

and even short-term relationships were few. Of the four young women/girls in the Palace, two sustained themselves as prostitutes (Utas 1999), while the third was a substance abuser suffering a mental disorder. I have no proof, but it is quite likely she was given shelter, food, drugs etc. in exchange for sexual favours to male Palace dwellers. The fourth was a young girl who was under protection of the informal leader of the Palace. It is hard to see youth like those in the Palace ever being reintegrated in larger society. Even if they were not part of an underclass sub-culture prior to the war, they were now on the margins of urban society permanently. Youth lived on the streets of Monrovia before the war as well, but in post-war Monrovia they greatly outnumbered the pre-war figures.[13] Leaving individual tragedies aside, on a sociostructural level these urban marginals form a highly volatile and dangerous group of people unlikely to hesitate if given the opportunity to pick up arms again.[14]

Rural – Sinoe County

At the other extreme of the scale of reintegration we find ex-combatant youth in rural Sinoe County in southern Liberia.[15] Mainly Sarpo and Kru people populate Sinoe County. The war clearly drove a wedge between the two populations. The first rebel group to emerge in the area was the NPFL. Initially, youth of both Sarpo and Kru origin joined its rank-and-file. However, as time passed the leaders of NPFL started to view Sarpos with increasing distrust. Sarpo peoples speak a language closely related to that of the Krahn population, the group from which President Samuel Doe originated, and which was favoured in both civil service and the army during his period in power, 1980-1990. The Krahn were thus envisioned as main enemies of the NPFL. A gradual expulsion of Sarpo fighters within the NPFL was followed by atrocities against Sarpo populations, who fled into the bush or into exile. Partly as a response, Sarpo peoples organised their own warring faction, the LPC. Initially the creation of LPC led to more atrocities against civilian Sarpos.[16] The LPC and NPFL fought over power in the county, and both factions carried out gruesome atrocities on civilians as a means to gain control.

In post-war Sinoe County, as I found it in 1998, ex-combatants originating from all over Liberia had assembled in the urban centre of Greenville. In the rural areas, ex-combatant youth were mainly of Kru or Sarpo origin (with a few

[13] There are no quantitative studies substantiating this statement. However, Monrovian residents maintain that this is the case.

[14] As became apparent already during my fieldwork, when elements loyal to the ULIMO-J leader Roosevelt Johnson repeatedly created problems in town (partly provoked by the security forces). A few times it developed into shootouts and during the September 18 battle, ex-combatant youth rearmed and again turned Monrovia into a battle zone. During that incident one among the Palace youths participated on R. Johnson's side and later escaped with him to Nigeria. In the aftermath of the battle another Palace dweller got picked up by security forces and tragically was executed.

[15] In rural settings studies with a specific focus on youth have been largely absent (except for studies of life cycles, see e.g. Ottenberg 1989; Riesman 1986). Paul Richards (1995; 1996a; 1996b; 1999; Peters & Richards 1998) work centering rural youth in Sierra Leone points out the urgent need for such studies.

[16] As such LPC was not a direct response to the NPFL, rather the LPC was a creation of people residing in Monrovia and Zwedru, the capital of Grand Gedeh County. Quite likely, a split between the citizens of Sinoe (Sarpo and Kru) was what the men behind LPC wished to obtain. A lasting outcome of the war has been that Sarpo peoples have been forced to harmonize with Krahn peoples.

Bassa), and hailing from Sinoe County itself. In contrast to the youth hanging out in Greenville, most youth in the rural areas had already returned to the villages. The process of spontaneous social reintegration was remarkably rapid here. In many cases ex-combatant youth had moved back to their home villages, often under the roof of their families. Discourses of reconciliation prevailed among the adult generation. Indeed, although sons and daughters had committed crimes in the area, even direct assaults on family and kin, 'they are our sons and daughters, so we have to forgive them', was the common explanation of how reconciliation was possible. Protection of self and family was a main incentive for youth to join the rebel forces in the first place, and this further enhanced forgiveness.

Reconciliation and reintegration programmes implemented by the international aid community played only a marginal role in rural Sinoe. Reconciliation and reintegration were mainly taking place spontaneously. During 1998, the Belgian Red Cross tried to establish programmes to speed up social reintegration in rural areas. In several rural towns they opened schools for skills training aimed at giving youth from the vicinity both theoretical and practical education. As part of the assessment team for this project I toured around in rural Sinoe and interviewed inhabitants, trying to locate needs in the communities. One conclusion was that there was no need to train carpenters, mechanics and electricians. In one town we found three carpenters, all three unemployed. The need for mechanics was equally limited. Only three cars were registered in the entire county. The need for other mechanics was also marginal. Electricity was unavailable, and even in Greenville town at the time the only sources were generators at the hospital and in three INGO compounds. Even under these limiting circumstances, 50 per cent of all youth (girls included) interviewed wanted to become mechanics. Despite the limitations, the Belgian Red Cross rushed the programme, going against our recommendations, and began to educate youth in just those trades for which there was no demand.[17] In fact, it is highly questionable whether any kind of programme was needed in the area because social reintegration was proceeding so well. Educating youth in skills for which they find no use only forges a class of educated, but disgruntled youth, again deceived by the world. Worse, it would be a further incentive for urbanisation, as many of these semi-educated youth would next try their luck in Monrovia, or other overcrowded urban environments, filled to the brim with unemployed people of rural origin.

As noted above, many of the young ex-combatants in Sinoe County had already by mid-1998 returned to their families and villages. They were resettling in the larger networks of extended families and, through that, in village life in general. In most cases they had cut off contacts with other ex-combatants and were no longer enmeshed in patron networks from the war years. Other vertical relationships had effectively replaced their dependency under rebel commanders. Even if it appeared that life was returning to the way it was during 'normal day', it should be observed that permanent changes had also taken place. For instance,

[17] The director did not have the slightest patience to understand local sociology. That the project hired an anthropologist was a requirement from Brussels, and our report was totally disregarded by him. Ignoring local officials, the local Red Cross administration and his own staff's advice, he soon managed to make himself and his NGO remarkably unpopular. Within a year the project was forced to close down.

there was an upsurge in marriage involving quite young men, or young couples living together in their own house. In tandem with this there was also a tendency for young men (and even boys, the youngest I heard of was 15) to farm their own land. Prior to the war it was rare to find men establishing themselves as individual farmers and family heads before they turned 25. They would work on the family farm or participate in communal farm activities but seldom worked for themselves. This suggests that the dividing line between childhood and adulthood has moved further down the age pyramid. The finding fits rather well with the 'traditional' idea of warriorhood as a path towards becoming a man, and being rewarded with a farm and a wife.

Semi-urban – Ganta

Ganta, the largest town in Nimba County, was a temporary settlement for many ex-combatant soldiers. Characteristically, groups of ex-combatants lived together in houses, either squatting or paying symbolic rent to the owner. From the onset of my fieldwork in Ganta I joined several groups of ex-combatants, but as I deepened my focus I chose one main group of people to work with. Paul and his friends were living in a house together, several wartime friends, their girlfriends and children. Their house was also a meeting-point for people of their kind, and it is in this socially extended form that I discuss 'Paul and his friends'. I knew Paul from my work in Côte d'Ivoire and our acquaintance proved instrumental in building trust. Quite soon I felt we could talk pretty openly about most issues, and they went out of their way to teach me about their post-war livelihoods, as well as about their lives as combatants during the civil war years.

Paul and his friends came mainly from Nimba and Bong Counties, and had histories of fighting for INPFL (Independent National Patriotic Front of Liberia), NPFL or both. Nimba County functioned as the primary pick-up area for the NPFL, with Bong County coming a close second. As the NPFL entered Nimba, the population in general saw it as a Nimba revolution against the government, which had persecuted Nimba people, in particular, following the failed coup attempt in 1985 (Osaghae 1996; Ellis 1999; AfricaWatch 1990). To join NPFL, or its sister movement INPFL, came naturally to most youth. The NPFL split soon after it entered Liberia, due to disagreement between Charles Taylor and Prince Johnson. Hailing from Nimba County, Johnson was the more popular of the two. After the split Johnson maintained command over most of the Libyan-trained soldiers (the core of the original NPFL) and further managed to enrol a large number of local youth in his force. In this fashion Johnson was more successful than Taylor during the primary phase of the war. In the long run, however, Taylor turned out to be a shrewder politician and outsmarted 'the soldier by profession' Johnson, who left soon after he managed to catch and kill President Doe (Huband 1998; Ellis 1999; Van den Boom 1995).

After the war came to a halt in 1996, Paul and his friends, for various reasons, ended up in Ganta. Even if they had plans to go back to their home-towns and villages, in the rural areas, these had not materialised by late 1998. To sustain themselves, Paul and some of the others were making mud bricks. The later part of 1998 saw the beginning of a construction boom in Ganta, and people were in dire need of construction material, primarily bricks. Making mud bricks on contract was a heavy and tedious job, but it paid quite well. Simultaneously with Paul and his friends a lot of others started off in the same line of business. The brick-making guild consisted predominantly of ex-combatant youth with close bonds to each other, and roots in the warring factions.

Typically three or four boys worked together on a contract basis. The building contractor was generally a private person, but work could also be carried out for churches, or schools. The contractor would allocate a spot where the soil was suited to extracting material for making bricks. He/she would also provide some shovels and some money in advance (alternatively rice, soup stock and a tin of sardines for a daily meal). The deals struck were simple enough; money was paid per brick after the work was complete. Generally it was agreed upon in advance how many bricks should be made. On the location the boys constructed a small hut thatched with palm leaves for shade and rain protection. To prevent theft, someone slept on the site overnight. During the rainy season it was not possible to make bricks, as they would not dry. However, as heavy showers were frequent, even towards the end of the dry season, banana leaves, and other leaves of similar size, were used to cover the bricks, preventing them from getting wet and subsequently cracking in the sun. A similar activity other ex-combatants were involved in was breaking rock (used in the foundation of houses or when constructing roads) in small quarries. A few also worked on large-scale projects such as EU-sponsored rice fields, earning 'a dollar a day'.

On the domestic side Paul and his friends were taking care of their backyard gardens, mainly for subsistence, but their wives and girlfriends sometimes sold the surplus products from a market table (*wallah*) in front of the house. Ex-combatant youth were also involved in other petty trades such as buying hard liquor, produced on sugarcane farms in the rural areas, and transporting it to Ganta, or even Monrovia. They would also buy cassava, rice, bush-meat from the countryside – depending on what was available in season – sold it in larger towns. Yet other ex-combatants were involved in petty trading activities such as money changing (indeed ex-combatants had close to a monopoly on that business – in general having some senior businessman backing them up), small scale diamond transporting, etc. Learning to do business was one of the positive side effects of the war years, as many young combatants, as well as their girlfriends, administered the selling of looted goods. Many continued to use the trade skills they had learnt during war in the post-war setting.

Earnest hard work was a key aspect of social reintegration in post-war society. Paul and most other ex-combatants worked hard towards achieving this goal. It was surprisingly seldom that other neighbours complained about ex-fighters misbehaving, and creating problems. All members of Paul's house went to church on Sundays, and many spent leisure time at church, doing Bible studies and other social activities, during the weeks. Even a renowned hard-core fighter, Alex,[18] was active in church. He spent a lot of time in the 'church business', being the accountant for a local parish. Religion, mainly in the form of Pentecostal churches, played a central role in Liberian society in normal times (Gifford 1993; Noonoo 1991). However, during the war years, churches became a central place to deal with war and exile experiences. Among Liberian refugees

---

[18] Alex is not talking a lot about morality but he believes in forgiving: 'You have to be both good and bad', he once told me, 'Today as I go to Monrovia, I say hello to the people I cut the ears off during the war'.

in the Ivory Coast, churches were the most important institutions organising refugee life (Utas 1997). In a different context Marc Sommers (2001a; 2001b) has noted the immediate appeal of Pentecostalism for young urbanites, creating bonds between people previously regarded as different. In that vein I argue that the inclusiveness of Pentacostal churches makes them a primary tool for reintegration in post-war society. Joining a local church is an attempt to ask for forgiveness and reacceptance from God and the local community equally.

Neighbours showed little direct contempt for ex-combatants. Even if many ex-combatants still abused alcohol and other drugs, and thus at times misbehaved, neighbours were often aware of the advantage of having them in the vicinity. During the war, civilians had learned the benefits of maintaining good contacts with high-rank military figures in the neighbourhood, and to a certain extent this paid dividends. The mere presence of ex-combatants living nearby served as a deterrent to thieves. As the thieves themselves were quite often also ex-combatants they formed part of an overlapping social network, and as such it was quite unlikely they would target an area protected by peers.

Even if Paul and his friends did not live in their home communities, they were still testing out the supportive capacity of old ties with kin and home. However, a great uncertainty prevailed. What would happen to them when they returned home? Would kin and community members punish them? Would they be blamed and stigmatised for what they and others had done during the war years? Paul and a few of the others talked with confidence about their family ties, but others were bitter, and blamed their parents for pushing them into the war in the first place. By this time many had become acutely aware that their war efforts had placed them in a much worse predicament than when they first joined.

In the lives of Paul and his friends it was the war-friend network that still dominated social ties. Many young ex-combatants lived together with the very friends they fought with. They worked together, and spent most of their leisure time with other ex-combatants. At the time, it appeared to be typical for the semi-urban setting (cf. remarks above on Greenville). In most cases the wartime families also remained intact. It was common to find a young man sharing a house with his friends, staying with one or two wives/girlfriends in a single room. Often these young ex-fighters had several children with different girlfriends. Another characteristic of this environment was the relative absence of adults. Except for neighbours, who had limited influence in any case, adults were largely absent, with one exception – the presence of 'big men'. Often 'big men' were the very same men who had commanded them in the rebel armies, but in some instances local patrons from outside the military hierarchy had regained influence. One needs to bear in mind that many of the commanders during the war years were youths in the same age range as the fighters themselves. These (youthful) 'big men' often maintained their standing within war networks, but it was more seldom that they managed to maintain any position of power in the larger society.

In 1998 young ex-combatants in the semi-urban areas were slowly preparing to move back towards their home communities.[19] They were not able, however,

---

[19] When I returned to Ganta in early 2000 I found that all, with the exception of two young girls, had left Paul's house. This is a clear indication that the resettlement/reintegration process was proceeding. I was told that Paul had again left for Danane trying to get on a resettlement programme to Canada. Later the same year I learned that he was back in Ganta.

to proceed too fast, but had to assess their situation carefully so as not to get stuck in any unbearable situation. Further, they were waiting to return home until they could bring something home to prove that they had managed well – that they had got something out of the experience. To return in rags was no option.[20] Many of the young ex-combatants in Ganta, including most of Paul's friends, saw education as an opportunity to make up with their families. Returning with an education might, quite likely, make up for other deficiencies, and thus provide an entry ticket to social acceptance. Another path available at the time was to take waged labour work. The plantation industry was slowly re-emerging as an employer. Alluvial mining was another business where young labour was plentifully needed. Likewise logging had become important in post-war Liberia. Cutting down the remaining rain forest might not be good for the country but for ex-combatant youth it was a job providing both a salary and renewed respect in society. To join the army was yet another path. In short they were back to the opportunity structure with which youth were familiar prior to the war (Jackson 1977; Richards 1996a).

Comparing the Cases of Reintegration

As we have seen above, there were differences in the opportunity structures for ex-combatants, depending on where along the sliding scale between urban and rural they were situated in the post-war environment. In the Monrovia case we saw that youth were being aided to get back into society by numerous international and national aid organisations. However, it seems that, whatever education or skills were taught, ex-combatants remained jobless and footloose. In rural Sinoe the situation was quite the opposite. Social reintegration seemed to be working well and with surprising speed. As I showed above, aid directed towards reintegration of youth in this setting might even harm such a process in the long term. Finally, in the semi-urban, or semi-rural, case of Ganta we followed a group of highly motivated ex-combatant youths, who were themselves seriously working towards re-acceptance and reintegration, in either pre-war homes or novel post-war environments. International donor community aid to ex-combatants should be context-specific, and begin by understanding the combatants themselves. It was striking – in Ganta 1998 – how few donors targeted ex-combatant youth at all.

Parts of the military structure remained intact in ex-combatant networks, and organisational skills were maintained within these networks.[21] For instance, the smooth operation, and general success, of the brick-making guild in Ganta rests on war networks. The boys comprising the brick-making guild were to a large extent ex-combatants, and when they organised their work they made use of organising skills they learnt in the military structures of the rebel armies. Their former commander could work as a contractor, or broker, between them and the buyer. Similar networks of ex-combatants were found in the gold and diamond

---

[20] Cf. urban refugees: they are often prepared to wait for several years, so that they can return with some kind of wealth and pride.

[21] Aid projects could make efficient use of that. Already many aid projects have ex-commanders high up in their organisations, who are making informal use of ex-combatants from their former military units. Many international organisations are either unaware they employ senior rebel commanders, or have chosen to ignore such facts.

mining, in the smaller (as well as some larger) logging projects, in sugarcane farming and on rubber, coffee and cocoa plantations. In larger corporations the wartime patrimonial structures were often broken down and replaced with civilian patron/client networks.

To have participated in the war, as opposed to not having done so, was clearly seen as a 'touchstone of fraternity' (Scott 1990:39). On the basis of war experience, ex-combatants remained part of a sub-culture with distinctive social codes and standards. Thus such a comradeship, or military 'buddy system' (Ben-Ari 1998:101), was employed for other means than fighting a war. I propose that military structures and discipline can be regarded as positive and if utilised with care can help to speed up demobilisation and reintegration. Skill of command from the national military is often highly rewarded in private corporations as well as in the civil service in the western world. It could certainly be used as such in Liberia, too. I equally express fear over aid projects further enhancing tendencies towards urbanisation, already a dominant aspect of Liberian development. During the early post-war years too much effort was spent on educating ex-combatants in too few skills. Carpenters, mechanics or electricians were flooding Liberia. Every single young woman was educated in soap making and in the process of tie-and-dye. How would they benefit from such skills? Would they all urbanise? If more and more Liberian youth urbanise, the risk is that they will end up in places like the Palace.

Reintegration or Re-marginalisation

As I briefly suggested in the introduction to this article, the data I have presented point towards a complex picture of reintegration. This is a typical NGO buzzword, but it does not tell us much about the social realities of a particular area. In rural settings, reintegration is a process clearly taking place. But in the other two settings reintegration is a more difficult issue to assess. One of the cornerstones of my work is the argument that the Liberian Civil War was partially an outcome of the structural marginalisation of youth. Due to economic crisis and increasing dependence on the central state in the 1980s an ever-growing number of young people in urban and semi-urban environments were excluded even from the possibilities of becoming adults. Possibilities to participate in the wage economy diminished and education ceased having any importance. With this crisis looming, many young men lost even the possibility to establish themselves as adults, by building a house, or getting married – even though they continued to become fathers, of children for whom they could not provide. Chronologically, they outgrew youth, but socially they became 'youthmen' (Momoh 1999).

The rebel factions were specifically successful in recruiting from the category of already marginalised and highly dissatisfied young urbanites and semi-urbanites. Is it thus strange that we see, in the post-war setting, few tendencies towards reintegration of youth in the urban case? Marginalisation appears to be the norm for a large proportion of young urbanites. Thus re-marginalisation and not reintegration is the natural outcome awaiting most ex-combatants. In the semi-urban case we see a tendency to both reintegration and re-marginalisation. Young ex-combatants work arduously to escape from the margin. They know very well that they risk ending up back there, because it is the place from which so many ex-combatants came. Enlistment in the armies, in the first place, was envisaged as a move away from the margin and into the centre of society – a means of integrating in society, even if by force. But it seems inevitable that many will be remarginalised at the end of the war, even if some, by striving especially hard, are successful in turning the tide. The war endeavour for some might actually have made a difference – enabling their integration. But for a large proportion of Liberian ex-combatants re-marginalisation, not reintegration, remains the only reality. Extreme poverty and lack of opportunities maintain the continuum of war and peace in Liberia.

Epilogue

During 1999 the security situation in Liberia deteriorated. Parts of Liberia experienced moments of unrest verging on war. Heavy shooting put civilians to flight. Even so, most observers regarded the war as closed. Yet by the end of 1999 upper Lofa County was experiencing the first of a series of armed incursions. By mid 2000, groups of insurgents were entering from neighbouring Guinea on a regular basis. Liberians saw the birth and growth of a new rebel movement, ironically named Liberians United for Reconciliation and Democracy (LURD). LURD rebels have since that time operated in Lofa County, on occasions advancing towards Monrovia. During the first half of 2002, LURD made a series of successful raids in Bong, Bomi and Montserrado Counties, temporarily taking control of the major towns, Gbarnga, Tubmanburg and Klay Junction, before troops loyal to the government were able to recapture them. In mid May 2002, an attack on President Taylor's birth place (Arthington, less than 20 kilometres from Monrovia) caused headlong panic in Monrovia. The tide changed, and during the autumn of 2002 LURD was forcibly driven back. However, in February 2003 LURD groups again captured Tubmanburg and Bopolu.[22] With a core of soldiers recruited from among Liberian exiles in Guinea, LURD has also been able to enlist young people from within Liberia. Similarly, the Armed Forces of Liberia (AFL), along with various governmental security forces and pro-governmental paramilitaries, have succeeded in drawing fresh support and recruitment among young Liberians, mainly from Monrovia and surrounding counties. It is highly conceivable that many of the young men and women written about in this text have taken part in these new developments.

In this renewed civil war (2000 and onwards) the Guinean government, despite its official denials, has been supporting and training LURD (see International Crisis Group 2003:10–12). There is little doubt that US support to the Guinean army has benefited LURD rebels (ibid., and Human Rights Watch 2002), and the US government stands firm in its wish to rid Liberia of Charles Taylor. Currently it would also appear that, since March 2003, the Ivorian government has supported a new rebel force MODEL[23] (Movement for Democracy in Liberia),

---

[22] Most observers believe that pro-government groups stage certain attacks so as to go about the business of looting, logging and diamond digging with impunity. It is also likely that the government makes use of these attacks so as to enable new political space in Monrovia. Thus it is difficult to verify what is rebel activity and what is actually government-sponsored.

[23] MODEL emerged as a separate movement from LURD only in April 2003, thus it is yet not clear what the objectives are. However, see their Declaration of Intent on *The Perspective* homepage: http://www.theperspective.org/newrebelgroup.html

active in south-eastern Liberia (International Crisis Group 2003: 20–24). Its presence is an outcome of an apparent split in the LURD leadership along the old ULIMO-J/ULIMO-K lines. By pointing to the involvement and intervention of other governments in Liberian affairs, Charles Taylor was equally active. Since the emergence of the RUF (Revolutionary United Front of Sierra Leone) in 1991, he has continued to meddle in that country's conflict. It is also quite clear that pro-Taylor militias have been very active in MPIGO (Mouvement Populaire Ivoirien du Grand Ouest) – the western rebel force engaged in the internecine struggle in Ivory Coast (International Crisis Group 2003: 15–20). The MPIGO is based in Danane, once the Ivorian stronghold of the NPFL.

LURD and MODEL finally reached Monrovia in July 2003. Taylor's troops were hemmed in parts of the city, fighting was fierce, and many civilians suffered. Under strong international pressure, Taylor left for exile in Nigeria. An interim government has been formed, while the guns have yet to quieten. Those who believe Taylor caused the war hope for peace. A more sober analysis suggests that the failure of impoverished young people to find a secure place in Liberian society will sustain a situation of 'no peace, no war'.

Endnote

* This essay refers to the period before resumption of hostilities and the peace accords of 2003.

References

Abdullah, I., et al. 1997, 'Lumpen youth culture and political violence: Sierra Leoneans debate the RUF and the civil war' *Africa Development*. xxii (3/4): 171–216

Abdullah, Ibrahim 1997, 'Introduction' Special issue on Lumpen culture and political violence: the Sierra Leone Civil War *Africa Development* xxii (3/4): 5–18

—— 1998, 'Bush path to destruction: the origin and character of the Revolutionary United Front/Sierra Leone' *The Journal of Modern African Studies* 36 (2): 203–35

AfricaWatch 1990, 'Liberia: flight from terror: testimony of abuses in Nimba County' *Liberia Studies Journal* (reprint) xv(1): 142–61

Ben-Ari, Eyal 1998, *Mastering soldiers: conflict, emotions, and the enemy in an Israeli military unit* New York: Berghahn Books

Bernat, J. Christopher 1999, 'Children and the politics of violence in Haitian context: statist violence, scarcity and street child agency in Port-au-Prince' *Critique of Anthropology* 19 (2): 121–38

Bledsoe, Carolyn 1990, 'The politics of AIDS, condoms and heterosexual relations in Africa: recent evidence from local print media' in Handwerker, Penn W. ed., *Births and power: social change and the politics of reproduction* Boulder, CO: Westview Press

Bourgois, Philippe I. 1995, *In search of respect: selling crack in El Barrio Philippe Bourgois* Cambridge: Cambridge University Press

Bucholtz, Mary 2002, 'Youth and cultural practice' *Annual Review of Anthropology*. 31: 525–52

Certeau, Michel de 1984, *The practice of everyday life* Berkeley: University of California Press

Chingono, Mark F. 1996, *The state, violence and development: the political economy of war in Mozambique, 1975–1992* Aldershot & Brookfield, VT: Avebury

Cruise O'Brien, Donal B. 1996, 'A lost generation? Youth identity and state decay in West Africa' in Werbner, Richard and Ranger, Terence eds, *Postcolonial identities in Africa* London: Zed Books

El-Kenz, Ali 1996, 'Youth and Violence' in Ellis, Stephen ed. *Africa now: people, policies and institutions* The Hague & London: DGIS & James Currey

Ellis, Stephen 1998, 'Liberia's warlord insurgency' in Clapham, Christopher ed. *African guerrillas* Oxford: James Currey

—— 1999, *The mask of anarchy: the destruction of Liberia and the religious dimension of an African civil war* New York: New York University Press

Ferguson, James 1999, *Expectations of modernity: myths and meanings of urban life on the Zambian Copperbelt* Berkeley: University of California Press

Gifford, Paul 1993, *Christianity and politics in Doe's Liberia*. Cambridge & New York: Cambridge University Press

Guyer, Jane I. 1995, *Money matters: instability, values, and social payments in the modern history of West African communities* Portsmouth, NH & London: Heinemann & James Currey

Hall, Tom and Montgomery, Heather 2000, 'Home and away: "childhood", "youth" and young people' *Anthropology Today*. 16 (3): 13–15

Hannerz, Ulf 1987, 'The world in creolisation' *Africa*. 57 (4): 546–59

Hannerz, Ulf 1996, *Transnational connections: culture, people, places* London & New York: Routledge

Hazlehurst, Kayleen Hazlehurst Cameron 1998, *Gangs and youth subcultures: international explorations* New Brunswick, NJ: Transaction Publishers

Honwana, Alcinda and De Boeck, Filip eds 2005, forthcoming, *Makers and breakers: children and youth in postcolonial Africa* Oxford & Trenton, NJ: James Currey & Africa World Press

Huband, Mark 1998, *The Liberian civil war* London & Portland, OR: F. Cass

Human Rights Watch 2002, 'Back to the brink: war crimes by the Liberian governent and rebels: a call for greater international attention to Liberia and the sub region' Washington, DC: Africa Division

International Crisis Group 2003, 'Tackling Liberia: the eye of the regional storm' Freetown/Brussels: International Crisis Group

Jackson, Michael 1977, *The Kuranko: dimensions of social reality in a West African society* London: C. Hurst

Jensen, Steffen 2001, 'Claiming community – negotiating crime: state formation, neighbourhood and gangs in a Capetonian township'. Unpublished PhD: Roskilde University

Keen, David 1998, *The economic functions of violence in civil wars*. Oxford & New York: Oxford University Press for the International Institute for Strategic Studies

Kynoch, Gary 1999, 'From the Ninevites to the Hard Livings Gang: township gangsters and urban violence in twentieth-century South Africa' *African Studies*. 58 (1): 55–85

La Fontaine, Jean S. 1970, 'Two types of youth group in Kinshasa (Léopoldville)' in Mayer, Philip ed. *Socialization: the approach from social anthropology* London: Tavistock Publications Limited

MacGaffey, Janet 1991, *The real economy of Zaire: the contribution of smuggling & other unofficial activities to national wealth*. Philadelphia, PA & London: University of Pennsylvania Press & James Currey

Marks, Monique 2001, *Young warriors: youth politics, identity and violence in South Africa* Johannesburg: Witwatersrand University Press

Momoh, Abubakar 1999, 'The youth crisis in Nigeria: understanding the phenonemon of the area boys and girls', Paper presented to the conference on Children and youth as emerging categories in Africa, Leuven

Noonoo, Kofi Aaba 1991, 'Relationship between children's self-esteem and their perception of parental behaviour and God images among Liberians and African-Americans' Unpublished PhD dissertation, Ann Arbor, MI: University Microfilms International

Osaghae, Eghosa E. 1996, *Ethnicity, class and the struggle for state power in Liberia* Dakar: Codesria

Ottenberg, Simon 1989, *Boyhood rituals in an African society : an interpretation* Seattle, WA: University of Washington Press

Panter-Brick, Catherine 2002, 'Street children, human rights, and public health: a critique and future directions' *Annual Review of Anthropology* 31: 147–71

Peters, Krijn and Richards, Paul 1998, 'Jeunes combattants parlant de la guerre et la paix en Sierra Leone' *Cahiers d'Ètudes africaines* 150–2 (xxxviii-2–4): 581–617

Rashid, Ismail 1997, 'Subaltern reactions: lumpens, students, and the left' *Africa Development* xxii (3/4): 19–44

Reno, William 1995, 'Reinvention of an African patrimonial state: Charles Taylor's Liberia' *Third World Quarterly* 16 (1): 109–20

—— 1998, *Warlord politics and African states* Boulder, CO: Lynne Rienner Publishers

Richards, Paul 1995, 'Rebellion in Liberia and Sierra Leone: A crisis of youth?' in Furley, Oliver, ed. *Conflict in Africa* London: Tauris Academic Studies

—— 1996a, *Fighting for the rain forest: war, youth and resources in Sierra Leone* Oxford: James Currey

—— 1996b, 'The Sierra Leone–Liberia boundary wilderness: rain forests, diamonds and war' in Nugent, Paul and Asiwaju, A.I. eds *African boundaries: barriers, conduits and opportunities* London: Pinter

—— 1999, 'The social life of war: Rambo, diamonds and young soldiers in Sierra Leone' *Track Two*

8 (1): 16–21

Riesman, Paul 1986 'The person and the life cycle in African social life and thought' *African Studies Review*. 29 (2): 71–38

Scheper-Hughes, Nancy 1992, *Death without weeping: the violence of everyday life in Brazil* Berkeley: University of California Press

Schneider, Eric C. 1999, *Vampires, dragons, and Egyptian kings: youth gangs in postwar New York* Princeton, NJ: Princeton University Press

Scott, James C. 1985, *Weapons of the weak: everyday forms of peasant resistance* New Haven, CT: Yale University Press

Scott, James C. 1990, *Domination and the arts of resistance: hidden transcripts* New Haven, CT: Yale University Press

Sesay, Max Ahmadu 1996, 'Politics and society in post-war Liberia' *The Journal of Modern African Studies* 34(3): 395–420

Sommers, Marc 2001a, *Fear in Bongoland: Burundi refugees in urban Tanzania* New York: Berghahn Books

Sommers, Marc 2001b, 'Young, male and Pentecostal: urban refugees in Dar es Salaam, Tanzania' *Journal of Refugee Studies* 14 (4): 347–70

Ssewakiriyanga, Richard 1999, '"New kids on the blocks": African-American music and Uganda youth' *CODESRIA Bulletin* (1 & 2): 24–8

Sykes, Karen 1999, 'After the "raskol" feast: youths' alienation in the New Ireland, Papua New Guinea' *Critique of Anthropology* 19 (2): 157–74

Utas, Mats 1997. *Assiduous exile: strategies of work and integration among Liberian refugees in Danane, the Ivory Coast.* Uppsala: Department of Cultural Anthropology

—— 1999, 'Girls' "loving business" – sex and the struggle for status and independence in Liberia' *Antropologiska Studier* (64–65): 65–76

—— 2003, 'Sweet battlefields: youth and the Liberian civil war' PhD thesis Uppsala: Department of Cultural Anthropology and Ethnology, Uppsala University

—— 2004a, 'Fluid research fields: studying ex-combatant youth in the aftermath of the Liberian Civil War' in Boyden, J and de Berry, Jo, eds, *Children and youth on the frontline: ethnography, armed conflict and displacement.* Oxford: Berghahn Books

—— 2005, forthcoming, 'Agency of victims: young women's survival strategies in the Liberian civil war' in Honwana, Alcinda and De Boeck, Filip eds *Makers and breakers: children and youth in postcolonial Africa* Oxford & Trenton, NJ: James Currey & Africa World Press

Van den Boom, D. 1995, *Bürger Krieg in Liberia* Münster: Lit

Virilio, Paul and Lotringer, Sylvere 1997, *Pure war* New York: Semiotext(e), Inc

9

Memories of Violence
Recreation of Ethnicity in Post-Colonial Zimbabwe[1]

BJÖRN LINDGREN

In the 2000 parliamentary elections, President Mugabe and his Zanu-PF govern-ment used an inverted form of the racial politics once used by British colonisers. In order to gain political support they played on the distinction between white colonial landowners and the black African landless. They were thereby able to justify occupations of white-owned commercial farms, while at the same time using violence against the opposition party MDC (Movement for Democratic Change). The same tactics were used in the 2002 presidential election, after which the government announced that its 'fast-track land reform' had come to an end. Attacks on the civilian population have continued, however, particularly by the Zanu-PF youth militia, instead of 'war veterans' as perpetrators of violence.

This is not the first time the president and the ruling party have resorted to violence in order to rule Zimbabwe. In this chapter I describe how Robert Mugabe and the ruling Zanu-PF party, shortly after independence in 1980, sent the Fifth Brigade to hunt down so-called dissidents in southern Zimbabwe, and how civilians in the Umzingwane district remember this violence. In practice, the brigade did not target 'dissidents', but the political opposition of the time and its supporters. In this conflict a politics was practised with ethnicity at its centre. Shona-speaking soldiers were used against Ndebele-speaking civilians, and thousands of people were killed.

To understand political violence in Zimbabwe today we need to take into account past injustices. This holds true not only for the colonial violence and land occupations to which Mugabe often refers (e.g., *New African* 2002 and 2003), but for the atrocities associated with the 'hunt for dissidents' for which the president and the Zanu-PF themselves were responsible in the 1980s. I argue that this violence was politically motivated, with Mugabe and the Zanu-PF playing on ethnicity as a means to achieve a one-party state. The violence was not primarily a conflict between army soldiers and dissidents, with the civilian population caught in-between, as it is sometimes portrayed (e.g. Ranger 1999: 1,

[1] This article is based on periods of fieldwork in southern Zimbabwe between 1997 and 2002. The fieldwork was mainly funded by the Royal Swedish Academy of Sciences. Apart from Paul Richards and my colleagues at Uppsala University, I would like to thank informants in Umzingwane district, as well as Don Handelman and Isak Niehaus, for valuable discussions and comments.

246ff). It was a tactic of warfare aimed at hitting both rival politicians in southern Zimbabwe and the civilian population supporting them.

I also suggest that the Zanu-PF political strategy provoked a reaction along ethnic lines in Matabeleland in southern Zimbabwe – cultural 'resistance' in Carolyn Nordstrom's (1997) sense of the term – that led to a re-creation of Ndebele ethnicity. This has made the period between 1980 and 1987, and especially the Fifth Brigade's atrocities in 1983 and 1984, constitutive of Ndebele ethnicity today. 'It is in creativity, in the fashioning of self and world that people find the most potent weapon against war', Nordstrom (1997: 4) writes in her study of Mozambique. Today, men and women in Umzingwane district explicitly identify themselves as Ndebele when remembering the atrocities.

Finally, I propose that narratives of atrocities have strengthened and spread feelings of Ndebeleness in southern Zimbabwe. Discussion of the Fifth Brigade was for a long time suppressed in public debate (e.g., Kaarsholm 1997, Werbner 1998), but has since the late 1990s been publicly voiced to new generations of Zimbabweans. Memory is the link between the past and identity. 'We are what we remember', as Fentress and Wickham (1992:7) put it. But it is above all when memories of violence are narrated in public that people together start to 'remake the world' and re-arrange social categories into evil and good (Das and Kleinman 2001, Malkki 1995:52ff).

In what follows, I give a short description of some of the societal categories that people in southern Zimbabwe may identify with. Thereafter I describe how violence in the liberation war continued after independence, and how politicians used ethnicity to achieve their goals. I then retell the stories of three men in Umzingwane district who held positions especially targeted by the Fifth Brigade: ex-Zipra guerrilla Akukho Khumalo, Zapu politician No Nyathi, and Headmaster Aliyase Moyo. I first describe how these men experienced the atrocities. Thereafter I turn to Terence Ranger's (1989, 1999) description of the violence carried out in neighbouring Matobo district, before I contrast Ranger's findings with the explanations the three men offer of the violence they experienced. I end by suggesting that a narrative of the Fifth Brigade's atrocities in terms of 'evil' Shona and 'good' Ndebele makes people's experiences of suffering understandable and easier to cope with, and that these atrocities have influenced the way people voted in the latest parliamentary and presidential elections.

'The Ndebele' and Other Categories of Belonging

In daily parlance, people in Zimbabwe talk of themselves as Ndebele if they speak Ndebele as their mother-tongue, and as Shona if they speak Shona as their first language. In the latter case, they may also refer to themselves as Zezuru, Karanga, Manyika, Korekore, Ndau, and Kalanga. This is a consequence of the linguistic classification of isiNdebele as an Nguni-language, in contrast to chiShona divided into six sub-categories (e.g., Bourdillon 1987:16ff, Bastin, Coupez, et al. 1999, SIL 2002). Out of the total Zimbabwean population of some ten and a half million people, roughly one and a half million speak Ndebele while about eight and a half million speak Shona or one of its sub-categories (Census 1994, SIL 2002).

The geographical concentration of Ndebele-speakers in Matabeleland is a result of the first Ndebele king Mzilikazi Khumalo's migration from eastern South Africa

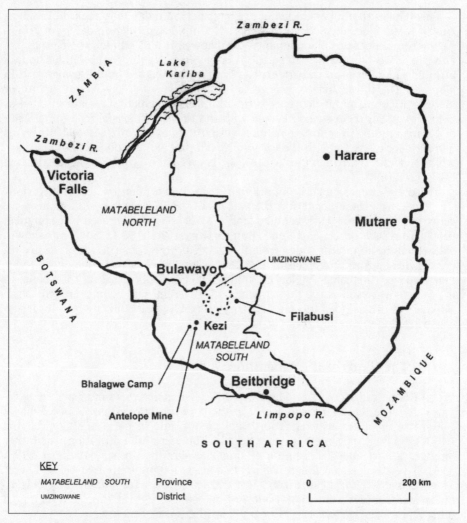

Map: Zimbabwe showing research area   *(© Per Nordesjö)*

to southern Zimbabwe in the 19th century. Historians differ in their representations of the formation of the Ndebele state, but in short Mzilikazi Khumalo left Shaka Zulu's emerging kingdom with a small Nguni-speaking group in about 1820 and ended up in what today is Matabeleland in Zimbabwe in 1840. When Mzilikazi and his followers had left Shaka, they were reinforced on their way north by, among others, various Sotho-speakers from South Africa, and later on by groups who would be labelled Shona-speakers (notably Karanga- and Kalanga-speakers) in today's Zimbabwe (see e.g. Cobbing 1976).[2]

---

[2] Mzilikazi and his followers probably got the name *amaNdebele* during their migration north by Sotho-speakers who called them *Matebele* (Hughes & van Velsen 1954), and are in early missionary writings referred to as the *Matabele* (Moffat 1835, Livingstone 1857). In 1870, Mzilikazi was

This implies that a person living in Matabeleland today may regard himself as Zimbabwean, Ndebele, and, for instance, Nguni, i.e. an Ndebele of Nguni origin. Apart from categories of nationality (Zimbabwean) and ethnicity (Ndebele), we may therefore talk about categories of origin (e.g. Nguni, Sotho, and 'Shona'), including more specific categories (e.g. Zulu within Nguni, and Karanga within 'Shona'). The most obvious way to tell if a person is of, say Nguni, Sotho, or 'Shona' origin, is by his or her *isibongo* (pl. *izibongo*), which often is translated as 'totem name' or 'clan name'. People with the *isibongo Khumalo*, for example, are of Nguni origin. They are sometimes referred to by themselves and others as 'pure' Ndebele. People with the *isibongo Nyathi* (buffalo) are often of Sotho origin, while a person with a name like *Moyo* (heart) often is of 'Shona' origin (see Lindgren, 2004).

These and other categories of belonging are drawn upon by people in various situations. Like the other terms, the category Ndebele has been continuously reconstructed since the 19th century, and may or may not be used to distinguish people from each other. As Terence Ranger (e.g., 1985, 1993, 1999) has shown, Ndebele and Shona ethnicities were to a high degree constructed, or rather reconstructed, during colonialism, i.e. they were 'invented' or 'imagined'. After independence, the category Ndebele could have been contrasted to 'the Shona' in a positive way, following the principal of 'different but equal', but the Fifth Brigade's atrocities ruled this out for many people. Instead ethnicity has since been constructed along quite hostile lines.

The 'End' of the Liberation War

When Rhodesia became Zimbabwe in 1980 after many years of armed struggle, war came to an end for some people in the country, but certainly not for all. In the provinces of Matabeleland North and South, and in parts of Midlands, war was to continue for almost another decade. The end of the liberation war rather 'brought a brief interlude, more a fleeting cease-fire than peace' (Werbner 1995: 196). The struggle for independence had been fought from two sides. Robert Mugabe had led Zanu (later Zanu-PF) and its armed wing Zanla from Mozambique with support from China, and Joshua Nkomo had led Zapu and its armed wing Zipra from Zambia with support from the Soviet Union.[3]

At independence, ex-combatants from both sides were to be demobilised or integrated into the new Zimbabwe National Army (ZNA), but for different reasons many refused. Instead, ex-combatants were involved in various violent acts, from 'campaigning' for Zanu-PF and Zapu prior to the elections in February 1980, to armed clashes between ex-Zanla and ex-Zipra groups. Both ex-Zanlas and ex-Zipras caused problems, but Zanu-PF politicians soon used the term 'dissident' for ex-Zipras only (Alexander 1998:152ff). The argument was that ex-Zipras were dissatisfied with the outcome of the elections and were now using arms to change it. However, many ex-Zipras felt forced to become 'dissidents' because of

---

[2] (cont.) succeeded by one of his sons, Lobengula, who reigned over the Ndebele state until the British took over after a battle in 1893, and finally after a rising in 1896.

[3] Zanu(-PF) stands for 'the Zimbabwe African National Union (-Patriotic Front)', and its armed force Zanla for 'the Zimbabwe African National Liberation Army'. Zapu stands for 'the Zimbabwe Africa Peoples Union', and its armed wing Zipra for 'the Zimbabwe Peoples Revolutionary Army'.

persecution within the new army (Alexander 1998:156ff, see also Alexander, McGregor and Ranger 2000a:180ff).

Prime Minister Robert Mugabe and Zanu-PF politicians soon started to blame Joshua Nkomo and Zapu politicians for being behind dissident activities. In August 1981, it was announced that North Korean instructors had arrived to train a Fifth Brigade which according to the press should 'wipe out dissidents and criminals', including those found in the army. The decision to form this brigade was taken already in October 1980 (Alexander 1998: 155, 157). Nkomo expressed worries in *The Chronicle* that the Fifth Brigade was to be used 'for the possible imposition of a one-party state' (CCJP/LRF 1997: 45). This was never quite accomplished, but Mugabe expressed the wish to establish such a state several times during the 1980s (Quantin 1992), and Zanu-PF held nearly every seat in Parliament during the whole of the 1990s (Saunders 2000:38).

By claiming that Nkomo and Zapu were behind dissident activities, something both Nkomo (1984:224ff) and dissidents have denied (Alexander 1998, Yap 2001:172ff), Mugabe and Zanu-PF created an excuse to take control over the country. In February 1982, they announced that arms had been found on properties owned by a Zapu company and around Zipra assembly points. Mugabe presented this as evidence that Zapu was planning a coup to overthrow the government. As a result, Nkomo and other Zapu ministers were dismissed from government, and Nkomo had to flee the country. Senior Zipra officers were subsequently arrested on charges of treason. Although ex-Zipra commanders Lockout Masuku and Dumiso Dabengwa were not found guilty in High Court, they remained in jail until 1986 (Alexander 1998:155f).

To be able to rule the country without political opposition, Mugabe and Zanu-PF hit at the 'infrastructure' of Zapu, that is the mainly Ndebele-speaking civilian population in Matabeleland. The State of Emergency that had been introduced by the Smith regime in 1965 was continuously renewed every sixth month until 1990. This granted the government extra-legal powers, such as to impose curfews in various areas of Matabeleland, and to detain people without trial (CCJP/LRF 1997:42). The government also enacted the Emergency Powers Regulations after an attack on Mugabe's residence in June 1982 involving ex-Zipras, and a kidnapping of six tourists blamed on dissidents but possibly carried out by South African agents (CCJP/LRF 1997:42ff). This act granted freedom from prosecution to government officials and security forces, as long as their actions were 'for the purpose of or in connexion with the preservation of the security of Zimbabwe' (quoted in CCJP/LRF 1997:44).

Gukurahundi: the Fifth Brigade's Atrocities

The government sent various armed forces and intelligence units to Matabeleland from 1980 onwards, including the Zimbabwe National Army (ZNA), Police Support Units (PSUs), the Central Intelligence Organisation (CIO), and the Police Internal Security Intelligence Unit (PISI). However, the most brutal and feared force was the Fifth Brigade. The total number of soldiers sent to Matabeleland during this period is difficult to estimate. But with the arrival of the Fifth Brigade, there were at least 5,000 soldiers in Matabeleland North in January 1983, and about 15,000 soldiers in Matabeleland South in April 1984

(CCJP/LRF 1997:46f, 56).[4] The Fifth Brigade itself can be estimated at about 2 500 to 3 500 soldiers.

These figures should be compared with the number of dissidents, estimated to be 'no more than 400 at their height' (Alexander 1998:166), although government sources would have it to be between 750 and 800. Of these dissidents some belonged to 'Super Zapu'. This group of South African-backed dissidents mainly operated in Southwest Matabeleland between late 1982 and mid-1984. Super Zapu probably consisted of fewer than a hundred members, but caused considerable problems in the area. At the time of the general amnesty in May 1988, in total, 122 dissidents turned themselves in (CCJP/LRF 1997:30, 34, 37, 47, Alexander 1998:166, 164).

Unlike other army units, the Fifth Brigade was directly responsible to Prime Minister Mugabe, and consisted almost solely of Shona-speaking ex-Zanla combatants. The soldiers were distinctively uniformed with red berets, used AK-47s with bayonets, and had radios incompatible with other army units. At its passing out parade in December 1982, Mugabe handed over a brigade flag with the name *Gukurahundi* (Alexander 1998:157f, CCJP/LRF 1997:45ff). The *chiShona* term *Gukurahundi* refers to the cleansing spring rains that rinse away dirt. Whether it was Mugabe's and the Fifth Brigade's intention or not, people in Matabeleland came to see themselves as the dirt to be rinsed away.[5] Indeed, the Fifth Brigade has been described as trained to target not soldiers but civilians (CCJP/LRF 1997:50ff), which some dissidents have confirmed. One comment was that: 'It was trained to reduce the Matabeleland population, it was just killing civilians' (Alexander 1998:167).

Statements by Robert Mugabe and other Zanu-PF ministers in the media at the time also indicate this. Mugabe said that 'we don't differentiate when we fight, because we can't tell who's a dissident and who is not' (*The Chronicle* 18 April 1983). Emerson Mnangagwa, likening dissidents to cockroaches and the Fifth Brigade to DDT, argued that 'the campaign against dissidents can only succeed if the infrastructure which nurtures them is destroyed' (*The Chronicle* 5 March 1983). And Enos Nkala referred to dissidents as 'Ndebeles who were calling for a second war of liberation' (*The Chronicle* 30 June 1980). In 1985, he further described Zapu as a murderous organisation' which 'must be hit so hard that it doesn't feel obliged to do the things it has been doing' (quotes taken from LCFHR 1986:52, CCJP/LRF 1997:54, 69, and Alexander and McGregor 1999:252, 249ff).

When the Fifth Brigade arrived in Matabeleland North in January 1983, it started, in Alexander's (1998:158) words, a 'grotesquely violent campaign against civilians, civil servants, party chairmen, and *occasionally*, armed insurgents' (my emphasis). Within six weeks, CCJP/LRF (1997:48) reports, 'more than 2,000 civilians had died, hundreds of homesteads had been burnt,

---

[4] CCJP/LRF refers to *Africa Confidential*, 11 April 1984, for the latter figure. Since *Africa Confidential* lists the movements of brigades, battalions, and units without giving the figure 15,000, I take it that CCJP/LRF has extracted the numbers of soldiers from the various troops.

[5] Richard Werbner (1991:161ff) reports on this interpretation in Bulalima-Mangwe district where people mainly speak *chiKalanga*, which is close to *chiShona*. People in Umzingwane district also refer to this translation, even though most people speak *isiNdebele* and not *chiShona*. Jocelyn Alexander (1998:158, fn.) did not find the interpretation in Nkayi district, although Merete Tonnesen at Aarhus University did (personal communication 21 December 2000).

and thousands of civilians beaten'. The brigade's attacks have been described as explicitly 'tribal' in nature, including forcing people to speak and understand *chiShona*, reference to 'Ndebele' raids against the 'Shona' in the distant past, and demanding people shout anti-Zapu slogans (Werbner 1991:169, 1995:198ff, 1998:92ff, Amnesty International 1993, CCJP/LRF 1997:50ff, Alexander 1998:157ff).

In January 1984, the Fifth Brigade moved into Matabeleland South while the Zanu-PF government deployed a strategy once used by the Smith regime: to starve out the enemy. A curfew was imposed in the province restricting movements in and out of the area. People had experienced three years of drought and were dependent on government and international organisations for food. The government stopped this relief, and closed all local shops in the area. This was done in an area with 400 000 inhabitants, of whom at most 200 were dissidents (CCJP/LRF 1997:56).[6] At the same time around 8,000 people were detained, of whom many were taken to Bhalagwe camp in Matobo district. Later, skeletons from this period were found in Antelope Mine (Amnesty International 1993, CCJP/LRF 1997:57).

The Fifth Brigade was withdrawn from service in late 1984 to be retrained at Mbalabala, situated in Umzingwane district. It was briefly in service again in 1985, but finally withdrawn from Matabeleland in 1986 (CCJP/LRF 1997:57). From late 1984 and onwards, violence was instead connected to the parliamentary elections held in July 1985. Again, the victims of this violence were 'almost invariably Ndebele speakers' (CCJP/LRF 1997:62). In the elections, Zanu-PF won an overwhelming victory, but Zapu retained all 15 seats in Matabeleland. In 1986, Zanu-PF started a move towards unity with Zapu, but talks broke down in 1987. In June that year, Minister Enos Nkala banned all Zapu rallies and meetings. In September, he banned Zapu as a political party and had all Zapu offices closed. The talks were then resumed, and ended with Robert Mugabe and Joshua Nkomo signing the Unity Accord in December 1987 (CCJP/LRF:72ff).

Memories of Violence: Experiences

As in the rest of Matabeleland, the *Gukurahundi* also hit at civilians in Umzingwane district. I will here give excerpts from three personal stories of how these atrocities were experienced, and later on how they are explained: firstly that of Akukho Khumalo, then that of No Nyathi, and finally that of Aliyase Moyo. All stories were related to me in English, and recorded on tape. Unlike information passed down via public media or oral tradition from one generation to another, these stories are memories of lived experience, painfully inscribed in mind and body of the person. The stories are individual and differ somewhat from each other. Yet, as I will show later on, they are also socially formed and constitutive of ethnic identity.

Akukho Khumalo became a Zipra soldier when he was in his early twenties. He was trained abroad and specialised in anti-aircraft defence during the

[6] According to the Lawyers Committee for Human Rights, people were eating less than 20 per cent of what they required. The food embargo hit particularly hard at elderly people and children, but how many actually died of starvation is difficult to estimate (LCFHR 1986:135ff, CCJP/LRF 1997:57).

liberation war. After independence he joined the Zimbabwe National Army, but he had to leave because of threats within the army itself. Like the majority in his situation, Khumalo never became a dissident but went home to his home area to farm. Today he lives together with a brother next to his late father's homestead. However, his reasons for leaving the army are pretty much the same as those described by dissidents (Alexander 1998).

> I could not be safe, and at some date I was threatened that I should leave the army. I left quietly, but I think that was an illegal discharge. I think that is why even now my life has not become straight. I was dismissed with nothing, not even a cent, just told to go: 'otherwise we kill you'. Now, that was during the time of the formation of the Fifth Brigade, and I had already collected from certain friends that there was a certain army that was being built up to deal with us.

When the Fifth Brigade arrived, Khumalo was at his home, situated in the area west of the Bulawayo-Beitbridge road, which was declared a curfew area. Although there was a severe drought, he was not allowed to buy or receive food from outside.

> People needed food from town [Bulawayo], but all the supplies were stopped. People coming from town were not allowed to bring food to their families, because it was believed that this food was to supply the dissident operation. They labelled this area [as] possessing a Zapu infrastructure which was nursing dissidents, and it became very painful to the lives of the mostly innocent and general people, because they could not have access to the food brought about by their people working in town.

The Fifth Brigade also detained, tortured, and killed people. As an ex-Zipra soldier having been forced to leave the army without honourable discharge, Akukho Khumalo felt himself a prime target, easy for the soldiers to label him as a 'dissident'.

> I became quite suspicious that if they could get me, then I would be in a very hard situation, and that's when I ran away from this area. In fact, I jumped by night to the other side of the road. I had problems getting transport to town, and I went by foot as far as Filabusi where I boarded a Masvingo bus and was taken as someone coming from Masvingo during the roadblock checks. And that's how I survived. I got to Bulawayo and stayed there until the curfew was lifted.

No Nyathi was not a Zipra soldier during the liberation war, but he actively supported the Zipra forces. He was arrested by Rhodesian soldiers several times in the late 1970s and finally detained for seven months at Gweru. After independence, he became a Zapu politician. The first day he met the *Gukurahundi* soldiers he had slaughtered a cow for his mother at his brother's homestead. 'I heard the radio say it was a curfew, which meant people mustn't move between six p.m. and six a.m.', he recalled. On that day, during daylight hours, Nyathi was to drive a friend and his parents home in their car.

> When I proceeded across the Lumene river, that's where I met them: the *Gukurahundi*. We had not been informed that they would be there. When I met them I was stopped, and I was asked to get out of the car, because there should be no movements of cars. I said that I had not heard anything of that sort. Then I was asked to lay down. I was beaten thoroughly, by a lot of them. From there, I was asked to reverse the car pushing it. The owner of the car and the parents were not allowed to touch the car. By then, they [the soldiers] were behind me, hitting me.

After a while No Nyathi was asked where he was going, and was allowed to continue. Before he drove away, some of the soldiers had already left. At a turn-off further ahead, the soldiers were waiting for him. 'They asked me to lay down again and I was beaten thoroughly.' After having been allowed to continue for the second time, Nyathi left the car and his passengers by the road and walked home.

> My shop was open at that time, because they were saying six to six. I never knew I was supposed to have closed the shop. Those who beat me at that side were going along the road. They found the shop open, [and] they asked whose the shop was. They went to my brother's homestead, where there was a function. There was beer and there was meat. They sent my children to come and call me from this side, and they told my children that if I was not going to go, my mother was going to be killed.

Nyathi decided to go to his brother's homestead. When he arrived he found his relatives and neighbours fighting each other, while the soldiers were watching.

> They were fighting among themselves, asked by the soldiers to fight. If they saw that you sort of tried to not fight hard, they were hitting you. When I got there they asked me: whose shop is that? I told them it was my shop. They said: who told you to open the shop? I said: I did not know that the shop was to be closed. I just heard it was six to six. They beat me again. They beat me a third time.

Aliyase Moyo has been a teacher his whole life. He was not a Zipra soldier during the liberation war, or a Zapu politician after independence. Yet, he was targeted by the Fifth Brigade. Moyo worked as headmaster at a school when the *Gukurahundi* came. Shortly after the soldiers had arrived in the district, 'dissidents' visited him at home and demanded he should cook for them. Prior to that, he had never encountered any dissidents.

> They said we should cook for them. These people were armed, so I did cook. Then the [Gukurahundi] soldiers came. In an hours time there were soldiers here asking me: did you see some people passing here? Then the correct answer was: yes, I saw them, and I did cook. If you said you did not cook, they killed you.

However, Aliyase Moyo did not believe the people he had cooked for actually were dissidents.

> They said they were dissidents, but as far as I am concerned I do not believe they were dissidents. No, I think they were disguised people. They were sent by the government also, to do the same business as the Fifth Brigade, the business of killing.

After Moyo had cooked for the 'dissidents' and been harassed by the *Gukurahundi* soldiers he went to a local police station to report what had happened. 'If you didn't report, you were killed', Moyo related. The police phoned the Fifth Brigade, who said they would take over the matter. Moyo was ordered to go home, where he met the *Gukurahundi* soldiers again. His wife and children had run away to Bulawayo. In the evening a lorry came to his homestead:

> They took me to the [Mzinyathini] camp. I stayed there for three days. They were beating people, and killing people. Of course, some were kind, some were cruel, some were killers. Some of them really told me they were sent by Mugabe to come and kill people. They told me that they were told to shoot, not to talk to anyone. But since they were also human beings, they said, it was much better to get a stick and beat a person to death. If you survive you survive, if you die you die.

Civilians as Caught In-between

Terence Ranger was one of the first scholars to carry out academic research on the atrocities in Matabeleland. After the amnesty in May 1988, he visited northern Matobo district, which is situated next to Umzingwane district in Matabeleland South. With his initial interrogation of the Fifth Brigade and the 'dissidents', Ranger paved the way for many other researchers who have dealt with the subject since then. However, in an early article from this time, Ranger (1989) made two points that today seem questionable. I would like to address these two points here, not least since Ranger (1999:1, 246ff) has repeated them ten years later.

Firstly, Ranger (1989:162ff) states that the atrocities in the mid-eighties were expressed as a 'balance of terror' where both the national army and the dissidents were blamed for the atrocities. In relation to this, Ranger (1989:163ff) also holds that the public support for the dissidents diminished from 1983 to 1988, and that people distinguished between 'good' and 'bad' dissidents personified in two men, Ndevu (the beard) and Gayigusu, both referred to by people in Umzingwane district.

Secondly, Ranger avoids dealing with Shona and Ndebele ethnicity, with reference to the atrocities, and stresses instead identities based on origin. Ranger (1989a:166, 167) emphasises 'the extraordinary ethnic variety of Matabeleland', he refutes the simple equation of 'ZAPU equals "the Ndebele"' (repeated in for instance Bhebe and Ranger 1995:31f), and he states with reference to an interview with a headman that 'nothing could be sillier than the "Shona" killing the "Ndebele" or vice versa'.

These two points are repeated in Ranger's (1999) historical account of the Matopo hills from the 1890s to the 1990s, where he again, and with reference to the CCJP/LRF report from 1997, emphasises that people in the northern part of Matobo district 'condemned dissidents and the Zimbabwean forces equally' (1999:246ff). Here, however, he does not mention the issue of ethnicity in relation to the atrocities at all, even if his informants sometimes do. Mrs Lesabe, former Member of Parliament for Umzingwane district, is for instance quoted as referring to a conversation with a man describing the atrocities as 'the ruling party against the Matabeles' (1999:260). Despite a strong focus on Ndebele ethnicity in other parts of the book covering the colonial period, Ranger does not treat ethnicity in relation to the atrocities.

However, the fact that people in Matabeleland South are Zimbabwean citizens, or that categories of origin exist, does not rule out the significance of ethnicity per se. Nationality, ethnicity, and origin are used by and ascribed to people in various situations, and in Umzingwane district Ndebele ethnicity is to a very high degree used, and ascribed to people, in situations relating to the atrocities. While Ranger describes people as civilians or of various origins caught in-between government forces and dissidents, people in Umzingwane district describe themselves very much as Ndebele in this context. They see themselves as Ndebeles who, on the order of Robert Mugabe and the Zanu-PF party, were harassed, mutilated, and killed by Shona soldiers of the Fifth Brigade.

Since Ranger (1989) wrote his first report on atrocities in Matabeleland South, new research has given a partly different picture of the atrocities. This includes Ranger's own involvement in Alexander and McGregor's study of the violence in

Matabeleland North (Alexander, McGregor and Ranger 2000a,b). This research shows that 'the balance of terror' was generally quite unbalanced in Matabeleland, with the Fifth Brigade and other army units causing much more harm than the dissidents (Werbner 1991:158ff, 1995, 1998:92ff, CCJP/LRF 1997:47ff, Alexander 1998:157ff, and Yap 2001:194ff). In Umzingwane district, people clearly express this imbalance. Moreover, the public support for the dissidents was probably very low from the beginning, and to the extent that civilians did support the dissidents it was more for personal than for political reasons (Alexander 1998:68f). What people in Umzingwane district supported were not dissidents, but Joshua Nkomo, Zapu and, during the liberation war, Zipra.

In addition, it seems by now to be clear that Zanu-PF politicians played on ethnicity both explicitly and implicitly in the media (Alexander and McGregor 1999, Yap 2001:215ff). More practically, they also formed the Fifth Brigade of Shona-speaking soldiers and sent it to Matabeleland. As mentioned, there are many descriptions of how these soldiers drew on ethnic sentiments when carrying out atrocities. Soldiers also used the Zanla mobilisation method *pungwe* from the liberation war, in which song and dance were accompanied with political education. However, in this context, as Alexander (1998:159) writes, 'the songs were in an unfamiliar language, the dance was forced, the slogans were anti-Zapu, and the "festivities" were accompanied by beatings and killings.'

In response to the politicians and soldiers' use of ethnic injustice, people in Umzingwane district have reacted by emphasising themselves as Ndebele in relation to the Shona in a new way. Since the late 1990s, narratives of the Fifth Brigade's atrocities have also entered the public debate.[7] In retrospect, we may conceive of the Fifth Brigade's atrocities as a 'critical event', after which 'new modes of action came into being which redefined traditional categories' (Das 1995:6). Today, some fifteen to twenty years after the atrocities, people narrate the atrocities by merging experiences in the past with explanations in the present. Analytically, I have already described memories of the atrocities as experienced in the past, and shall now turn to memories of the atrocities as explained in the present.

Memories of Violence: Explanations

When people narrate past experiences in the present, they do not only recall information, they engage in a meaning-making practice where individual experiences are connected to larger political and economic processes (White 2000). Since the government of Zimbabwe has not recognised the atrocities, or compensated people for their hardships and losses, there is little public room for individual healing. Instead, Ndebele-speakers make sense of their suffering by relating individual pain to collective belonging. People strive to find 'a voice in

---

[7] In 1997, the Catholic Commission for Justice and Peace handed over a report on the Fifth Brigade's atrocities to Robert Mugabe (CCJP/LRF 1997). This report was leaked to a South African newspaper, which wrote a news story on the subject and published almost the entire report on the internet (*The Weekly Mail and Guardian* 2–8 May 1997). Thereafter, several Zimbabwean newspapers and magazines wrote on the atrocities. See *Zimbabwe Independent* 15–22 May and 6–12 June 1997, *Zimbabwe Standard* 4–10 May and 18–24 May 1997, *The Sunday Mail* 11 May 1997, *The Sunday News* 11 May 1997, *The Financial Ghazette* 15 May 1997, *Horizon* June 1997, and *Parade* June 1997. See also Werbner (1998:95), and Alexander & McGregor (1999:256f).

community with other voices' (Das and Kleinman 2001:4). This leads to a certain standardisation of narratives concerning the Fifth Brigade, and especially regarding the explanations of the atrocities.

For instance, when Mugabe and Nkomo signed the unity accord in 1987 it was agreed that the atrocities should stop, but also that Nkomo's Zapu party should cease to exist. Some people in Matabeleland have criticised Nkomo for signing the agreement, but many people who experienced the violence themselves hold that Nkomo saved the 'Ndebele'. A *nyanga* ('traditional doctor') in Umzingwane district argued that Nkomo did what he had to do, 'It was right. He saved the Ndebele. We would have been finished', he explained. And an elderly teacher in the district likewise held, 'It was a good thing, because if he hadn't done it we would not have been living. He knew his people were suffering, that they were eliminated, that they were killed.'

In contrast to Terence Ranger's (1989, 1999) description of people's reactions to the violence in Matobo district, people in Umzingwane district define themselves as Ndebele when they relate to the atrocities, as in the example of the *nyanga* and the teacher above. By expanding the individual to the collective, they make sense of their own suffering. Moreover, many people also equate the Ndebele with the Zapu party, and some further hold that the 'Shona' indeed did kill the 'Ndebele'.

According to Akukho Khumalo, the ex-Zipra soldier, the Fifth Brigade was built up by Robert Mugabe and Zanu-PF to eliminate Joshua Nkomo and Zapu.

> [Mugabe and Nkomo] came to be very sharply opposed, and Zanu thought it wise to eliminate the people of Zapu so that they could be ruling freely, one over the other. They decided to formulate a strategy of bringing about an army more loyal to the Zanu-PF, and that's why they formed the Fifth Brigade. Now, with the formation of the Fifth Brigade, they pretended as if, or let me see, yes, I am all right, they pretended as if there were a lot of dissidents existing in Matabeleland South.

Like many others in Umzingwane district who identified themselves with Zapu and Zipra and regarded Joshua Nkomo as their Ndebele leader, Khumalo strongly connects Zanu-PF with 'the Shona' and Zapu with 'the Ndebele'.

> The operation of the Fifth Brigade was built on torturing and killing the people of this part of the country, in particular, I could say, in Matabeleland. The elections of 1980 showed that nobody in Matabeleland was voting for Zanu, and very few people in Mashonaland were voting for Zapu. The ruling people, most of whom were Shona, were supposed to have these people who were talking Ndebele, most of whom were Zapu, to be silenced because they were causing discomfort to them.

Thus, Akukho Khumalo and many others in Umzingwane district do connect, and even equate, the Ndebele with Zapu, which seems to be the case also in Nkayi and Lupane districts in Matabeleland North (Alexander, McGregor, and Ranger 2000a).[8] In fact, politicians like Enos Nkala, who was active in Zanu-PF while Zapu still existed, are referred to as 'lost Ndebeles'. Instead of looking for differences between Zapu and the Ndebele, Khumalo and other victims of the atrocities look for similarities. By equating Zanu-PF with the Shona, and Zapu with the Ndebele, they connect their own individual suffering to larger political and economic processes.

---

[8] See also Alexander and McGregor (in preparation) on local interpretations of the atrocities in Nkayi and Lupane districts in Matabeleland North, and Ranger's (1996) comments on Alexander and McGregor's work.

No Nyathi, the former Zapu politician, also equates the Shona with the Zanu-PF and the Ndebele with Zapu. Moreover, he names the Shona as the perpetrators and the Ndebele as the victims. When asked who was responsible for the atrocities, Nyathi held the *Gukurahundi* soldiers responsible for the atrocities rather than the 'dissidents', and behind them the Zanu-PF party rather than the government, which after independence consisted of both Zanu-PF and Zapu politicians.

> I would say it was the *Gukurahundi* [who was responsible for the atrocities] because, as I am saying, a dissident was an Ndebele person. The *Gukurahundi* was Shona people. ... There was a government, but Zanu had this Fifth Brigade to go against the *amaNdebele* who were said to be Zapu. Why was the Fifth Brigade Shona people only? Because Zanu was Shona, Zapu was Ndebeles. It was something which was formed for this killing, because after the killing it went off. It is no longer there.

The attitude that President Mugabe, Zanu-PF, and the Shona wanted to kill Joshua Nkomo, Zapu and the Ndebele is, as Veena Das puts it in her definition of a 'critical event', a redefinition of traditional categories. The view of the 'Shona' as killers and the 'Ndebele' as victims did not exist prior to the atrocities. What is important here is not how I, as a researcher, categorise things or events, but how people in Matabeleland do it. One can, of course, rearrange existing categories without reference to the 'Shona' and the 'Ndebele', and regard Mugabe and Nkomo as Zimbabwean politicians, Zanu-PF and Zapu as political parties, and people as citizens. However, such an arrangement of categories is not often encountered in Umzingwane district.

In fact, the statement that the Shona were killing the Ndebele is commonly put forward quite bluntly. According to Aliyase Moyo, the teacher who was taken to the Mzinyathini camp, the *Gukurahundi* soldiers did not just happen to be Shona labelling Ndebele as dissidents. The very aim of the Fifth Brigade was to hit at the Ndebele as a people.

> These people [the *Gukurahundi* soldiers] were organised in so much that they really wanted to finish the *amaNdebele* people. They wanted to kill us. That was their primary aim, and that was their command. And when they came here, some people were really beaten to death. At the moment, I can say we are a bit confused ourselves. What we were fighting for [in the liberation war] was freedom, to liberate everybody, whether the white man or an African man. When this went on like that, it seems that this type of freedom was obtained for the *maShona*. And I'm sure even now the *amaNdebele* are frozen. They are not free, as the *maShona*.

Scholars have for a long time held that human beings use cognitive schemata to comprehend complex information when remembering the past (Garro 2001). This is not least true for people retelling emotionally charged experiences of violence in narratives. More individual schemata are then related to broader, cultural schemata. As White (2000:498) puts it, 'stories create cognitive scaffolding that allows people to fill in unspoken assumptions and make connections to existing cultural schemata.' In southern Zimbabwe, individual experiences of the Fifth Brigade's atrocities are made into collective history, and life stories are regarded as tokens of ethnic identity. From a cognitive perspective, we may say that people in Matabeleland construct the relevance of their stories for themselves by expanding individual schemata built on experience of violence to cultural schemata explaining the atrocities.

Violence, Ethnicity, and Memory

David Keen (1999:89) has pointed out the importance of studying the relation-ship between those orchestrating and carrying out violence with the civilian population who are not engaged in fighting. The Fifth Brigade's atrocities were not simply a by-product of warfare between army soldiers and dissidents but a tactic of warfare, intended to destroy self-esteem, in order to control political will and weaken civil support of Zapu (cf. Nordstrom 1997 on Mozambique). Although politicians cannot foresee future events, evidence suggests that people in Matabeleland did not only 'believe' that the atrocities were 'orchestrated' by 'Zanu-PF's leaders' (Alexander, McGregor, and Ranger 2000b:322ff), but that the atrocities, in fact, were orchestrated by Mugabe and the Zanu-PF.

The political instability in Zimbabwe after independence and the persecution of soldiers within the army certainly influenced later developments in the country (Alexander 1998:151). But why were only Zipra and not Zanla guerrillas labelled 'dissidents', and why were mainly Ndebele-speakers persecuted within the army? The case remains that Robert Mugabe accused Joshua Nkomo of being behind dissident activities, that Nkomo had to flee the country, that ex-Zipra officers were detained from 1982 and onwards, and that Zapu was banned as a political party in 1987. The Zanu-PF government further renewed the State of Emer-gency, enacted the Emergency Powers Regulation, and sent the Fifth Brigade to Matabeleland. In addition, it imposed curfews, stopped drought relief food, and closed shops in southern Zimbabwe.

In reaction to the atrocities, people in Matabeleland have 'resisted' violence and oppression by re-creating Ndebele identity through a rearrangement of old categories, where the 'Shona' are viewed as perpetrators and the 'Ndebele' as victims. This redefinement of categories is a response to the Zimbabwean govern-ment's oppression of its subjects in Matabeleland. While the government-controlled press had an important role in spreading political leaders' explicit and implicit ethnic rhetoric throughout the country, people experienced such senti-ments first hand in connection to extreme violence in Matabeleland. Both these processes provoked reactions along ethnic lines, giving people outside Matabele-land a justification for the atrocities on ethnic grounds, and people inside Matabeleland an explanation as to why they were targeted, and a rationalisation of their experiences of suffering.

When the *Gukurahundi* arrived in Matabeleland, the soldiers hit especially hard at ex-Zipra soldiers, Zapu politicians, and people like headmasters, such as Khumalo, Nyathi, and Moyo. These people are mainly male, but men and women with other occupations were harassed too. As often is the case in civil wars, the Fifth Brigade hit at civilians in their homesteads, targeting private arenas (cf. Turshen 1998). While some women fled with their children outside the curfew area others stayed at home, and some of these women were not only beaten but also raped (see Tonnesen 2001:56ff, 114ff). These women experienced gendered violence that differs from Khumalo, Nyathi, and Moyo's experiences of violence.

Yet, women often give similar explanations of the atrocities to those of the men. For example, during the preparations for the parliamentary elections in June 2000, a businesswoman in her fifties said, 'The *Gukurahundi* was sent to kill the *amaNdebele*. They were sent by the government. Our president sent them.' An elderly retired male farmer explained, 'They started to kill the Ndebele people. ...

He [Mugabe] didn't want Nkomo to be a [political] leader. ... He wanted one party only.' And a woman in her mid-forties related, 'They came here to kill people only, to destroy their homelands. There was only *Gukurahundi* here in Matabeleland. They were not in Mashonaland.'

In the long run, the Fifth Brigade's atrocities have heightened the awareness of being Ndebele at the expense of being Zimbabwean or, for that matter, 'Nguni'. That is, it has heightened the awareness of ethnicity at the expense of nationality and origin. Further, in relation to the atrocities, people tend to refer to themselves as Ndebele, rather than as men or women of different age or occupation. Memory, as Fentress and Wickham (1992:25) write, not only has to retrieve information, it also 'identifies a group, giving it a sense of its past and defining its aspirations for the future'. Many people in Umzingwane district now equate the Shona with Zanu-PF and the Ndebele with Zapu, and hold that the Shona were torturing, raping, and killing the Ndebele.

The Parliamentary and Presidential Elections

In recent years, people in Matabeleland have experienced the violence of the Zanu-PF youth militia as a recapitulation of the political violence carried out in the 1980s. Despite Mugabe and Zanu-PF's rhetoric on 'whites' and the re-occupation of their farms, most of those who have been murdered in the political violence since early 2000 are 'black' MDC politicians and supporters (Zimbabwe Human Rights NGO Forum 2001, 2002). Several civil servants accused of being MDC have also been targeted (McGregor 2002). During the local elections in Umzingwane district in September 2002, the 'green bombers', as the militia also are called, were not only dressed in green uniforms. 'They had red berets', as a woman said, 'just like the *gukurahundi*' (Lindgren 2003).

The Fifth Brigade atrocities have also been used in the political rhetoric against the Zanu-PF. In April 2001, between the parliamentary and presidential elections, Morgan Tsvangirai visited the mass graves left by the Fifth Brigade in Kezi, situated in Matobo district in Matabeleland South, and declared: 'This was a barbaric operation by Zanu-PF and its leadership. ... MDC will obviously want to see justice being done if it comes to power' (*The Daily News* 9 April 2001).

The opposition party MDC sprang out of the labour movement in the late 1990s, and it is often portrayed as having strong support from workers. In the parliamentary elections in June 2000, it received many votes in Zimbabwe's two major cities, Harare and Bulawayo. However, the party also received many votes in the two Matabeleland provinces. The same pattern applied to the presidential election in March 2002. Morgan Tsvangirai had his strongest support in Harare and in Bulawayo, but also in the two provinces Matabeleland North and Matabeleland South. He further received many votes in the country's third largest city Mutare, and in the province of Manicaland in which Mutare is situated (Zimbabwe Government On-Line 2000, MDC 2002).

Although the support for MDC in the major cities may partly be explained by the party's link to the labour movement and class-consciousness, the support for MDC in the two Matabeleland provinces demands another explanation. The re-creation of ethnicity and the heightened awareness of being Ndebele fit this picture. People in Matabeleland who identified themselves as Ndebele, and who never got the opportunity to participate in nation-building after independence, found in the MDC a broader platform to challenge Robert Mugabe and the Zanu-PF party.

Not surprisingly, people in Bulawayo have lately started new organisations that promote 'Ndebele' interests. One example is the Vukani Mahlabezulu Cultural Society, an organisation educating youth in Ndebele culture and tradition. Another one is Imbovane Yamahlabezulu, a pressure group working for the release of, in their view, political prisoners arrested during the Fifth Brigade era. And a third example is Zapu 2000, a political movement dissatisfied with the Zanu-PF government's 'discrimination' against the Ndebele. Similar initiatives exist in the countryside. At a chief's meeting in Umzingwane district in June 2001, funds were collected to create courses in 'Ndebele culture' in order to teach youth who they are and where they come from. And in November 2002, a traditional cultural exchange festival was planned for December with visiting chiefs from South Africa.

Indeed, some people did clearly not vote *for* Morgan Tsvangirai and the MDC in the elections, but rather *against* Robert Mugabe and the Zanu-PF party. Prior to the parliamentary elections, a commentator in Bulawayo related that 'people would vote for a cockroach' rather than for Robert Mugabe. Around the same time, a group of men at a beer hall in Umzingwane district were discussing the coming elections. The news of emerging political violence was directly related to the Fifth Brigade's atrocities. A man in his fifties burst out: 'That thing is so much in our heart. No one will ever forget it!' And a year later, after the elections had been held, a man explained why the district's MDC candidate MaKhumalo was voted into parliament instead of Zanu-PF's candidate Mrs Lesabe: 'People didn't vote for MaKhumalo because they like her. They voted for her because they don't like the present government. Even if it was a dog, they would have voted for it.'

Similar to how the Zanu-PF accused Zapu of trying to overthrow the government in the 1980s, the ruling party has also accused the MDC of plotting. In February 2002, presidential candidate Morgan Tsvangirai and two other MDC-leaders were charged with planning to kill Mugabe. The trial was first set for 11 November 2002, but was then postponed until 3 February 2003. Many people in southern Zimbabwe do not believe the accusation to be true, not because it is unlikely that someone would try to kill the president, but because that person would be dead if he tried and failed. A middle-aged man said:

I know these guys. I experienced the Fifth Brigade. They are not playing. If he [Morgan Tsvangirai] really had tried to murder the president, he would not have existed today. He would have been dead. It [the trial] will be postponed, and postponed, and postponed again. It will take five years, at least. They just want to disturb MDC people.

In this way, 'old' and 'new' conflicts in Zimbabwe are intertwined, with one feeding the other through political processes and memories of violence. In each conflict politicians have played on categories of belonging based on race and ethnicity. As a consequence, ethnicity has become related to nationalism in new ways. During colonialism, Ndebele ethnicity and Zimbabwean nationalism were compatible with each other. After independence, Ndebele-speakers were stigmatised as 'dissidents' and marginalised from nation building. Today, memories of the Fifth Brigade's atrocities have led to a portrayal of the Shona as perpetrators of violence and the Ndebele as victims. Although the war of independence officially ended with Rhodesia becoming Zimbabwe in 1980, and though the political violence in Matabeleland allegedly ceased with the Unity Accord in 1987, people in southern Zimbabwe have been living in a state between war and peace for several decades now. Memories of current political violence will make future politics. Through the social work of memory, war and peace are intertwined threads, connecting generations.

References

Africa Confidential 1984, 'Zimbabwe: fear is the key' *Africa Confidential* 25 (8)

Alexander, J. 1998, 'Dissident Perspectives on Zimbabwe's Post-Independence War' *Africa* 68 (2): 151–82

Alexander, J. and McGregor, J. 1999, 'Representing Violence in Matabeleland, Zimbabwe: press and internet debates' in Allen, T. and Seaton, J. eds, *The Media of Conflict: war reporting and representations of ethnic violence* London: Zed Books

Alexander, J., McGregor, J. and Ranger, T. 2000a. *Violence and Memory: one hundred years in the dark forests of Matabeleland* Oxford: James Currey

Alexander, J., McGregor, J. et al. (2000b). 'Ethnicity and the Politics of Conflict: the case of Matabeleland' in Nafziger, E. W., Stewart, F. and Väyrynen R. eds, *War, Hunger, and Displacement: the origins of humanitarian emergencies* Oxford: Oxford University Press

Alexander, J. and McGregor, J. (in preparation), 'Democracy, Development and Political Conflict: rural institutions in Matabeleland North after independence'

Amnesty International 1993, *Amnesty International World Report* London: Amnesty International

Bastin, Y., Coupez, A. et al. 1999. *Continuity and Divergence in Bantu Languages: perspectives from a lexicostatistic study* Tervuren, Musée Royal de L'Afrique Centrale

Bhebe, N. and T. Ranger, eds, 1995, *Society in Zimbabwe's Liberation War* Harare: University of Zimbabwe Publications

Bourdillon, M. 1987, *The Shona Peoples: an ethnography of the contemporary Shona, with special reference to their religion* Gweru: Mambo Press

CCJP/LRF 1997, *Breaking the Silence, Building True Peace: a report on the disturbances in Matabeleland and the Midlands 1980–1988.* Harare: The Catholic Commission for Justice and Peace and the Legal Resources Foundation of Zimbabwe. www.hrforumzim.com/frames/inside_frame_reps.htm Available: 18 May 2003

Census 1994, *Zimbabwe National Report 1992* Harare: Central Statistical Office

Cobbing, J. 1976, 'The Ndebele under the Khumalos 1820–1896' Unpublished thesis. Department of History, Lancaster University

Das, V. 1995, *Critical Events: an anthropological perspective on contemporary India* Oxford: Oxford University Press

Das, V. and Kleinman, A. 2001, 'Introduction' in Das, V., Kleinman, A., Margret, L., Ramphele. M. and Reynolds, P. eds, *Remaking a World: violence, social suffering, and recovery* Berkeley: University of California Press

The Daily News 2001, 'Tsvangirai Tours Mass Graves of Gukurahundi Victims', 9 April.

Fentress, J. and Wickham, C. 1992, *Social Memory* Oxford: Blackwell

Garro, L. 2001, 'The Remembered Past in a Culturally Meaningful Life: remembering as cultural, social, and cognitive process' in Moore, C. and Mathews, H. eds, *The Psychology of Cultural Experience* Cambridge: Cambridge University Press

Hughes, A. J. B. and van Velsen, J. 1954, 'The Ndebele' in Kuper, H., Hughes, A. J. B. and van Velsen, J. eds, *The Shona and Ndebele in Southern Rhodesia* London: International African Institute. Vol. IV

Kaarsholm, P. 1997, 'Inventions, Imaginings, Codifications: authorising versions of Ndebele cultural tradition' *Journal of Southern African Studies* 23 (2): 243–58

Keen, D. 1999, 'Who Is It Between? 'Ethnic War' and Rational Violence' in Allen, T. and Seaton, J. eds, *The Media of Conflict: war reporting and representations of ethnic violence* London: Zed Books

LCFHR 1986, *Zimbabwe: wages of war* New York: Lawyers Committee for Human Rights

Lindgren, B. 2003, 'The Green Bombers of Salisbury: elections and political power in Zimbabwe' *Anthropology Today* 19 (2): 6–10

Lindgren, B. (2004). 'The Internal Dynamics of Ethnicity: clan names, origins, and castes in southern Zimbabwe' *Africa* 72(4): 173–93

Livingstone, D. 1857, *Missionary Travels and Researches in South Africa* London: John Murray

Malkki, L. 1995, *Purity and Exile: violence, memory, and national cosmology among Hutu refugees in Tanzania* Chicago: The University of Chicago Press

McGregor, J. 2002, 'The Politics of Disruption: War Veterans and the Local state in Zimbabwe' *African Affairs*, 101: 9–37

MDC 2002, 'Results Presidential Elections'. Movement for Democratic Change press. http://www.mdczimbabwe.com/archivemat/archive.htm Available: 18 May 2003

Moffat, R. 1940 [1835], *Robert Moffat's Visit to Mzilikazi in 1835* Witwatersrand: Witwatersrand University Press

New African. 2002, 'We Won't Be a Banana Republic', September

New African. 2003, 'Zimbabwe. The Land has come back', February

Nkomo, J. 1984, *The Story of My Life*. London: Methuen

Nordstrom, C. 1997, *A Different Kind of War Story* Philadelphia: University of Pennsylvania Press

Quantin, P. 1992, 'The General Elections in Zimbabwe: a step towards a one-party state?' in Baynham, S. ed., *Zimbabwe in Transition* Stockholm: Almqvist & Wiksell

Ranger, T. 1985, *The Invention of Tribalism in Zimbabwe*. Gweru: Mambo Press

—— 1989, 'Matabeleland Since the Amnesty' *African Affairs* (88)

—— 1993, 'The Invention of Tradition Revisited: the case of colonial Africa' in Ranger, T. and Vaughan, O. *Legitimacy and the State in Twentieth Century Africa* London: Macmillan

—— 1996, 'Violence and Memory: Zimbabwe, 1896–1996' *BZS Zimbabwe Review* 96 (3): 1–15

—— 1999, *Voices from the Rocks: nature, culture and history in the Matopos hills of Zimbabwe* Bloomington IN and Oxford: Indiana University Press and James Currey

Saunders, R. 2000, *Never the Same Again: Zimbabwe's growth towards democracy 1980–2000* Harare: Strand Multiprint

SIL International 2002, *Ethnologue: languages of the world* SIL International

Tonnesen, M. 2001, 'When Leaves Became Roots and Roots Became Leaves: Local Perspectives on the Matabeleland Conflict and its Aftermath' Master's Thesis Århus University

Turshen, M. 1998, 'Women's War Stories' in Turshen, M. and Twagiramariya, C. eds, *What Women Do in Wartime: gender and conflict in Africa* London: Zed Books

The Weekly Mail and Guardian. 1997, 'Nightmare of Mugabe's Matabele Atrocities'. Johannesburg, 2–8 May

Werbner, R. 1991, *Tears of the Dead: the social biography of an African family* Edinburgh: Edinburgh University Press

—— 1995, 'In Memory: a heritage of war in southwestern Zimbabwe' in Bhebe, N. and Ranger, T. eds, *Society in Zimbabwe's Liberation War* Harare and London: University of Zimbabwe Publications and James Currey, Vol. 2

—— 1998, 'Smoke from the Barrel of a Gun: postwars of the dead, memory and reinscription in Zimbabwe' in Werbner, R. ed., *Memory and the Postcolony* London: Zed Books

White, G. 2000, 'Histories and Subjectivities' *Ethos: journal of the society for psychological anthropology* 28 (4)

Yap, K. 2001, 'Uprooting the Weeds: Power, Ethnicity, and Violence in the Matabeleland Conflict 1980–1987', PhD thesis, Amsterdam, University of Amsterdam

Zimbabwe Government On-Line. 2000, 'Election 2000 results'. *www.gta.gov.zw/headlines/main_update_page.htm* Available: 18 May 2003

Zimbabwe Human Rights NGO Forum 2001, 'Human Rights and Zimbabwe's June 2000 Election'. www.hrforumzim.com/frames/inside_frame_special.htm Available: 18 May 2003

Zimbabwe Human Rights Forum 2002, 'Human Rights and Zimbabwe's Presidential Election: March 2002'. www.hrforumzim.com/frames/inside_frame_special.htm Available: 18 May 2003

10

Belonging in Nowhere Land
The Tibetan Diaspora as Conflict

ÅSA TILJANDER DAHLSTRÖM

The Tibetan diaspora is about 40 years old now and any changes of the situation are not within sight. The Chinese People's Liberation Army occupied the Tibetan capital Lhasa in 1959. Tibet had slowly been invaded over the ten previous years, and Lhasa was the last Tibetan stronghold of any political importance. The inhabitants tried to defend their city and during ensuing riots at least a thousand deaths occurred, and many more were imprisoned. About 80,000 Tibetans fled to neighbouring countries over the years following the Chinese takeover. The language, and the Tibetan Buddhism, have been targets of repression and there have been reports of large numbers of political prisoners.[1] In this chapter I explore some of the 'small details' that followed the Sino-Tibetan conflict: lost roots, divided families, alienation and homelessness, and their outcomes, as for example in new ways of constructing necessary kin networks.

For many Tibetans the diaspora situation makes it hard to 'come to peace' with life and mind.[2] Among the reasons for this is that the 'common past', on which the politicised identity is based, is not only common but also highly individual, and that the future is experienced as unclear and to a large extent outside of one's control. I argue that the diaspora is to be seen as a continuation of the Sino-Tibetan conflict. In this perspective the diaspora represents the geography of conflict – a 'solution' that carries with it the impossibility of a solution, that is, of 'peace'. The diaspora constitutes a critique of the very concepts of 'peace' and 'solution'.

The chapter is based on fieldwork among college and university students[3] who stay in Tibetan boarding schools and student homes.[4] These hostels make very

[1] Numbers from Barnett & Akiner (1994) and from *Human Rights Practices for 1998 Report*. It is difficult or impossible to get the correct number of casualties during the Lhasa riots in 1959.

[2] This is not to be seen solely as an English expression. To have 'peace of mind' is considered a major goal in life for a Buddhist. See for example Dalai Lama (1991), Sakya (1990).

[3] I conducted three months of fieldwork with the students during the autumn of 1996. Interviews and informal discussions were done entirely in English because of lack of language skills on my part, but also due to the students being more used to discussing some issues in English than in Tibetan. Certain concepts in Tibetan and their use were also discussed. The study was completed later on with fieldwork in Bylakuppe Tibetan Settlement in 1998.

[4] The boarding schools, Tibetan Children's Villages (with several branches around India), are sponsored mainly by foreign aid. Here children can stay and get a more Tibetan-oriented education.

good starting points to explore what the diaspora means to young Tibetans. To grow up in a hostel, orphaned or with kin and family far away, often means a life on the periphery of an already marginalised society. The students themselves talk about this in terms of an institutionalised suffering 'for a good cause'. At the same time, they find the hostels absolutely necessary, in order to 'keep the Tibetan culture', as they put it.

Kinship metaphors are used in order to explain the predicaments of the hostel youth. To know your own kin is potentially problematic in Tibetan circumstances, due to the diaspora situation *per se*, as well as the fact that family names (if any) are seldom used. The local knowledge of kinship is difficult to maintain in the diaspora and subsequently there is an often-expressed fear of forgotten kin ties and particularly of unknowingly venturing into incestuous relationships. Parents and relatives are furthermore very important as keys for employment, as it is crucial to be introduced by someone when applying for work. Without this 'presentation' it is assumed to be very hard or impossible to get work. It has become increasingly common for students to 'adopt' younger pupils, whom they henceforth support, as a self-imposed duty, through their school years. Later on he or she may introduce the protegé to a future employer. These kinds of constructive solutions, together with fears of unconscious incest, are to be interpreted as signs of how the diaspora situation is experienced – as a fragile life in someone else's place, in a situation that is neither peace nor war. This is a permanent impermanence likened to *bardo*, the intermediate state between death and rebirth (Dhondup 1994). The younger generations seem to rely on themselves rather than on the older generation, something that must be considered a major change regarding the gerontocratic character of Tibetan society (Sakya and Emery 1990, Taring 1986).

With the diaspora situation, a growing gap arises between Tibetans living in Tibet and those living in India. The language develops in different directions and Tibetans with various backgrounds have problems understanding each other, linguistically as well as mentally. Border-crossings become mental as well as geopolitical and bring testimonies of alienation, mutual mistrust and disappointment. A diaspora-as-conflict perspective will be useful in order to understand processes and tensions within the Tibetan diaspora, and in its relations with the homeland.

Background

The Chinese People's Liberation Army invaded Tibetan territory in 1949 and slowly gained increased control over the country. The Tibetan government, led by the young fourteenth Dalai Lama, and with hardly any army of its own, could not do much to stop the invaders. Due to rumours of Chinese threats to eliminate the Dalai Lama a clash came in Lhasa in 1959 and many civilians lost their lives in the following riot. The Dalai Lama and members of his family and of the government managed to escape from Lhasa and travelled through the mountains

---

[4] (cont.) There are also four Central Schools for Tibetans with boarding facilities. The boarding schools are all very popular and have a reputation for providing a good education. They are run by Tibetans but are under the supervision of the Indian Central Board for Secondary Education. The student homes (Youth Hostels) are established in many Indian college and university towns and besides providing students with room and board they aim at keeping them together in a Tibetan atmosphere.

down to India. Since then hundreds of thousands of Tibetans have done the same, and each week people still arrive in India as refugees. Dharamsala, situated in the Himalayan foothills of Himachal Pradesh, serves as a capital-in-exile, but there are Tibetan settlements all over India and the largest are in the south. Tibetans also live in Nepal, Bhutan, Europe, Australia and the US. The Dalai Lama has become a strong symbol of Tibetan liberation struggle over the years (particularly since receiving the Nobel Peace Price in 1989) and of Tibetan Buddhism as the reincarnation of Chenrezig, the Bodhisattva of Compassion, and the spiritual leader of the major Tibetan Buddhist order *Gelug-pa*.

From the Chinese point of view Tibet has always been a part of China, although this statement is contradicted by the fact that China claims to have 'liberated' Tibet from its 'old feudal rule' (Schwartz 1992). The degree of suppression inside Tibet has changed over the years. It has been extremely severe at times and, for example, during the Cultural Revolution (1966-76) the loss of Tibetan lives was considerable. Nowadays lack of educational and work opportunities for Tibetans are considered the most serious threats in the long run, together with the restrictions on religious practice and on the use of the Tibetan language. The Chinese policy is to 'modernise' Tibet, Tibetan language and Buddhism have come to symbolise backwardness. Protests from the Tibetan side are not allowed and any attempts are punished with long prison sentences. The underground protest organisations often concentrate on the spread of information, that is, the Tibetan version of history together with the UN Declaration of Human Rights. Visible protests occur either directly in the form of stone-throwing, or indirectly through use of foreigners, who are asked to bring the Tibetan case to the UN and the international community, in order to force the Chinese at least to discuss the issue with the Tibetan side (Dorje 1998 pers. comm., Lhamo 1996 and 1998 pers. comms, Schwartz 1992).[5] The Chinese always have been, and still are, consistent in their refusal to discuss the status of Tibet and insist that the case is an internal Chinese issue.

The Tibetan diaspora is affected by many internal conflicts. The community has an elected government representing the Tibetan nation and led by the Dalai Lama. An ongoing democratisation project is subject to much criticism, particularly the system of representation, and a clause on the possibility of removing the Dalai Lama. The system of representation (which for lay people is based on geographical belonging in the homeland and for the monastic community on both geographical and order or religious belonging) seems to be based on a presumption of historical or emotional connections with the homeland that do not correspond with real feelings of belonging. To remove the Dalai Lama as the political leader is to many Tibetans a contradiction in terms, as he embodies all leadership by virtue of his divinity and knowledge. From this point of view it is impossible (unthinkable) to tell politics apart from Buddhism. The democracy project is legitimised through the use of Buddhist metaphors, for example in speeches by the Dalai Lama. Another conflict concerns the means of liberation struggle (armed versus non-violence) in the fight against the Chinese for a free Tibet. The Dalai Lama has been known world-wide for his non-violence policy

---

[5] Schwartz shows in his article how the notion of 'modernity' plays an important part for both sides in the Chinese-versus-Tibetan discourses. 'Modernity' has come to stand for two completely different views on the ideal Tibetan society of the future.

based on *satyagraha*, Mahatma Gandhi's philosophy of truth.[6] The non-violence policy is established in the exile Tibetan Constitution. Some other groups – both in Tibet and in the diaspora – try, however, to pursue armed struggle as the only way of dealing with the Chinese, with reference to Yassir Arafat and the PLO as the model. Some of these groups have tried to organise themselves into political parties, which is controversial, since their programmatic belief in armed struggle actually makes them non-constitutional. Some of these group-ings within the diaspora are based on other belongings, such as religion (the Bonpos[7]), ethnicity (the *Chushi Gangdruk*, a Khampa[8] organisation) and gender (Tibetan Women's Association). Like the large Tibetan Youth Congress, the latter offers no political alternative in the usual sense but formulates critique against the exile government and is respected for this, more or less. Any attempts to raise issues other than the preservation of Tibet and Tibetan culture, for example women's rights issues, are severely criticised as factional-ism by the political and religious establishment (for example DeVine 1993, Senge 1995).

To keep the community Tibetan is expressed as crucial for survival, and this aim permeates politics and education particularly. Schooling is a sensitive topic, as it highlights questions of the future; should the main aim be to prepare for a life in India or in liberated Tibet sometime in the future? The students complain either that what they find is a too Indianised education, or that what they call an education is useless for the current prospects of a life in India or abroad. The teachers react by blaming the students for being lazy and 'softened' by a convenient life in India (for example Dhondup 1994, Gyatso 1993 and Goldstein-Kyaga 1993).

My suggestion is that these conflicts may be understood in terms of conflicting ways of constructing notions of collective identity. Personal experiences of the homeland and the diaspora seem to be an important component behind the individual notion of what it means to be Tibetan, of the meaning of Tibetan democracy, of the right for someone politically to represent somebody else, of the contents of a Tibetan education, and so on. My study among Tibetan students is placed within this frame of interpretation.

---

[6] *Satyagraha* is a Sanskrit word that is difficult to translate. It stands for non-violent strategies to weaken the centralised power in order to 'restore the truth'. *Satyagraha* is based on the ideas developed by Mahatma Gandhi that the weaker party may act from the conviction of being closer to the truth than the other side. The weaker party hence has to convince the other party of the legitimacy of their claims for the sake of a higher justice (see for example Fischer 1962). The present Dalai Lama refers to Mahatma Gandhi as a role model for liberation struggle (Dalai Lama 1991).

[7] Bonpos practise Bon, the second largest Tibetan religion. There are many different scholarly theories on Bon. It used to be regarded as a pre-Buddhist religion that was gradually suppressed. Nowadays it is more common to view Bon as a religion that developed simultaneously with Buddhism and with many points of similarity (Kvaerne 1993). I have elsewhere developed the idea that it may be relevant to see Bon as an alternative to Buddhism, that is, as a deliberate choice not to be part of the Buddhist society (Tiljander Dahlström 1997:11). The Bonpos have their own settlements and leadership in exile, although the Dalai Lama is considered the religious head of Bon as well.

[8] Kham is a part of Tibet (in the Southeast) disputed by the Chinese and the Lhasa leadership of Tibet. A Khampa originates from Kham, but not all Khampas maintain their Khampa belonging (see Peissel 1972, Tiljander Dahlström 1997).

Home and Diaspora

The Tibetan nation,[9] as defined by diaspora politicians, covers all Tibetans in the world regardless of where they live. In reality only Tibetans living outside of Tibet and China are, for example, able to vote, and the degree of importance the imagined community has for people inside the country varies, depending on, for example, political standpoint and education.

It is common that studies have an emphasis on either 'Tibet' or 'the diaspora/exile society'. It is problematic to obtain permission for research inside Tibet and this makes it uncommon for fieldwork to be conducted both inside and outside of the country. To the individual researcher Tibet and the diaspora may seem like two different worlds that turn out to have fewer common features than expected. I prefer to discuss the situation in terms of a Tibetan 'diaspora'[10] instead of the more common 'exile society'. Diaspora studies have grown significantly during the late 1990s, and several other Tibetanists prefer to use this term (Anand 2000, Korom 1997, Nowak 1984, Venturino 1997). This is partly because of the different connotations of the concepts: a diaspora is spread all over the world and its members have left their (mythical or real) homeland for various reasons, both voluntary and involuntary. An exile society implies, to me, a more united (i.e. less dispersed) group of people arriving in an exile situation more or less involuntarily. More important, however, is the fact that 'diaspora' seems to be preferred by many Tibetans, because it seems to imply more personal and group agency to be a member of a diaspora than to be a refugee in exile (Diary 1996).[11] The Tibetans use the term *kyabchor-pa* (literally 'protect-take care of-person') for 'refugee'. 'The Tibetan diaspora' is in Tibetan *Bod me tsen jol du dampa* (literally 'Tibetans scattered abroad'), but the English term seems to be more commonly used among some groups, such as students and politicians. Other concepts of collective belonging are also common within the diaspora, such as *nang-pa* ('Buddhists'), and on another level for example *grong-pa* ('farmers'), or *chos-pa* ('belonging to the monastic community'), two categories that are mutually exclusive.

The Greek word 'diaspora' originally means 'the dispersal of (the Greek) people due to colonisation', from the verb *speiro* ('to sow') and *dia* ('over'). Safran (1991) defines 'diaspora' as follows: expatriate minority communities (1) that are dispersed from an original 'centre' to at least two 'peripheral' places; (2) that maintain a 'memory, vision or myth about their original homeland'; (3) that 'believe they are not – and perhaps cannot be – fully accepted by their host country'; (4) that see the ancestral home as a place of eventual return, when the time is right; (5) that are committed to the maintenance or restoration of this homeland; and (6) of which the group's consciousness and solidarity are 'importantly defined' by this continuing relationship with the homeland (Safran 1991:83). Robin Cohen has a similar definition, although he adds the tolerance for pluralism of the host country as a criterion (1997:26). Cohen speaks in terms of five types of diasporas, where the Jewish is axiomatic. The Jewish represents

---

[9] To imagine Tibet as a nation is to a large extent a post-1959 phenomenon; this will be more thoroughly discussed later on in this chapter (see also Anand 2000).

[10] I here follow Cohen´s (1997) example and use the terms diaspora and diasporas without capital D.

[11] The experienced similarity between the Jewish and the Tibetan diaspora has led the Dalai Lama to seek contact with Jewish leaders (see Katz 1991).

the 'victim diasporas', which embrace a 'homeland' on the same territory as another victim diaspora, the Palestinian (Cohen 1997, Boyarin and Boyarin 1993). The other four are 'labour diasporas' (like the Indian), 'imperial diasporas' (for example, the British), 'trade diasporas' (the Chinese, the Lebanese) and 'cultural diasporas' (the Caribbean, or Paul Gilroy's 'Black Atlantic', see Gilroy [1993] and Cohen [1997]). To Cohen the five labels are to be seen as pointing to certain features rather than as attempts to essentialise. Labelling is anyhow problematic, as I will show with the Tibetan case.

Diasporic practices (such as, in this case, leaving the homeland and seeking refuge elsewhere) cannot be reduced to epiphenomena of nation-states and imperialism (see Clifford 1994, Said 1984), not even in the case of the Tibetan diaspora. Tibetans used to live and travel all over Central and South Asia for business and pilgrimage reasons, regardless of geopolitical borders. The map of possible and impossible routes was based on knowledge of terrain and altitudes, water and food availability, shelters or friendly hosts for the night and risks of robbers or wild animals. The next valley could be like a foreign country, far away from home and inhabited by strangers with incomprehensible tongues. It might be impossible to know whether a return home could ever be made, and a move within the country might involve a lifetime of longing for a distant home (see for example Sakya and Emery 1990). 'Home' was a certain village or camp in a certain valley under the jurisdiction of a monastery or an estate. Individual belonging was based on the family and kin group or the religious community, collective belonging on being a Buddhist under the Dalai Lama. Before the Chinese army challenged the existence of Tibet the government in Lhasa had no real political power in remote parts like Kham and Amdo (Peissel 1972). The Chinese occupation made the notion of the 'homeland' important and hence self-definition as a diaspora possible. What we may call 'the diasporic mind' existed already – the view of the world as open for travels in order to obtain or leave something, a mental map of availability and risk. The diaspora, though, was not born until the 'homeland' was challenged, thus formulated. Diasporas always embody critique, in one way or the other, against politicised definitions of the 'homeland', and they always comprehend an agenda of their own. While the diasporic mind is ontological, diasporas are political: they consist of and reflect memories, imaginations, and visions of possible lives. The two concepts are not synonymous. 'The diasporic mind' can be found within a country where means of communication, due to (for example) destroyed or absent infrastructure (in the European sense of the word), are scarce and hazardous. 'Diasporas', on the other hand, are the outcome of opposition against politicised definitions of borders and states. I find it problematic to label in the way Cohen does. The Tibetan trade diaspora and the cultural diaspora (by the latter I mean the area Tibetan-speaking Buddhists have inhabited since historical time, stretching from Kashmir, in India to Szechwan, in China, and from Mongolia to northern India) came into existence with modern political mapping. The trade diaspora is also the outcome of politicised economy and land-use.

The third of Safran's criteria concerns feelings, within the diaspora, of not being fully accepted by the host country. This means that Tibetan/Indian relationships form an important part of the diaspora issue. Although Tibetans now live in many countries, India remains the main host for the diaspora. India and Tibet have old connections – commonly referred to – that are based on religion. Most refugees seem to feel welcome in India, despite some political anti-foreigner moves and a few racist riots. Few Tibetans seriously consider working within Indian society, though. The policy to keep the diaspora together, and Tibetan 'shyness' in comparison to Indian 'outspokenness', is said to be the reason. The number actually applying for Indian citizenship in order to work for Indian companies etc. is not known, however.

The notion of 'home' is another focus in my study. 'Home' is an important concept within the Tibetan diaspora as it is a keyword to the past as well as to the future, to dreams and visions as well as to everyday reality (cf. Safran's second [1991] criterion). Furthermore a focus on the individual 'home' balances the collective 'homeland' and 'diaspora'. The Tibetan word for 'home' is *nang*, which literally means 'inside' or 'the interior'. The term is connected to *nang-pa*, 'inside person', which means 'Buddhist'. The term for 'outside' has in a similar way a connection to the term for 'non-Buddhist' or 'foreigner': *phyi-pa* or 'outside person' (*phyi* means 'outside' or 'backwards'). 'Tibet' is in Tibetan *Bod*, but when referred to as 'the homeland' the concept used is *pha-yul*, literally 'fatherland'. The word *yul* primarily signifies a 'country' (in general), or an 'inhabited land', but it also indicates the countryside as opposed to the urban areas (Das 1994). According to Ekvall (1968) *yul* is antithetical to *hbrog*, which means 'high pasturage', a term for the landscape inhabited by the nomads (*hbrog-pa*). This would indicate that *pha yul* is the 'fatherland' of the settled – the inhabitants connected with sedentary farming. The proper term for the homeland of the nomads should be *pha-hbrog*, but it seems not to be in use any longer (Dhondup 1999, pers. comm.). In, for example, some Tibetan tax records *bod-pa* ('Tibetans') and *hbrog-pa* ('nomads') are listed separately. When referring to all people living in Tibet, the term *bod-kha-ba* ('Tibetan part ones') was used (Ekvall 1968). In the diaspora the term *bod-pa* is used for all Tibetans, maybe due to the search for a sharper national and ethnic identity. The internal differences, commonly referred to among Tibetans inside Tibet, are said to be between 'settled' (*she-chak*) and 'nomads' (*hbrog-pa*), and monks/nuns (*chos-pa*) (Dhondup 1994, Lhamo 1996 and 1998 pers. comms). In contemporary diaspora 'settled' and 'nomads' are often referred to as *grong-pa* ('farmers') in general, due to their common current occupation. The different concepts of belonging are reflected in the wide variety of ideas of the past, and imaginations of the future, that dwell in the contemporary diaspora.

The insight that notions of 'home', and related terms like 'citizenship' and 'belonging', may bear significantly different meanings for men or women, hetero- or homosexuals, 'blacks' or 'whites', rich or poor; is crucial to anthropology, as many have pointed out (Rosaldo 1993, Cohen 1985). Spivak has shown how 'home' in many cases means different things to Indian men and women. For the man the home is a sign of who he is, it is connected to his power and social position and it means economic security. The woman is never the owner of the house and her belonging there is based on marriage (she belongs to the husband's family). She may be circulated among the men like a commodity, from house to house. 'Home', 'security' and 'rights' mean different things to her (Spivak 1993: 162). Violent and traumatic memories may also influence experiences of home, as Lawrence Langer shows in an interview with a Holocaust victim, called George. George survives the Holocaust, and later on moves to the U.S. He marries and has a home together with his wife, but he cannot get rid of the feeling that a home 'is something you lose' (Langer 1995:21). His loss, in this case, is of the security and nourishing tranquillity of a home that he remembers from his childhood. Each night he is chased, and eventually shot dead, by the Germans, again and again. His nightmares even make his home an unsafe place for him. To lose one's home, an experience shared by many people in diaspora, may also have deep impact on the conception of 'home', such as long-lasting feelings of being insecure, of '...not to be at home in one's home' (Adorno 1978).

Experiences of 'home', and of 'diaspora', are simultaneously deeply personal and highly collective. A life in the diaspora may be very different, depending on age, gender and class. Notions of the past and the future that are important parts of the diasporic collective identity often vary considerably between, for example, a young person and an elderly one. 'Home' may be differently interpreted depending on a nomadic or settled family background. During his fieldwork among Warlpiri in Central Australia, Michael Jackson (1995) noticed how his own notion of 'home' was other than the Warlpiris'. The European (settled) notion of home is about 400 years old; it developed with the rise of the bourgeoisie in the 17th century. Before that, 'home' connoted a place, a village, or a group of kin (Jackson 1995:86). The term 'home' originally means 'village', 'settled country', in for example English, Swedish, German and Greek. With the rise of the bourgeoisie, says Berger, the term came to encompass a code of domestic morality, safeguarding the property of the family, which included the women (Berger 1984:55). The simultaneous development of the term 'homeland' served in a similar way to implant feelings of patriotism, persuading men to die in wars not of their own interest (ibid.:55). 'Home' has then come to mean 'house', to an extent that it has become a root metaphor that has created a certain '[...] Eurocentric bias to see all human existence from the perspective of the sedentary cultivator or householder [...]' (Jackson 1995:86). Jackson had to deliberately try to free himself from routines, determined boundaries, timetables and fixed addresses in order to understand the Warlpiri concept of 'home'. He came to explore the notion as something made, not given, and as a mode of activity rather than a bounded entity (ibid.:149). The Warlpiri 'home' is a place *in* the world, rather than a place cut off from it (ibid:99). Other authors have written about the nomadic non-sedentary world-view in terms of 'nomadic science' (Clastres 1974), and of deliberate resistance to the state among stateless societies (Granero 1986). There is also a discussion on 'the nomadic mind' as an outcome of 'modernity', meaning, by this, any kind of involuntary changes in people's lives, such as war, environmental disasters or socio-economical conditions (for example Berger et al. 1973, Kondo 1996, Lavie 1996, Malkki 1995, Rutherford 1990).

Tibetan Kinship and Belonging

As noted, new 'constructions' of kinship have developed in the Tibetan diaspora. Kinship and marriage rules are, however, traditional matters of debate among both Tibetans and Tibetologists. Descent as well as locality rules in Tibet seem to have been, and still are, flexible (Aziz 1973, Thakla 1996). The lineage system is frequently attributed to Tibet by Western scholars as well as by Chinese scholars (Xiaolin Guo 1994, pers. comm.), despite the fact that in reality it seldom seems to be found outside of Amdo. Within the extended family exogamy is strictly maintained. Cousins (parallel and cross) are considered as siblings and the same word is used for male cousin and brother (*cho-choe*), and female cousin and sister (*acha*). In English Tibetans often say cousin-sister and cousin-brother when they want to be specific.[12]

The literature often emphasises the ethnic endogamy among Tibetans (discussed in Corlin 1975:17). In the Tibetan diaspora of today ethnic endogamy is not strictly maintained, or so it seems. To the students I have talked to, marriage with an Indian partner seems to be unlikely, while marriage with an American or European is desirable to some and unthinkable to others. In Tibet, marriage rules are probably even less strict, as a marriage to a (presumably atheist) Chinese partner is possible and generally does not involve any religious commitments. Fjeld (1998) shows how family background (the family's *kyesa*; the belonging in the hierarchical division in nobility, commoners and polluted) is still a valid social determinant in Tibet. Restrictions on relations between people with different *kyesa* basically concerns marriage, though, rather than everyday life social interaction.[13] The 'ideal' family consists of husband and wife from the same *kyesa* together with the husband's parents and grandparents, any children and unmarried aunts and uncles.[14] Decision-making within the family should be the responsibility of the older generations and in this regard age seems to be more important than gender. A life as a single is possible and highly respected as long as it involves religious devotion, work within the family or business enterprises.

I would say that rather than group endogamy the important criterion for being 'Tibetan' is religion (being a Buddhist), and to some extent occupation. Most Tibetans are more or less dependent on trade for their everyday survival. At least someone in the family is occupied with trade in one way or another and this often forms the basis of the family economy. 'Tibetans', whether they call themselves Sherpa, Nyeshangte or Tibetan, are well known all over South Asia and as far away as Hong Kong for their roadside petty commodity business. Many set up their own shops, hotels, restaurants or carpet manufacture. Young Tibetan students often prefer business studies. The importance of Buddhism and trade as self-defining criteria is apparent, for example, in the way the differences between Tibetans and others sometimes are expressed in terms of 'lazy' and 'cheating' Indians and 'atheist' Chinese in contrast to 'hard-working' (business-minded, successful), 'honest' (in business) and 'religious' (Buddhist) Tibetans.

To recognise kin and family is potentially difficult for all Tibetans due to the many fragmented families, the loss of kin connections and the separation of generations during or after the escape of large groups to India. Family names are seldom used, which adds to the problem. The use of a combination of two personal names is the most common, occasionally with an addition of a name of the family estate, if any. Diemberger (1993) shows in her article on Tibetan

---

[12] Diemberger (1993) claims in her study on Khumbo, a Tibetan people in NE Nepal, that the system stresses the closeness of kin ties through people of the same gender. This means that parallel cousins are equated to siblings and parallel aunts and uncles to parents, but cross-cousins and -aunts/uncles are referred to by different terms and not equated to siblings or parents. This contradicts the information I have got from Tibetans in India.

[13] The word *kyesa* (*sKyes sa*) derives from the term used for 'family background' during the Chinese Cultural Revolution in Tibet, *kyegung* (*sKyes Gungs*). Someone's *kyesa* was very important during this period of time (1966-76).

[14] This is the traditional concept of an ideal family. In reality practice as well as ideals might have changed, at least in urban surroundings.

Khumbo in Nepal how knowledge of kinship and family history forms an important part of women's power in society. It is likely that the changed possibilities of kinship control in the diaspora situation have affected women's power, but there are no studies on this as far as I know.

Life at the Hostels for Youth

India is a huge country where travel is tiresome and time-consuming. The settlements are to a large extent situated way out in the countryside. This, together with the fact that many diaspora Tibetans are children and youth with no accompanying adult relatives, has led to a situation in which generations often stay separated from each other. In other words, many young Tibetans have experienced a life at a Tibetan Hostel or a boarding school (my estimation is that at least 60% of those under 20 years of age have stayed in a hostel for a period of time). Few Tibetans live in cities (where high schools, colleges and universities are situated), which means that a majority of the students have to stay at hostels (the only exception of some significance is the Tibetan settlement in Delhi). The distances to the families often make it impossible to visit home more than once or twice a year, at the most. Some students have their families in Tibet, which means that they can go home once every ten years or so, if they are lucky. During my fieldwork I came to spend a lot of time at Hostels, particularly the ones presented below. The 'Youth Hostel culture' includes typical features, such as the creation of new, fictive, kin networks. The students are often concerned about family making and child rearing, as they have little experience of this, and these concerns affected our discussions. The diaspora/Tibet relations and the situation in Tibet are among other issues close to the hearts of many Tibetan young people.

The two 'Tibetan Youth Hostels' I visited, one for girls and one for boys, are situated in a middle class area south of the city centre of a South Indian university town. The students are generally second- or third-generation refugees, with a few exceptions. A majority have lived in hostels since early childhood. The parents of the students live in the Karnatakan settlements (such as Bylakuppe and Mundgod), or in Dharamsala, Arunachal Pradesh, West Bengal, Bhutan, Nepal or Tibet. The settlements in Karnataka are about 7–15 hours away from town, by bus; Dharamsala is reached in three days by train; and places in Bhutan or Northeast India take at least five days to reach. This means that some of the students are able to go home during holidays but many have to stay in town, unless they join a friend in his or her place or on a trip somewhere.

The girls, about 45 in total, live in a quite comfortable house with several small rooms where three to seven girls live together. A hostel warden, a harsh middle-aged woman, and the old cook live here to look after the girls. Upstairs is a dining-hall where all the students eat, and where they can watch television in the afternoons. Each time I pass the dining hall at least some of the girls are watching the seemingly endless song-and-dance Hindi movies. Otherwise the lives of the girls take place in the small rooms they share with others, sitting on the beds with their colourful bedsheets, leaning on quilt and pillow in order to chat, eat or do their homework. The girls hardly go anywhere. They say the nightmarish daily bus-rides in the extremely crowded city buses to and from college or university are too tiring. For the girls there is a curfew at seven o'clock in the evening.

The boys' hostel is a small house with only a few big rooms and a kitchen. Currently 23 boys live in this house. It is very crowded and the students complain about lack of privacy and the difficulty of studying in the noisy atmosphere. There is no hostel warden in this hostel. Quite a few of the boys have bikes or scooters and go wherever they want to. They constantly come and go, on their way downtown to stroll around for a while or to see a movie. There is no curfew for the boys.

Very few of the students claim to be involved with diaspora politics, 'We are too far away from Dharamsala, and we never get any information about what happens', they tell me. One of the boys I talk to works with the Tibetan Youth Congress locally, but the majority seldom claim to have an opinion on the political issues I try to bring up: 'If we follow His Holiness (the Dalai Lama) he guides us right. It is as simple as that', they explain to me.

During the time I spent at the hostels it happened only three times that I talked to a boy alone (the same person); otherwise it was close to impossible to meet the boys other than in a group. The discussions I had with the girls generally took place in their rooms and we were usually three or four sitting together on the beds. I guess with me being a woman, I felt comfortable talking in small groups with the girls, and the boys felt uncomfortable talking to me alone. For this reason, and because of the friendship I felt with some of the girls, I came to spend much more time with the girls than at the boys' hostel. In order to protect the identities of the students I have changed their names.

Vicarious Suffering

The inhabitants of the hostels are all college or university students, aged 19 to 23. Several of the students I talked to go to teacher's training courses or work on their Bachelor of Arts degree, mostly in order to join a teacher's training course later. Only one boy I met took arts courses without any real professional plans. By far the most popular are the business programmes and the computer courses. The students refer to the fact that business and agriculture are the most common ways to make a living in the diaspora. The need for knowledge in business administration, agro-business and accountancy is obvious, they tell me. 'Tibetans do well already but they can do better. Our parents are not educated, so we can make a change', Kalsang says. Language studies are other favourites. Many students consider themselves to be good at languages and quite a few mention good teachers in these subjects. Mathematics, on the other hand, seems to be disliked by everybody: 'I just don't understand it', 'Tibetans don't understand mathematics!' are common comments. Besides this, most of the students tell me that they like to study and try to be ambitious: 'As it is the Tibetan community that pays for my studies I simply have to do my best.' Most students have scholarships administered by the Tibetan Department of Education in Dharamsala. The scholarships are supposed to cover half the expenses and the parents have to pay the other half. The educational possibilities of the children therefore depend on the economic standing of the parents.

The atmosphere at the schools is another problem often mentioned. The students are afraid of the teachers and the gap between the two statuses seems huge. The teaching methods are considered very old-fashioned. The problem with the Indian teachers and schools derives, according to the students, from the old British school system with its emphasis on hierarchy and discipline. Many of the students also blame the problems on what they call 'the Tibetan nature', meaning that Tibetans are very shy and silent and never dare to ask any questions, particularly not if there are frank and talkative Indians in the same classroom. Especially Tibetan girls have 'a shyness problem', the boys tell me. The girls never say that about themselves. To them all Tibetans are shy (in comparison to Indians and Westerners). Dhondup tells me that at her first school in Bylakuppe the Indian teacher always shouted at the Tibetan pupils to speak louder and '[...] he made us feel ashamed of ourselves by making us read the same paragraphs over and over again. I think that made us even more shy.'[15] In Tibetan the students describe themselves as 'polite' and 'discreet' (*gha tsempo*) rather than 'shy' in its English meaning, that is, the connotation changes with the change of language. To be 'discreet' and 'polite' are important virtues in the Tibetan society. Fjeld (1998) shows how in a contemporary Lhasa locale, Tibetan definitions of Tibetan culture focus on certain traditions (like the celebration of *Losar*, with the Great Prayer Festival), and on discreet and polite behaviour. An often-stressed difference between Chinese and Tibetans is that the Chinese are rude and not discreet (ibid.). In the diaspora it is more common to stress that the Chinese lack of religion makes the great difference.

Although studies are considered necessary many of the students express problems related to their education. Almost everyone mentions that the lack of guidance poses a huge problem to many young Tibetans. As they grow up, away from their families, decisions regarding, for example, what kind of school or which topics to choose have to be taken by the student him/herself. Parents seldom have any education themselves and face many difficulties when they try to relate to the education of their children. It is mostly the same with the 'hostel parents' (the staff of the hostel, usually one man and one woman); those at the girls' hostel speak neither English nor Hindi and have no schooling. Their lack of schooling is a qualification for the appointment as they are supposed to be 'as Tibetan as possible' (Topagyal 1994). According to the students, hostel life prepares them more for a life in Tibet than for a professional career in India, something experienced as frustrating by many of them.

Parents and relatives are also important when a young person applies for work, particularly within the Tibetan administration. Without these kinds of connections it is more difficult to get a good position. Students originating in remote places (Tibet or Bhutan) often have to take major life decisions by themselves, like whom to marry and when. Tsering, a girl from Bhutan, tells me it takes four days for her to go to her maternal home and that letters often disappear on the way: 'So I never get any advice. I could even marry my own cousin brother by mistake!' she says with a giggle. To marry a cousin is just about the worst that might happen. Part of the problem with 'not getting any advice' concerns the risk of marrying the wrong person, or encountering a relative without recognising him/her. The major problem is, however, that without a kin network you are on your own, without support in case of trouble. The students themselves have found a solution to this. Already at a young age,

---

[15] Among Tibetan teachers it seems to be quite common to use the sense of shame (*ngo-tsha*) as a method to keep order in the classrooms (Labiesse 1995).

when she stayed at Tibetan Children's Village in Upper Dharamsala, Lhamo decided to help her even younger orphaned friend Lhakpa. She promised to take care of Lhakpa as well as she could, with money when needed, and in the future to present her to possible employers. This is called 'to adopt a friend'. The students agree this is common among the children at the TCV boarding schools, a creative solution among children left to take care of themselves.

Lhamo has lived in hostels since she was seven years old. Many of the students have spent most of their life in hostels of this kind. Some of the boys tell me: 'If we try to see something good in this we can tell you that we are strong and take responsibility for ourselves and each other. Another truth is that many of us feel depressed and frustrated. We miss our families, we don't get any guidance in life and the lack of privacy in this house just drives us crazy sometimes.' Living in a hostel is suffering, they say. But they have a reason to suffer. Students also have to 'suffer' for the sake of living up to the 'suffering' of their parents, who personally experienced the occupation and the building up of the diaspora society, and therefore 'suffered the most'.

The Location of Home

I came to India together with my husband, my brother and his girlfriend. This fact caused many comments and questions, particularly from the girls. They are very fascinated by our love relationships and asked many questions about how we met, if my husband proposed properly and what our parents think about my brother and his girlfriend living together without being married. Families and marriage were favourite topics of discussion. The ideal family in their minds seems to be something of a mixture between Jane Austen (whom they apparently read in school) and the families in Hindi movies, two ideal types with amazing similarities: a rich man and a poor woman (or vice versa) meet each other and several complications follow before the happy ending, including the arrival of two healthy children. This common teenage talk after a while turns into a much more serious discussion on issues really close to their hearts. Dolma says to me one day: 'Do you think I can have a family of my own? I never experienced family life. What kind of parent will I be? I hardly remember my own mother and I know nothing about a mother-child relationship.' Tsering and the others talk to me about the same kind of concerns. The only thing they know for sure, they say, is that they will do anything to keep the children with them at home. Lhamo tells me: 'My children will not go through the same terrible experiences as I did when my parents left me at TCV (the boarding school) when I was seven years old. I was homesick and cried every night. It was particularly bad when other parents came to visit their children, I always ran away and hid until they left.' When I ask if they think the situation will be different for them when they themselves become parents, Tenzing, who grew up with her family in a nearby settlement, seems to be convinced of a changed situation in the future. The others hesitate. 'I am not sure I want to marry, I don't know where I will get work. But I don't mind being by myself', says one of them (Tsering).

The reason for this hesitation about marriage lies with the pressure to work for the Tibetan community wherever needed, regardless of family needs. This means that a wife and husband might get work in different parts of India and in such a situation it may be the only solution to keep any children at boarding school. It is not only the diaspora situation *per se* that has resulted in the boarding-school solution, but the way the society is organised. As a solution it may have come easily to mind in the diaspora, given the fact that in old Tibet it was common to place even very small children in monasteries far away from the parents, in cases where the children were predestined to become monks, nuns or servants at monasteries, or if the child was orphaned and alone. Children were also, to some extent, sent to schools in India already before 1959 (*Jetsun* Pema 1997:38). This does not suggest, however, that it is an easy decision to send a child away to boarding school. It is regarded as a major dilemma in life for many young Tibetans, as well as for their parents.

The students generally feel obliged to work for the Tibetan community after finishing their exams, as their education is sponsored more or less for this reason, but also because they want to stay and play their part within the community. Teaching and business seem to be preferred. The students claim it would be hard for them to work on administrative and political issues as they are so isolated from diaspora politics: 'We never know what is going on and get no information from Dharamsala', says Kalsang. No student I have talked to mentions the Indian labour market as a possibility. Tsering gives me a typical answer when I ask her where she would like to live and work in the future: 'I want to work with the Tibetan community in Dharamsala. If I cannot do that I want to live in Denmark!'. On my question why she picked Denmark, she tells me she has a sponsor there and hence developed an interest in the country. To stay in Indian society is out of the question for Dolma. Some other girls, for example Nyima, have grown up with Indians and feel more at home with Indian society. Nyima is the only one to wear a *salwar kameez* (Indian woman's dress). The others wear trousers and T-shirts just like me. The *chuba* (Tibetan woman's dress), commonly seen in Dharamsala, is here regarded more like a work uniform.

During our discussions in the girls' hostel we came to spend quite a lot of time talking about childhood memories. In combination with discussions on our future lives this led us to think about where 'home' is. I have often noticed that the question 'Where do you come from?' always provides two different answers when posed to Tibetans. The first, immediate, answer is 'Tibet'. Later on, when we know each other better, the answer to the same question is 'Bylakuppe', 'Dharamsala', 'Mundgod' or some other place in India or a neighbouring country. Now I realise it is the same with questions on the future. After the answer 'Tibet' there are second answers, like 'Dharamsala', 'I wouldn't mind staying in this city' and even 'Denmark'. Tibet is the obvious answer, but as Tibet is a concept and symbol, but not a real place for the students, the future in their minds is located somewhere closer to themselves. Somehow Denmark seems to be a more real place than Tibet. Tsering has colour pictures and letters from Denmark, and occasionally she hears about the country on the news. Tibet is little more than old darkened pictures of dead relatives and some family memories. 'You never hear about Tibet on the news. I don't even know what it looks like!' as Tsering says. To these students Tibet is a somewhat unreal place, always located somewhere else in time and space. Tibet is, however, very important as their 'own' history, as a vision (of a possible future), and as a reason. The student hostels are necessary in many ways but one important and often repeated argument for hostels is that Tibetans must stay together in order to keep the Tibetan nation.

Some of the boys tell me they tend to think of this when they feel frustrated in the crowded hostel, as suffering for a reason is an easier suffering.

The diaspora situation means that the 'home' of the future is seldom the same as 'home' of the past. Parents, grandparents and children have different 'homes' in their minds. Tibet is a common point of reference for the older generations. But 'home' for them seems to be where the Dalai Lama is, first and foremost. Second most important is to stay close to family and friends, if at all possible. For many of the girls at the hostel the 'home' of the past is located somewhere in the magic land of childhood, in a refugee settlement in the mountains of Southern India, or on a hill slope in Arunachal Pradesh. Jamyang invokes the same bright eyed look when talking about the little family house along a dusty road in Bylakuppe, as I imagine I have when talking about the cottage of my childhood summers. The present 'home' is, for most of them, among friends at the hostel. Their childhood 'home' is too far away, too unknown or maybe too connected with a major loss experienced at a young age.

Going Back 'Home'

One day the girls ask me if I want to see 'someone from Tibet'. I find the expression a bit strange but agree. Of course, I certainly want to meet someone from Tibet. I later found out that this girl, Lhamo, currently is the only girl at the hostel to be born in Tibet. Her parents brought her to Dharamsala when she was six years old, and dropped her at the TCV boarding school: 'They told me they planned to go away for five or six days to see a relative. They never came back, so after a while I realised they had returned to Lhasa. How I was angry with them! I felt terribly homesick. But when I grew older I understood they did this because they wanted me to get a Tibetan education. In Tibet there is only Chinese education.'

Lhamo thinks she got a good education at the TCV, but she tells me she had no adults around and that this was problematic, she had no one to turn to in confidence: '[...] so instead we tried to talk to each other about our problems, it made them easier to bear, but of course we couldn't solve each other's problems'. Lhamo was preoccupied with thoughts about her family, she says. She wanted to know what it would be like to be part of a family and self-evidently to belong somewhere. Her memories of her parents and their home were fading. After a while it became absolutely necessary for her to go back to see them: 'I wanted to know about my home and my parents and to experience family-life. I had stayed in a hostel for so long!' she explains.

So Lhamo went back to Lhasa. She stayed with her parents[16] and managed to get work as a tourist guide. The Chinese government promises work to everyone who returns but in reality there are very few jobs, and most young people end up hanging around 'the tea-stalls' smoking, drinking and doing minor crimes, according to Lhamo. The work as a tourist-guide is an opportunity open to

[16] Lhamo's father works for a company owned by the Chinese government. Apparently his employers wanted him to make Lhamo come and stay in Tibet, as it looked bad for a daughter of a government employee to be living in India. Lhamo's mother is a business woman and has over the years managed to see Lhamo in Dharamsala a few times as she holds a so-called 'business passport' for Nepal.

Tibetans from India who speaks good English. 'Indian' guides are popular among foreign tourists as they are supposed to know more about the situation in Tibet. But the government is suspicious of them and Lhamo later on realised she was being followed by security people.[17] She liked her job, though, and all the practical arrangements surrounding her return were solved quite easily.

Mentally, it was much more difficult to adjust to the new situation. Lhasa felt like a very foreign place to Lhamo. Her closest neighbours were suspicious and asked her why she had come back instead of being in India to do some good 'in return for the money His Holiness had spent on my education'. Even worse was the meeting with the parents: 'It was such a big difference between me and the rest of the family. We couldn't understand each other. They speak a different language as they mix Tibetan with Chinese, which I don't understand. I mix Tibetan with English and Hindi, which they don't understand; they constantly blamed me for speaking too fast. I was considered stupid, as I don't speak Chinese. They also found me far too frank and I said many "forbidden" things. I said "marriage" and they thought that was very bad, and my sister and mother blushed all over, can you imagine!' Other misunderstandings emerged from the fact that Tibetan parents count on all the young to obey them; it is important to show respect to older people. Lhamo was used to making all decisions herself, and many conflicts derived from her parents trying to decide for her. She was, for example, not allowed to stay overnight at a girlfriend's place, something she found absolutely ridiculous.

It was not easy to make new friends in Lhasa and Lhamo felt increasingly lonely: 'I had many acquaintances but no real friends.' Her childhood friend from the neighbourhood went to study in China and came back '[...] completely different, he never speaks to his parents and says he doesn't understand Tibetan anymore. He doesn't like us who come from India.' It is very easy to recognise foreign Tibetans in Lhasa, not only by the absence of the red cheeks and because of the accent but also mentally, she says. Friends of the same age were very immature compared to Lhamo and her friends in India:

> They are dependent on their parents; they never dare to do anything on their own. They know nothing about Tibet or the Western world, only China exists for them. They are not interested either. They find us very inquisitive and cheeky. And we find them naïve and credulous. You can fool them anywhere. I guess that's why they don't know about Tibet. They never study history at school. And they are so superstitious and always just talk about the next life and what will happen then. We don't do that in India. In the countryside it is even worse. Some are satisfied with their lives, but others are dissatisfied and feel like they are controlled.

The other girls at the hostel have occasionally talked about the difference between them and the 'Tibetans', as they call them. Many tell stories about sisters or brothers who married Tibetans and how troublesome this is. Lhamo says this is partly due to differences in the view of marriage; in Tibet people marry when they are very young and often the marriage ends in divorce. Divorce is accepted in Tibet while it is looked down upon among Tibetans in India. Lhamo herself has decided to marry an Indian Tibetan. She will definitely avoid

---

[17] It is no longer possible for foreign Tibetans to work as tourist guides in Tibet. The Chinese authorities cancelled this opportunity due to accusations of subversive activities among the foreign guides (information from Fjeld, September 1997).

the problems that come with a 'mixed marriage', as they call it. 'There is such a difference in the way we think, I have experienced that myself, and these marriages often end in divorce.'

It was the pressure to marry that finally made Lhamo decide to go back to India. Her parents wanted her to stay and take care of them, and had started to look for a suitable husband. Lhamo felt lonely. Lhasa was a strange place to her and she was scared of her parents' marriage plans. Finally she left, without telling anyone. 'When I was happily back in India it felt like coming home. I realised Dharamsala is home for me', she says. 'It is painful of course, now that I have learned to know my family I really miss them sometimes.' It was easier when the memories of the family were vague, she says, but she is anyhow happy she made the trip. Now she has completely different feelings for the country, she says, and a much deeper understanding for the suffering of the Tibetan people. Everything she has heard about the situation proved to be true, she tells me.

Before I heard Lhamo's story I had not realized how wide the gap is between Tibetans inside and outside of Tibet. I had heard the girls' talk about 'mixed marriages' between exiles and Tibetans from Tibet, and how they refer to Lhamo as 'the one from Tibet', but I had never thought about the consequences until I heard Lhamo's story. There seems to be a growing alienation among the students I met. 'Home' can be many places and the word means different things to each generation. The fact that young people to a large extent grow up apart from their families and other adults is considered (by themselves) as the reason for possible future problems with parenthood and relationships. Fear of losing home and belonging due to a diaspora situation is expressed in terms of 'lack of guidance in life' and risks of unconscious incest.

The Tibetan Diaspora as Conflict

This chapter has shown how the diaspora world is formed and experienced by Tibetan college students in their twenties, and how their various notions of 'home' and 'diaspora' differ from those of their parents and grandparents. The individual experiences of belonging and alienation are expressed in terms of kinship, while the collective experiences are expressed as 'suffering' (because of the greed and atheism of China, for the sake of the liberation, etc.) and 'struggle' (to keep the own culture, to spread information about the situation, etc.). The diaspora is hierarchically organised and this organisation offers a position primarily according to the place a person occupies within the 'right' kin networks. To have the 'right' *Kyesa* (family background or class) is important in this regard. An 'adoption' system, among the students and created by themselves, constitutes an alternative 'support network'; one of the ideas in 'adoption' is that the older introduces his/her protégé to future employers. Closeness to Dharamsala, the diasporic heart, is another factor that determines present and future chances. The duty is to serve wherever a contribution is demanded. Individual needs are not considered important.

This politicised identity is, however, not unchallenged. Examples of disputed issues are the constitutional non-violence policy, the systems of political representation and the place for women's rights and minority issues within the diaspora. The individual experiences and notions of 'home' and 'belonging' seem to be of vital importance for the way the 'Tibetan identity' is regarded and constituted. The duty to sacrifice for the sake of a common cause, with a disputed meaning, is an important reason behind internal Tibetan conflicts. The experience of 'suffering' for the cause of the 'struggle' is transferred from parent to child. The students I met have to 'suffer' for the sake of legitimising the 'suffering' of their parents. Their expressed wish is to break with this by fighting for the right to keep their future children with them. This may be interpreted as an awareness of this 'legacy of suffering', as well as a wish to gain 'peace of mind'. From this perspective the diaspora means a continuation of the Chinese-Tibetan conflict. To live in diaspora is to live the conflict.

The notion of the 'homeland' is part of the diaspora definition and so is the potential challenge to the situation of being 'at home', as an order or necessity to move somewhere else can arrive at any time. Belonging in diaspora includes a notion, with a mythic dimension, of a 'homeland' but not necessarily of being 'at home' anywhere. Within this lies the dilemma of exile and diaspora: the 'homeland' is a notion rather than a territory. The 'homeland' of the diaspora is never actually there to find. There might be, as in the Tibetan case, a place with the same name, but it never answers to the expectations of a 'homeland'. As Lhamo found out, not even having a family in the homeland is enough to make it a 'homeland'. Thus the diaspora simultaneously unsettles and constitutes the very notion of autochthony. I have no intention to deny any rights to a home-land based on moral, political or other claims. What I have discussed is the arena of myths, visions, memories and dreams that constitute a 'homeland'.

The idea of the eventual return to this 'homeland' is part of being in a diaspora. The maintenance of the diaspora situation hence contains a contra-diction in terms; the 'homeland' is not available for returning. Any resettlement or re-migration comprehends this contradiction, which is what makes these issues so problematic. To the diaspora-as-conflict 'peace' is neither to be found in re-migration nor in staying. On an individual level it is possible to learn to live in the diaspora, irrespective of where it is located in the geographical sense. On the collective level diaspora constitutes a critique of the very notions of 'peace' and (conflict) 'resolution'. 'The national order of things' (Malkki 1995) we tend to take for granted is no settled or inevitable condition.

References

Adorno, Th. 1978, *Minima Moralia – Reflections from a Damaged Life* London: Verso

Amnesty International 1996, *People's Republic of China: Persistent human rights violation in China* London: Amnesty Press

Anand, D. 2000, 'Travel-Routing Diaspora ... Homing on Tibet'. Paper presented at the 16th European conference on Modern South Asian Studies, Edinburgh 6–9 September

Aziz, B.N. 1973. 'Some Notions about Descent and Residence in Tibetan Society', in Fürer-Haimendorf, Ch. von ed., *The Anthropology of Nepal* Warminster: Aris & Phillips.

Barnett, R. and Akiner, S. eds 1995, *Resistance and Reform in Tibet* London: Hurst & Company

Berger, J. 1984, *And Our Faces, My Heart, Brief as Photos* London: Writers and Readers Publishing Cooperative

Berger, J., Berger, B. and Kellner, H. 1973, *The Homeless Mind* Harmondsworth: Penguin Books

Boyarin, D. and Boyarin, J. 1993, 'Diaspora: Generation and the Ground of Jewish Identity' *Critical Inquiry* 19: 693–725

Clastres, P. 1977 (1974), *Society Against the State. Essays in Political Anthropology* New York: Zone Books

Clifford, J. 1994, 'Diasporas'. *Cultural Anthropology* 9 (3): 302–38

Cohen, A.P. 1985, *The Symbolic Construction of Community* London: Tavistock

Cohen, R. 1997, *Global Diasporas: An Introduction* London: University College London Press

Corlin, C. 1975, 'The Nation in Your Mind. Continuity and Change among Tibetan Refugees in Nepal' Ph.D. thesis, University of Göteborg

Dalai Lama 1991, *Freedom in Exile* New Delhi: Rupa & Co.

Das, V. 1994, 'The Anthropological Discourse on India: The Reason and Its Other' in Borofsky, R. ed., *Assessing Cultural Anthropology* New York: McGraw Hill

DeVine, C. 1993, *Determination. Tibetan Women & The Struggle for an Independent Tibet* Toronto: Vauve Press

Dhondup, K. 1994, 'Dharamsala Revisited – Shangrila or Sarajevo?' *Tibetan Review* 7

Diemberger, H. 1993, 'Blood, sperm, soul and the mountain. Gender relations, kinship and cosmovision among the Khumbo (N.E. Nepal)' in del Valle, Th. ed., *Gendered Anthropology* New York: Routledge

Du Rietz, A. 1997, 'Den Tibetanska Diasporan. Ett folks kulturella överlevnad' Unpublished C-thesis, University of Lund

Ekvall, R. B. 1968, *Fields on the Hoof: nexus of Tibetan nomadic pastoralism* New York: Holt, Rhinehart & Winston

Fischer, L. ed. 1962, *The Essential Gandhi. His Life, Work, and Ideas* New York: Vintage Books

Fjeld, H.E. 1998, 'Representing the Past: Some Perspectives on Change and Continuity in the Former Nobility in Lhasa. Conference proceedings', 5th Nordic Conference on Tibet, Moesgård, Denmark 1997

Gilroy, P. 1993, *The Black Atlantic. Modernity and Double Consciousness* London: Verso

Goldstein-Kyaga, K. 1993, *The Tibetans – School for Survival or Submission. An Investigation of Ethnicity and Education* Stockholm: HLS Förlag

Granero, F.S. 1986, 'Power, Ideology and the Ritual of Production in Lowland South America' *Man* 21 (4)

Gyatso, S. 1993, 'The Crisis of Tibetan Language in Exile' *Tibetan Review* 9

Human Rights Practices for 1998 Report. http://www.usemb.se/human(human1998/china.html

Katz, N. 1991, 'A meeting of Ancient people: Western Jews and the Dalai Lama of Tibet: Searching out the Jewish Secret for Surviving Exile' http://www.jcpa.Org/jl/hit20.html

Kondo, D. 1996, 'The Narrative Production of "Home", Community and Political Identity in Asian American Theatre' in Lavie, S. and Swedenburg, T. eds, *Displacement, Diaspora, and Geographies of Identity* Durham, NC: Duke University Press

Korom, F.J. 1997, 'Introduction: Place, Space and Identity: The Cultural, Economic and Aesthetic Politics of Tibetan Diaspora' in Korom, F.J. ed., *Tibetan Culture in the Diaspora* Wien: Verlag der Österreichischen Akademie der Wissenschaften

Kvaerne, P. 1993, *Bon, Buddhism and Democracy* Copenhagen: NIAS Report No.12

Jackson, M. 1995, *At Home in the World* Durham, NC: Duke University Press

Labiesse, Ch. 1995, The paradox of Tibetan education in exile *Tibetan Review* 8

Langer, L.L. 1995, *Admitting the Holocaust. Collected Essays* New York: Oxford University Press

Lavie, S. 1996, 'Blowups in the Borderzones: Third World Israeli Authors' Groping for Home' in Lavie, S. and Swedenburg, T. eds., *Displacement, Diaspora, and Geographies of Identity* Durham, NC: Duke University Press

Leach, E.R. 1973, 'Complementary Filiation and Bilateral Kinship' in Goody, J. ed., *The Character of Kinship* Cambridge: Cambridge University Press

Lopez, Jr. D.S. 1994, 'New Age Orientalism: The Case of Tibet' *Tibetan Review* 5

Malkki, L.H. 1995, *Purity and Exile. Violence, memory, and national cosmology among Hutu refugees in Tanzania* Chicago: University of Chicago Press

Nowak, M. 1984, *Tibetan Refugees: youth and a new generation of meaning* New Brunswick, NJ: Rutgers University Press

Peissel, M. 1972, *Cavaliers of Kham. The Secret War in Tibet.* London: Heinemann

Pema, Jetsun 1997, *Tibet-Mystery: an autobiography* Shaftesbury: Element Books

Rosaldo, R. 1993, *Culture & Truth. The Remaking of Social Analysis.* Boston, MA: Beacon Press

Rutherford, J. 1990, 'A Place Called Home: Identity and the Cultural Politics of Difference' in Rutherford, J. ed., *Identity. Community, Culture, Difference* London: Lawrence & Wishart

Safran, W. 1991, 'Diasporas in Modern Societies: Myths of Homeland and Return' *Diaspora* 1 (1): 83–99

Said, E. 1984, 'Reflections of Exile' *Granta* 13: 159–72

Sakya, J. and Emery, J. 1990, *Princess in the Land of Snows. The Life of Jamyang Sakya in Tibet* Boston, MA: Shambala

Schwartz, R. 1992, 'Democracy, Tibetan Independence and Protest Under Chinese Rule' *The Tibet Journal* 17 (2): 3–27

Senge, Geshe J. 1995, 'Role Models. Letter to the press' *Tibetan Review* 12

Spivak, G. Chakravorty 1993. *Outside in the Teaching Machine* Oxford: Oxford University Press

Stein, R.A. 1972, *Tibetan Civilization* Stanford, CA: Stanford University Press

Taring, R. Dolma, 1986, *Daughter of Tibet* New Delhi: Rupa & Co.

Thakla, N. Lhamo. 1996, 'Women in Tibetan Community' *Tibetan Review* 1

Tiljander Dahlström, Å. 1997, 'Belonging in Exile. Experience and Conflict in the Tibetan Diaspora' Licentiate thesis, Department of Cultural Anthropology, Uppsala University

Topagyal, T. 1994, 'A Mismanagement of Human Resources' *Tibetan Review* 10

Venturino, S. 1997, 'Reading Negotiations in the Tibetan Diaspora' in Korom, F.J. ed., *Constructing Tibetan Culture. Contemporary Perspectives* Quebec: World Heritage Press

11

Who Needs a State?
Civilians, Security & Social Services in North-East Somalia[1]
BERNHARD HELANDER

The shape and content of institutions delivering social services in countries and territories where the state has collapsed is an issue that only very recently has begun to generate systematic interest. Taking a cue from Christoplos' argument that questions are often phrased around what 'we' can do for 'them' (Christoplos 1998), this paper tries to take a look at what it is that 'they' do for 'them', and what are the challenges faced in doing so. Christoplos very convincingly demonstrates that research is generally more concerned with the future democratic impact on 'civil society' than with what the civil society actually accomplishes. Granted the point, one has, nevertheless, to keep in mind that operating social services in a war-torn society invariably has to confront complex issues like security. This essay takes as its point of departure a very straightforward question: to what extent can the emergent civil society in post-war Somalia play a positive role in promoting or enhancing security? To deal with this question in a way that may shed light more generally on the role and importance of the so-called civil society (a term that will be given a more workable definition as we go on) there are a number of fundamental, conceptual issues to be taken into account. One such issue concerns, of course, the very nature of civil society in a context where there is no state. Another such conceptual concern is the definition of security itself where I will dwell on how local concepts of security are, paradoxically, both more narrow and yet more encompassing than what we normally understand by the word. I shall argue that unless one takes such locally constructed concepts into account the rationales underlying the decisions made by single households cannot be grasped. I shall draw largely on my own material from North-east Somalia (the so-called Puntland State of Somalia) where I have conducted research since 1995.

---

[1] This chapter is an edited version of an essay by Bernhard Helander entitled 'Getting things done in Somalia: civilians, security and social services', *Antropologiska Studier*, 66–7, 128–40. I have taken the liberty to alter the title, and to add three final sentences, to link the conclusion to the theme Bernhard would have discussed at greater length had he been able to complete the chapter he envisaged. I have also incorporated some footnotes in the text (PR).

A Sad Story

The Somali scenario may not need much introduction. Since the overthrow of the military regime in January 1991, the country has lapsed into a form of stable statelessness maintained by a delicate equilibrium between different fiefdoms (Menkhaus 1998). The positions appear so cemented that it has prompted the French president to comment that Somalia constitutes a 'dangerous example' to the rest of the world.[2] In brief, Somalia has, in the eyes of some, come to epitomise a war-torn, fragmented society.

Years of attempts to recreate the Somali republic, by the UN, by neighbouring states, by donor countries, and by other Arab League nations, have only contributed to accelerate the fission of factions and polities, and created unattainable but attractive ideals at the national level for local politicians to dream about. In recent years, attempts by outsiders to forge a centralised state have gradually subsided and given way to an increased interest in what is now termed 'local administrative structures'. Some such involvement is in the form of technical support to train and help local administrators of different kinds to carry out their tasks. Other involvement is of a more dubious kind and comes in the form of money, and sometimes ammunition and weapons primarily from some of the other countries in the region, for example the long-standing support for rival militias in southern Somalia from Ethiopia and Eritrea.

I shall not dwell longer on the history of state collapse; the above reflections have been outlined merely to give an idea of the general directions of events as seen from the horizon of outside actors. A good guide to the different enclaves of the former Somali Republic are the studies carried out by United Nations Development Office for Somalia (UNDOS).[3] The increasingly opaque political landscape, traversed by an extremely flexible system of clans and obscure business and international interests, is, in its Byzantine complexity, parallelled only by the severity of the recurrent shortages of food, droughts and floods. If the political situation of Somalia may appear elusive, the mass of refugees the situation has triggered is all the more tangible. A rough estimate is that about one million Somalis live in internal displacement and about as many reside in different forms of foreign exile. In some neighbouring countries this mass exodus has been viewed as a direct security threat and Kenya has repeatedly closed its border to Somalia. Indeed, the general impression that the mere word Somalia invokes is a gloomy one.

Resisting and Rebuilding

In view of the many failed attempts to re-create stability through diplomatic and other forms of external involvement it is of some interest to ask to what extent there are social forces within the country that may possess the requisite strength to alter the political scenario. When viewed from the perspective of stable local communities, with groups of actors striving in a multitude of directions, the

[2] AFP, May 12 1999.

[3] See, for instance the reports by B. Helander on Bari region and on Puntland, by R. Marchal on the Lower Shabeele region, and by K. Menkhaus on Awdal region, all available online from the UNDOS web site, http://www.undos.org.

image of Somalia is indeed less gloomy (Helander 1998a). In vast parts of the country the war is history and people are more concerned with their everyday affairs of making a living than with the political struggles of political and commercial elites. It is in the concerns that ordinary people have with finding export markets for their livestock, struggling for the education of their children, seeking to combat disease, or finding fuel for household consumption that we find a demand for social services and political regularity, regardless of who it is that may organise it. So much of social service that we normally expect to be under the control of authorities is organised in neighbourhoods, by ad-hoc committees or by local business people that one actually can hear people wonder 'What will be left for the government to do when it comes back?' To give one example: in the northern commercial capital of Puntland – Bosaaso – largely spared from fighting, the pre-war power grid stands intact and is operated by the mismanaged remnants of a former government power company. Yet, the bulk of supply of electricity comes from private generators with cables spanning roof tops and cross-cutting every back yard of the city, sold and distributed according to a variety of tariffs and forms of cooperation.

The inventiveness and entrepreneurial skills displayed at the level of daily life can also be seen in local political action throughout the rest of the Somali Republic. The country's many small political enclaves are ruled by a constantly changing system of home-made governance where a city, a village or a few districts join together to create rudimentary taxation systems or set up a local police force. Solutions at the political level have a very short lifespan and tend to collapse in the fierce competition that they often inspire. In a competitive political climate, whenever a mayor is appointed and a taxation system initialised, other 'mayors' and 'tax collectors' will eventually also make claims to legitimacy. In Bosaaso in 1996 there were three competing candidates for the position of governor. The United Nations agency UNICEF had decided to make the city the venue for a widely publicised 'Day of the African Child' and hordes of journalists arrived. While two of the gubernatorial rivals declared a truce during this period, a third wrote threatening letters to the international visitors assembled. Having been refused entry to the main banquet he opened fire over the Bosaaso night sky with an anti-air craft gun. No journalist ever reported this tension since the other two governors – who were attending the banquet – quickly explained that the explosions were fireworks in honour of the occasion.

Travelling down the main tarmac road in the same part of the country gives ample illustration of how the political competition gives rise to – and opportunity for – fiscal initiative. At times I have counted as many as forty-eight checkpoints along the road, each demanding its share of the cargo that passes by. Some of these are set up by cities along the road, others by clans, others again by local thugs.

Two Types of Security

To have basic subsistence and social service catered for is indeed a very basic form of security and it is one of the top priorities for most people. Talking about subsistence and access to social service in general, people often use the phrase 'the daily bill' (*mashruuca*) and it is ranked in formal ranking exercises as equally important as the politico-military concept 'security' (*nabad-suugada*). The way in which people see the connections between their search for their daily bill and the overall security situation varies considerably between different social categories. Business people are those who most loudly lament the lack of law and order. While huge investments in sophisticated hardware for telecommunications are made, it is clear that investment in more labour-intensive activity such as manufacturing plants and food processing is deemed unwise. The fear that a large workforce would raise demands for yet more relatives to be employed seems to be a crucial concern, and there are indeed many examples of enterprises that have ended in that way. For many rural people the collapse of the state has meant that market support structures for their produce have disappeared. Livestock on the hoof, which is the principal export article, requires an extensive system of compulsory veterinary services. In the absence of state control, livestock prices have dropped to roughly half the price received before the war and a long ban on import of Somali livestock by one of the principal importing countries did not help to improve the earnings.

In other sectors the new situation appears to imply very little change compared to the pre-war situation. The main health services, for instance, are those offered by private clinics and pharmacies. There is such a demand for health care that there are now examples of physicians returning from exile to take up practice in their old country. As of Spring 1999 I estimated there were no less than twenty-seven qualified physicians working in Puntland. The pre-war figure for the same area was one. Contrary to what used to be the case, doctors and nurses can now work without competition from the government hospitals. The quality of this private health system is of course debatable, but this is nothing new. The education system gives a more mixed picture. The best measure of school attendance rates in a society lacking a census is that of smaller, preferably, rural communities. I have carried out an investigation in three different localities, scattered over the three Northeastern regions of Puntland and the average enrolment of children in grades one to eight tended to be about 40 per cent.[4] While this figure comes close to the pre-war figures it should be noted that the almost complete absence of secondary schools and all other forms of further education considerably affects the overall picture. But it is the very nature of the schools that do exist which it is important to observe. Nearly all those I have visited have a background in a small group of parents, unemployed teachers, and sometimes a local NGO, starting and continuing to operate the school on a voluntary basis. An added incentive has often been the food for work supplied by the World Food Programme, and the more successful schools have in many cases also been able to draw in some form of outside support from aid agencies or donors in the Gulf states. For the vast majority of schools, however, modest school fees meet the main part of the running costs.

Three Dimensions of Somali Civil Society

It is such small networks of professionals and concerned individuals who get

---

[4] The three regions covered were Bari, Nugaal and Muddug. At the time of my survey Puntland had not yet claimed the Sool and Sanaag regions, over which it now has a border dispute with its neighbour Somaliland.

together under some form of organisational umbrella in order to 'get things done' that is the key focus of this essay. One can pick almost any place in Somalia today and find a wide range of more or less formalised networks consisting of individuals, intellectuals, professionals, businesspeople, elite women and local politicians. Within themselves, many such networks have enough potential power and influence to make a lasting impact on the social environment in which they exist. Yet it appears that some factors constrain this potential from being traded in for real development of security in the political-military sense. The interesting task, therefore, is to highlight the conditions that support and mitigate the influence that the civil society has in Somalia.

I shall look specifically at three different dimensions of constraining and supporting factors. The first concerns the political culture in which they operate; the history of Somalia without a state is now so long that new patterns of political preferences have been firmly established and these affect the possibility for any form of action. A second question concerns the nature of these networks: what are the factors that promote internal efficiency and cohesion and what are the threats to this? Thirdly I shall pay attention to the external interfaces that these networks have. How do they liaise with the business community? What relations do they have with the international agencies? What role is played by relatives abroad and other international contacts?

The Political Culture in Which the Civil Society Operates

One of the major legacies of a civil war on the level of daily social life is the disastrous impact on trust. The ability of people to believe, with a certain degree of security, in an expected response from others, or simply to believe in other people is, indeed, a scarce commodity in Somalia today. Any opinion expressed or action performed must always be positioned in the political landscape. People feel a strong need always to know things like the clan identity of public figures. If such knowledge is withheld, the action or statement will mostly be entirely disregarded. It is widely believed that it is only within a rather limited sphere of intimate relationships that some degree of trust can be taken for granted. For commercial, public, and political purposes it is therefore usually necessary to balance membership in organisations' ruling bodies to avoid suspicions of favouring only one's own clan or family. However, a recurrent problem in Somali political culture is that by spreading trust to other groups, one also erodes support from within one's own group. Serious political actors must therefore always strive to maintain a balance between actions aimed at the public good and actions aimed to please their own kin group. In local and regional governments this is relatively easily achieved by distributing important seats to members of different clans and subclans, thus making sure that each group will have their own route of access to means supposedly controlled by that government. Private companies often maintain a similar type of strategy but for a different purpose. The ruling bodies of larger commercial enterprises are with few exceptions composed of completely unrelated people. This is meant to ensure that no one with corporate function favours his or her own clan. In fact, in business life there is a great deal of hesitation about doing business with relatives. The general feeling is that better deals are to be had when dealing with non-relatives.

NGOs, school boards, and other forms of social organisation have to consider the constraints of trust that characterise the wider political culture within which they operate. However, the solutions are not as unambiguous as those current in political and corporate life. Rather, newly formed organisations where neither commercial success nor political power are the chief aims require a lot of goodwill and support to gain momentum. Such demands usually require that key actors enjoy each others' trust and, given what I have described above, it is hardly surprising to find that a large majority of formalised organisations, at least initially, are founded by rather close relatives. As time and activities progress, there is a need to extend the social base of the organisation. This has to be done both to earn the trust of potential donors and in order actually to be able to carry out any activities.

Let me give one example. There is a small NGO in Northeast Somalia that I have followed for a number of years. Although there is a preponderance of members from a majority clan, the core members are not all related but they all belong to a sphere of intellectuals in itself seen as having a certain political bias, closely allied to that of the majority clan. The ambition of the NGO is to work with environmental issues and in the fisheries sector. Interestingly, it has chosen to focus its work on an area far away from the provenance of most of the key members. It operates an ambitious support programme for local fishermen belonging largely to unrelated clans. A major reason for this choice of location of activities was that one of the NGO members works for an international agency pledged to give its support only as long as it could be guaranteed not to accrue to relatives of the NGO board.

When the NGO initiated its activities in one fishing village it was met with understandable suspicion. 'What's in it for you?', was a more or less explicit question it had to handle. With time suspicions faded, but it continued as an undercurrent whenever the programme changed focus or sought to expand to other areas along the coast.

At the same time, the group has come to experience reduced trust within the majority clan. Even other intellectuals regularly interacting with the group have shown signs of distrust towards it. The problems are several. Many members of the majority clan have fishing villages, too, that they feel ought to have been eligible for support from this NGO. Others feel there must be some kind of hidden agenda behind both the facts that a generous grant was obtained from an international agency and that activities have been located in such a remote, and almost inaccessible, area.

The net result of this group's ambitious plans is that today they have little chance of getting their funding from the international agency renewed and in consequence will have to close the programme in the area. Fishermen there, in turn, are likely to interpret the termination as a sign that their initial suspicion was correct and the NGO will be seen as a failure by the community of similar bodies in the area.

It is important to emphasise that the type of trust I have talked about above is exclusively in the political arena. There are other fields of life where trust remains comparatively uneroded. The business sector, for instance, has built an international system for transfer of remittances and payments so that money can be transferred through a telephone call from any spot on the earth to any village in Somalia.

The Nature of Somali Civil Society

Let us turn briefly to consider another dimension of Somali civil society, namely its very constitution and definition. I have so far talked somewhat vaguely about networks of professionals and intellectuals and I have elsewhere argued that, ironically, the more such groups avoid formalisation, the more efficient they can be (Helander 1998b). The so-called logic of bureaucracy forces highly formalised groups into internal competition over meagre resources, exhausting their momentum on petty details such as appointments to junior positions. What is of some interest in the present context is to consider more broadly how the civil society defines itself and is defined by others in a situation where there is no state. There is a growing body of literature seeking to define civil society, and while there is no consensus between the different definitions, they all hinge, as Goran Hyden has recently shown (Hyden 1997), on a particular configuration of relations to the state. Although there is no formal state in our case here, there are local authorities representing a certain degree of power. The actors highlighted so far are very often, as individuals, highly critical of these authorities. Yet they themselves belong to the circle of people appointed to offices within such authorities. Indeed, many of the individuals working in the organisations I deal with in this essay have been asked to take up work with the newly founded government of Puntland, but have decided to turn down such offers. In a sense, then, the more active parts of the civil society can be said to be defined, in part, by their oppositional standing.

However, this opposition works both ways. While distrust of the government's leadership style and its competence in general is something that helps cement together small groups of active individuals, they cannot use that as a *raison d'être* for their very activities. The minute a group or an individual says that 'we want to play a role in organising this aspect of social life because we are better equipped to do so than the government' it would immediately be interpreted as a challenge to the government power itself. There have been many examples of that kind, not least in the attempts to form a medical association for Puntland, something that was initially met with great distrust from the government. For the same reason, large-scale activities have to be avoided since the scale itself would be threatening to the government. However, if large-scale activities are offered in the form of commercial services they appear politically less threatening and more understandable to the population at large. Many business ventures running social services such as veterinarians, water suppliers and city planners operate on very narrow profit margins, and would, anywhere else in the world, be seen as 'NGOs' rather than companies. At the same time it may be argued that the need to cloak popular movements as business ventures effectively limits the areas that are open for activities. Again, the form of security that the civil society is able to address is in the sphere of the daily bill, not security as controlled by the political and military establishment.

From the overall perspective of this essay where we are interested in the ability of civil society positively to influence security, it is disappointing to realise that the nature of constraints effectively seems to block popular movements with that aim. This is perhaps most clearly illustrated by the many cases of harassment that journalists in the local papers have to endure throughout the country. Arrests, confiscated equipment, and public defaming have become automatic responses to papers and radio stations reporting on things that those for the moment in power would rather remain hidden.

The Interface with Outside Actors

It goes without saying that for the majority of locally formed organisations the primary ambition is to get funding and whatever activities they plan are always second to that aim. The very term 'NGO' acquired a bad ring in Somalia during the UN intervention when the number of NGOs mushroomed uncontrollably. There are still a good number of organisations that are acutely aware of the shifting agendas of foreign donors and that rapidly adjust their own priorities accordingly. When 'women's issues' are the rule of the day, the foreign visitor will find a host of very articulate local organisations ready to take up work in that field. If the foreign concern is repatriation of refugees, freshly formed 'repatriation societies' will crop up. It is probably unavoidable that with a largely unemployed and rapidly growing urban population there will for every sincere initiative exist a larger number of less scrupulous set-ups. As long as casual visitors are ready naïvely to distribute funds without setting up systems of accountability, these types of organisations will continue to exist. There are no limits to the inventiveness of such scams. Relatives abroad are often relied upon to establish contacts with new, unsuspecting, donors.

But the existence of such problems does not diminish the importance of outside support and contact for the more authentic parts of the civil society. I have long argued in a series of reports and recommendations to different agencies that there is a need to expand and alter the type of support that the civil society now receives from development funds. Rather than seeing local NGOs as groups from whom one simply invites tenders to hire as local implementing agencies, there is a need to support the organisational format itself. The Somali civil society exists in a kind of vacuum where they connect only with the rhetoric of potential funding agencies from the West. In so far as such contacts lead to interaction with new ideas on organisational formats, these ideas derive from Western or Northern histories and contexts. For instance, when the EU a couple of years ago wanted to help the local Chamber of Commerce in Bosaaso with a twinning programme, the counterpart became a Chamber of Commerce in the UK. Similarly when a group of physicians started to form a medical association, the model for its bye-laws became the ordinance of the Italian medical society. However, much like the organisations and associations in any society, contacts with developments and solutions in neighbouring and similar countries are needed. The local medical association could have much to learn from the Ethiopian medical association and the completely uncontrolled labour market would benefit from some of the experiences of trade unions elsewhere in Africa.[5]

Yet, maintaining substantial international contacts is the exclusive right of the political and military elites. And given Duffield's thesis that 'developmentalists' are unable to analyse or understand local power configurations (Duffield 1996) we should not expect foreign aid to play any significant role in changing these

---

[5] The medical association of Puntland has recently set up its own homepage on the Internet. See http://www.angelfire.com/sd/pma. See also the vibrant 'Puntland Intelligentsia Network' at http://www. puntin.org.

conditions. It is of some significance to note that very few of the persons possessing political power in Somalia today actually reside in the country. They are firmly rooted in the Somali diasporas all over the world and their children and families do not live under the conditions that the rest of the country does. Naïve outsiders frequently ship members of the political elite across the globe, in order to attend 'peace conferences' (Prunier 2000).[6] High-level contacts between such individuals and their counterparts in other countries can be established and cultivated. We do not have to bring up here the nature of the contacts that have prevailed between such elites in Somalia and their counterparts elsewhere in Africa and Asia. But we should point out that while various militias over the years have enjoyed generous international support, civil society has been left unaided. Again, this constraint means that whatever it is that local organisations want to achieve, they will of necessity be confined to their own locality and lack access to a wider sphere of debate, support and example.

One should be cautious not to bluntly write off the potential impact that internationally sponsored meetings may have on local politics, however. Although the purpose of such meetings is to re-create the Somali republic, the context sometimes offers opportunities for civilian actors to interface directly with the political processes in their respective enclaves. In a recent Djibouti meeting the minister of the interior of Puntland has been appointed chairman despite the fact that Puntland has officially decided to boycott the meeting. While this prompted the president promptly to sack him, it opened up a possibility for re-configuration of constellations in the internal power struggles in Puntland. The strong opposition against the government in segments of the civil society attending the meeting, has now found a strong ally in one of that very government's former big men.

Conclusion

Civilians determined to engage in delivery of services in areas where there is no state do not operate outside politics. Rather, their ambitions are intrinsically linked with local power struggles and face the risk of becoming construed as claims to political power. As I have shown here, opposition against those in power may indeed also help define a common stand and positions. The Somali civil society finds itself in an ambiguous position. It cannot gain sufficient political strength to negate the force of the political and military establishment and its influence on security in the conventional sense is therefore limited. It can, however, provide security in the Somali sense of 'the daily bill'. But lasting success in such endeavours requires political stability. Positive development of subsistence and social services does to some extent affect the political climate by enhancing socio-economic stability. At the same time, such developments may increase political competition and therefore, paradoxically, have a negative effect on political security. With every positive move of civil society to increase its ability to deliver security in the form of social services, the point comes closer where

[6] At the time of writing this was the thirteenth of a sequence of international conferences aimed to create an exile government for Somalia, this time based in Djibouti (http://www.somalia-rebirth.dj/index.html). The fact that the major players have refused to attend the conference has not halted the stream of funding from the EU and UN. Some donors are keen to create the semblance of a climate that will allow mass deportation of Somali refugees from Europe (EU 2000).

such services demand a more coherent control of political and military security. This, in turn, is seen as a threat by those in power and tends to gradually increase the chasm between those struggling to deliver social services and those who control the political field. It is thus very important for the international community to understand the delicacy of the balancing act it must perform. The UN system, international financial institutions, and bi-lateral donors have a built-in bias to work with state-like mechanisms, but this may mean unwittingly strengthening self-appointed and violent gate-keepers at the expense of civil society. Civilian groups and service providers need direct support to ensure that they are in a position to assert pressure through which the re-emergent Leviathan will be domesticated.

References

Christoplos, I. 1998, 'Humanitarianism and local service institutions in Angola' *Disasters* 22:1–20

Duffield, M. 1996, 'The symphony of the damned: racial discourse, complex political emergencies and humanitarian aid' *Disasters* 20:173–93

EU 2000, 'The Council of the European Union. General Secretariat, Permanent Representatives Committee/ Council' *Implementation of the Action Plans for Afghanistan and the Region, Iraq, Morocco, Somalia and Sri Lanka* Brussels: Document No: 7429/00 JAI 32 AG 40

Helander, B. 1998a, 'Somaliland: example or exception?' *News from Nai*, 2

—— 1998b, 'Finns det ett civilt samhälle i Somalia? (Is there a Civil Society in Somalia?)' *Utsikt mot utveckling*, 2

Hyden, G. 1997, 'Civil society, social capital, and development: dissection of a complex discourse' *Studies in Comparative International Development* 32:3–30

Menkhaus, K. 1998, 'Somalia: political order in a stateless society' *Current History* 97 (619) 220–24

Prunier, G. 2000, 'Somalia re-invents itself' *Le Monde Diplomatique* (English edition), 12 April

APPENDIX
Bernhard Helander's Bibliography

Compiled by
MICHAEL BARRETT

Helander, Bernhard 1984, *Notions of Crop Fertility in Southern Somalia* Uppsala: Kultur-antropologiska Institutionen, Uppsala Universitet

Helander, Bernhard 1986a, *Death and the End of Society: Official Ideology and Ritual Communication in the Southern Somali Funeral* Uppsala: Uppsala University

Helander, Bernhard. 1986b, 'Individualitet som mysticism i Somalia' *Antropologiska Studier*. (38–39): 30–34

Helander, Bernhard 1986c, 'Individuality as Mysticism: On the Concept of Burji', Paper presented to the Proceedings from the Third International Conference of Somali Studies', Rome

Helander, Bernhard 1986d, 'Islamiska fundamentalister är bättre på utveckling' [Islamic Fundamentalists – Better on Development] *SIDA-Rapport* (9): 18–20

Helander, Bernhard 1986e, 'The social dynamics of southern Somali agro-pastoralism: a regional approach' in Conze, P. and Labahn T. eds, *Somalia: Agriculture in the Winds of Change* Saarbrucken-Shafbrucke: Epi Verlag

Helander, Bernhard 1986f, *The social dynamics of southern Somali agro-pastoralism: a regional approach* Uppsala: Kulturantropologiska Institutionen, Uppsala Universitet

Helander, Bernhard 1987, *Gender and Gender Characteristics as a Folk Model in Southern Somali: Social Classification and Symbolism* Uppsala: Kulturantropologiska Institutionen, Uppsala Universitet

Helander, Bernhard 1988a, 'Death and the End of Society: Official Ideology and Ritual Communication in the Southern Somali Funeral' in Cederroth, Sven, Corlin, Claes and Lindström, Jan eds, *On the Meaning of Death: Essays on Mortuary Rituals and Eschatological Beliefs* Uppsala & Stockholm: Uppsala University; Almqvist & Wiksell International

Helander, Bernhard 1988b, 'Incorporating the Unknown: The Power of Southern Somali Medicine' in Jacobson-Widding, Anita and Westerlund, David eds, *Culture, Experience and Pluralism: Essays on African Ideas of Illness and Healing* Uppsala & Stockholm: Uppsala University; Almqvist & Wiksell International

Helander, Bernhard 1988c, 'Smutsa ner händerna! [Get to the bottom of it!]' *SIDA-Rapport* (1): 27–28

Helander, Bernhard 1989a, 'Den somaliske familien' in Schakt, J. ed., *Somalia*. Oslo: Utlendingsdirektoratet

Helander, Bernhard 1989b, 'Somalier i Sverige [Somalis in Sweden]' in Svanberg, Ingvar and Runblom, Harald eds, *Det mångkulturella Sverige: en handbok om etniska grupper och minoriteter* Stockholm & Uppsala: Gidlund; Centrum för multietnisk forskning, Uppsala Universitet

204   Bernhard Helander

Helander, Bernhard 1990a 'Getting the Most Out of It: Nomadic Health Care Seeking and the State in Southern Somalia' *Nomadic Peoples* 25 (7): 122–32

Helander, Bernhard 1990b 'Mercy or Rehabilitation? Culture and the Prospects for Disabled in Southern Somalia' in Bruun, Frank J. and Ingstad, Benedicte eds, *Disability in a Cross-Cultural Perspective* Oslo: University Dept. of Social Anthropology

Helander, Bernhard 1990c 'Reflektioner kring en slaktad kamel: härstammningsregler, ideologi och erfarenhet i södra Somalia' in *Årsbok 1990*, Annales Societatis Litterarum Humaniorum Regiae Upsaliensis. Uppsala: Kungl. Humanistiska Vetenskaps-Samfundet i Uppsala

Helander, Bernhard 1991a, 'Somali' in Levinsson, D. ed., *Encyclopaedia of World Cultures* New Haven, CT: Human Relations Area Files

Helander, Bernhard 1991b, 'The Somali Family' in Barci, K. and Normark, S. eds, *Somalia: A Historical, Cultural and Political Analysis* Uppsala: Life and Peace Institute

Helander, Bernhard 1991c, 'Vad är ett ord? Extension och illusion i somaliskt släktskap. [What is a word? Extension and illusion in Somali Kinship]' *Häften för kritiska studier* 24 (3): 34–41

Helander, Bernhard 1991d, 'Words, Worlds, and Wishes: The Aesthetics of Somali Kinship' *Cultural Anthropology* 6 (1): 113–20

Helander, Bernhard 1992 'Samtal i ett somaliskt apotek: stora världens lösningar på små människors problem [Conversations in a Somali pharmacy: Big world's solutions to small people's problems]' *Socialmedicinsk Tidskrift* 69 (9–10): 450–9

Helander, Bernhard 1993a, 'An anthropological study of washing slabs, washing habits and washing sites in the Lake Zone Regions, Tanzania' Stockholm: Socialantropologiska institutionen, Sektionen för utvecklingsstudier, Stockholms Universitet

Helander, Bernhard 1993b, 'Fyra Farliga Fällor i Fält: En svensk(s) antropologisk(a) forskningsetik?' in Dahl, Gudrun and Smedler, Ann-Charlotte, eds, *Det respektfulla mötet: ett symposium om forskningsetik och antropologi [Stockholms universitet 25–27 november 1991]* Stockholm & Uppsala: Humanistisk-samhällsvetenskapliga forskningsrådet (HSFR); Swedish Science Press [distributör]

Helander, Bernhard 1994, 'Somalisk islam som världsbild och enande kraft' in Svanberg, Ingvar and Westerlund, David eds, *Majoritetens islam: om muslimer utanför arabvärlden.* Stockholm: Arena

Helander, Bernhard 1995a, 'Antropologi [Anthropology]' in Rylander, Kristina ed., *Att studera Afrika: En litteraturvägledning.* Uppsala: Nordiska Afrika Institutet

Helander, Bernhard 1995b, 'Disability as Incurable Illness: Health, Process, and Personhood in Southern Somalia' in Ingstad, Benedicte and Reynolds Whyte, Susan eds, *Disability and Culture* Los Angeles, CA: University of California Press

Helander, Bernhard 1995c, 'Overvejelser omkring alternative forligsmodeller i Afrika' [Reflections on alternative models for conflict resolution in Africa] *Den Ny Verden.* 28(2): 41–54

Helander, Bernhard 1995d, 'Probleme bei der Konfliktlösung in Afrikanischen Staaten: Uberlegungen zu alternativen Ansätzen der Versöhnungsarbeit und -forschung' [Problems in conflict management in African states: Considerations regarding alternative approaches in resolution work and research] *Antimilitarismus Information.* 25(12): 70–77

Helander, Bernhard 1995e, 'Somalia: Aid fuels the conflict' *News from Nai* 1995(3)

Helander, Bernhard 1995f, 'Vulnerable Minorities in Somalia and Somaliland' *Indigenous Affairs.* (2): 21–23

Helander, Bernhard 1996a, 'The Hubeer in the Land of Plenty: Land, Labor, and Vulnerability among a Southern Somali Clan' in Besteman, Catherine and Cassanelli Lee V. eds, *The Struggle for Land in Southern Somalia: The war behind the war* Boulder, CO & London: Westview; Haan

Helander, Bernhard 1996b, *Power and Poverty in Southern Somalia* Uppsala: Kultur-antropologiska Institutionen

Helander, Bernhard 1996c, 'Rahanweyn Sociability: A Model for other Somalis?' in Andrzejewski, Bogumil Witalis, Hayward, R. J. and Lewis, Ioan M. eds, *Voice and Power: the culture of language in North-East Africa: essays in honour of B.W. Andrzejewski.* London: School of Oriental and African Studies, University of London

Helander, Bernhard 1997a, 'Clanship, Kinship, and Community among the Rahanweyn' in Adam, Hussein M. and Ford, Richard eds. *Mending Rips in the Sky: Options for Somali communities in the 21st Century* Lawrenceville, NJ: Red Sea Press

Helander, Bernhard 1997b, 'Ethnographic Authority for Sale: Another Day in the Life of a Self-Proclaimed Cultural Expert' *Antropologiska Studier* 56–57

Helander, Bernhard 1998a, *Bari Region: Local administrative structures, political tendencies and prospects for technical support* Nairobi: United Nations Development Office for Somalia

Helander, Bernhard 1998b, 'The Emperor's New Clothes Removed: A Critique of Besteman's "Violent Politics and the Politics of Violence"' *American Ethnologist* 25 (3): 122–32

Helander, Bernhard 1998c, 'Finns det ett civilt samhälle i Somalia?' [Is there a civil society in Somalia?] *Utsikt mot utveckling* (2)

Helander, Bernhard 1998d, 'Somaliland: Example or Exception?' *News from Nai* (2)

Helander, Bernhard 1999a, 'Can Civil Society Play a Role in Enhancing Security in Somalia?' *International Migration, Development & Integration* 99–107

Helander, Bernhard. 1999b, 'Power and Poverty in Southern Somalia' in Anderson, David and Broch-Due Vigdis, eds, *The Poor Are Not Us: Poverty and pastoralism in Eastern Africa* Oxford & Athens, OH: James Currey, Ohio University Press

Helander, Bernhard 1999c 'The Puntland State of Somalia: Stratagem or Steps Towards Good Governance?' Nairobi: United Nations Development Office for Somalia

Helander, Bernhard 1999d, 'Somali Islam as World View and Uniting Force' in Westerlund, David and Svanberg, Ingvar eds, *Islam outside the Arab World* Richmond: Curzon

Helander, Bernhard 2000a, 'Getting Things Done in Somalia: Civilians, Security, and Social Services' *Antropologiska Studier* 66–67: 128–40

Helander, Bernhard 2000b, 'Will there be peace in Somalia now?' *American Diplomacy* 5 (4)

Helander, Bernhard 2001, 'The Arta group: Faction or Government?' *Bulletin of the Anglo-Somali Society* (Spring)

Helander, Bernhard 2003, *The Slaughtered Camel: Coping with Fictious Descent among the Hubeer of Southern Somalia* Uppsala: Uppsala University Press

Helander, Bernhard nd-a, 'Beggars Don't Cry ...' A Somali Saar Poem

Helander, Bernhard nd-b, 'Rumours of Rain: Ideas of Centralisation, Social Fragmentation and the Nature of Power in Post-Government Somalia' *Africa*

Helander, Bernhard nd-c, 'The Slaughtered Camel: Coping with Fictitious Descent among the Hubeer of Southern Somalia' PhD: Uppsala University

Helander, Bernhard ed. nd-d, *Speaking to Power: The Roles of Academics in the Somali War* Uppsala: Nordic Africa Institute

Helander, Bernhard. nd-e, 'Weak Nobles, Strong Commoners and Poetic Combats: A Paradox of Bodily Strength among the Hubeer of Southern Somalia' in Ovesen, J. ed., *African Text and Context* Stockholm: Almqvist & Wiksell International

Helander, Bernhard and Hassan Awad Duaale 1984, 'Notions of crop fertility among dry-farmers of the Bay Region' Paper presented to the Proceedings of the Second International Congress of Somali Studies, Hamburg

Helander, B, et al. 1989, *Training in the Community for People with Disabilities* Geneva: WHO

Helander, Bernhard and Lena Hagberg 1993, *Somalier: Grundinformation* [Somalis: Basic Information] Norrköping: Statens Invandrarverk

Helander, Bernhard, Hagberg, Sten and Unge, Roy 1996, 'Lokala Konfliktlösningsmetoder i Afrika: Antropologiska perspektiv på lokala strukturer och institutioner för konflikt-lösning och konfliktförebyggande', *Säkerhet och Utveckling i Afrika*. Stockholm: Utrikes-departementet

Helander, Bernhard, in cooperation with Mohamed Haji Mukhtar and I. M. Lewis 1995, *Building Peace from Below: A critical review of the District Councils in the Bay and Bakool regions of southern Somalia* Uppsala: Life and Peace Institute

Index